The U-Boat Commanders

Dedicated to Jo and Mark Robinson

The U-Boat Commanders

Knight's Cross Holders 1939–1945

Jeremy Dixon

'I was fascinated by the operation of a U-boat... every single man was an indispensable part... every submariner, I am sure, has experienced in his heart the joy of the task entrusted to him.'

Großadmiral Karl Dönitz, Commander-in-Chief of U-boats

Pen & Sword
MILITARY

AN IMPRINT OF PEN & SWORD BOOKS LTD.
YORKSHIRE – PHILADELPHIA

First published in Great Britain in 2019 by Pen & Sword Books Ltd
Pen & Sword Military
An imprint of
Pen & Sword Books Ltd
Yorkshire – Philadelphia

Copyright © Jeremy Dixon, 2019

ISBN 978 1 52671 873 0

The right of Jeremy Dixon to be identified as Author of this work has been asserted by him in accordance with the Copyright, Designs and Patents Act 1988.

A CIP catalogue record for this book is available from the British Library

Typeset in Ehrhardt MT & 10/12
by Aura Technology and Software Services, India

Printed and bound by TJ International Ltd, Padstow, Cornwall

Pen & Sword Books Ltd incorporates the Imprints of Aviation, Atlas, Family History, Fiction, Maritime, Military, Discovery, Politics, History, Archaeology, Select, Wharncliffe Local History, Wharncliffe True Crime, Military Classics, Wharncliffe Transport, Leo Cooper, The Praetorian Press, Remember When, White Owl, Seaforth Publishing and Frontline Publishing.

For a complete list of Pen & Sword titles please contact

PEN & SWORD BOOKS LTD
47 Church Street, Barnsley, South Yorkshire, S70 2AS, England
E-mail: enquiries@pen-and-sword.co.uk
Website: www.pen-and-sword.co.uk

Or

PEN & SWORD BOOKS
1950 Lawrence Rd, Havertown, PA 19083, USA
E-mail: Uspen-and-sword@casematepublishers.com
Website: www.penandswordbooks.com

Contents

Acknowledgments

I would like to thank John Preece, who proofread the book and offered advice, and I must thank family and friends for their continued support, which include my mum and dad, my sister and my two nephews together with Paul Budden, Lisa Castle, Jared Copeland-Gregory, Alex Curran, Ricky Delamare, Ann Driscoll, Paul and Claire Fairbrass, Laura Fisher, Mark Framp, Dan Fraser, Rod Fraser, Rob French, Colin Harris, Shirley Hedley, Sue Hollands, Lorraine Horsnell, Candy and Nick Isles, Matt Jackman, Lauretta Kelly, Julia Macintosh, Sophie McLoughlin, Debra and David Mills, Colin Neve, Barbi Preece, Nathan Pearce, David Ross, Jackie Snowling, Alison Stringer, Anne Taylor and Ben Tip.

Many of the photographs in this book are from my own collection and some are from the archive of *Deutsches Wehrkundearchiv* and *Veit Scherzer*.

Introduction

This book gives the accounts of those U-boat commanders who won the Knight's Cross and its higher grades during the Second World War. Included in this study is *Großadmiral* Karl Dönitz: although not a U-boat commander during the war, he was the commander of all U-boats, and from 1943 was Commander-in-Chief of the German Navy and named Hitler's successor in his Last Will and Testament, and played a major role in the U-boat war.

There were approximately 7,320 Knight's Crosses awarded during the Second World War, and 318 of the recipients were from the German Navy (*Kriegsmarine*), 144 were from the U-boat service (U-*bootwaffe*), and of these 122 were U-boat commanders. These Knight's Cross holders were responsible for the sinking of 1,790 ships for a total of 9,099,552 shipping tons during the Second World War.

The Knight's Cross (*Ritterkreuz*) was one of the highest decorations any man could receive, awarded for extreme acts of valour and for outstanding leadership, to all ranks of the German armed forces (*Wehrmacht*) during the Second World War. Few awards captured the respect and admiration of the German public as the Knight's Cross.

Hoffmann postcards of Günther Prien and Erich Topp. (Author's collection)

Postcards were produced during the war of many of the recipients, especially those who had been awarded the higher grades.

The Knight's Cross was a highly-respected decoration especially among U-boat men. In fact crews took great pride if their captain became a recipient and sometimes it was added to the boat's insignia, and captains would often joke about having an 'itchy neck', which could only be cured by the red, white and black ribbon of the Knight's Cross.

Of the 122 recipients of the Knight's Cross among U-boat commanders, some were awarded the higher grades: twenty-three received the Oakleaves (*Eichenlaub*), three received the Swords (*Schwertern*) and two, Albrecht Brandi and Wolfgang Lüth, were awarded the much prized Diamonds (*Brillanten*).

The Knight's Cross could be awarded for a number of reasons. The amount of shipping tonnage sunk by the commander, for excellent leadership and bravery, for continued attacks on the enemy even if the situation was hopeless. Or in the case of Günther Prien, the first U-boat commander to be awarded the Knight's Cross, it was for his skill in sinking the battleship *Royal Oak* in Scapa Flow. Sometimes the award would be made after a personal recommendation from the Commander-in-Chief of the Navy or a senior Admiral. It was a great honour and usually the whole boat would celebrate their commanders' award.

Knight's Cross with Oakleaves, Swords and Diamonds

Albrecht 'Cherry' BRANDI
Fregattenkapitän
12 ships sunk, 31,689 tons

Knight's Cross: Awarded on 21 January 1943, as *Kapitänleutnant* and as commander of *U-617* after sinking enemy ships with a total of 39,575 tons. He was the 148th recipient of the *Kriegsmarine* and the 79th U-boat commander to be awarded the Knight's Cross.

Knight's Cross with Oakleaves: Awarded on 11 April 1943, as *Kapitänleutnant*, and the 224th recipient while still commanding *U-617* after sinking three enemy ships which included the minelayer HMS *Welshman* on 1 February 1943. The award was presented by *Großadmiral* Dönitz at *Führer* Headquarters '*Wolfschanze*' in Rastenburg, East Prussia in April 1943.

Knight's Cross with Oakleaves and Swords: He became the 66th recipient of the Swords and the 5th U-boat commander on 9 May 1944, as *Kapitänleutnant* and as commander of *U-380* after sinking a steamship and the destroyer HMS *Puckeridge* while operating in the Atlantic and the Mediterranean. The award was personally presented to Brandi by Hitler at the Berghof, Obersalzburg on 20 May 1943.

Knight's Cross with Oakleaves, Swords and Diamonds: Awarded on 24 November 1944 to become the 22nd recipient as *Korvettenkapitän* and as commander of *U-967* after sinking the US escort destroyer USS *Fechteler*. The presentation was made at the Reich Chancellery in Berlin by Hitler in early January 1945.

Albrecht 'Cherry' Brandi was one of only two U-boat commanders to be awarded the Diamonds to the Knight's Cross, the other being *Kapitan zur See* Wolfgang Lüth. Brandi was born on 20 June 1914, in Dortmund. He was the sixth and youngest child of Ernst and Clara Brandi, and his father was a mining director of the United Steelworks. After the completion of his schooling the young Albrecht

(Author's collection)

joined the *Reichsmarine*, which became the *Kriegsmarine* in 1935. He received his basic training aboard the sail training ship *Gorch Fock* and became a midshipman. In September 1935, he was posted to the light cruiser *Karlsruhe* where he continued his training and he then attended the Naval Academy in Flensburg-Mürwik – graduating in March 1937 as a *Fähnrich zur See*.

In April 1937, he was appointed Watch Officer aboard a minesweeper and as part of the 1st Minesweeping Flotilla he saw action during the Polish campaign. He was commissioned as a *Leutnant zur See* in April 1938 and was promoted to *Oberleutnant zur See* in October 1939. At the beginning of 1940 he applied to join the U-boats but was refused, in May he was appointed commander of the minesweeper *M-1*, part of the 1st Minesweepers Flotilla. In April 1941 he began his U-boat training; his second attempt to transfer to submarines had been accepted. Once he had completed his training he waited for his orders. In December 1941 he was assigned to *U-552* commanded by *Kapitänleutnant* Erich Topp, and it was while with Topp that Brandi learnt how to become a successful U-boat commander.

In April 1942, Brandi was given command of *U-617*, leaving his base in Kiel for his first patrol on 29 August 1942. He sank four merchant ships during this patrol which lasted until 7 October 1942, when he arrived at his new base in St. Nazaire. These included the British tanker *Athelsuktan*, sunk with the loss of her captain, six naval staff members, thirty-five crew, seven gunners and two passengers. He was promoted to *Kapitänleutnant* on 1 October, and he left for the Mediterranean the following month, to start his second patrol. In order to get to his destination in the shortest time he had to navigate through the Straits of Gibraltar, a heavily-guarded stretch of water. Brandi decided to surface at night with engines stopped and let the strong current of the Straits take him through. It was working when a Sunderland flying boat spotted *U-617* and dropped two depth charges, but they missed and *U-617* slipped away undamaged. On 19 November Brandi attacked a British convoy in which many ships were destroyed or damaged but these reports were unconfirmed. He then spent four hours being depth-charged in which almost eighty depth charges were dropped but he managed to get away. During his third patrol he torpedoed and sank the naval tug HMS *St. Issey* on 28 December north-east of Benghazi with loss of the entire crew. On 13 January 1943, he attacked three ships and explosions were heard and one steamer was claimed as sunk. On the 15th he sank two more ships, the Greek SS *Annitsa* and the Norwegian MV *Harboe Jensen* which was hit by two torpedoes on the port side, broke in two and sank immediately. Five crew members and one gunner jumped overboard and survived, being picked up by one of the escort ships.

On 1 February 1943, he sighted the British minelayer HMS *Welshman* a few miles off the Maltese coast. She was an important target, as *Welshman* had been used to lay mines as part of the defence of Malta. Although he was about 1,200m away he fired all four torpedoes and waited. At approximately 18:45 Brandi heard two explosions and the enemy ship appeared to be thrown in the air. There were other smaller explosions and at 20:40 the captain gave the order to abandon ship: 155 men were dead and around 120 survived. Four days later Brandi sank two more ships, the Norwegian SS *Cornona* and *Henrik*, who had been part of Convoy AW22. The patrol ended on 20 July 1943 when Brandi reached Toulon.

On his eighth patrol he sank the British destroyer HMS *Puckeridge* on 6 September; she was hit by two torpedoes and sank within eight minutes. Sixty-two men were lost.

Brandi receiving his Knight's Cross with Oakleaves from Adolf Hitler. (Author's collection)

On 12 September 1943, whilst patrolling on the Moroccan coast *U-617* was attacked by a Sunderland flying boat. Brandi's crew managed to shoot the aircraft down but not before it dropped three bombs which exploded so close to the submarine that it was badly damaged. Brandi gave the order to abandon ship but not before he gave orders to lay charges and scuttle the boat. Brandi and his crew rowed ashore and landed on the Spanish coast and were interned. He was taken to an officers' internment camp near Cadiz where he managed to escape and made his way home via France with the assistance of a car and false papers. By the end of November he was back in Germany and appointed commander of *U-380*.

After only one patrol his boat was destroyed on 11 March 1944 whilst in port, during an air raid by the 9th USAAF. In April he was given command of *U-967*, a Type VIIC boat. On 5 May he sank the escort destroyer USS *Fechteler*: his torpedo hit amidships and the explosion lifted the ship out of the water and she broke in two. One officer and twenty-six ratings were lost. In June Brandi became ill and had to return to base. He was mentally exhausted, and *Oberleutnant zur See* Heinz-Eugen Eberbach took over his command. Brandi soon recovered and by July had been appointed Chief of Operations, being attached to the Commanding Admiral of the Eastern Baltic Sea Area, *Vizeadmiral* Theodor Burchardi. In June 1944, he was promoted to *Korvettenkapitän*, and six months later he reached the rank of *Fregattenkapitän*.

In January 1945 he was appointed Chief of the Small Naval Combat Unit in Holland. He was captured by the Allies in May 1945 and briefly interned. Brandi became an

HMS Welshman *was completed in August 1941 and made about eight supply runs to Malta in 1942. She was struck by two torpedoes, capsized and sank by the stern about 45 miles east-north-east of Tobruk, Libya, on 1 February 1943.* (Author's collection)

architect and later governor of the province of Westphalia before he died on 6 January 1966, after a long illness. His funeral was held in Dortmund and attended by West German Navy personnel and surviving crewmates from *U-617*. His close friend, former *Fregattenkapitän* Reinhard Suhren, described Brandi as a 'Knight without fear or failings.'

Other awards:
1 Apr 1939: Long Service Award 4th Class
Apr 1940: Iron Cross 2nd Class
Apr 1940: Iron Cross 1st Class
Apr 1940: Minesweepers Badge
8 Oct 1942: U-boat War Badge
29 May 1943: Italian Medal for Military Valour in Silver
Jul 1944: U-boat War Badge with Diamonds
1945: U-boat Combat Clasp in Bronze

Wolfgang August Eugen LÜTH
Kapitän zur See
47 ships sunk, 225,756 tons
2 ships damaged, 17,343 tons

Knight's Cross: Awarded on 24 October 1940, as *Oberleutnant zur See* and as commander of *U-138* of the 1st U-boat Flotilla, for sinking 49,000 shipping tons in a period of twenty-seven days. He was the 19th U-boat commander to be awarded the Knight's Cross and the 42nd recipient from the *Kriegsmarine*.

Knight's Cross with Oakleaves: Awarded as *Kapitänleutnant* and as commander of *U-181* on 13 November 1942, for sinking thirteen ships totalling more than 81,000 shipping tons. As the 142nd recipient he was presented with his Oakleaves by Hitler on 30 January 1943 at a ceremony at *Führer* Headquarters '*Wolfschanze*' in Rastenburg, East Prussia.

Knight's Cross with Oakleaves and Swords: He became the 29th recipient on 15 April 1943, as *Kapitänleutnant* and as commander of *U-181*, for sinking over 100,000 tons of shipping. The Swords was presented to Lüth at *Führer* Headquarters '*Wolfschanze*' in Rastenburg, East Prussia at the same time with his Diamonds.

Knight's Cross with Oakleaves, Swords and Diamonds: Awarded on 9 August 1943, as (Scherzer)
Korvettenkapitän and as commander of *U-181*, to become the 7th recipient of the Diamonds and the 1st U-boat Commander to win the award. The award was presented personally by Hitler on 25 October 1943 at *Führer* Headquarters '*Wolfschanze*' in Rastenburg, East Prussia together with *Korvettenkapitän* Robert Gysae, Erich Topp and Reinhard Suhren.

Wolfgang Lüth was one of the most successful U-boat commanders of the Second World War, sinking over 225,000 tons of shipping and ranking second overall. He was born on 15 October 1913, in Riga, Latvia and was the fourth son and youngest child of August and Elfriede Lüth. His father owned a small business in Riga, producing knitwear. Among his customers was the Imperial Russian Army; it is possible that during the First World War Russian soldiers may have been wearing Friedrich Lüth's clothing. Nevertheless during the First World War his father was interned in Siberia and the young Wolfgang together with his mother and four brothers and sisters were evacuated, to German. In 1921 the Lüth family returned to Riga, where Wolfgang was educated, and in 1933 the family returned to Germany.

In April 1933, Lüth joined the *Kriegsmarine* and was assigned as a recruit to a small island called Dänholm on the Baltic coast for basic training. He spent three months training hard, dressed in a field-grey jacket, boots and a helmet. He lived in barracks, drilled on parade grounds, ran in formation, and scrambled through netting and obstacles whilst being screamed at by instructors. Finally on completion of the course Lüth was allowed to wear naval uniform. In June 1933, he became an officer cadet and served aboard the sail training ship *Gorch Fock*, and later on the light cruiser *Karlsruhe*. In April 1935, he entered the Naval College in Flensburg and in October 1936, was commissioned as a *Leutnant zur See*. Lüth, because he was born in Riga, was an *Auslandsdeutscher*, a German national living abroad. He was of medium height; slender with a rather large nose and a strong Baltic accent, and when he smiled he revealed a wide gap between his two front teeth and couldn't help but stand out in a crowd. He was distinctive rather than handsome and once during a lecture at the naval college he was told that he had the typical facial features of a Bavarian noble family. This amused him no end.

In May 1938, he was promoted and the following month begun training at the U-boat School in Neustadt-Holstein. In July he was appointed Second Watch Officer aboard *U-27* and in October he reported aboard *U-38* as First Watch Officer. He was quick to learn and was a good student but he was also an enthusiastic supporter of the National Socialists, and made his political feelings known. It was unusual for a naval officer to be so politically outspoken and this must have alienated him for a time among other young officers, but it must have helped in his career advancement. On 15 November 1939, Lüth was attached to *U-13* under *Kapitänleutnant* Heinz Scheringer, serving as his deputy during a patrol off the north-east coast of England, in the Newcastle area. From December 1939 he took command of *U-9* and left Kiel for his first patrol on 16 January 1940. On the 18th he sank his first ship, the Swedish SS *Flandria*, and just two hours later he claimed his second victory, another Swedish ship, the SS *Patria*. In February 1940, he left Wilhelmshaven for minelaying operations in the Moray Firth. He claimed one ship, the British tanker *San Tiburcio* which hit one of his mines and on 11 February he sank another east of the Orkney Islands. On 4 April 1940 he again left Wilhelmshaven for his fourth patrol where he took part in Operation *Hartmut*, the early preparations for the German invasion of Denmark. On the 20th he made an unsuccessful attack on the Polish destroyer *Blyskawica*. The patrol ended on 24 April when *U-9* sailed into Kiel. In May 1940 he left Kiel to patrol the Dutch and Belgian coasts and on the 9th he sank a French submarine and two days later sank the Estonian SS *Viiu* and later the same day sank the British SS *Tringa*. This ship was hit aft by one torpedo and sank immediately. Sixteen men were killed including her captain. He then returned to the North Sea and on 23rd near Zeebrugge *U-9* torpedoed and sank the Belgian SS *Sigurds Faulbaums*, a captured German ship. *U-9* was then spotted by Allied destroyers and subjected to depth-charge attacks for several hours, before returning to base on 30 May 1940.

During August and September 1940, Lüth served on *U-138*, a training boat for new commanders. He left Kiel on 10 September to operate in the North Channel and on 20th encountered a convoy and sank three ships, the tanker SS *New Sevilla*, SS *Boka* and SS *Empire Adventure*. In a second attack, early on the 21st, he sank the SS *City of Simla*, a British passenger steamer of 10,138 tons. Of her passengers 153 were rescued, only one crew member and two passengers being lost. He returned to his home base on 26 September. On 21 October he was given command of *U-43*, a Type IXA submarine, taking over from *Kapitänleutnant* Wilhelm Ambrosius. He left Lorient on his first patrol on 17 November 1940, to carry out weather-boat duties and on 2 December he sank two ships. Four days later Lüth attacked a convoy west of Ireland and sank the SS *Skrim* and returned to base on 17 December. His next patrol was delayed when *U-43* sank at her moorings in Lorient because one of the valves was left open and allowed water to leak into the bilges over a number of hours, and the torpedo hatch had also been left open. It took three months to refit the boat.

Finally, on 11 May 1941, *Kapitänleutnant* Lüth took *U-43* out, and within four days he had sank a fishing vessel, killing all the crew. The ship wasn't a threat to anyone: Lüth just wanted some 'target practice'. On 1 June, he headed in the western North Atlantic, and five days later sank the Dutch SS *Yselhaven*. She was struck by two torpedoes and sank within two minutes about 60 miles east of Newfoundland. The master and eight crew members were lost. The remaining crew who had abandoned the ship were in two lifeboats but one of them with fifteen occupants was never seen again. The remaining survivors were picked up by the Finnish SS *Hammarland* on 15 June. Lüth then sank the British MV *Cathrine* south-west of Ireland. He returned to base on 1 July. His next patrol, his third as commander of *U-38*, was unsuccessful and he returned to base on 23 September. On 10 November, Lüth set out on his next patrol and was joined by four other boats. On 28 November Lüth sighted a convoy and attacked, sinking the munitions ship SS *Thornliebank*, *U-43* being slightly damaged by the explosion. On the evening of the 30th, Lüth sank the SS *Ashby* and two days later sank the SS *Astral*. On his last patrol with *U-43* he sank three more ships, the SS *Maro*, SS *Chepo* and SS *Empire Surf* before returning to Kiel on 22 January 1942.

He oversaw the overhaul and refitting of *U-43* before taking over as commander of *U-181* on 12 April 1942. On 12 September, Lüth took out his new boat on its first patrol in the South Atlantic. After a few days *U-181* was attacked by aircraft, and after a ten-hour hunt and more than thirty depth-charges, managed to escape. Lüth took his boat across the Equator and within the next few weeks had sunk four more ships. On the morning of 15 November, *U-18* was spotted on the surface by a British destroyer and was attacked, Lüth managed to crash-dive and escape. Over the next twelve days Lüth sank another seven ships, and on his way back to base on 2 December he sank the SS *Amaryllis*, east of Cape St. Lucia. Lüth arrived in Bordeaux on 18 January 1943, and after sinking thirteen ships he was awarded the Knight's Cross with Oakleaves. On 23 March, Lüth took *U-181* out on another patrol together with four other boats, which included *U-404* commanded by Knight's Cross holder *Kapitänleutnant* Otto von Bülow and *U-571* commanded by another Knight's Cross holder, *Kapitänleutnant* Helmut Möhlmann. The boats sighted a convoy and *U-404* and *U-662* sank four ships between them, Lüth continued southwards, and on 11 April sank the SS *Empire Whimbrel* with two torpedoes and gunfire. Lüth took his boat through the South Atlantic and round the Cape and eventually arrived at the southern end of the Mozambique Channel. There on 11 May he sank the South African SS *Harrier*, which was torpedoed and disintegrated in a massive explosion: there were no survivors. He then moved into the Indian Ocean, and on 2 July sank SS *Hoikow*, which was hit by two torpedoes and sunk by the bow within three minutes. Of her passengers and crew of 149, only four survived. In the next eight days *U-181* sank three more ships. Over the next few days Lüth encountered very bad weather and had to call off an important rendezvous with other boats. He did, however, surface and signal another boat, *U-197*, and explained the situation, and *U-197* signalled back that she was under attack and was unable to submerge. Lüth went to help, but couldn't find *U-197*. Reluctantly he abandoned the search and headed home. He finally reached Bordeaux on 14 October 1943, after a patrol that had lasted 206 days. Whilst on patrol he had been awarded the Swords and the Diamonds to his Knight's Cross, and Lüth had nominated two members of his own crew for the Knight's Cross, his chief engineer *Kapitänleutnant* Carl-August Landfermann and his Second Watch Officer *Oberleutnant zur See* Johannes Limbach, both of whom received the award for their achievements.

On 15 January 1944, Lüth was appointed chief of the 22nd U-boat Flotilla, and on 17 July he was reassigned as a division officer at the Naval School at Flensburg. He was promoted twice during his time at Flensburg and on 15 September, he became the youngest *Kapitän zur See* in the German Navy, at just thirty years old. On 30 April 1945,

Wolfgang Lüth wearing his Knight's Cross with Oakleaves and Swords, April 1943. (Author's collection)

The last resting place of Kapitän zur See *Wolfgang Lüth, accidently shot by a German sentry in Flensburg on 14 May 1945.* (Author's collection)

Hitler committed suicide in Berlin, and named *Großadmiral* Dönitz as his successor. On 8 May, Dönitz appointed Lüth as Commandant of the Naval School – six days later Lüth would be dead.

On the night of 14 May 1945, Lüth was walking from the headquarters of *Großadmiral* Dönitz to the Commandant House in the Naval School, along a dark and narrow walkway called the Black Path. It was a windy and rainy night and the sentries outside the school and surrounding area were young, wet, tired and jittery, and they had been ordered to shoot to kill. Lüth himself had issued the order; all sentries were to only challenge once and then shoot. At approx. 00:30 hours Lüth approached a young sentry called Matthias Gottlob, who was only eighteen. His orders were to stop and challenge some of the most senior officers of the *Wehrmacht* as they walked to the two buildings. He couldn't see up the path because it was so dark. He suddenly heard footsteps and shouted, 'Halt!' down the pathway, as he was directed to do, 'Who is there?'. The footsteps stopped, but there was no answer. The sentry took the rifle in his hands and shouted again. Still no answer. This time he pointed his rifle down the path and screamed at the top of his voice, 'Halt, who is there?'. Again there was no answer. He put the rifle to his shoulder and fired. Within a few seconds the sergeant of the guard ran towards the sentry. He asked Gottlob who had he shot: the young sentry didn't know. They both saw a body on the ground, as they slowly walked along the path. It was seen to be wearing a leather coat and a white scarf – it was Lüth, with a bullet wound to the head.

The next day Dönitz convened a board of enquiry to find out what happened. Everyone among the Germans were in shock, nobody could believe it. Was it an accident? Was it suicide? Some thought the British had killed him. The verdict was that Lüth had not heard the challenge made by Gottlob because of the wind in the trees, making such a noise. Gottlob was young and inexperienced and had shot, just as he had been ordered to do. Dönitz ruled that it had been a tragic accident and nobody was to blame. The theory of suicide was quickly rejected. On 16 May 1945, Lüth was given a Nazi state funeral – the last of the Third Reich. The Allied authorities had granted Dönitz permission. The coffin was covered with a swastika flag and had a guard of honour. Dönitz read the eulogy, '... Wolfgang Lüth, we now take leave of you.'

Lüth was a gifted U-boat commander but he wasn't always liked by his crew. He was very prudish and nagged his men to get married and to have children, and if they were married then he nagged them to stay faithful. He would restrict them to the boat so they couldn't go ashore and visit bordellos, and he would often follow his officers around to make sure they did not cheat on their wives. He was described by one U-boat commander as 'the craziest man I ever met.'

Other awards:
31 Mar 1937: Long Service Award 4th Class
6 Jun 1939: Spanish Cross in Bronze
25 Jan 1940: Iron Cross 2nd Class
18 Feb 1940: U-boat War Badge
15 May 1940: Iron Cross 1st Class
1 Nov 1941: Italian War Cross with Swords
26 Jan 1943: U-boat War Badge with Diamonds
15 Apr 1943: Honorary Dagger of the Navy
12 Oct 1944: U-boat Combat Clasp in Bronze

Knight's Cross with Oakleaves and Swords

August Wilhelm <u>Otto</u> KRETSCHMER
Fregattenkapitän
47 ships sunk, 274,418 tons
5 ships damaged, 37,965 tons

Knight's Cross: Awarded on 4 August 1940, as *Kapitänleutnant* and as commander of *U-99*, part of the 7th U-boat Flotilla, for sinking 117,000 shipping tonnes. He became the 7th U-boat commander and the 23rd *Kriegsmarine* recipient of the award.

Knight's Cross with Oakleaves: Awarded as *Kapitänleutnant* and as commander of *U-99* on 4 November 1940 to become the 2nd U-boat commander to receive the Oakleaves, in recognition of sinking over 200,000 shipping tonnes. The presentation was made by Hitler during a special ceremony on 13 November 1940 at the Reich Chancellery, Berlin.

Knight's Cross with Oakleaves and Swords: Awarded on 26 December 1941 as the 5th recipient as *Korvettenkapitän* and still commander of *U-99*, for sinking over 274,000 tonnes of shipping. The presentation was made whilst Kretschmer was a prisoner-of-war at Bowmanville Prison Camp in Ontario, Canada by the camp commandant.

Otto Kretschmer was the most successful U-boat commander of the Second World War, responsible for the sinking of forty-seven ships, for a total of 274,418 tonnes. He earned

(Author's collection)

the nickname 'Silent Otto', both for his successful use of the silent running capability of U-boats as well as for his reluctance to transmit radio messages during patrols. His total is more incredible due to the fact that he was captured by the Allies in March 1941, spending the rest of the war as a prisoner.

Kretschmer was born on 1 May 1912, in Heidau, Lower Silesia, the son of a local teacher. At the age of seventeen he spent eight months living in Exeter, England, where he learnt to speak English. He joined the *Kriegsmarine* as an officer cadet in April 1930, and attended various courses aboard different ships. In June 1932, he served aboard the survey vessel *Meteor* for navigation training and in October 1934 was commissioned as a *Leutnant zur See* and in December he transferred to the light cruiser *Köln*. In January 1936, he transferred to the U-boat service, where he received extensive training and in June was promoted to *Oberleutnant zur See*. In October 1937, he took command of *U-23*, a Type VIIA U-boat. He spent the next eighteen months patrolling off the Spanish coast, as part of the German forces taking part in the Spanish Civil War.

In June 1939 he was promoted to *Kapitänleutnant* and in August Kretschmer took *U-23* out of Wilhelmshaven and headed for the North Sea where he performed minelaying duties. He returned a few days shortly after the German invasion of Poland began, and set out again on more minelaying duties. In late September 1939, he took part in his first war patrol against the British navy in the area of the Orkneys. He sank his first ship, the British SS *Glen Farg*, on 4 October and during his next patrol he claimed another ship, the Dutch SS *Scotia*. For his next patrol he operated off the coast of Scotland and the Orkneys and on 11 January 1940, he sank the Norwegian SS *Fredville* and the following day the Danish tanker MV *Danmark*. During the next two patrols Kretschmer sunk another five ships, including the destroyer HMS *Daring*, for a total of 18,000 tons.

Kretschmer left for the Atlantic in June 1940, and headed for Norwegian waters, but it was to be a short patrol. He had been warned not to enter certain areas around the Norwegian coast which were being patrolled by the battleship *Scharnhorst*. However, in avoiding a British submarine he inadvertently wandered into this prohibited area and was attacked by an aircraft from the *Scharnhorst*. *U-99*'s periscope was damaged during the attack – badly enough for Kretschmer to go in for repairs at Wilhelmshaven. Two days later, with a repaired periscope Kretschmer set out once again and crossed the North Sea and on towards the Hebrides. On 5 July 1940, he sank the Canadian SS *Magog* by torpedo. After the sinking Kretschmer ordered *U-99* to surface and approached the lifeboats. He gave a bottle of brandy to the ship's captain and wished him well. Two days later *U-99* sank two more ships and the British SS *Humber Arm* the following day. In the early hours of 12 July, he sank the Greek SS *Ia* and six days later he sank the British SS *Woodbury*. Again Kretschmer surfaced near the survivors' rafts and gave out blankets; he then headed for base in Lorient.

During his next two patrols Kretschmer sank a total of ten ships and damaged another three. By the end of his fourth patrol he had sunk a total of over 71,000 shipping tons. On 10 October, *U-99* left port for the west coast of Ireland, and on the evening of 3 November sank the SS *Casanare*. Kretschmer then sank the armed merchant cruiser HMS *Laurentic*. The *Laurentic* was struck by two torpedoes, although three were actually fired at her, the second failed to explode. Kretschmer fired a third which entered into the hole the first torpedo had made. When the armed merchant cruiser HMS *Patroclus* approached to pick up survivors she was fired at too by Kretschmer, and was hit by three torpedoes.

After crash-diving to escape a Sunderland flying boat, Kretschmer surfaced and fired another torpedo at the stricken *Laurentic*. The torpedo struck her stern and ignited the depth charges stored there, causing the ship to sink within two minutes. Two officers and forty-seven ratings were lost. At 18,724 tons, HMS *Laurentic* was one of the largest ships sunk during the war. A destroyer had spotted *U-99* and Kretschmer had to act quickly if he was to sink HMS *Patroclus*. He fired his fifth torpedo which had no effect so he fired a sixth which broke the ship in two, the stern capsized and the bow sank slowly. The commander, six officers and forty-nine ratings were lost. On 5 November, *U-99* sank the British tanker MV *Scottish Maiden* and three days later returned to port. On 27 November, Kretschmer took out *U-99* for his seventh patrol and sank another four ships in five days. On 7 December *U-99* had sunk the Dutch SS *Farmsum* in heavy seas and had been damaged herself during the attack. Kretschmer was about to give the order to surface to make repairs when three destroyers were sighted. *U-99* had to dive, and was subjected to fifty depth charges before the destroyers moved away. With one engine out of action and the periscope not working, Kretschmer had no choice but to head for his home port.

On 22 February 1941, Kretschmer took *U-99* out for his eighth and last patrol. He sank two ships, the British whaling factory ship *Terje Viken* (at the time the largest ship of her type in the world at 20,638 tons) and the British tanker *Athelbeach* on 7 March, and sank another six ships from Convoy HX112 on 16 March, and that same day he was promoted to *Korvettenkapitän*. Shortly after midnight on 17 March, with all of his torpedoes expended, Kretschmer moved away from the convoy. *U-99* was then spotted by a destroyer and he gave the order to dive but it was too late: the boat was attacked with depth charges. As a result *U-99* was badly damaged and sank to 720ft. With leaks appearing, Kretschmer had little choice but to surface. As the destroyers moved closer, Kretschmer made the decision to scuttle his boat by opening all hatches. When the destroyer HMS *Walker* approached and started to lower a boat *U-99* had still not sunk, so the Chief Engineer went back on board to flood the ballast tanks. He was never seen again. Three of his crew, including the Chief Engineer, were lost and Kretschmer along with the remaining members of his crew were picked up by HMS *Walker*.

The 18,724-ton armed merchant cruiser HMS Laurentic, *sunk by Kretschmer on 3 November 1940.* (Author's collection)

Kretschmer spent almost seven years as a prisoner-of-war in the hands of the British at No. 1 POW Camp Grizedale Hall. In 1943, the German High Command tried to rescue Kretschmer, during a plan called Operation *Kiebitz* but it failed. Kretschmer spent the last four years in captivity in Canada at Bowmanville POW Camp. Whilst in captivity, on 1 September 1944 he was promoted to *Fregattenkapitän*. He finally returned to Germany in December 1947, and like so many surviving German naval veterans joined West Germany's *Bundesmarine*. He joined the newly-formed service in 1955 and rose to the rank of *Flottillenadmiral* in December 1965. He retired from the service in September 1970, and was often interviewed for television and radio, and appeared in the British TV documentary series *The World at War*.

While on holiday in Bavaria on 5 August 1998, Kretschmer died in a boating accident on the Danube, while celebrating his fiftieth wedding anniversary.

Other awards:
2 Oct 1936: Long Service Award 4th Class
17 Oct 1939: Iron Cross 2nd Class
26 Oct 1939: Return of Memel Commemorative Medal
9 Nov 1939: U-boat War Badge
17 Dec 1939: Iron Cross 1st Class
20 Dec 1939: Commemorative Medal of 01 Oct 1938
1941: U-boat War Badge with Diamonds

Reinhard 'Teddy' Johann Heinz Paul Anton SUHREN
Fregattenkapitän
19 ships sunk, 96,444 tons
4 ships damaged, 28,907 tons

Knight's Cross: Awarded on 3 November 1940, as *Oberleutnant zur See* and as First Watch Officer on *U-48* in recognition of his part in the sinking of almost 200,000 tonnes of shipping. The award was requested by the commander of *U-48*, *Kapitänleutnant* Heinrich Bleichrodt, and was presented to Suhren by *Kapitän zur See* Hans-Georg von Friedeburg to become the 20th U-boat recipient.

Knight's Cross with Oakleaves: Awarded as *Oberleutnant zur See* on 31 December 1941, as commander of *U-564*, to become the 56th recipient, for his outstanding achievement of sinking nine ships, which included two totalling 11,596 tonnes. He was presented with his award at *Führer* Headquarters '*Wolfschanze*' in Rastenburg, East Prussia by Hitler in January 1942.

Knight's Cross with Oakleaves and Swords:
Awarded on 1 September 1942, as *Kapitänleutnant* (Scherzer)

and as commander of *U-564*, to become the 18th recipient, and the 3rd naval officer, for sinking a total of ten ships during three patrols in the Atlantic. The Swords were presented by Hitler at a ceremony at *Führer* Headquarters '*Wolfschanze*' in Rastenburg, East Prussia on 25 October 1943.

Reinhard Suhren was born on 16 April 1916 in Langenschwalbach, Hesse, the second of three children of Geert Suhren and Ernestine Ludovika Suhren. His younger brother Gerd was also awarded the Knight's Cross on 21 October 1940, during which time he was serving as chief engineer aboard *U-37*. Upon receiving his school certificate the young Suhren was accepted on a sailing course at the Hanseatic Yacht School in Neustadt-Holstein. During the course at the school, the students had to learn to march, and it was during these marches that a boy yelled at Suhren, 'Hey Reinhard, when I look at you marching, it reminds me of a Teddy bear.' Later that same boy met Suhren again during his basic training and greeted him with the words, 'Hey Teddy, it's you'. The nickname 'Teddy' would stay with Suhren throughout his entire career. For his basic training he was attached to the 2nd Company of the Ship Division at Stralsund, in the Baltic from April 1934 until June 1935.

With his basic training over Suhren was accepted as a naval cadet and began training as an officer at the Flensburg-Mürwik Naval Academy in March 1937. He attended courses in navigation, gunnery, communications and as a torpedo officer and was commissioned as a *Leutnant zur See* in April 1938. On 28 August, he transferred to the U-boat school and in November was appointed Second Watch Officer aboard *U-51* as *Leutnant zur See*, under the command of *Kapitänleutnant* Ernst-Günther Heinicke. In April 1939, he was promoted to *Oberleutnant zur See* and transferred to *U-48* as First Watch Officer. He served under the command of *Kapitänleutnant* Herbert Schultze for five patrols, under *Korvettenkapitän* Hans Rudolf Rösing for two patrols and finally under *Kapitänleutnant* Heinrich Bleichrodt. It was during his time under Bleichrodt that Suhren made a name for himself. As First Officer he was also Torpedo Officer and played a key role in the sinking of almost 200,000 shipping tons. Bleichrodt had been awarded the Knight's Cross by Dönitz for his achievements but he insisted that his First Officer who had assisted him was also honoured. He argued that the success of *U-48* was more attributable to Suhren than himself as commander. In fact Bleichrodt said he wouldn't wear his Knight's Cross unless Suhren was also honoured. With the support of another U-boat commander, Engelbrecht Endraß, the Knight's Cross for Suhren was approved in November 1940.

On 3 April 1941, Suhren took command of *U-564*, a Type VIIC boat, part of the 1st U-boat Flotilla, operating out of Kiel. During a training patrol he rescued a crew of a German aircraft that had ditched in the Baltic. For his first war patrol as commander of *U-564*, Suhren left Kiel for the North Atlantic on 17 June 1941. On the 23rd he made contact with Convoy HX133 south of Greenland and managed to sink one ship before losing contact with the convoy. On the 26th Suhren re-located the convoy, and in the early hours of the 27th he sank two ships, the Dutch SS *Maasdam* and the British MV *Malaya II* and damaging a third, the Norwegian tanker MV *Kongsaard* just east of Cape Farewell. He again lost contact with the convoy soon after and although he sank another ship on 29 June, and after numerous attempts to make contact with any other convoys he returned to base at Brest on 27 July.

Suhren took *U-564* out again on its second patrol on 16 August and was directed towards Convoy OG71, but failed to find any ships. On 22nd Suhren sighted two ships west of Oporto, the steam tug *Empire Oak* and the Irish SS *Clonlara*: both were torpedoed and sunk. In the early morning of the 23rd, Suhren sank the corvette HMS *Zinnaa* before heading back to Brest. For his next patrol he joined *Brandenburg* Group, in a patrol near Cape Farewell. On 4 October, a convoy was sighted by reconnaissance aircraft, but was soon lost. Suhren then headed to Gibraltar to await the departure of Convoy HG75. On the morning of 24 October, Suhren torpedoed and sank three ships and a few days later he returned to port. Suhren had by this time sank a total of nine ships and had damaged another, for this achievement he was awarded the Oakleaves on New Year's Eve and was promoted to *Kapitänleutnant* the next day.

He sank only one ship during his next patrol, the Canadian tanker MV *Victolie* on 11 February 1942. She was hit by one torpedo amidships, and although the crew of *U-564* observed how her crew abandoned ship in the lifeboats they were never found and forty-seven men were lost. On 4 April, he left Brest and began his sixth war

Reinhard Suhren with his brother Gerd, also a Knight's Cross holder, who served as Chief Engineer aboard U-37 and survived the war. He died on 6 May 1991. (Author's collection)

patrol, reaching the coast of Bermuda on the 27th. He sank the British SS *Ocean Venus* on 3 May and the next day he damaged the SS *Eclipse* and the following day damaged the SS *Delisle* off the Florida coast. He sank three more ships before returning to base on 6 June 1942. His next patrol took him to the Caribbean, where on 19 July he attacked Convoy OS34, together with *U-108* and *U-654*. Suhren sank the British SS *Empire Hawksbill* and the MV *Lavington Court*. He had to wait a month before his next success, on 19 August he sank two ships, the *British Consul* and the *Empire Cloud*. He claimed another on 30 August before heading back to base, and on the way he sank the Norwegian tanker *Vardaas*. He finally reached Brest on 18 September, to be given the news that he had been awarded the Swords and had been promoted to *Korvettenkapitän*.

Suhren was appointed instructor with the 2nd U-boat Training Division on 26 October 1942, and transferred to the 22nd U-boat Flotilla as Chief of Staff, under *Korvettenkapitän* Wilhelm Ambrosius. During the last year of the war he served as Officer Commanding U-boats in Norway with the rank of *Fregattenkapitän*. He was taken prisoner by the British in Oslo, Norway and released from an internment camp in Neustadt-Holstein on 16 May 1946. Suhren was asked many times to join the *Bundeswehr*, the armed forces of West Germany. He always refused, saying that he couldn't serve in a navy which looked down upon all former soldiers of the *Wehrmacht*. On 25 August 1984, Suhren died of stomach cancer in Halstenbek near Hamburg. Among those who attended his funeral were Herbert Schultze, Erich Topp, Otto Kretschmer, Klaus Bargsten, Hans Meckel and Peter-Erich Cremer. The *Bundeswehr* provided an honour guard as a mark of respect. According to his will his remains were buried at sea where *U-564* was lost. His old boat had sunk on 14 June

1943, north-west of Cape Ortegal. He was an excellent commander and few were better qualified for a first command than Suhren who had achieved the unique feat of winning the Knight's Cross despite being only a First Watch Officer.

Other awards:
5 Apr 1939: Long Service Award 4th Class
25 Sep 1939: Iron Cross 2nd Class
20 Dec 1939: Commemorative Medal of 01 Oct 1938
21 Dec 1939: U-boat War Badge
25 Feb 1940: Iron Cross 1st Class
Mar 1942: U-boat War Badge with Diamonds
30 Jan 1944: War Service Cross 2nd Class with Swords
1944: U-boat Combat Clasp in Bronze
1945: U-boat Combat Clasp in Silver

Erich TOPP

Fregattenkapitän
36 ships sunk, 198,650 tons
4 ships damaged, 32,317 tons

Knight's Cross: He became the 75th recipient of the *Kriegsmarine* to be awarded and the 33rd U-boat recipient on 20 June 1941, as *Oberleutnant zur See* and as commander of *U-552*, 7th U-boat Flotilla, for sinking fourteen ships in the Atlantic for a total of almost 90,000 tons.

(Author's collection)

Knight's Cross with Oakleaves: He became the 87th recipient on 11 April 1942, as *Kapitänleutnant* and as commander of *U-552*, 7th U-boat Flotilla, for sinking thirteen ships for a total of 68,303 tons. He was the 12th naval recipient of the award, which was presented to him by Hitler at *Führer* Headquarters *'Wolfschanze'* in Rastenburg, East Prussia in June 1942.

Knight's Cross with Oakleaves and Swords: Awarded whilst still *Kapitänleutnant* and as commander of *U-552* on 17 August 1942, to become the 17th recipient inrecognition for sinking six ships for a total of 20,994 tons, and for damaging a further three. Hitler presented Topp with the Swords at *Führer* Headquarters *'Wehrwolf'* at Vinnitsa in the Ukraine, being the third naval officer to win the award.

Erich Topp was the third most successful U-boat commander of the Second World War, sinking thirty-six ships for a total of 198,650 tons. He was born on 2 July 1914, in Hannover, the son of an engineer. He joined the *Reichsmarine* on 1 April 1934, and went through the usual training onboard the sail training ship *Gorch Fock* and the light cruiser *Karlsruhe*, before entering the Naval Academy at Mürwik.

Topp was commissioned as a *Leutnant zur See* in April 1937, and appointed adjutant on board the *Karlsruhe*. On 5 October, he entered the U-boat School in Neustadt and in November the following year was appointed First Watch Officer on *U-46*, under the command of *Kapitänleutnant* Herbert Sohler. Promoted to *Oberleutnant zur See* in April 1939, his first war patrol was on 3 October 1939, when *U-46* headed out of Kiel into the Atlantic. Topp took part in two more patrols and *U-46* sank two ships.

On 5 June 1940, Topp was given command of *U-57*, a Type IIC boat. He left Bergen for his first patrol on 11 July, and by the 17th, he had sunk two ships, the Swedish *O.A. Brodin* and the British SS *Manipur*. He then headed back to Bergen. He sank a single ship during his next patrol, and on 14 August left Lorient for the coastal waters of Scotland. Just after midnight on the 24th, Topp attacked Convoy OB202, and sank the British SS *Cumberland* and SS *Saint Dunstan* and damaged another, the SS *Havilder*. During the evening of the 25th he sank the British tanker MV *Pecten* and soon after returned to port. He was then ordered to sail *U-57* from Bergen to Kiel. On 3 September whilst near the entrance to the Kiel Canal at Brunsbüttel, *U-57* was rammed by the Norwegian SS *Rona*. The boat sank and six crew members were drowned. Topp was later cleared of all blame. However, he was without a boat and was placed on the reserve list for the next two months.

On 4 December 1940, much to Topp's relief, he was appointed commander of *U-552*, a Type VIIC built by Blohm und Voss in Hamburg. He took the boat out on its first trials and then finally on 18 February 1941, he left for the North Atlantic. Within a few days Topp sighted Convoy OB289 and pursued it for three days. He managed to catch the convoy and fired seven torpedoes at various targets, but the torpedoes failed to detonate –

fairly common at the time. Then on 1 March he sank the British tanker SS *Cadillac* north-east of Rockall: thirty-eight crewmen lost their lives, only four were rescued. The following day an aircraft spotted Convoy OB292, leaving the North Channel and *U-552* formed part of a patrol that consisted of seven boats. On the 10th, Topp sank the Icelandic steam trawler SS *Reykjaborg* by gunfire south-east of Iceland. With faulty torpedoes Topp had no choice but to return to St. Nazaire.

Topp was promoted to *Kapitänleutnant* in early April 1941 and left for his next patrol on the 7th, and headed for the North Atlantic, where on the 27th he sank two ships, the British steam trawler HMS *Commander Horton* and the MV *Beacon Grange*. The following day a convoy was sighted, and in the afternoon Topp torpedoed the tanker MV *Capulet*. She was left burning and abandoned, until *U-201* sank her. Before returning to port Topp sank the British passenger ship SS *Nerissa*, bringing his total to eleven   (Author's collection)

ships sunk. His next patrol took him to the coast of Ireland, where he sank the British SS *Ainderby* on 10 June, two days later he sank the British merchant ship *Chinese Prince* and despite thick fog and strong winds Topp managed to sink another ship before heading back to port. On his next patrol Topp was directed towards Convoy SC42 but heavy air cover and the strengthening of escort ships made sinking any ships very difficult. Then when another convoy was sighted, Topp had teamed up with four other boats but because of radio interference any such attack could not be coordinated. On 18 June he sank the British SS *Norfolk* after firing two torpedoes, but only one crew member was lost. He continued to hunt for convoys and on 23 August he sank the Norwegian SS *Spind* and on 21 September whilst east-north-east of Cape Farewell he torpedoed and sank the American SS *T.J. Williams* with the loss of seventeen crew, and the same day he sank two other merchant ships, the Panamanian *Pink Star* and the Norwegian tanker *Barbro*, with loss of all her crew. He returned to St. Nazaire on 5 October.

On his next patrol Topp sank the destroyer USS *Reuben James*, which was escorting Convoy HX156. When the torpedoes hit, the ship exploded and split in two, the forward section sinking immediately and the stern staying afloat for five minutes. All the officers were killed. It was the first US naval vessel lost in the war, two months before the attack on Pearl Harbor. Topp was never reprimanded over the incident, as it was felt that no U-boat commander could be expected to identify an American vessel that had been blacked out at night and was escorting a British convoy. When news reached Hitler in the Reich Chancellery he was unconcerned and still in a good mood after his victories in Russia. In private, however, Topp was keenly aware of what he had done; he knew how politically explosive the sinking of a neutral ship might become. He had no qualms about international law but he felt remorse, even after the war, for taking the lives of those who were technically, at the time, non-combatants.

On Christmas Day 1941, Topp left port for the area near Gibraltar but was later ordered together with two other boats to assemble near the Azores. On 15 January 1942, Topp sank the SS *Dayrose* and three days later sank the SS *France Salman*. He was more successful during his next patrol, which began on 7 March in US waters. Topp torpedoed the tanker MV *Ocana* and it was left to burn until it was sunk by a minesweeper. On 3 April, Topp sank the SS *David H. Atwater* by gunfire. Although the ship was sinking *U-552* continued to fire, killing many of the crew as they struggled to launch the lifeboats – only three members of the crew survived. By 10 April Topp had sunk five more ships and had now brought his total to twenty-nine. During his next two patrols Topp would add another seven ships to his total. Awarded the Swords in August he was promoted to *Korvettenkapitän* the same day, Topp became the third most successful U-boat commander of the war.

In September 1942, Topp was assigned to training duties ashore; the High Command couldn't afford to lose a man of his calibre and experience. Later he took command of the 27th U-boat Flotilla where he stayed until August 1944. He was promoted to *Fregattenkapitän* in December and was involved in the commissioning of the new Type XXI boat for which he wrote the battle instructions before he took command of *U-3010* in March 1945. He was made commander of *U-2513* in April, and left Kiel for his one and only patrol with his new boat he had to make an emergency dive to avoid an aircraft attack and then in early May took the boat to Horton, where he surrendered to British forces on 9 May. Released from captivity in August 1945, he joined the *Bundeswehr* in March 1958. He was Chief of Staff at NATO's Military Committee in Washington DC, and in

October 1963 was appointed Chief of Staff in command of the fleet, and served from July 1965 as Deputy Director in the Naval Staff. He retired in December 1969, with the rank of *Konteradmiral*. In 1990 he published one of the most philosophical accounts of the U-boat war ever written, entitled *The Odyssey of a U-boat Commander*. He died in Süßen, a district in Göppingen in Baden-Württemberg in southern Germany, on 26 December 2005.

Other awards:
1 Apr 1939: Long Service Award 4th Class
Jan 1940: Iron Cross 2nd Class
Sep 1940: Iron Cross 1st Class
7 Nov 1939: U-boat War Badge
11 Apr 1942: U-boat War Badge with Diamonds
30 Jan 1944: War Service Cross 2nd Class with Swords
Sep 1944: War Service Cross 1st Class with Swords

Knight's Cross with Oakleaves

Heinrich Carl Bernhard Rudolf 'Ajax' BLEICHRODT
Korvettenkäpitan
25 ships sunk, 152,320 tons
2 ships damaged, 11,684 tons

Knight's Cross: Awarded on 24 October 1940, as *Kapitänleutnant* and as commander of *U-48* for his success in the North Atlantic for the sinking of thirteen ships including the British ships *City of Benares* and HMS *Dundee* for a total of 71,501 shipping tons. He became the 18th U-boat recipient of the award.

Knight's Cross with Oakleaves: Awarded on 23 September 1942, after sinking twekve ships which included the *Tuscan Star* and with a total tonnage of 80,819 as *Kapitänleutnant* and as commander of *U-109*, becoming the 125th recipient, and

Above: Bleichrodt as the 125th recipient of the Knight's Cross with Oakleaves, September 1942. (Author's collection)

Left: (Scherzer)

presented to him by Hitler in September 1942, at *Führer* Headquarters '*Wehrwolf*' at Vinnitsa, Ukraine.

One of the most successful U-boat commanders of the war, Heinrich Bleichrodt sunk twenty-five ships for a total of more than 152,000 tons making him the fourteenth most successful U-boat commander of the Second World War. He was born on 21 October 1909 in Berga, Sangerhausen and entered the *Reichsmarine* in January 1933. He received his commission on 1 April 1935 as a *Leutnant zur See* and was made platoon commander and then company officer. Two years later, after another promotion, Bleichrodt was appointed Watch Officer on board the sail training ship *Gorch Fock*.In July 1939 he was assigned to the heavy cruiser *Admiral Hipper*, and three months later he began his U-boat training now with the rank of *Kapitänleutnant*. He was appointed Watch Officer on *U-8* in March 1940, and in June was transferred to *U-34* under *Kapitänleutnant* Wilhelm Rollmann.

On 29 August 1940, Bleichrodt took over command of *U-48* from *Korvettenkapitän* Rudolf Rösing, and began his first war patrol on 8 September. On 15 September he sank the sloop HMS *Dundee* west of Ireland, the only escort ship of Convoy SC3. Six officers and six ratings were lost. The same day he also sank the Greek merchant ship *Alexandros* and the British *Empire Volunteer*. Three days later he sank the British passenger ship SS *City of Benares*, the flagship of Convoy SC3. This 11,000-ton liner was crowded with 400 passengers; among these were 90 English children who were being resettled in Canada to escape the Blitz. During the chaotic rush to abandon ship some of the lifeboats were released onto those already in the water and they crashed down on the occupants, killing many including some of the crew. The lifeboats that did get away drifted for days in the icy, rough seas before being found – altogether about 300 passengers, including 70 children, were lost. The sinking evoked outraged in Britain, and the impact was heightened by the release of the grim lifeboat stories of the thirteen children who had survived. As a result, the British government cancelled the Children's Overseas Resettlement Scheme. Having no idea of the pain and suffering he had caused, Bleichrodt went on to sink another British freighter the following night. He returned to Lorient on 25 September, having sunk the British SS *Blairangus* and damaged the Norwegian SS *Broompark*, which was later sunk by *U-552*. On 5 October 1940 he went to sea again and had a very successful patrol, sinking eight ships and returning to Kiel on 27 October having sunk over 43,000 shipping tons. One of these ships was the Norwegian *Brandanger* which was hit on the port side in the engine room by a single torpedo. Two crewmen died on watch below and four men drowned when they fell overboard during the launch of their lifeboat. The master and the twenty-three other survivors were picked up from their lifeboat by HMS *Clarkia* and were landed at Liverpool on the 15th. He sank two British merchant ships on the 17th; he claimed another the following day and sank the British tanker *Shirak* about 90 miles south of Rockall on the 20th. On 24 October Bleichrodt was informed by radio that he had been awarded the Knight's Cross in recognition of his success in sinking fifteen British ships.

On 5 June 1941, he was appointed commander of *U-109*, leaving for his first war patrol in his new boat on 28 June, and began to patrol north-west of Morocco. The patrol lasted until August and was unsuccessful; he either could find no trace of the convoys or was driven off by destroyers. In October, he left once again for the Atlantic, and was ordered to the area south-east of Cape Farewell to join other U-boats. Again he returned to base unsuccessful on 18 November. In December 1941, Bleichrodt left

HMS Dundee *was a sloop built at Chatham Dockyard in 1933. She was sunk by a torpedo fired from* U-48 *at 00:25 hours on 15 September 1940 while on escort duty with Convoy SC3 west of Ireland.* (Author's collection)

port to take part in Operation *Paukenschlag* in the Western Atlantic, being one of five boats. He headed for Newfoundland Bank, and on 19 December made an unsuccessful attack on a tanker. Two days later however he sank the British SS *Thirby* off Cape Sable. On 1 February 1942, he sank the British SS *Tacona Star* 387 miles north of Bermuda. She was struck by two torpedoes and the second hit her amidships in the engine room, causing the most damage, and the ship sank by the bow in less than four minutes. The Germans reported that the crew were seen to abandon ship in lifeboats, but they were never seen again and ninety-seven men were lost. Four days later he sank the Canadian tanker MV *Montrolite*, she sank by the stern within five minutes with the loss of the master, twenty-six members and one gunner. Bleichrodt sank the Panamanian SS *Halcyon* by gunfire the day after.

During his next patrol he operated in US waters and between April and May 1942 he sank a further three ships. On 18 July, *U-109* was attacked by a Junkers Ju 88, which had misidentified it. *U-109* managed to crash-dive and escape undamaged. Bleichrodt headed south and sank two more ships, and from August operated west of the Gulf of Guinea. In September Bleichrodt sank the SS *Ocean Might* and just before midnight on the 6th sank the British MV *Tuscan Star*. She was hit on the starboard side at the engine room and the hold by two torpedoes and sank after sixteen minutes, with the loss of fifty-one people. By the end of his fifth and final patrol as commander of *U-109*, Bleichrodt had sunk twelve ships.

On 14 October 1943 Bleichrodt was promoted to *Korvettenkapitän* and in December he suffered a breakdown whilst at sea. He radioed U-boat headquarters to request permission to return to port, but this was at first denied. On New Year's Eve he radioed again and insisted that he return to port and handed over command of *U-109* to his First Officer who brought the boat back to St. Nazaire. Bleichrodt was relieved of his command and given leave: he was exhausted. In July 1943 he returned to duty as a tactical training officer with 27th U-Boat

Flotilla and in February 1944 he was transferred to the 2nd U-Boat Training Division. In July he was appointed Commander of 22nd U-Boat Flotilla at Gotenhafen and Wilhelmshaven and in October was promoted to *Fregattenkapitän*. Bleichrodt surrendered to the Allies in May 1945 and was held until 25 September 1945 on war crimes charges which went to back to September 1940 when he torpedoed the SS *City of Bernares*. He was accused of knowing that the ship was full of evacuees. Bleichrodt denied all charges and even refused to apologise to the survivors – he was eventually acquitted. He died in Munich on 9 January 1977.

Other awards:
1 Jan 1938: Long Service Award 4th Class
25 Jul 1940: Iron Cross 2nd Class
24 Sep 1940: U-Boat War Badge
25 Sep 1940: Iron Cross 1st Class
1 Nov 1941: Italian War Cross with Swords
Oct 1942: U-Boat War Badge with Diamonds
1 Jan 1945: War Service Cross 2nd Class with Swords

<u>Otto</u> Erich August von BÜLOW
Korvettenkäpitan
15 ships sunk, 72,570 tons
2 ships damaged, 16,689 tons

Knight's Cross: Awarded as *Kapitänleutnant* and as commander of *U-404*, on 20 October 1942, after sinking 54,834 shipping tons. In the course of four patrols he sank twelve ships, including the destroyer HMS *Veteran*, and damaged another two.

Knight's Cross with Oakleaves: Awarded on 26 April 1943, as *Kapitänleutnant* and as commander of *U-404*, becoming the 234th recipient after sinking three ships for a total of 17,736 shipping tons. The presentation of his Oakleaves was made by Hitler at his military headquarters '*Wolfschanze*' in Rastenburg, East Prussia on 4 July 1943.

Born on 16 October 1911 into an aristocratic family in Wilhelmshaven, von Bülow joined the *Reichsmarine* in April 1930 as an officer cadet and began his training aboard the light cruiser *Emden* in October. Later in October he was transferred to the 'pocket battleship' *Deutschland* where he continued his training. He was commissioned as a *Leutnant zur See* in January 1935 and was appointed a company commander with the 6th Naval Artillery Battalion in September.

Promoted to *Oberleutnant zur See* in June 1936, he was appointed Watch Officer in April 1937, and then Flak   (Scherzer)

(Scherzer)

Officer on board the battleship *Schleswig-Holstein*. In March 1939 he was made company commander in the 5th Naval Artillery Battalion in Pillau and on 1 June was promoted to *Kapitänleutnant*. On 4 September 1939 he was made commander of the Naval Flak Battalion at Pillau and in November 1940 he was appointed commander of *U-3* of the 21st U-Boat Flotilla, where he continued his training as a U-boat commander. In August 1941 he was made commander of *U-404* and in January 1942 he left Kiel for his first war patrol. On 5 March, he sank the American SS *Collamer* off the coast of Nova Scotia. She had lost contact with Convoy H178 in heavy seas, and was unable to maintain full speed. She was hit by one torpedo which exploded amidships, causing the boilers to explode and killed the engine room crew of three officers and four men. A second torpedo struck and the ship began to sink quickly, seven more were lost. On 13 March he sank the Chilean merchant ship *Tolten*. The neutral ship was struck near the bridge by a single torpedo and sank within six minutes off the coast of New Jersey. Bülow had reported that the ship was zigzagging and was identified as a Chilean ship only after the attack. Twenty-seven of her crew were lost: there was only one survivor. He sank the American *Lemuel Burrows* and three days later sank the British tanker *San Demetrio*. In May 1942 he saw action in the Atlantic area for the second time; his first victim was the American merchant ship *Alcoa Shipper*, followed in June by another six ships, which included the Norwegian *Moldanger* which was struck on the port side amidships in the engine room, killing two of the crew. The ship sank after being struck by another torpedo and the explosion killed eleven men who were lowering a lifeboat. Fourteen crew members were killed and there were thirty survivors. He sank the American SS *West Notus* on 1 June and two days later sank the Swedish SS *Anna*. On 24 June he sank the Yugoslavian merchant ship the *Ljubica Matkovic* about 44 miles east of Cape Lookout. The following day he sank two more ships, the Panamanian SS *Nordal* and the American *Manuela*, about 75 miles east of Cape Lookout. On 11 September von Bülow attacked and damaged the Norwegian tanker *Marit II* and the following day damaged the Norwegian tanker *Daghild*. His last success during this patrol was the destroyer HMS *Veteran*, which he sank on the morning of 26 September with the loss of all the crew. Bülow had fired three torpedoes at the destroyer, and she was struck by two of them and sank immediately.

On 23 April 1943 von Bülow attacked the escort carrier HMS *Biter*. However, he was convinced that he had attacked the USS *Ranger*. Von Bülow and his crew waited to see if they had been successful and when they heard four separate explosions they were convinced they had scored a hit. Von Bülow even contacted his headquarters and informed them that USS *Ranger* had been destroyed, without checking first. It wasn't until after the war that the truth was known; the official records showed that von Bülow had in fact attacked the *Biter* – unsuccessfully as it turned out. He was promoted to *Korvettenkapitän* in June 1943 and in September was commander of the 23rd Flotilla with its headquarters in Danzig and then from February 1945 in Bremerhaven and

HMS Veteran *was struck by two torpedoes and sank immediately with the loss of her commander, eight officers and 150 ratings on 26 September 1942.* (Author's collection)

Hamburg. On 8 April 1945 von Bülow took command of one of the newly-commissioned Electro U-boats and together with other highly decorated-commanders including Schnee, Cremer, Emmermann, Witt and Topp, set out in an attempt to turn the tide in the battle of the Atlantic – without success. During the last weeks of the war von Bülow commanded the Naval Battalion in Neustrelitz, Plön and finally in Mürwik. He was captured by the British on 23 May 1945 and spent almost three months in captivity. In July 1956 he joined the *Bundesmarine*, and became the commander of the 3rd Destroyer Squadron with the rank of *Kapitän zur See*. Von Bülow retired from active service in 1970, and died on 5 January 2006 in Hamburg.

Other awards:
2 Oct 1936: Long Service Award 4th Class
1 Apr 1942: Long Service Award 3rd Class
6 Apr 1942: Iron Cross 2nd Class
6 Apr 1942: Iron Cross 1st Class
1942: U-Boat War Badge
Apr 1943: U-Boat War Badge with Diamonds
20 Apr 1944: War Service Cross 2nd Class with Swords

Karl DÖNITZ
Großadmiral

Knight's Cross: Awarded on 21 April 1940, to become the 5th member of the *Kriegsmarine* to be awarded as *Konteradmiral* and as Commander-in-Chief of U-boats in recognition of his excellent leadership and success against the British Royal Navy and Allied merchant shipping.

(Author's collection)

Knight's Cross with Oakleaves: Awarded as *Großadmiral* and Commander-in-Chief of the *Kriegsmarine* on 6 April 1943, to become the 223rd recipient of the award for his continued success as commander of U-boats. The award was presented to him by Hitler at the Berghof in May/June 1943.

Karl Dönitz was commander of all U-boats during the Second World War and from 1943 he was *Großadmiral*, Commander-in-Chief of the *Kriegsmarine* and subsequently became Hitler's successor in May 1945. Dönitz was born on 16 September 1891, in Grünau near Berlin, he was the son of an engineer, and joined the Imperial Navy in 1910, becoming an officer three years later. When the First World War began, he served on the light cruiser *Breslau* until March 1916, when shortly after being promoted to *Oberleutnant zur See*, he was temporarily assigned as airfield commander at the Dardanelles. He requested a transfer to the submarine forces and from October 1916 served as Watch Officer on *U-39*, and from February 1918, he served as commander of *UC-25*. On 5 September, he transferred as commander to *U-68*, operating in the Mediterranean. On 4 October his boat was sunk by the British and he was taken prisoner.

During the interwar period Dönitz remained in the *Reichswehr*, the Weimar Republic's armed forces. In January 1921, he was promoted to *Kapitänleutnant* and by 1928 he was commander of torpedo boats with the rank of *Korvettenkapitän*. In September 1933, he was promoted again and the following year he was put in command of the light cruiser *Emden*, a training vessel for young officer cadets. On 1 September 1935, he was promoted to *Kapitän zur See* and was placed in command of the first U-boat flotilla. By November 1937, he was convinced that a major campaign against merchant shipping was practicable and began pressing for the conversion of the German fleet to U-boats. He pointed out to *Großadmiral* Raeder, the Commander-in-Chief of the Navy, and to Hitler, that destroying Britain's fleet of oil tankers would starve the Royal Navy of supplies needed for its ships. Dönitz believed that the strategy to group several submarines together to form a 'Wolf Pack' was the best way to destroy enemy shipping. It was an idea he had from his First World War days.

Dönitz could not convince Raeder and the two often argued over funding priorities. Hitler wasn't really interested, giving more time to his closer associates like Hermann Göring and Heinrich Himmler. Like Hitler, Raeder believed that the German navy needed to build up its strength and needed to build more ships, huge battleships. On 28 January 1939, Dönitz was promoted to *Kommodore* and appointed Commander of Submarines. When the Second World War began, the *Kriegsmarine* was not prepared for war. Although it had increased its capital ships, Dönitz only had fifty-seven U-boats, many of which were short-range, and only twenty-two were of the new Type VIIs. He had to make do with what he had, while being harassed by Raeder and Hitler calling on him to dedicate boats to attacking British warships. These operations had mixed success. The British aircraft carrier HMS *Courageous* and the battleship HMS *Royal Oak* were sunk, but the battleship HMS *Nelson* managed to escape all U-boat attacks and was damaged by aircraft of the Italian air force in September 1941, and during the Normandy landings she struck a mine which had been laid by a U-boat in 1939. She was repaired and returned to duty in early 1945. HMS *Barham* was sunk off the Egyptian coast in November 1941 by *U-331*, which managed to escape and its commander *Kapitänleutnant* Hans-Diedrich Freiherr von Tiesenhausen was awarded the Knight's Cross.

Promoted to *Konteradmiral* in October 1939, Dönitz was promoted to *Vizeadmiral* in September 1940, and after the fall of France he gained U-boat bases at Lorient, Brest, St. Nazaire and La Rochelle. By 1941, Dönitz had the new Type VIIC U-boat, which were much improved although merchant ships had greatly increased, the U-boats had improved torpedoes and much better operational planning which led to an increase in shipping being sunk. By December 1941, America was in the war and Dönitz immediately planned to target shipping along the east coast of the United States, known as Operation *Paukenschlag* (Drumbeat). He only had nine of the large Type IX boats but it had dramatic results as the US Navy was entirely unprepared for anti-submarine warfare, and at the beginning committed every imaginable mistake. British shipping loses drastically increased.

On 14 March 1942, Dönitz was promoted to *Admiral* and by the end of the year production of Type VII U-boats had increased, and Dönitz was able to conduct mass attacks by groups of U-boats – his 'Wolf Packs'. Allied shipping losses mounted considerably and there was concern for a time about the state of British fuel supplies. On 30 January 1943, Dönitz was promoted to *Großadmiral* and took over from Raeder as Commander-in-Chief of the *Kriegsmarine*. However by mid-1943 the war in the Atlantic had turned against Germany, but Dönitz pushed for increased U-boat construction and he believed that further technological developments would tip the war once more in Germany's favour, and he shared this view with Hitler.

Dönitz continued to play an important role in the war, proving himself an able tactician in directing the Battle of the Atlantic. The submarine fleet probably came closer than any other weapon to winning the war for Germany, sinking some 15 million tons of Allied shipping and threatening to cut off the supply of food and fuel to Britain. However, U-boat losses increased, thanks to the Allies breaking the Enigma code, the entry of America into the war, improved anti-submarine ships and the fact that the U-boat losses were so great that production was unable to replace them in sufficient numbers.

In the final days of the war, with Hitler in his underground bunker in Berlin, unable to leave, suicide was his only escape. Until then his official successor had been Hermann Göring, but he and Himmler had betrayed Hitler, with Himmler offering to surrender to the Western Allies, which

Dönitz as Commander-in-Chief of the German Navy, here wearing his Knight's Cross with Oakleaves. (Author's collection)

Dönitz with his adjutant Korvettenkapitän *Walter Lüdde-Neurath, leaving the Flensburg government building in May 1945.* (Author's collection)

was declined. Both were expelled from the Party. On 29 April 1945, Hitler wrote his last will and testament and named *Großadmiral* Dönitz as his successor. Dönitz would be the new Reich President of Nazi Germany and Supreme Commander of the Armed Forces. On 1 May, Dönitz announced by radio that Hitler had fallen and had appointed him as his successor. The following day the new government fled to Flensburg-Mürwik. During these final weeks, Dönitz devoted all of his efforts to ensure German troops would surrender to the British or Americans and not the Soviets. He feared the Soviets would be vengeful and would carry out reprisals, so he had hoped to strike a deal with the Western Allies.

The Dönitz government came to an end on 23 May 1945, when the British arrested him. Much to his own surprise he was told he would be a defendant at a war crimes trial held at Nuremberg. There, together with the likes of Göring, Speer, Hess, Kaltenbrunner, Ribbentrop and others of Hitler's regime, he was accused of war crimes. He received the lightest sentence of those given prison sentences, ten years. Exactly ten years later he was released from Berlin's Spandau Prison. He retired to the small village of Aumühle in Schleswig-Holstein, where he wrote two books. In 1973, he appeared in the ITV documentary *The World at War*, and in later life he made every effort to answer correspondence and autograph postcards for collectors and admirers. He was unrepentant about his role in the war, and firmly believed that he acted correctly and always in the interests of his country. Karl Dönitz died of a heart attack on 24 December 1980, in Aumühle. His funeral was attended by hundreds of former membersof the *Kriegsmarine* but the West German government banned the wearing of uniforms and honours. However, a number of naval officers disobeyed this and there were over a hundred holders of the Knight's Cross in attendance.

Carl EMMERMANN
Korvettenkapitän
26 ships sunk, 152,080 tons

Knight's Cross: Awarded on 27 November 1942, to become the 69th U-boat recipient as *Kapitänleutnant* and as commander of *U-172*, for the sinking of fifteen ships for a total of just over 88,000 shipping tons.

Knight's Cross with Oakleaves: For continued actions in the Atlantic and in recognition of sinking a further ten ships, as *Kapitänleutnant* and as commander of

U-172 on 4 July 1943. The presentation was made personally by Hitler on 23 December 1943, at his military headquarters '*Wolfschanze*' in Rastenburg, East Prussia.

(Scherzer)

Carl Emmermann was the 13th most successful U-boat commander of the Second World War, sinking twenty-six ships for a total of 152,080 shipping tons. He was born in Hamburg on 6 March 1915, and entered the German navy as an Officer Candidate on 8 April 1934. From September 1934, he trained aboard the light cruiser *Karlsruhe* and at the outbreak of war found him in a posting at the Naval Academy at Flensburg-Mürwick. Commissioned as a *Leutnant zur See* in April 1937, he was promoted to *Oberleutnant zur See* in April 1939 and in September 1940 he joined the 1st U-boat Training Division and two months later, as *Oberleutnant zur See* he was appointed Watch Officer aboard *U-A*. This was a 1,300-ton boat built in Germany for the Turkish Navy under the name *Batiray*. With the outbreak of war, however, she was taken over by the *Kriegsmarine*.

Under the command of *Korvettenkapitän* Hans Eckermann *U-A* left Kiel on 25 February 1941, for the North Atlantic: Emmermann's first war patrol. *U-A* was one of seven boats which formed a patrol line to intercept Convoy OB292 just west of the British Isles on 5 March. *U-A* torpedoed and damaged the SS *Dunaff Head*, but it soon returned to port. On its next patrol *U-A* was unsuccessful. Promoted to *Kapitänleutnant* in October 1941, Emmermann took command of *U-172*, a Type IXC boat, in November. His first patrol out of Kiel on 22 April 1942 was an eleven-day shakedown patrol which took the boat to Lorient to join the 10th Flotilla. His first war patrol began on 11 May, when he left Lorient to operate in the Caribbean; it was to be very successful. En route he sank the British tanker MV *Athelknight* on 27 May and on 3 June he sank the American SS *City of Alma* and two days later the SS *Delfina*. On the morning of the 8th he sank the American MV *Sicilen* off Isla Beata in the Dominican Republic. Within the next fifteen days he sank another five ships and in early July made his way back to port. During the journey he sank the American SS *Santa Rita* by torpedo and gunfire, arriving back at Lorient on 21 July.

His next patrol took him to the South Atlantic, together with three other boats. From 26 August they operated against Convoy SL119, and continued towards the Equator. They arrived at their operational area off Cape Town in early October. On the 7th Emmermann sank two ships, the American SS *Chicsaw City* and the MV *Firethorn*, sinking another ship the following day. On the 10th, he spotted the British troopship the SS *Orcades*, a converted liner, and attacked her, firing two torpedoes. The *Orcades* was struck by both torpedoes; the crew and passengers began to abandon ship, whilst lowering her life-boats into the rough sea. One capsized, with the loss of thirty-eight lives. There had been 1,300 people on board, including women and children. The captain and some volunteers stayed on board and made temporary repairs and the *Orcades* headed slowly back to Cape Town. However, two hours later Emmermann attacked the *Orcades* again. He fired three more torpedoes at the liner and she sank in less than three minutes. At 23,456 tons, she was the largest ship sunk in the waters off the Cape. Emmermann returned to Lorient and by the time he arrived he had added four more ships to his ever-growing total. The following day he sank the Greek SS *Pantellis* about 40 miles south-west of Cape Town. She was struck on the starboard side forward of amidships by a single torpedo and sank by the bow in two minutes after a boiler explosion. Twenty-eight crew members were lost, with only five surviving. On 31 October Emmermann sank the British merchant ship *Aldington Court* and on 2 November he claimed the British SS *Llandilo*. She was sunk south-east of St. Helena with the loss of the master, twenty crew members and three gunners.

On 21 February 1943, Emmermann took *U-172* out to operate in the Western Atlantic where he joined other U-boats west of the Azores. He sank the British SS *City of Pretoria* which was struck by two torpedoes on 4 March, and sank after a large explosion. There were no survivors; all of the 145 crew were lost. One of the passengers was the Third Officer James Whyte, who had survived fifty-one days on a lifeboat after the sinking of the *City of Cairo* by *U-68* on 6 November 1942. Emmermann went onto sink another four ships before returning to his home base where he claimed another four ships during his next patrol in the South Atlantic. On 11 August Emmermann was ordered to rendezvous with *U-604* and *U-185* in order to transfer fuel and stores from *U-604* which had been seriously damaged in an aircraft attack a few days before. During the transfer a US Navy Liberator attacked the ships. Emmermann managed to dive *U-172*, while the other two boats remained on the surface. The Liberator made two unsuccessful attacks and upon making a third it was shot down by *U-185*. Emmermann took twenty-three of *U-604*'s crew back to Lorient.

From 1 November 1943, Emmermann was appointed Chief of the 6th U-boat Flotilla in St. Nazaire. On 28 August 1944, he became chief of the *'Erprobungsgruppe Type XXII'*

Emmermann waving from the conning tower of his U-boat. (Author's collection)

('Testing Group Type XXII'), and was promoted to *Korvettenkapitän* on 1 December. He wrote the battle instructions for the new Electro Type XXII boats. He took command of *U-3037* in March 1945, a Type XXI, for just four weeks but never took the boat out on a war patrol. During the last month of the war he commanded the 31st Flotilla in Hamburg, and like so many U-boat men he took part in infantry duty around the area of Hamburg, and became commander of Naval Battalion '*Emmermann*'. He was captured by British forces in May 1945, and was released on 2 September the same year. He returned to Germany where he studied engineering and became a successful businessman. He died in Celle, Lower Saxony on 25 March 1990.

Other awards:
5 Apr 1938: Long Service Award 4th Class
19 Mar 1941: Iron Cross 2nd Class
2 Aug 1941: Iron Cross 1st Class
2 Aug 1941: U–Boat War Badge
1 Oct 1943: U–Boat War Badge with Diamonds
1 Sep 1944: War Service Cross 2nd Class with Swords
1 Oct 1944: U–Boat Combat Clasp in Bronze

Engelbert ENDRAß
Kapitänleutnant
22 ships sunk, 118,528 tons
4 ships damaged, 25,491 tons

Knight's Cross: Awarded on 5 September 1940, the 12th U-boat recipient, as *Oberleutnant zur See* and as commander of *U-46*, for actions in the Atlantic where he sank eight ships for a total of 59,895 tons, which inlcuded the British armed merchant cruiser HMS *Dunvegan Castle*.

Knight's Cross with Oakleaves: He became the 14th recipient on 10 June 1941, as *Kapitänleutnant* and as commander of *U-46* for continued actions in the North Atlantic, where he sank another twelve ships for a total of 49,686 shipping tons. The Oakleaves were presented to him by Hitler at *Führer* Headquarters '*Wolfschanze*' in Rastenburg, East Prussia on 29 June 1941.

Engelbert Endraß was the twenty-third most successful U-boat commander of the Second World War, sinking a total of 118,528 tons of shipping. He was born in Bamberg, a small town in Upper Franconia on 2 March 1911, and began his naval career as an Officer Candidate with the 10th Company of 2nd Ships Battalion in the Baltic in April 1935. From June he was

(Scherzer)

assigned to the Ships Artillery School, and in March of the following year he attended the naval Academy in Flensburg-Mürwik.

In October 1937, he joined the U-boat force, and after his training was complete he joined *U-47* in December 1938 as a *Leutnant zur See*, being assigned as First Watch Officer under *Kapitänleutnant* Günther Prien. Endraß was promoted to *Oberleutnant zur See* in April 1939 and his first patrol began on 19 August, when *U-47* left Kiel for operations west of the Bay of Biscay. A few days later war was declared, and his boat sank two ships before returning to base. On 8 October, *U-47* left Kiel for a special operation to Scapa Flow – which is probably the most famous single incident in Second World War U-boat history. Prien sank the British battleship HMS *Royal Oak* during the night of 13/14 October 1939. Endraß would later be awarded the Iron Cross 1st Class for his part in the incident – he fired the torpedoes that sank the ship.

On 1 June 1940, Endraß was appointed commander of *U-46*, taking over from *Kapitänleutnant* Herbert Sohler, who had been relatively unsuccessful, sinking only two ships in five patrols. Endraß would be far more successful than his predecessor, sinking three times as many ships in just his first patrol. Endraß left port on 1 June 1940, heading in the area of Cape Finisterre, near Spain. On the 6th he sank the British armed merchant cruiser HMS *Carinthia* west of Galway Bay. She was struck aft by a single torpedo and was seen by the Germans turning, apparently uncontrolled in circles and dropped her depth charges from the stern. Another torpedo was fired about thirty minutes later but missed and was answered by gunfire from *Carinthia*. Endraß decided to leave the area as the ship was settling by the stern and the crew had begun to abandon ship. Only four men were lost during the attack, and the *Carinthia* was taken in tow the next day, but sank about 34 miles off Bloody

Foreland. Three days later he sank the Finnish SS *Margareta*. Within the next eight days he had sunk three more ships and damaged another. On 22 June Endraß made an unsuccessful attack on the aircraft carrier HMS *Ark Royal*, which was heading for Gibraltar.

In August he sailed from Bergen and headed towards the British Isles where for three days he chased Convoy HX62 without success. On 16 August he damaged the Dutch SS *Alcinous* and on the 20th he damaged the Greek SS *Leonides M. Valmas*, so much so that when it arrived in port after being taken in tow it was declared a total loss. He went onto sink the British armed merchant cruiser HMS *Dunvegan Castle* on 27 August. His first torpedo struck the ship and detonated alongside the generating rooms, stopping the engines and cutting all power in the ship. She was a sitting duck, and the second torpedo hit the engine room, and within a few minutes the ship s had sunk. Before his patrol ended he had claimed three more ships – taking his total to ten.

Endraß in an official photograph shortly after he had been presented with his Oakleaves. Note his officer's sword at his side. (Scherzer)

On 23 September, Endraß left for the area west of the British Isles: it was to be a short patrol. On 26th he sank two ships, but the following day two of his crew were washed overboard and drowned, and he headed for St. Nazaire, arriving on 29 September. An investigation cleared Endraß of all blame. He headed once again for the British Isles. He soon located Convoy SC7, and on the evening of 18 October, he sank three ships. Within two days he sank a further two ships, both from Convoy HX79. On the 25th, *U-46* was attacked by three Hudson aircraft: one of the planes scored a direct hit on the stern, blowing a hole in the outer plates. One crewman was killed and Endraß had no choice but to head for his home port of Kiel. On 12 February 1941, with his boat repaired, Endraß headed out for another patrol, which was short and uneventful, and returned to port in March. His next patrol was more successful. He set out on 15 March for an area south of Iceland. He sank two ships, the Swedish SS *Ligunia* on 29 March and the tanker MV *Castor* two days later. He later sank another ship and damaged the British SS *Alderpool* in the early hours of 3 April. By the end of this patrol he had sunk a total of twenty-one ships.

In July 1941 Endraß was promoted to *Kapitänleutnant* and on 25 September, took command of *U-567*, a Type VIIC, and headed for the North Atlantic. He was ordered to join a patrol group east of the Newfoundland Bank. On the 31st, they sighted Convoy HX156, and *U-552* and *U-567* both made attacks but were unsuccessful. After days of searching for the convoy Endraß returned to port. On 18 December, he once again headed out for operations in the North Atlantic and was directed to join three other boats, which were hunting for Convoy HG76, which they quickly found. On the 21st Endraß sank the Norwegian SS *Annavore* north-east of the Azores. However, *U-567* was soon spotted by the convoy's escorts. HMS *Deptford* illuminated the U-boat withstarshell and began to carry out a series of depth-charge attacks. After the third attack a large double underwater explosion was observed. HMS *Deptford* was satisfied *U-567* had been sunk and returned to the convoy: there were no survivors and no wreckage was ever found.

Other awards:
5 Apr 1939: Long Service Award 4th Class
6 Jun 1939: Spanish Cross in Bronze
25 Sep 1939: Iron Cross 2nd Class
17 Oct 1939: Iron Cross 1st Class
19 Dec 1939: U-Boat War Badge
18 Jul 1941: U-Boat War Badge with Diamonds
1 Nov 1941: Italian War Cross in Silver

Friedrich GUGGENBERGER
Kapitänleutnant
17 ships sunk, 66,848 tons
1 ship damaged, 6,003 tons

Knight's Cross: Awarded on 10 December 1941, as *Kapitänleutnant* and as commander of *U-81* for actions in the North Atlantic and for the sinking of the British aircraft carrier HMS *Ark Royal* on 13 November 1941, to become the 91st recipient of the *Kriegsmarine*.

Knight's Cross with Oakleaves: Awarded on 8 January 1943, to become the 171st recipient as *Kapitänleutnant* and as commander of *U-81* for continued actions in the

(Scherzer)

Atlantic where he sank another ten ships. The award was presented to him during a special ceremony at Hitler's headquarters '*Wolfschanze*' in Rastenburg, East Prussia on 31 January 1943.

Born in Munich on 6 March 1915, Friedrich Guggenberger began his career with the *Kriegsmarine* on 8 April 1934. After attending various training courses, which included time aboard the sail training ship *Gorch Fock* and the light cruiser *Emden*, he attended the Artillery School in Wilhelmshaven before joining he U-boat service in January 1939. He had received his commission as a *Leutnant zur See* in April 1937 and was promoted to *Oberleutnant zur See* in April 1939.

In January 1940, he was appointed First Watch Officer on board *U-28*, under the command of *Kapitänleutnant* Günter Kuhnke. In February he left for his first patrol for operations in the English Channel where *U-28* sank two ships. In May he went out on a second patrol, this time in the Atlantic, where *U-28* sank three ships as part of a group commanded by Günther Prien. In November, Guggenberger was given command of *U-81*, a Type VIIC boat, built by Bremer Vulkan. After conducting sea trials he took *U-81* to Trondheim, arriving on 1 August. He then carried out a short patrol which was unsuccessful.

On 27 August, he left for operations in the North Atlantic joining Group *Markgraf* near Iceland. On 1 September he was promoted to *Kapitänleutnant*, then eight days later he sank the British SS *Empire Springbuck* and the following morning sank the British SS *Sally Maersk* before returning to Brest on 19 September. He departed from Brest for his next patrol on 4 November, as part of a U-boat group, and headed for the Mediterranean. He passed through the Straits of Gibraltar, and by the 12th a convoy had been sighted, moving westwards, returning from Malta and heading to Gibraltar. As well as the battleship HMS *Malaya*, the convoy included the aircraft carriers HMS *Ark Royal* (22,600 tons) and HMS *Argus*.

On 13 November *U-205* made the first attack, firing three torpedoes at the *Ark Royal*, but they missed. Six Swordfish aircraft flew out but failed to find *U-205* or *U-81*, which was also in the area. At noon the same day, Guggenberger approached the British warships and fired a spread of four torpedoes at HMS *Malaya*. As the *Ark Royal* manoeuvred into the wind for her aircraft to land and take-off she was hit by one of the torpedoes, the other three missing. The torpedo detonated beneath the protection system and caused extensive damage along the hull. The explosion flooded the starboard boiler room, blew open the bomb-lift doors beneath the bridge. With most of the electrics out of action or destroyed the crew had to try and make repairs with only small lanterns for light. *Ark Royal* immediately assumed a 10-degree list, and the crew started to be taken off the ship. They had been fighting a losing battle. By 17:00 the list was now at 17 degrees and with the boiler and engine rooms flooded she had no power. The *Ark Royal* was taken in tow, but fourteen hours after the attack she sank, with the loss of only one member of the crew.

Guggenberger returned to La Spezia, and was met by cheering crowds; he had sunk the greatest prize of any U-boat captain. He went onto make another thirteen patrols with

HMS Ark Royal, *22,600 tons, one of the largest ships to be sunk by a German U-boat in the Second World War. She was hit on 13 November 1941, by a single torpedo which struck her amidships and sank whilst under tow. Miraculously only one rating from a crew of 1,488 was lost.* (Author's collection)

U-81, all in the Mediterranean, during which he sank fourteen vessels, for a total of 49,697 tons. This included the Free French anti-submarine trawler FFL *Vikings* on 16 April 1942 and the 6,500-ton British merchant ship *Maron* on 13 November. In January 1943, he took command of *U-847*, a Type IXD2, which was used as a training boat. From February to May 1943 Guggenberger served as a staff officer, attached to the staff of the Commander-in-Chief of U-boats, Karl Dönitz. Then he was given command of *U-513*, a Type IXC boat built by Deutsche Werft, Hamburg. He took her out on 18 May for operations in the South Atlantic. On 21 June, he sank the Swedish merchant ship SS *Venezia* and on the 25th damaged the US tanker SS *Eagle*. On 1 July, he took *U-513* southwards and on that day sank the SS *Tutòia*, and on 3 August he sank the SS *Elihn B. Washburne*. On the 16th, shortly after sinking the SS *Richard Caswell*, *U-513* was spotted by a US Navy Mariner flying boat. The aircraft made two direct hits on the U-boat, sending it down bow-first. There were only seven survivors, who included Guggenberger; forty-six men were lost. The seven survivors spent one day in a lifeboat before being picked up by the US seaplane tender USS *Barnegat*. Guggenberger was seriously wounded, and had a long stay in hospital before being transferred to Fort Hunt, New York for interrogation. On 25 September 1943, he was transferred to a prisoner-of-war camp at Crossville, Tennessee, and finally to Papago Park POW Camp near Phoenix, Arizona in late January 1944.

On 12 February 1944, Guggenberger and four other U-boat commanders escaped from the camp. They were later recaptured in Tucson, Arizona. Later Guggenberger was one of twenty-five prisoners who escaped on the night of 23/24 December. On 6 January they were all recaptured, less than 10 miles from the Mexican border. Guggenberger was transferred to

Camp Shanks, New York in February 1946 and then to a prisoner-of-war compound in the British Zone of Germany near Münster. He was released from captivity in August that year.

He went on to become an architect, and joined the *Bundesmarine* in February 1956. He later served as Deputy Chief of Staff on NATO Command AFNORTH for four years. He retired on 31 October 1972, as a *Konteradmiral*. On 13 May 1988, he went for a walk in the forest near Erlenbach am Main from which he never returned. His body wasn't found for two years, and his death is still a mystery.

Other awards:
08 Apr 1938: Long Service Award 4th Class
23 Mar 1940: Iron Cross 2nd Class
08 Jul 1940: U-Boat War Badge
19 Sep 1940: Iron Cross 1st Class
10 Mar 1942: Italian Bravery Medal in Bronze
29 May 1943: Italian Bravery Medal in Silver
00.00.1943: U-Boat War Badge with Diamonds

Robert GYSAE
Korvettenkapitän
25 ships sunk, 146,815 tons
1 ship damaged, 2,588 tons

Knight's Cross: Awarded on 31 December 1941, as *Kapitänleutnant* and as commander of *U-98* in recognition of his success in sinking ten ships for a total of 56,727 tons. He became the 99th recipient of the *Kriegsmarine* and the 43rd U-boat recipient of the Knight's Cross.

(Scherzer)

Knight's Cross with Oakleaves: He became the 250th recipient on 31 May 1943, as *Kapitänleutnant* and as commander of *U-177* for actions in the South Atlantic and the Indian Ocean after sinking fourteen ships. The award presentation was made by Hitler at the '*Wolfschanze*' in Rastenburg, East Prussia, on 25 October 1943, during the same ceremony that Wolfgang Lüth was presented with his Diamonds.

Robert Gysae was responsible for the sinking of twenty-five ships, for a total of 146,815 tons, which made him the fifteenth most successful U-boat commander of the Second World War. He was born on 4 January 1911, in Berlin-Charlottenburg, and entered the *Reichsmarine* in April 1931. From June of that year, he attended various courses, which included serving on the sail training ship *Niobe*, the light cruiser *Karlsruhe* and from April 1934, he attended the Ship Artillery School in Kiel. From September 1934, he served as Watch Officer on board the torpedo boats *Albatros* and *Leopard*, and was commissioned as a *Leutnant zur See* in April 1935 and in January 1937 he was promoted to *Oberleutnant zur See*. From September, he served on the Staff of the Fleet Commander *Vizeadmiral* Rolf Carls, and in October the following year he was appointed commander of the torpedo boat *T-107*. In October 1939, shortly after his promotion to *Kapitänleutnant*, he was appointed Torpedo Flotilla Chief.

In October 1940, Gysae transferred to the U-Boat service and became commander of *U-98*, a Type VIIC boat. He left Kiel in March 1941, for the Atlantic where he sunk four ships before returning to Lorient on 13 April. During the patrol he sank the British merchant ship *Koranton* on 27 March, which was struck by a single torpedo and immediately sank about 320 miles south of Reykavik, with the loss of all its crew. Gysae went on to sink two ships the Norwegian merchant ship *Helle* and the British SS *Welcombe* on 4 April, and five days later he sank the Dutch SS *Prins Wilhelm II*. His next patrol began on 11 May, when he left port for the North Atlantic, where he joined three other boats to form a patrol line near Greenland. In the morning of the 13th, he sank the British armed merchant cruiser HMS *Salopian* and by 21 May had sunk a further two ships. He was then asked to assist the battleship *Bismarck*. The plan was for the *Bismarck* and the heavy cruiser *Prinz Eugen* to break out into the Atlantic via the Denmark Strait, and then a group of U-boats would form a patrol line, and after the two ships had passed through the U-boats would deal with any British warships that were shadowing them. However, the plan was changed because *Bismarck* had been damaged by HMS *Prince of Wales* in the Battle of the Denmark Strait on 24 May. *Bismarck* would make for St. Nazaire whilst *Prinz Eugen* would head south-west. This decision would, however, prove fatal for the battleship. *U-98* was one of six boats called upon to assist *Bismarck* into the comparative shelter of the Bay of Biscay. The U-boat group was then ordered to form a patrol line running north-west from Cape Ortegal, but this was delayed due to bad weather. On the evening of 26 May, the boats that still had torpedoes were ordered to assist, but again heavy seas and high winds prevented them from finding the battleship. By the end of the following morning the *Bismarck*, the pride of Germany, had been sunk. During his next patrol he sank two more ships, both British steamers, on 9 July. The SS *Designer* was struck in the foreship by one of two torpedoes fired and sank after six minutes north-north-west of the Azores with the loss of the master and sixty-one crew members. The SS *Inverness* was struck by a torpedo and sank with the loss of six men. During his next four patrols Gysae sank only four ships which included the British SS *Biela*. After a chase of more than 100 miles she was struck by a third torpedo about 400 miles south-east of Cape Race. She developed a heavy list after being hit and the crew was seen to abandon ship in three lifeboats and several rafts. *Biela* broke in two and sank after being struck by a fourth torpedo. The survivors from the ship were never seen again; a total of forty-nine men were lost.

On 3 March 1942, he took command of a new boat, *U-177*, a Type IXD2 built by AG Weserof Bremen. His first patrol in his new boat proved to be successful. He left Kiel for the South Atlantic on 17 September and from early November was patrolling off the coast north of Cape Town. There he sank the Greek SS *Aegeus* on 2 November, and the British tanker SS *Scottish Chief* on the 19th, and the following day sank the SS *Pierce Butler*. On the 28th Gysae sank the British troop transport the RMS *Nova Scotia* with the loss of the master, ninety-six crew members, ten gunners, eight military and naval personnel, five passengers, eighty-eight South African guards and 650 Italian internees. There were 194 survivors. By the end of the patrol he had sunk a total of eight ships and had damaged another in just over one month. His next patrol was also a success and after leaving again for the South Atlantic in April 1943, Gysae took *U-177* to the Cape Town area once again as part of a group of seven U-boats. On 28 May, he sank two ships, the US SS *Agwimonte* and the Norwegian tanker MV *Storaas*. He claimed another three vessels in July and was promoted the same month to *Korvettenkapitän*. On 5 August he sank the Greek SS *Efthalia Mari*, struck by two torpedoes and sank after just eight minutes east of Madagascar. Gysae questioned the survivors and left the area: only one crew member had been killed aboard the ship.

In January 1944, he was appointed commander of the 25th U-boat Flotilla, a training flotilla based at Gotenhafen. During the last month of the war, Gysae commanded the *Marinepanzerjagd-Regiment 1*, a naval anti-tank regiment. He surrendered to Allied troops on 8 May 1945, and was held in an internment camp in Eidenstädt, being released the following month. He joined the *Bundesmarine* in July 1956, serving for four years as naval attaché in the United States. From February 1967, he served for three years as commander of Naval Division North Sea. He retired on 31 March 1971, with the rank of *Flotillenadmiral*. He died on 26 April 1989, in Wilhelmshaven.

Other awards:
02 Oct 1936: Long Service Award 4th Class
06 Jun 1939: Spanish Cross in Bronze with Swords
20 Dec 1939: Commemorative Medal of 01 Oct 1938
31 May 1940: Iron Cross 2nd Class
15 Apr 1941: Iron Cross 1st Class
31 May 1941: U-Boat War Badge
25 May 1943: Italian War Cross with Swords
00.00.1943: U-Boat War Badge with Diamonds
25 Jun 1943: Wound Badge in Black
01 Sep 1944: War Service Cross 2nd Class with Swords
01 Oct 1944: U-Boat Combat Clasp in Bronze

Reinhard HARDEGEN
Korvettenkapitän
22 ships sunk, 115,656 tons
5 ships damaged, 46,500 tons

Knight's Cross: Awarded as *Kapitänleutnant* and as commander of *U-123*, to become the 44th U-boat recipient, on 23 January 1942, for actions in the Atlantic where he was responsible for sinking fourteen ships for a total of 74,680 tons.

Knight's Cross with Oakleaves: Awarded on 23 April 1942, as *Kapitänleutnant* of *U-123*, becoming the 89th recipient, for continued actions in the Atlantic as part of the 2nd U-Boat Flotilla. He was presented with the award by Hitler at *Führer* Headquarters '*Wolfschanze*' in Rastenburg, East Prussia, in June 1942 together with *Kapitänleutnant*

Erich Topp. After the ceremony the two men were invited to dinner with Hitler where Hardegen caused great embarrassment by criticizing the lack of priority given to the U-boat war, causing Hitler to react angrily. Before leaving Hardegen received a reprimand from Operations Chief *Generaloberst* Alfred Jodl, to which Hardegen replied, 'The *Führer* has a right to hear the truth, and I have a duty to speak it'.

Born on 18 March 1913, in Bremen, Reinhard Hardegen was one of the most successful U-boat commanders of the Second World War, being the twenty-fourth most successful, sinking twenty-two ships for a total of 115,656 shipping tons. His father taught at the local secondary school or *Gymnasium*, and was one of a group that contributed to the conservative mind-set of the *Reichsmarine* crews in the 1920s and 1930s.

(Author's collection)

Hardegen was a Protestant and a skilled yachtsman by the time he was in his teens. He was recommended to the *Reichsmarine* by a former merchant naval officer, war hero and family friend *Kapitänleutnant* Paul König. He was accepted by the *Reichsmarine* on 1 April 1933, and served onboard various ships, including the sail training ship *Gorch Fock*, and made the usual round-the-world cruise as a cadet. From June 1934, he attended the Naval Academy at Flensburg-Mürwik and after being commissioned was assigned to naval aviation where he became a pilot. In 1936, Hardegen crashed and was seriously injured; he spent six months in hospital and as result suffered from internal stomach bleeding, and had to have a special diet and among other things had a shortened right leg. On 1 October he was commissioned as *Leutnant zur See* and was promoted to *Oberleutnant zur See* in April 1938. He continued to fly and during the Polish campaign he flew coastal missions and once Poland fell in November 1939 Hardegen transferred to the U-boat Service.

On 19 August 1940, he was appointed Watch Officer aboard *U-124*, under *Kapitänleutnant* Georg-Wilhelm Schulz. During this time he trained as a U-boat commander, taking part in two war patrols and in the sinking of six ships. With his training complete Hardegen was promoted to *Kapitänleutnant* on 1 December and the next day took command of *U-147*, a Type IID boat. At first his boat was a training vessel attached to the 22nd U-boat Flotilla, but finally in February 1941 his boat was made operational. On 22 February, Hardegen left Kiel for the west of Scotland to begin his first war patrol as a U-boat commander. On the second day of the patrol two torpedoes failed to detonate against a large ship, and he had to make an emergency dive after mistaking a destroyer for a merchant ship. During the dive, the tower hatch was damaged, and Hardegen had to resurface, but with the fast-approaching darkness of the night they weren't spotted and the repair was successful. On 27 February, he sank the Norwegian SS *Augrald*, and a few days later he attacked two freighters, only to find that his torpedoes failed to detonate yet again. Hardegen decided to return to port, the accident with the tower hatch had caused a leak and he seemed to have faulty torpedoes – he had little choice. He returned to Kiel on 12 March. He was informed that he would be getting a new boat and command of

U-147 would pass to his First Watch Officer, *Oberleutnant zur See* Eberhard Wetjen. The crew presented Hardegen with his commander's pennant and with the original flag at date of commissioning. Whilst under the command of Wetjen, *U-147* made two patrols and sank three ships. On 2 June 1941, in the North Atlantic she was depth-charged and sunk by the British destroyer HMS *Wanderer* and the corvette HMS *Periwinkle* with the loss of all hands.

On 16 May, he was given command of *U-123*, a Type IXB boat. He hoped this command would bring him more success. His boat was part of Operation *Paukenschlag*, the targeting of shipping along the coast of America. He left for operations in the Central Atlantic on 15 June 1941. On 20 June, he sank the neutral vessel the Portuguese SS *Ganda* by gunfire, mistaking it for a British freighter. Dönitz later ordered all references to the sinking deleted from the logbook of *U-123*. Hardegen proceeded southwards, and on 27 June spotted Convoy SL76, and closed in. He sank two ships, the British SS *PLM 22* and the Dutch SS *Oberon*. He sank another ship on the 29th, the British SS *Rio Azul* which broke in two when she was struck by a torpedo and sank with the loss of thirty-three men. Hardegen was then attacked with depth charges from a Sunderland aircraft. Escaping without damage *U-123* continued south and sank the SS *Auditor* on 4 July. From the 10th, *U-123* operated off Freetown but without success. Hardegen then joined more U-boats to form a wolf pack and they went after Convoy HG69, but once again without success. Hardegen, out of torpedoes, returned to Lorient.

For his next patrol he left for the Atlantic on 14 October, to operate west of Ireland. A convoy was found and on the 20th, he damaged the armed merchant cruiser HMS *Aurania*. This would be Hardegen's only success during the patrol, although other convoys were spotted, and four ships sunk, none were sunk by *U-123*. He returned to base. On 23 December, Hardegen took *U-123* out of port and headed for the Western Atlantic, as part of Operation *Paukenschlag*. Five boats were sent towards the American coast to sink as much Allied shipping as possible. He was ordered to penetrate the inshore area around New York City. He placed his boat on the ocean floor and waited for darkness, then proceeded into New York harbour on 15 January 1942. He found very little merchant traffic, and managed only to sink one vessel, the British tanker *Coimbra*, before making his way back out to sea. On 12 January, he sank the British SS *Cyclops* south of Halifax, and on the morning of the 14th he sank the Panamanian tanker MV *Norness*. He then proceeded south along the south coast, submerging during the day and surfacing at night. During the night of the 19th, Hardegen sank three ships and damaged another. During the journey home, he sank a further two ships near Bermuda, to bring his total to eight ships sunk and two damaged. He reached Lorient on 9 February 1942.

On 2 March, Hardegen left port and headed out to US waters to launch another successful attack against Allied shipping. He took *U-123* to the Newfoundland area, and turned south and on the 22nd he sank the US tanker SS *Muskogee* and two days later sank the British tanker MV *Empire Steel*, which was carrying gasoline: she burned for five hours before sinking and there were no survivors. On the 17th Hardegen sank the American Q-ship USS *Atik*, mistaking her for a merchant freighter. He surfaced to finish off the ship with his deck guns, only to find the *Atik* trying to ram him and opening fire on him with her guns. Hardegen made his escape on the surface, but *U-123* was hit eight times and a crew member was killed. Hardegen then submerged and finished off the *Atik* with a single torpedo. On 2 April, he torpedoed and damaged the tank SS *Libre* and on the morning of the 8th, off Jacksonville, Florida, Hardegen attacked two US tankers, the SS *Oklahoma* and the SS *EssoBaton Rouge*, both ships being damaged.

On 9 April, *U-123* sank the SS *Esparta* and on the 11th he sank the US tanker SS *Gulfamerica* by torpedo and gunfire. With the ship still burning, Hardegen spotted the USS *Dahlgren*, a destroyer, closing in on his position and Hardegen was forced to crash dive. He found himself on the bottom, only 60ft under the surface, when the American destroyer dropped six depth charges. The U-boat was seriously damaged and Hardegen believed the destroyer would return for another attack, so he ordered all secret code books and machines destroyed and ordered the crew to abandon the boat. As he was about to open the tower hatch to allow the crew to escape, he was gripped by a paralysing fear and was unable to proceed with the evacuation. Luckily for him the destroyer failed to drop any more depth charges and moved away. This allowed *U-123* to make repairs and slowly move to deeper waters. Between 2 and 17 April Hardegen had sunk five ships and had damaged another three, and on his return journey to Lorient he received a signal to say he had been awarded the Oakleaves. Shortly after arriving in Lorient Hardegen underwent a medical examination, and much to his shock he was relieved of command: his old flying injury had caught up with him. The medical report stated he was not fit for duty aboard a U-boat. On 1 August 1942, he took up duties as an instructor with the 27th U-boat Training Flotilla in Gotenhafen.

Kapitänleutnant *Hardegen is presented with the Knight's Cross by Dönitz shortly after his arrival at Lorient on 9 February 1942, after completing another war patrol.* (Author's collection)

In March 1943, Hardegen was appointed Chief of U-boat Training whilst attached to the Torpedo School at the Naval Academy. He was promoted to *Korvettenkapitän* in March 1944 before taking up a position with the Torpedo Weapons Department in October. Here he oversaw the testing and development of new acoustic and wire-guided torpedoes. On 12 February 1945, he served as battalion commander in the 6th Naval Infantry Regiment. He took part in fierce fighting against British troops in the area around Bremen; most of the officers in his unit were killed. Hardegen later admitted that his own survival was due to his stay in hospital with a severe case of diphtheria. For the last few days of the war and for a time after he served on the Staff of *Großadmiral* and later Reichs President Dönitz at Flensburg, where he surrendered to British troops in late May 1945. He was released from an internment camp on 9 November 1946. He would have been released much earlier but he had for a time been mistaken for an SS officer with the same name. It took him almost eighteen months to convince the Allied interrogators of his real identity.

Hardegen became a businessman, and in 1952 he started an oil trading company, which became a great success. He also served as a Member of Parliament for the Christian Democrats in his home town of Bremen for thirty-two years. He celebrated his 100th birthday in March 2013, in good health, and was still playing golf and driving a car. Reinhard Hardegen, the last of the so-called 'aces of the deep' died at the age of 105, on 9 June 2018.

Other awards:
02 Nov 1936: Pilots' and Observers' Badge
01 Apr 1937: Long Service Award 4th Class
18 Sep 1940: Iron Cross 2nd Class
18 Nov 1940: U-Boat War Badge
23 Aug 1941: Iron Cross 1st Class
07 May 1942: U-Boat War Badge with Diamonds
20 Apr 1944: War Service Cross 2nd Class with Swords

Werner Friedrich Wilhelm Adolf HARTMANN
Kapitän zur See
26 ships sunk, 115,337 tons

Knight's Cross: Awarded on 9 May 1940, as *Korvettenkapitän* and as commander of *U-37*, in recognition of his successes during three patrols in the Gibraltar area, the English Channel and around the coast of Norway where he sank nineteen ships for a total of 78,560 shipping tons, to become the 4th U-boat recipient.

Knight's Cross with Oakleaves: On 5 November 1944, he became the 645th recipient, as *Kapitän zur See* and Leader of U-boats in the Mediterranean. It was for his success as commander of *U-198* when he sank seven ships for a total of 36,778 shipping tons, off the coast of Africa and Madagascar, before he took over his new post.

Werner Hartmann was credited with sinking twenty-six ships for a total of 115,337 shipping tons to make him the twenty-fifth most successful U-boat commander of the

Second World War. He was born on 11 December 1902, in Silstedt near Wernigerode, Harz, Werner Hartmann was the third child of Albert Hartmann, an evangelic pastor from Wernigerode, and Helene Hartmann, neé Wernicke. The young Hartmann attended the local *Volksschule* from 1909 to 1914 and later he went to a *Gymnasium* in Magdeburg, equivalent to a secondary school.

On 1 April 1914, Hartmann joined the Royal Prussian Cadet Corps in Oranienstein near Diez. Initially he served in the *Vorkorps* or pre-corps, a training unit for potential officers, and was later transferred to the Berlin Military Academy in April 1917. Then four years later he began his naval career with the *Reichsmarine*. On 1 October 1925 he was commissioned as a *Leutnant zur See* and began his training, which included on board the cruiser *Berlin*, and his basic training was at

(Scherzer)

Stralsund in the Baltic Sea he later attended the Naval Academy in Mürwik. In July 1927 he was promoted to *Oberleutnant zur See* and by October was serving as commander of the torpedo boats *Seeadler* and *Albatros*, before being transferred to the U-boat service in October 1935. He had been promoted to *Kapitänleutnant* in October 1933 and was promoted to *Korvettenkapitän* in July 1937.

Hartmann commanded *U-26* during the Spanish Civil War, patrolling Spanish waters from 1937 to 1938, with Günther Prien serving as his First Watch Officer. In October 1938, he was Flotilla Chief of the 6th U-boat Flotilla, and from October 1939 was also appointed commander of *U-37*, a Type IXA boat. He left port for his first patrol soon after his appointment and was part of a five-boat patrol. Together with *U-42*, *U-45*, *U-46* and *U-48*, they awaited orders south-west of Ireland, and then took up their new positions west of Portugal. On 8 October, Hartmann sank the Swedish ship the SS *Vistula* and the Greek SS *Aris* four days later. On the 15th he sank the French SS *Vermont* by gunfire. By the next day the five U-boats which had left port had been reduced to only three, *U-42* and *U-45* having been sunk. The three remaining boats sighted Convoy HG3 near the coast of Portugal and moved in for the attack. On the afternoon of the 17th, Hartmann sank the SS *Yorkshire*, and on the 24th sank another three ships. The *Yorkshire* was struck by two torpedoes from the stern tubes and sank about 160 miles west-north-west of Cape Finisterre. The master, twenty-four crew members and twenty-three passengers were lost. The survivors, 105 crew members and 118 passengers, were picked up by the US SS *Independence Hall*. On his return journey to port he sank the Greek SS *Thrasyvoules*, arriving in Wilhelmshaven on 8 November.

His next patrol began on 28 January 1940, when he left for the Atlantic to operate off the coast of Ireland. En route to the operational area he sank two ships. He was then ordered to carry out a special mission. He had to land in Ireland two *Abwehr* (German Military Intelligence) agents, Ernst Weber-Drohl and Wilhelm Preetz, who were to intensify anti-British sentiments. He completed the mission on 8 February and two days later sank the Norwegian SS *Silja* and the British fishing vessel *Togimo* the following day. Hartmann then took *U-37* south to take part in the third attempt at controlled wolf-pack operations. On the 17th he sank another ship, and the following day he added two more to his tally, before returning to base. He once again left Wilhelmshaven for another patrol on 30 March, and sank the Swedish tanker MV *Sveabourg* and the Norwegian merchant ship *Tosca* on 10 April and two days later he sank the British merchant ship *Stancliffe*, which was struck on the starboard side just forward of the bridge by a single torpedo about 50 miles north-north-west of Muckle Flugga, Shetlands. The ship sank within eight minutes. The master and twenty-one crew members were lost. The U-boat went alongside a lifeboat and Hartmann gave orders for the survivors to receive cigarettes and a bottle of rum. The sixteen survivors in the lifeboat made it safely to land a few days later.

From May 1940, he served on the staff of the Commander of U-boats, and in November was appointed commander of 2nd U-boat Training Division in Gotenhafen. On 1 April 1941 he was promoted to *Fregattenkapitän* and in December, Hartmann was appointed Chief of the 27th U-boat Flotilla, and in November 1942 took over as commander of *U-198*, a Type IXD2. His first patrol began on 9 March 1943, when he left Kiel for operations in the Indian Ocean. On 1 April during his patrol he learnt that he had been promoted to *Kapitän zur See*. By the middle of May, he reached his operational area, off the east coast of South Africa. On 17 May, he located Convoy LMD 17 off Cape Saint Lucia and sank the SS *Northmoor*. Shortly after the sinking, *U-109* was attacked by a Catalina flying boat and was slightly damaged, but *U-109* managed to knock out one of the aircraft's engines with her deck guns. Hartmann continued his patrol, and made for an area south of the Mozambique Channel, where he sank the MV *Hopetarn*. On 5 June, he sank the SS *Dunra*, 190 miles off Durden and the following day sank the SS *William King*. After refuelling from his supply ship, Hartmann had no success until 6 July, when he sank the SS *Hydraios* and the SS *Leana*. After being depth-charged on the 11th by a Ventura aircraft and then chased by another aircraft, *U-198* succeeded in avoiding any damage. Hartmann's final success came on 1 August, when he torpedoed and sank the SS *Mangkalihat*, from Convoy BC 2. He then returned to port.

On 16 January 1944, Hartmann was appointed Leader of U-boats in the Mediterranean, and from August served as Operations Leader of the *Kleinkampfverband* (Small Task Force – naval special forces) of the Navy in Italy. He served for a time with the *Volkssturm* in Danzig, before taking up command of the 6th Naval Grenadier Regiment in February 1945, taking part in defensive actions against the British. He was captured near Schleswig-Holstein and spent several months in a British internment camp, being released in December 1946. He joined the *Bundesmarine* in July 1956 and commanded the 1st Naval Training Regiment in Glückstadt until his retirement with the rank of *Kapitän zur See*, in March 1962. Hartmann died of a pulmonary embolism on 26 April 1963 in Esseln, Waldeck.

Other awards:
02 Oct 1936: Long Service Award 4th to 3rd Class
01 Apr 1939: Long Service Award 2nd Class
21 Aug 1939: Spanish Naval Service Cross in White
00 Sep 1939: Spanish Service Cross in Silver 2nd Class
08 Nov 1939: Iron Cross 2nd Class
08 Nov 1939: Iron Cross 1st Class
07 Dec 1939: U-Boat War Badge
00.00.1944: U-Boat War Badge with Diamonds

Werner Gustav Emil HENKE
Korvettenkapitän
25 ships, 157,064 tons
2 ships damaged, 7,954 tons

Knight's Cross: Awarded as *Oberleutnant zur See* and as commander of *U-515* on 17 December 1942, for actions in the Atlantic where he sank ten ships for a total of 71,677 tons, to become the 73rd U-boat recipient.

Knight's Cross with Oakleaves: Awarded on 4 July 1943, as the 257th recipient, as *Kapitänleutnant* and as commander of *U-515* for further actions in the Atlantic. The Oakleaves were presented to him by Hitler during a special ceremony at the '*Wolfschanze*' in Rastenburg, East Prussia on 4 July 1943.

(Scherzer)

Werner Henke was the twelfth most successful U-boat commander of the Second World War, sinking twenty-five ships for a total of 157,064 shipping tons. He was born on 13 May 1909, in Rudak, a small village just outside Thorn, situated on the Vistula River about 110 miles north-west of Warsaw and 100 miles south of Danzig. His father Hugo was a state forestry official and at the time of Henke's birth it was a typical German town, but two years after the First World War it became part of Poland.

Henke entered the *Kriegsmarine* as an Officer Candidate on 8 April 1934. He attended the Naval Academy at Murwik from April 1935, and served for a time on the 'pocket battleship' *Admiral Scheer* and was commissioned as a *Leutnant zur See* in October 1936. On 3 May 1937, Henke was appointed Company Officer, attached to the 5th Naval Artillery Battalion. He attended the Coastal Artillery School at Swinemünde from May 1937 and was promoted a year later. He spent the next two years stationed in Pillau naval base, before being assigned to the battleship *Schleswig-Holstein* in May 1939. In September he participated in the first action of the Second World War in the Battle of Westerplatte, the first engagement during the invasion of Poland. From May 1940, he served as First Watch Officer on board the escort vessel *Lech*, part of the 1st U-Boat Flotilla. In November he was transferred to *U-124*, where he served as Second Watch Officer and later as First Watch Officer, under the command of *Kapitänleutnants* Wilhelm Schulz and Johann Mohr, taking part in five patrols. He was promoted to *Oberleutnant zur See* in February 1941 and from November attended various training courses, including a commander's course and torpedo training in Gotenhafen.

In February 1942, Henke was appointed commander of *U-515*, a Type IXC, and left Kristiansand on 15 August for operations in the Western Atlantic. He patrolled off the coast of Trinidad and on 12 September torpedoed and sank two tankers, the Panamanian *Stanvac Melbourne* and the Dutch *Woensdrecht*, struck by two torpedoes. The crew abandoned ship in lifeboats and were picked up the following night by two US patrol vessels. The *Woensdrecht* broke in two after being hit by three more torpedoes. While the stern sank, the forepart was towed to Trinidad, where she was declared a total loss and later scrapped. Four more ships were sunk in the same area. On the 13th the British SS *Ocean Vanguard* and the Panamanian SS *Nimba*, on the 14th he sank the British SS *Harborough* by torpedo and gunfire, and the Norwegian MV *Sörholt* the following day. He continued to claim more ships over the next few days, and by the end of his patrol he had sunk a total of ten ships. His next patrol began on 7 November, in the Central Atlantic. After four days *U-515* was attacked and damaged by aircraft and in the evening Henke sighted a British cruiser force 150 miles south of the Cape. However, he was soon driven off by the destroyer escorts before he could make an attack. But Henke persisted and in the early hours of the 12th, he sank the British destroyer depot ship HMS *Hecla*, firing a spread of four torpedoes. She was struck in the engine room. Three more torpedoes were fired to 'finish off' the ship, which sank with the loss of 279 lives: there were 568 survivors. *U-515* was then spotted by HMS *Venomous* but managed to escape. Henke then joined a U-boat group, and just north of the Azores he sank the troopship SS *Ceramic* just after midnight on 7 December. She had been hit initially by one torpedo and then within a few short minutes she was struck by two more in the engine room below the waterline. The engines stopped and the call came to abandon ship. The crew clambered into eight lifeboats, it was cold, the sea was rough and there was poor visibility due to the darkness. The *Ceramic* stayed afloat for three hours and was then struck by two more torpedoes, which broke her in two and she sank. Of 656 passengers on board, there was only one survivor, Sapper Erich Munday, who was picked up by *U-515*. On the 23rd Henke began the journey home, arriving in Lorient on 6 January 1943.

On 21 February, Henke was ordered to take *U-515* to a position west of the Azores. En route, he sank the British MV *California Star* and picked up its Second Officer as a prisoner. Henke joined a group and hunted for Allied convoys, without success, at least not for Henke. It wasn't until 9 April that Henke was successful when he sank the French MV *Bamako* off the coast of Dakar. *U-515* was attacked by a *Catalina* flying boat on 29 April, but Henke managed to dive and escape. The following day Henke sank four ships and on 1 May he claimed three more, the British SS *City of Singapore*, the Belgian MV *Mokambo* and the SS *Clan MacPherson*. Then before Henke set course for Lorient, he sank the Norwegian MV *Corneville* off Accra on 9 May.

During his next patrol *U-515* was damaged by the frigate HMS *Tavy* and had to return to port. Promoted to *Kapitänleutnant* on 16 July 1943, he took out his repaired boat, joining *Schill I* Group, for patrols near Lisbon on 9 November. On the 18th, *U-515* damaged the British sloop HMS *Chanticleer* and continued to search for more convoys. Henke had to stop off for repairs on 22nd, and then headed towards the Canary Islands two days later. From early December Henke was operating south of Freetown, where he sank three ships in just seven days. He then headed for base, but on the way his batteries, which had been damaged, failed and *U-515* had to be escorted to Lorient by two German minesweepers. Henke now had time for some welcome leave while his boat was being repaired.

On 30 March 1944, he left for operations near West Africa, in what would be his last patrol. On 8 April, *U-515* was located off the Azores by an Avenger aircraft from the escort carrier USS *Guadalcanal*. Depth charges were dropped but *U-515* escaped, and contact was lost. Later the next morning Henke ordered *U-515* to surface and was immediately spotted by an aircraft, which dropped depth charges but they fell short. The boat dived as more aircraft and two destroyers, made for the area, more depth charges were dropped and for two hours *U-515* and her crew listened and waited until the enemy ships left the area.

HMS Chanticleer, *struck by a torpedo fired by* U-515 *about 250 miles east-northeast of San Miguel, Azores, on 18 November 1943. She was towed to Ponta Delgado, where she was declared a total loss. In 1946 she was sold for scrap and broken up at Lisbon.* (Author's collection)

At noon the following day, USS *Pope* established contact with *U-515* and dropped three depth-charges, which seriously damaged the U-boat. Henke ordered repairs and leaks were plugged, but three further attacks re-opened them and *U-515* began to flood. She then started to rise, and broke surface very close to the American destroyer USS *Chatelain*. She opened fire, at very short range and then aircraft attacked with rockets. The boat sank in minutes, and Henke and forty-four members of the crew were rescued – sixteen men drowned.

Henke was interned along with his crew in the interrogation centre known as PO Box 1142 in Fort Hunt, Virginia. A British propaganda broadcast had falsely accused Henke of shooting British survivors of the troopship SS *Ceramic* in December 1942. Henke believed the British wanted to try him as a war criminal. The commandant of the interrogation centre took advantage of this news and threatened to hand Henke over to British authorities unless he cooperated fully with them. At first he agreed to tell them everything they asked but later he went back on his promise. On 15 June 1944, fearing that he might be extradited to England, Henke, according to official reports, made a dash for the fence of the interrogation centre and began to climb. He was ordered to stop a number of times and when he ignored these warnings a guard shot at him with a machine-gun. Henke was hit several times in the leg, arm and body and was fatally wounded in the head. He was posthumously promoted to the rank of *Kapitänleutnant* and is buried in the cemetery in Fort George G. Meade, Maryland.

Other awards:
08 Apr 1938: Long Service Award 4th Class
06 Jun 1939: Spanish Cross in Bronze
17 Sep 1939: Iron Cross 2nd Class

23 Oct 1940: Commemorative Medal of 01 Oct 1938
04 May 1941: U-Boat War Badge
04 Oct 1941: Iron Cross 1st Class
00.00.1943: U-Boat War Badge with Diamonds

Hans-Günther LANGE
Kapitänleutnant
2 ships sunk, 935 tons
1 ship damaged, 20 tons

Knight's Cross: Awarded on 26 August 1944, as *Kapitänleutnant* and as commander of *U-711*, part of the 12th U-Flotilla, for his leadership during seven war patrols in the area of the North Atlantic.

Knight's Cross with Oakleaves: Awarded as *Kapitänleutnant* and as commander of *U-711* on 29 April 1945, for continued actions in the North Sea area.

Hans-Günther Lange was born on 28 September 1916 in Hannover and entered the German Navy in April 1937. He served as an Officer Candidate with the 3rd Company of II *Schiffsstammdivision* in Stralsund on the Baltic Sea. From June 1937 he attended various training courses on board the sail training ship *Gorch Fock* and the battleship *Schlesien*. In May 1938, he was promoted to *Fähnrich zur See* and continued with his training, attending the Naval College in Mürwik until March 1939. In July he was promoted to *Oberfähnrich zur See* and was commissioned as a *Leutnant zur See* the following month.

(Scherzer)

Lange then served as a company officer in the XIV. *Schiffsstammdivision* from October and in April 1940 served as Watch Officer on the torpedo boat *Jaguar*, seeing action during the Norwegian campaign.

In September 1941, Lange transferred to the U-boat service, with the rank of *Oberleutnant zur See* and after three months of training was assigned as First Watch Officer on board *U-431*. Whilst under the command of *Kapitänleutnant* Wilhelm Dommes he took part in four war patrols against Allied shipping in the area near Tobruk. In July 1942 he began his training as a U-boat commander and after two months, with his training complete, he took command of *U-711*. In March 1943, he finally took his new boat out on its first war patrol. It was a short patrol, without success and he returned to port on 30 April. His second patrol was as part of the 11th U-boat Flotilla and once again was unsuccessful, returning to base in Ankenes on 18 June 1943.

On 22 July, *U-711* left for operations in northern waters, and together with *U-302* and *U-354* patrolled as *Wiking* Group, searching for Soviet convoys. None were sighted until 21 August, when *U-302* and *U-354* attacked a convoy, damaging one ship and sinking another. Lange and *U-711*, however, did not take part in the attacks. From 4 to 6 September *Wiking* Group continued its search for convoys, now supported by *U-255*, but nothing was located. On the 24th Lange was ordered to shell the wire-tapping station at Pravdy, on Nasen Island, and four days later he also shelled the wire-tapping station at Blagopoluchiya, Novaya Zemyla. He returned to port on 30 September, after the loss of a crew member overboard.

In March 1944, Lange left port for Trondheim for operations against Allied convoys near Iceland. As part of *Blitz* Group, *U-711* joined in the attacks on Convoy JW58, but they proved unsuccessful, and Lange returned to Hammerfest on 6 April. On 11th, he was ordered to Narvik, where his boat was made ready for another patrol. Two days later he sighted the Norwegian fishing vessel *Solvoll* about 200 miles west of the Lofoten Islands. She was stopped and found to have five men, one woman and two children aboard who had escaped from occupied Norway. One of the men jumped overboard when the boat was stopped, but he was fished out of the water. The Germans then placed a boarding party aboard, but the boat developed engine trouble the next day and had to be sunk by gunfire. On 14 April the passengers were landed at Lødingen and were held in a Gestapo prison until the end of the war. On 24th, he left for operations as part of *Kiel* Group, which along with *Donner* Group was deployed against Convoy RA59, which had been located by German aircraft. His next three patrols were unsuccessful. On 1 August Lange was promoted to *Kapitänleutnant* and on the 23rd, he joined a patrol line, and made various unsuccessful attacks on a Soviet task force. Later that same day, Lange fired torpedoes at the Soviet battleship *Archangelsk* (the former HMS *Royal Sovereign* and a sister-ship to HMS *Royal Oak*), and the Soviet destroyer *Zarkij*, east of Bear Island, but the attack was unsuccessful.

For his next patrol, which began on 7 September, Lange was operating in the Kara Sea with *U-739* and *U-957*. He made at least six attacks on Convoy VD1, all of which were unsuccessful due to torpedo defects. The three boats then landed a party on Sterligova Island on 24 September and destroyed a wireless station. He then returned to base. On 9 February 1945, Lange took *U-711* out of Narvik to intercept a convoy south of Bear Island. Howeverm he was unable to make an attack and joined *U-968* and *U-992* in further attacks against a different convoy. On the morning of the 14th Lange sank the SS *Horace Gray* and claimed another shortly after but it remains unconfirmed. On the 17th, both *U-711* and *U-968* attacked another convoy and Lange sank the corvette HMS *Bluebell*. She was struck in the stern by an acoustic torpedo, known as a Gnat. The corvette blew up as the torpedo detonated her depth charges and she sank in less than thirty seconds about 30 miles east-north-east of the Kildin Islands. Of the ninety-one officers and men aboard, only one survived. Lange then moved westwards, with air support, to Bear Island Passage in the hope of finding contact with a convoy but this proved unsuccessful. As for Lange and *U-711*, they returned to port on 24 February. His next two patrols were much the same as the others, chasing convoys but never managing to make a successful attack. On 22 March 1945, Lange torpedoed the Soviet armed trawler *BPS-5* off the Kola Inlet, damaging her stern. On 19 April, during his last patrol, again near the Kola Inlet, he sank a small steamer. On 2 May, Lange was ordered to take *U-711* to Harstad: for him and his crew the war was over. Two days later, aircraft from the Fleet Air Arm of the Royal Navy attacked the naval installation at Kilbotn near Harstad. *U-711* was moored alongside the MV *Black Watch*, and as a result of the attack both ships were sunk. Forty men from the *U-711* were on board the *Black Watch* and were killed when she blew up. A skeleton crew of twelve men – probably those on watch aboard the U-boat – cut her loose and sailed off, but the boat sank a couple of hundred metres away from the depot ship although all twelve men managed to escape. Lange wasn't on board during the attack and survived. He was taken prisoner by British forces on 8 May 1945 and was briefly interned.

Lange joined the *Bundesmarine* in October 1957, and took part in the construction of a new German U-boat force within NATO. He commanded the 1st U-boat Squadron from April 1961 until October 1963, and from January 1964 he was commander of the entire U-boat force. Later he held several staff positions, and ended his career on 30 September 1972. He lived in retirement in Kiel until his death on 3 April 2014, at the age of ninety-seven.

Other awards:
07 Jun 1940: Iron Cross 2nd Class
12 Dec 1940: Iron Cross 1st Class
03 Apr 1941: Long Service Award 4th Class
24 Dec 1940: Destroyer War Badge
00 Oct 1943: U-Boat War Badge
11 May 1944: German Cross in Gold
00.00.1944: U-Boat War Badge with Diamonds
00.00.1945: U-Boat Combat Clasp in Bronze
00.00.1945: U-Boat Combat Clasp in Silver

HMS Bluebell *was searching for U-boats off Kola Inlet ahead of Convoy RA64 on 17 February 1945 when she was hit by a torpedo fired from* U-711. *She blew up when the torpedo struck, detonating her own depth charges, and sank in less than thirty seconds.* (Author's collection)

Georg Fritz Christian LASSEN
Korvettenkapitän
26 ships, 156,082 tons
5 ships damaged, 34,419 tons

Knight's Cross: Awarded on 10 August 1942 as *Oberleutnant zur See* and as commander of *U-160*, part of the 10th U-boat Flotilla, for actions in the Atlantic and Indian Oceans resulting in the sinking of over 66,012 shipping tonnes.

Knight's Cross with Oakleaves: He became the 208th recipient on 7 March 1943 as *Kapitänleutnant* and as commander of *U-160*, for continued actions in the Atlantic and Indian Oceans after sinking a further nine ships for a total of 52,056 shipping tonnes. He was presented with the Oakleaves during a ceremony at *Führer* Headquarters '*Wolfschanze*' in Rastenburg, East Prussia by Hitler on 4 July 1943.

(Scherzer)

Georg Lassen was born in Berlin on 12 May 1915, and was the tenth most successful U-boat commander of the Second World War, responsible for the sinking of 156,082 shipping tons. He joined the *Kriegsmarine* in April 1935, and on completion of his training was assigned to the light cruiser *Leipzig* as Signals Officer and as adjutant with the rank of *Leutnant zur See*.

In April 1939, he began his training as a U-boat commander and in August was assigned as First Watch Officer on board *U-29*, under the command of *Kapitänleutnant* Otto Schuhart. When the Second World War broke out, *U-29* was operating in the English Channel as part of the 2nd U-boat Flotilla. Lassen was promoted to *Oberleutnant zur See* in October and took part in seven war patrols with *U-29*, sinking a total of twelve ships, including the British aircraft carrier HMS *Courageous*. From January 1941, Lassen took over as commander of *U-29*, and during this time it served as a training vessel.

On 16 October 1941, Lassen was appointed commander of *U-160*, a Type IXC boat built in Bremen. During operational training at Danzig, on 14 December, several members of his crew were killed in an accidental fire. On 1 March 1942, Lassen left Heliogland in the North Sea, for the Western Atlantic, and *U-160* went initially to the Newfoundland area and then moved south, to patrol off the US east coast. On the 27th, Lassen sank the Panamanian SS *Equipoise* about 60 miles south-east of Cape Henry. She was struck by a torpedo on the starboard side, blowing out the bottom of the ship, causing her to sink within two minutes. Lifeboats were launched by the crew, but one of them capsized when it hit the water and the other was launched without anyone in it. Nine survivors climbed aboard the empty boat, but the severely-injured master died shortly afterwards and was buried at sea. Forty-one men were lost. Lassen then moved to off to the coast of Cape Hatteras, where he sank the MV *City of New York* on the 19th and the British SS *Rio Blanco* on 1 April. On 11 April, he sank the British passenger ship SS *Ulysses*, about 45 miles south of Cape Hatteras. The stern was struck by one torpedo and then another hit the engine room. While the crew abandoned ship, *U-160* went around the ship and fired another torpedo that hit amidships and caused the ship to sink in thirty minutes. The master, 189 crew members, five gunners and ninety-five passengers were later picked up by the USS *Manley*.

His next patrol took him to the central Atlantic, where he patrolled off the coast of Trinidad. Whilst off the coast of Tobago, he sank three ships on 21 June, and then moved onto Venezuela where he sank the Dutch SS *Telamon* on the 25th. Lassen sank the British tanker *Donovania* near Trinidad on 21 July. He had been chasing the tanker for more than four hours when he was finally able to fire a torpedo which struck the ship, and she sank by the stern in shallow water after being hit by a second torpedo. Three crew members and one gunner were lost, the remainder of the crew were rescued by a British motor torpedo boat and the USS *Livermore*. By the end of his second patrol he had sunk eleven ships for a total of 66,012 shipping tons. Promoted to *Kapitänleutnant* on 1 September Lassen continued to be successful. On 23 September 1942 he left port and headed out for the Caribbean, arriving just off the coast of Trinidad in mid-October. On the 16th he torpedoed two ships, sinking the British SS *Castle Harbour* and damaging the SS *Winona*. In November he spotted a convoy and during three separate attacks on 3 November, he sank four more ships. One of the ships was the Dutch *Bintang*. She was struck by two torpedoes on the port side amidships about 650 miles east of Trinidad. The explosions that followed destroyed both port lifeboats, while the others went down with the ship, so the survivors climbed on the rafts. Only four of the five rafts were eventually found and there were fifty-one survivors: twenty-two were lost. By the end of the patrol, he had sunk another four vessels, bringing his total to nineteen ships. After some well-deserved

leave, Lassen took *U-160* out on patrol to the South Atlantic as part of *Seehund* Group, together with *U-182*, *U-506* and *U-516*. The group assembled near the Cape Verde Islands and then sailed to St. Helena. On 8 February 1943, Lassen sank the US SS *Roger B. Taney*. He took *U-160* on to the Cape Town area and along the southern coast and then north up the east coast of South Africa. On 3 March, he sighted Convoy DN21, and in three attacks, sank four ships and damaged two. On the 8th, he sank the US SS *James B. Stephens* and three days later sank the SS *Aelbryn* near Durban. He then began his return journey, reaching Lorient on 10 May.

From 15 June 1943 until January 1945, Lassen was attached to the Training Division in Pillau, part of the 1st U-Boat Flotilla, where he served as a tactics instructor, training new U-boat commanders. Lassen was promoted to *Korvettenkapitän* in April and from the 15 April he took command of the *Pretoria*, a converted hospital ship. He transported 2,000 wounded and 200 refugees from Pillau to Stettin in Germany, to escape the Soviets, together with the coffins of former

Kapitänleutnant *Lassen*, the 208th recipient of the Knight's Cross with Oakleaves, presented for his continued service in the Atlantic and Indian Oceans by Hitler on 4 July 1943. (Author's collection)

Reich President and *Generalfeldmarschall* Paul von Hindenburg and his wife, and the regimental colours from the Tannenburg Memorial.

In May, Lassen was ordered to Flensburg, the headquarters of the new President of Germany, *Großadmiral* Dönitz. He was put in command of a makeshift battalion known as Works Battalion *Lassen*. On 31 August 1945, he was taken prisoner by British troops and was briefly interned. He died in Calviá, Mallora, Spain on 18 January 2012. He was ninety-six years old. His ashes were scattered in Santa Ponça Bay, together with the ashes of his wife.

Other awards:
05 Apr 1939: Long Service Award 4th Class
26 Sep 1939: Iron Cross 2nd Class
26 Oct 1939: Return of Memel Commemorative Medal
20 Dec 1939: Commemorative Medal of 01 Oct 1938
18 Jul 1940: U-Boot War Badge
18 Jul 1940: Iron Cross 1st Class
22 Oct 1944: U-Boot Combat Clasp in Bronze
22 Oct 1944: U-Boot War Badge with Diamonds

Heinrich Christian Wilhelm LEHMANN-WILLENBROCK
Fregattenkapitän
25 ships, 179,125 tons
2 ships sunk, 15,864 tons

Knight's Cross: Awarded on 26 February 1941 as *Kapitänleutnant* and as commander of *U-96* as part of the 7th U-Boat Flotilla, for sinking ten ships for a total of 90,183 shipping tons.

Knight's Cross with Oakleaves: Awarded on 31 December 1941, as the 51st recipient and as *Kapitänleutnant* and as commander of *U-96* in recognition of his continued success and for sinking a total of ten ships for a total 63,478 shipping tonnes. He was presented with the award by Hitler on 12 January 1942, at *Führer* Headquarters '*Wolfschanze*' in Rastenburg, East Prussia.

Heinrich Lehmann-Willenbrock gained widespread recognition when one of his patrols was documented and publicized by an accompanying member of a propaganda company, Lothar-Günther Buchheim. The story of *U-96* was eventually made into a mini-series called *Das Boot*, in which Lehmann-Willenbrock was portrayed by Jürgen Prochnow. Born on 11 December 1911 in Bremen, he was the sixth most successful U-boat commander of the war sinking twenty-five ships for a total of 179,125 shipping tons. Like most of the early U-boat commanders he was

(Author's collection)

A signed photograph of Kapitänleutnant *Heinrich Lehmann-Willenbrock wearing his Knight's Cross with Oakleaves.* (Wehrkundearchiv)

a professional naval officer, having joined the *Reichsmarine* as an officer cadet in April 1931. Lehmann-Willenbrock was commissioned as a *Leutnant zur See* in April 1935 and attended the usual training courses at the Naval Academy and aboard the light cruiser *Karlsruhe*. He served as Watch Officer onboard the sail training ship *Horst Wessel* from February 1937, having been promoted *to Oberleutnant zur See* a month earlier. He served on the ship for two years before applying to join the U-boat arm.

Lehmann-Willenbrock began training as a U-boat commander in April 1939, and on completion he was appointed commander of *U-8*, a training vessel in Kiel. He took command of *U-5* during the early stages of the Polish campaign watching for Polish shipping escaping to Britain and in October was promoted to *Kapitänleutnant*. On 4 April 1940, he took *U-5* out of Kiel to take part in Operation *Hartmut*, the German invasion of Denmark and Norway. From the 9th he was ordered to support German transports and naval forces landing troops and prevent any interference from British warships. He was ordered to join the 8th U-boat Group, and engage British forces moving down the Norwegian Sea from the north, but he made no contact. He returned to Wilhelmshaven on 19 April.

On 14 September 1940, he was appointed commander of *U-96*, a Type VIIC boat built in Kiel. His first patrol began in early December when he left for the area west of the North Channel. On the 11th he sank the British passenger ship the SS *Rotorua* with the loss of the master, four naval officers (including a commodore), fourteen crew members, one passenger and two gunners. Later that same evening he sank the Dutch SS *Towa*. The following day he sank two more ships, and on the 14th he sank the British passenger ship MV *Western Prince* and damaged the British SS *Empire Razorbill* by gunfire. His second patrol was short and he sank two ships, the SS *Oropesa* and the SS *Almeda Star*, both passenger liners. The *Almeda Star* was sunk on 17 January 1941. She was chased by *U-96* and three torpedoes were initially fired which missed, another was soon fired and this also missed, but the fifth torpedo struck the ship amidships. She did not sink and another two were fired and then she was attacked using the deck guns: she sank by the bow soon after being hit by the guns. Lifeboats were seen on the deck and although approximately fifteen incendiary shells had hit the ship the small fires soon went out. So Lehmann-Willenbrock fired another torpedo which struck the forepart and caused the ship to sink by the bow within three minutes. Seven destroyers were ordered to search for the 360 people aboard, but no-one was ever found.

Lehmann-Willenbrock left Kiel on 30 January 1941, to begin his third tour south of Iceland. On 13 February, he sank two stragglers from Convoy HX106 south of Iceland. On the 18th he sank the British SS *Black Osprey*, and on the 22nd, he sank another ship from Convoy OB287, the British tanker SS *Scottish Standard*. On the 23rd he sank another ship, and two more the following day, to bring his total to twelve ships sunk. On 12 April 1941, he left for his next patrol, and it soon became clear it was going to be a hard one. Very few ships were spotted and it was suspected that the convoys were being re-routed. Finally on the 18th, a convoy was sighted by *U-125* south of Reykjavik, and all boats were directed to it – one was *U-96* which sank three ships. A few days later another convoy was sighted but contact was lost. Lehmann-Willenbrock decided to head for port. On the way back, *U-96* sank the SS *Empire Ridge*, reaching St. Nazaire on 22 May. His total now stood at eighteen ships sunk and two damaged. During his next patrol again very few ships were spotted until 29 June when he sank the British troopship SS *Anselm*. She was struck by two torpedoes and sank within twenty-two minutes, which was just enough time for the crew to launch all but one of the lifeboats. Nonetheless, four crew members and 250 of the service personnel aboard were lost. *U-96* returned to port on 9 July.

On 2 August, *U-96* left for the central North Atlantic, and was immediately directed towards Convoy OG70, but couldn't find it. Between the 6th and 10th, *U-96* and ten other boats searched for Convoy HG68 and that wasn't found either. From 1 September, *U-96* was with *Kurfüst* Group and was directed towards Convoy OG73 but was unable to make contact. *U-96* returned to port on 12 September. Lehmann-Willenbrock left St. Nazaire on 27 October for the Atlantic, together with *U-133*, *U-552*, *U-567*, *U-571* and *U-577*. They were ordered on the 30th to the Newfoundland Bank where they were to operate as *Stosstrupp* Group. On the 31st, Convoy HX156 was sighted and whilst searching for it, *U-96* encountered Convoy OS10 and sank the SS *Bennekon*. Lehmann-Willenbrock then joined *Störtebecker* Group near the Azores from 5 November, but a week's search proved fruitless. On the 10th, the group was ordered west to the central North Atlantic, and again they found nothing. Then, on the 22nd, *U-96* was ordered to the Gibraltar area where she refuelled and made ready to enter the Mediterranean. On 31st she was located by a

Lehmann-Willenbrock together with the crew of U-96. (Author's collection)

U-256, *September 1944.* (Author's collection)

Swordfish aircraft and was bombed and slightly damaged. Lehmann-Willenbrock decided to head for port, arriving in St. Nazaire on 6 December.

On 31 January 1942, *U-96* headed out to operate in the Nova Scotia and Cape Cod area, where on 19 February it sank the MV *Empire Seal* and in the early hours the following day sank the US MV *Lake Osweya.* Two days later *U-96* sank the Norwegian SS *Torungen* by torpedo and gunfire and then during the evening sank the tanker MV *Kars.* On the 26th Lehmann-Willenbrock was promoted to *Korvettenkapitän*, but had no further success until 9 March when he sank the MV *Tyr* west of Sable Island. He returned to port on 23 March – his last patrol. On 1 May, he was appointed Chief of the 9th U-boat Flotilla in Brest. He briefly took command of *U-256* on 3 September 1944, leaving Brest for Trondheim, but went further south and landed at Bergen on 17 October, without engaging any shipping. He then took command of the 11th U-Boat Flotilla on 11 December, being promoted to *Fregattenkapitän* a week later.

He surrendered to Allied troops in May 1945 and was briefly held in custody, returning to West Germany in May 1946. He worked for a time salvaging ships on the Rhine, then in 1948 he moved to Buenos Aires where he worked as a skipper on several ships. In March 1959, he showed great courage as skipper of the freighter *Inga Bastian* when he and his crew saved the lives of fifty-seven sailors from a burning ship. In 1969, he became captain of the German nuclear research ship *Otto Hahn*, a post he held for over ten years. He later became the Chairman of the U-boat Comrades Association in Bremen for many years, whose headquarters bears his name to this day. Lehmann-Willenbrock died on 18 April 1986 in Bremen.

Other awards:
02 Oct 1936: Long Service Award 4th Class
20 Apr 1940: Iron Cross 2nd Class
31 Dec 1940: Iron Cross 1st Class
02 Jan 1941: U-Boat War Badge

01 Nov 1941: Italian War Cross with Swords
00.00.1942: U–Boat War Badge with Diamonds
08 May 1942: Wound Badge in Black
30 Jan 1944: War Service Cross 2nd Class with Swords
19 Oct 1944: U–Boat Combat Clasp in Bronze

Heinrich Otto Moritz LIEBE
Fregattenkapitän
34 ships sunk, 187,267 tons
1 ship damaged, 3,670 tons

Knight's Cross: Awarded on 14 August 1940 as *Kapitänleutnant* and as commander of *U-38*, as part of the 2nd U-boat Flotilla, for the sinking of seventeen ships for a total of 76,169 shipping tonnes.

Knight's Cross with Oakleaves: *Kapitänleutnant* Liebe became the 4th U-boat commander to be awarded the Oakleaves on 10 June 1941 as Commander of *U-38*, in recognition of sinking a further fifteen ships for a total of 103,470 shipping tonnes. The award was presented by Hitler at his headquarters in Rastenburg, East Prussia, the '*Wolfschanze*', on 29 June 1941.

Heinrich Liebe was the fourth most successful U-boat commander of the Second World War, sinking thirty-four ships for a total of 187,267 shipping tons. He was born on 29 January 1908, in Gotha, Thüringia. Liebe joined the *Reichsmarine* in April 1927, and after his basic training was commissioned as a *Leutnant zur See* four years later. He attended various other training courses over the next few years, which included service aboard the First World War battleship *Schleswig-Holstein*. In October 1933 he was promoted to *Oberleutnant zur See* and from December 1935 to September 1936, attended the Naval Academy at Flensburg-Mürwik, before being appointed commander of *U-2*, whilst attached to the U-boat School.

From April 1938, Liebe was the Commandant of the U-boat School in Neustadt, Holstein, and then on 24 October, already a *Kapitänleutnant* he was appointed commander of *U-38*, a Type IXA boat. On 19 August 1939, Liebe took *U-38* from Wilhelmshaven to operate west of Lisbon, where, on 6 September *U-38* was shot at by the British SS *Manaar*: there was an exchange of fire and the ship was sunk – it was one of the first actions by a U-boat in the Second World War. The next day Liebe was ordered to return to port and on the way back he sank the British tanker MV *Inverliffey*. On 14 November Liebe took *U-38* out on another patrol, on the north-west coast of Norway. He then moved (Scherzer)

southwards and sank the British SS *Thomas Walton*, and by the 13th had sunk another four ships, which included the Danish merchant ship *Argentina*: her entire crew of thirty-three was lost. His next patrol began on 26 February 1940, and ended on 5 April, and during this time he sank a total of six ships. On 8 April, he left port to take part in Operation *Hartmut*, the invasion of Denmark and Norway. He joined the 5th U-boat Group and took *U-38* to the north-east of the Shetland Islands, and later moved to operate against British naval forces. On the 18 April, *U-38* attacked the cruiser HMS *Effingham* but the attack failed because of defective torpedoes. On the 19th Liebe took *U-38* to Norwegian waters, and two days later he sailed to the coast of the Shetlands Islands but had no success. He returned to Wilhelmshaven on 27 May.

On 6 June 1940, *U-38* left for operations south of Ireland, and after Liebe delivered an agent there on the 12th, he sank the Greek SS *Mount Myrto*. The next day he sank two more ships, both from Convoy HX48, and then took *U-38* east to patrol the area at the western entrance to the English Channel. On the 20th, he sank the Swedish SS *Tilia Gorthon* and on the 21st sank the SS *Luxembourg*, and the following day sank the Greek SS *Neion*, before returning to port on 2 July. His sixth patrol began on 1 August, off the North Channel. In the evening of the 7th *U-38* attacked Convoy HX61 and sank the British troopship the SS *Mohamed Ali El-Kebir*, with the loss of ninety-two: there were 766 survivors. On the 11th he sank the British SS *Llanfair*. From 13 to 16 July, together with *U-46* and *U-48*, Liebe attempted to add to his score by sinking ships from Convoy HX62 but had no success. On the 31st, however, he sank the British SS *Har Zion*, a straggler from Convoy OB205, carrying 1,000 cases of spirit and 120 tons of fertiliser. She was struck by two torpedoes amidships and sank by the stern north-west of Bloody Foreland. The master, thirty-four crew members and one gunner were lost. The sole survivor was Seaman Osman Adem. On 1 October Liebe sank the British passenger ship MV *Highland Patriot* with the loss of only three crew members.

Liebe's last patrol with *U-38* began on 9 April 1941, when he left Lorient for the South Atlantic. On 4 May, he sank the SS *Japan* from Convoy OB310, and the following day he sank the MV *Queen Maud*. Low on fuel, he left the convoys and was refuelled by the supply ship *Egerland*. He then sailed to the Freetown area where he sank five more ships in just eight days. By 7 June, Liebe was ready to rendezvous once again with his supply ship, but she had been sunk. He now had to return to port, and during the journey he sank the SS *Kingston Hill* south-west of the Cape Verde Islands. He reached Lorient on 26 June.

In July 1941, Liebe was assigned to the staff of the Commander-in-Chief of the *Kriegsmarine*, *Großadmiral* Erich Raeder and from 1943 was *Großadmiral* Karl Dönitz. In August 1944, he was transferred to the staff of the Commander of U-boats, *Generaladmiral* Hans-Georg von Friedeburg – a post he kept until the end of the war. Liebe was promoted to *Fregattenkapitän* on 17 September 1944. After the war he joined the German Hydrographical Institute, and later returned to his hometown in the Soviet sector of German to live with his parents. He refused to train Soviet submariners, and perhaps as a consequence of his refusal he was only employed in menial posts, and was never used to his full potential. Liebe died on 27 July 1997, in Eisenbach, Germany.

Other awards:
02 Oct 1936: Long Service Award 4th Class
20 Apr 1937: German Olympic Medal

08 Oct 1939: Iron Cross 2nd Class
16 Dec 1939: U-Boat War Badge
06 Apr 1940: Iron Cross 1st Class
02 Dec 1941: Italian War Cross with Swords
00.00.1941: U-Boat War Badge with Diamonds
03 Sep 1944: War Service Cross 2nd Class with Swords

Karl-Friedrich MERTEN
Kapitän zur See
27 ships sunk, 170,151 tons

Knight's Cross: Awarded on 13 June 1942 as *Korvettenkapitän* and as commander of *U-68* for sinking eleven ships in the North Atlantic for a total of 63,000 shipping tons.

Knight's Cross with Oakleaves: He became the 147th recipient of the Oakleaves on 16 November 1942, as *Korvettenkapitän* and as commander of *U-68* in recognition for sinking sixteen ships for a total of 107,000 shipping tons. Hitler personally presented him with the Oakleaves together with Wolfgang Lüth on 30 January 1943, at *Führer* Headquarters '*Wolfschanze*' in Rastenburg, East Prussia. The following day Merten left Hitler's headquarters for the Hotel Kaiserhof where he was awarded the U-boat Badge with Diamonds by *Großadmiral* Raeder.

Below left and right: (Scherzer)

Karl-Friedrich Merten was an outstanding U-boat commander and was responsible for sinking twenty-seven ships for a total of 170,151 shipping tons, making him the seventh most successful U-boat commander of the Second World War. He was born on 15 August 1905, in Posen, now in Poland. His father, also Karl-Friedrich, was Mayor of Elbing from 1910, but was forced out of office in 1934 for refusing to join the Nazi Party. He had an older brother and sister who died before he was seven years old, and had a younger brother Klaus who became a *Feldwebel* in the army, but who died on the Eastern Front in 1942.

In April 1918, at the age of twelve he was sent to the Royal Prussian Cadet House in Köslin, which became a boarding school following the First World War. There he attended until his graduation in March 1926. He then joined the *Reichsmarine* soon after and underwent his basic military training with the 5th Company of the II. *Schiffsstammdivision* in Stralsund. He trained on board various training vessels and sailed on the first training cruise of the light cruiser *Emden* in November 1926. It began in Wilhelmshaven and took him around Africa, Indonesia and then on to Japan and the west coast of North and South America. Following the cruise, which ended in March 1928, Merten attended cadet training at the Naval Academy until March 1929. Here he learnt navigation, naval infantry, gunnery and officer training. Shortly after he was commissioned as a *Leutnant zur See* in October 1930, Merten was assigned as Gunnery Officer on the light cruiser *Königsberg*, and from 1932 served as a gunnery instructor at the Naval Academy. During this time he attended various training courses, including an anti-aircraft instructor's course at Wilhelmshaven from February 1932. In December, Merten was posted to the gunnery training ship *Bremse*, serving as the Second Gunnery Officer.

In April 1933, he was promoted to *Oberleutnant zur See* and a year later was married in Wiesbaden. He then served with the staff of the commander of minesweepers and at the same time was the Second Watch Officer aboard the torpedo boat *T-156*, until January 1934. Merten was then posted to the light cruiser *Karlsruhe* in September 1935, serving for almost two years as the Second Gunnery Officer and Watch Officer. In April 1936 he was promoted to *Kapitänleutnant* and from March 1937, he served briefly as the anti-aircraft gunnery officer aboard the light cruiser *Leipzig* and in the same position back on the *Karlsruhe*. He participated in the navy's non-intervention patrols during the Spanish Civil War.

In July 1939, Merten was posted as a cadet training officer on board the battleship *Schleswig-Holstein*, and when the Second World War began he took part in the bombardment of the Polish base at Danzig in September. On 7th, he led the *Schleswig-Holstein*'s naval infantry in the battle of Hel, and it was for this action that he was awarded the Iron Cross 2nd Class. In April 1940, he volunteered to join the U-boat service. He was soon accepted and his training started at the torpedo school in Flensburg-Mürwik, and was posted to the 1st U-boat Training Division on 1 July 1940. On 30 November, Merten joined the crew of *U-38*, under the command of *Kapitänleutnant* Heinrich Liebe, as Watch Officer. He took part in one war patrol during which two ships were sunk.

On 11 February 1941, he took command of *U-68*, a Type IXC submarine, built in Bremen. Promoted to *Korvettenkapitän* in April he left Kiel on his first patrol on 30 June, for operations in the central North Atlantic. For three days he took part in a failed convoy operation. Then on 24 July, he was directed to another convoy, OG69, west of Ireland where he attacked a corvette but without success. He returned to his new base in Lorient on 1 August. For his second patrol, which began on 11 September, Merten headed out for the Southern Atlantic and on to to the Ascension Islands then on to Cape Verde. During the patrol he sank four ships, totalling 23,697 tons, which included the British SS *Silverbelle* and the SS *Bradford City*, which he sank on 1 November 1941. On the 13th, *U-68* was resupplied by the auxiliary cruiser *Atlantis* under the commander of *Kapitän zur See* Bernhard Rogge. Once supplies had been transferred to *U-68*, Merten conducted a number of mock attacks on *Atlantis* for training purposes. On 23 November, Merten received reports that *Atlantis* had been sunk by HMS *Devonshire* while resupplying *U-126*; almost 300 sailors were rescued including Rogge. Two days later the survivors were transferred to the refuelling ship *Python*. On 30 November *U-58* met with *Python* for refuelling and to stock up on torpedoes. During the operation a ship was sighted just as *U-68* had finished the transfer. Within a few minutes HMS *Dorsetshire* opened fire on *Python*, but *U-68*, still in the process of storing the new torpedoes, was not in a position for combat. Merten, however, managed to submerge but holding the boat at periscope depth was almost impossible. *Python* was hit by *Devonshire* and sank. The cruiser, unaware of *U-68*'s difficulties, left the area. Merten ordered the boat to surface and rescued the survivors; those that couldn't fit in below were towed in lifeboats to a rendezvous point with *U-124* and *U-129*. Apparently, following the first salvo from *Devonshire*, *Python*'s crew had chosen to scuttle the ship to avoid unnecessary casualties. The survivors were unloaded from the U-boats to another vessel and onto safety. Merten therefore decided to return to port, he reached Lorient on Christmas Day 1941.

His third patrol began on 11 February 1942, when he left port for the Central Atlantic. The patrol took *U-68* to the West African coast and lasted for sixty days, covering 10,995 nautical miles. Merten sank a total of seven ships during this patrol, including three on 17 March. The next patrol, his fourth he sank another seven ships, in a patrol that lasted fifty-six days. On 5 June he sank the American tanker SS *L.J. Drake* sailing towards Puerto Rico when she was struck by three torpedoes and immediately exploded. Afterwards all that remained were pieces of wreckage and, unsurprisingly, there were no survivors. On the 10 June he sank three ships, the British SS *Surrey*, MV *Ardenvohr* and the MV *Port Montreal*. Five days later Merten sank the French tanker *Frimaire*. She was struck by three torpedoes, capsized and sank by the stern north-east of Barranquilla, Colombia. Merten had seen French nationality markings without the yellow border for the Vichy government and correctly identified the tanker, but did not know about neutral traffic in the area and assumed that the ship had been seized and was en route to Panama. Only after the sinking was he told this had been a Vichy French tanker operating under Portuguese charter and he shouldn't have made the attack. *U-68* returned to base on 10 July. For his next patrol Merten took *U-68* to join *U-156*, *U-172*, *U-504* and the U-tanker *U-459*, and they sailed out of port as *Eisbär* Group. Between September and October the group sank more than 100,000 shipping tons off the coast of South Africa. Merten sank eight ships, which included four in one day, for a total of 48,196 tons. On 19 October Merten began his journey home, and on 6 November he sank the British passenger ship SS *City of Cairo*, south of St. Helena. *U-68* surfaced among the lifeboats and Merten spoke to the survivors, gave them a compass and apologised for sinking their ship. It was almost a month before they were picked up by a German ship. Merten reached Lorient on 6 December; it was to be his final patrol. (In September 2013, divers from Deep Ocean Search managed to recover fifty tons of silver from the wreck. The value of the recovery was worth around £40 million.)

On 19 January 1943, Merten was appointed deputy commander of the 26th U-boat Flotilla. On 1 March, he took over as commander of the 24th U-Boat Flotilla, and during this time he found himself in frequent conflict with the *Gauleiter* of East Prussia, Erich Koch. In July 1944, Koch had ordered 6,000 Hitler Youth to man defensive positions around Memel against the advancing Red Army. Merten ordered the youngsters to be evacuated and *Großadmiral* Dönitz had to act as a mediator and calm down the furious *Gauleiter*. On 12 March 1945, Merten was posted to *Führer* Headquarters in Berlin as a liaison officer. He was put on the staff of *Fliegendes Sondergericht West* (Flying Special Court-Martial West). This was created by Hitler in response to the American capture of the Ludendorff Bridge over the Rhine at Remagen. A bridge that should have been blown up but its commander failed to so and was executed. Anyone who failed to carry out one of Hitler's orders would be tried by court-martial and executed. Merten had been promoted to *Fregattenkapitän* in January 1944 and on 15 April 1945 he was promoted to *Kapitän zur See*, and together with other officers he travelled to Upper Bavaria to the so-called Alpine Fortress. It was there that he was taken prisoner by US forces and held in captivity in Biessenhofen until 29 June 1945.

In October 1948, Merten was arrested by the French authorities and accused of wrongfully sinking a French tanker in June 1942. He was held in custody until 8 March 1949 at Chercho-Midi prison, Paris. He was acquitted on 10 September 1949. He attended the funeral of *Großadmiral* Dönitz on 6 January 1981. On 14 September 1984, he attended a reunion of the survivors of the City of Cairo, which was attended by seventeen survivors. In 1986, Merten published his book *Wir* U-*Boot fahrer sagen 'Nein!' So war dis nicht* ['We U-boat sailors say "No! It was not like this"']. He died of cancer on 2 May 1993 in Waldshut-Tiengen in Baden-Württemberg.

Other awards:
02 Oct 1939: Iron Cross 2nd Class
30 Dec 1941: Iron Cross 1st Class
02 Oct 1936: Long Service Award 4th Class
21 Dec 1936: Olympic Badge of Honour 2nd Class
01 Apr 1938: Long Service Award 3rd Class
20 Apr 1938: Spanish Cross in Bronze
20 Dec 1939: Commemorative Medal of 01 Oct 1938
02 Aug 1941: U-Boat War Badge
09 Oct 1942: High Seas Fleet War Badge
30 Jan 1943: U-Boat War Badge with Diamonds
30 Jan 1944: War Service Cross 2nd Class with Swords
29 Oct 1944: War Service Cross 1st Class with Swords

Johann MOHR
Korvettenkäpitan
29 ships sunk, 135,751 tons
3 ships damaged, 26,167 tons

Knight's Cross: Awarded on 27 March 1942, as *Korvettenkapitän* and as commander of *U-124*, part of the 2nd U-boat Flotilla after sinking fourteen ships for a total of 57,659 shipping tons.

Knight's Cross with Oakleaves: Awarded as *Kapitänleutnant* and as commander of *U-124* on 13 January 1943 to become the 177th recipient, for his continued success against enemy shipping, in particular for sinking thirteen ships in the Atlantic, the Mediterranean and off the coast of Africa. The presentation of the Oakleaves was made by Hitler in February 1943 at his military headquarters in Rastenburg, East Prussia, the '*Wolfschanze*'.

(Scherzer)

Johann Mohr was one of a handful of U-boat commanders who spent their entire U-boat career on a single boat. He sank twenty-nine ships for a total of 135,751 tons, making him the seventeenth most successful U-boat commander of the Second World War. Mohr was born on 12 June 1916, in Hannover and entered the *Reichsmarine* in April 1934, as an Officer Candidate and was attached to the 4th Company of II. *Schiffsstamabteilung* (Ships' Cadre Battalion) in the Baltic. Here he underwent basic training and would later serve on board the light cruiser *Karlsruhe*, the 'pocket battleship' *Deutschland* and he attended the Naval Academy at Flensburg.

In April 1937 he was commissioned as a *Leutnant zur See* and served on the staff of the Commander of Armoured Ships. In April 1939 he was promoted to *Oberleutnant zur See* and two years later he transferred to the U-boat Service and was assigned to the 1st U-boat Training Division. He continued with his training and in September 1940, was assigned to *U-124* as Second and later First Watch Officer under the command of *Kapitänleutnant* Wilhelm Schulz. He participated in six patrols with Schulz, during which time *U-124* sank nineteen ships. On 1 September 1941, Mohr became the youngest *Kapitänleutnant* in the *Kriegsmarine*, and a week later he succeeded Schulz when he was named commander of *U-124*. He left for operations in the North Atlantic on 16 September, to begin his first patrol as commander. He soon sighted Convoy OG74 north-north-east of the Azores. On the 25th Mohr sank the SS *Empire Steam*, which was struck by two torpedoes north-north-west of the Azores. Four crew members, two gunners and two stowaways were lost. The master, twenty-four crew and two gunners were picked up by HMS *Begonia* and landed at Milford Haven on 30 September. During the early hours of the following day he sank two more ships, the SS *Petrel* and the SS *Lapwing*, and in the evening that same day he sank the British SS *Cervantes*. With all torpedoes expended, he returned to port. His next patrol began on 30 October, and lasted until 29 December, and he sank just two ships, but one was the British light cruiser HMS *Dunedin*, which was sunk south-west of St. Pauls Rocks on 24 November. It was also during this patrol that Mohr became involved with the incident surrounding the sinking of the German raider *Atlantis* together with *U-68* and *U-126* (for more on this incident see Karl-Friedrich Merten).

Johann Mohr wearing his Knight's Cross seated on one of the deck guns of his U-boat. (Wehrkundearchiv)

His next patrol was more successful. Mohr left Lorient on 21 February 1942 to operate in US waters. On 14 March, he sank the tanker MV *British Resource* north of Bermuda, with the loss of forty-six. On the 17th he sank the Honduran banana boat SS *Ceiba* east of Cape Hatteras. Over the next six days *U-124* claimed another five ships sunk and three damaged before returning to port on 10 April. Mohr left for operations in the North Atlantic on 4 May together with *U-94*, *U-96*, *U-406*, *U-569* and *U-590*, to take part in a planned group-operation *Hecht*, in the area of the Newfoundland Bank. A convoy was sighted on 11 May, and the next day *U-124* sank four ships, which included the British catapult-armed ship SS *Empire Dell*. The *Hecht* Group continued their patrol line and by 25 May, they were being refuelled at a rendezvous point 600 miles south of Cape Race. On the 31st, *U-590* sighted another convoy, but as the weather deteriorated the operation against the convoy was cancelled. On 8 June, *U-124* sighted Convoy ONS-100 in the central North Atlantic, and the following day sank the French corvette *Mimrose*. She was struck on her port side by one torpedo about 600 miles south-east of Cape Farewell. The torpedo struck near the engine room and flooding caused the boilers to explode. The corvette sank by the stern within three minutes with most of the crew being killed by the detonations of her depth charges. Her loss wasn't noticed by the other escorts until morning. The commander, sixty French sailors and six British sailors were lost. On the 10th, *U-124* made her final attack on the convoy and sank the British SS *Dartford* east of Newfoundland. The operation was terminated on 17 June and the next day Mohr began the journey back to his home port. During the journey home he sank the US SS *Seattle Spirit* on the morning of the 18th and reached port eight days later. Mohr wrote poetry during his patrols and he wrote this verse whilst on the journey back:

> *The moon night is as black as ink*
> *Off Hatteras the tankers sink*
> *While sadly Roosevelt counts the score*
> *Some fifty thousand tons. Mohr.*

Mohr and his crew had some well-deserved leave before beginning their next patrol on 25 November, when they headed for the Central Atlantic, to an area east of the Caribbean. The patrol lasted until 13 February 1943, and Mohr sank a further five ships, including four in a single day, before returning to Lorient. After restocking with food and torpedoes, Mohr left port on 27 March, for his sixth and last patrol. He headed for the Freetown area and soon sighted Convoy OS45. On 1 April he was promoted to *Korvettenkapitän* and on the evening of the following day he sunk two ships, the British SS *Katha* and SS *Gogra*. In the early hours of the 2nd, *U-124* was located by escort ships from the convoy and was depth-charged by the sloop HMS *Black Swan* and the corvette HMS *Stonecrop*. Mohr had been slow to react; he chose to wait until the ships were almost upon him before giving the order to dive. Two patterns of depth charges from both ships resulted in the loss of *U-124*. There were no survivors: fifty-three men were dead.

Other awards:
08 Apr 1939: Long Service Award 4th Class
06 Jun 1939: Spanish Cross in Bronze
26 Oct 1939: Return of Memel Commemorative Medal
29 Nov 1939: Iron Cross 2nd Class
04 May 1941: Iron Cross 1st Class
04 May 1941: U-Boat War Badge
13 Jan 1943: U-Boat War Badge with Diamonds

<u>Rolf</u> Christian Detlef MÜTZELBURG
Kapitänleutnant
19 ships sunk, 81,961 tons
3 ships damaged, 17,052 tons

Knight's Cross: Awarded on 17 November 1941, as *Kapitänleutnant* and as commander of *U-203* in recognition of his success in the Atlantic where he sank ten ships for a total just over 41,000 tons.

Knight's Cross with Oakleaves: Awarded as *Kapitänleutnant* on 15 July 1942, to become the 104th recipient, as commander of *U-203* for continued success in the Atlantic

(Scherzer and Author's collection)

where he sank a further eight ships and damaged another three. He was presented with the Oakleaves by Hitler at his headquarters '*Wehrwolf*' at Vinnitsa in the Ukraine.

Born in Kiel on 23 June 1913, Rolf Mützelburg was the son of a naval officer, and he joined the *Reichsmarine* on 1 April 1932. He attended the usual training courses from October 1932 to March 1936, being commissioned as a *Leutnant zur See* in January 1936. On 28 September 1936 he was assigned to the minesweeper *M117* and served as First Watch Officer. He was promoted in October 1937 to *Oberleutnant zur See* and appointed adjutant to the commander of the 2nd Minesweeper Flotilla. From February 1938 until August 1939 he underwent further training which included attendance at the Naval Academy where he learnt about navigation, torpedoes and naval artillery. In September 1939, Mützelburg took over as commander of the 12th Minesweeper Flotilla, and at the same time he underwent training at the U-boat school in Flensburg.

In January 1940, he was promoted to *Kapitänleutnant* and transferred to the U-boat service, and in June he took command of the training boat *U-10*, succeeding *Oberleutnant zur See* Joachim Preuss, whilst stationed in Pillau, and attached to the 21st U-boat Flotilla. Then from November 1940 to January 1941 he served on *U-100*, gaining valuable experience as a commander from her captain, *Kapitänleutnant* Joachim Schepke.

On 19 February 1941, Mützelburg took command of *U-203*, a Type VIIIC boat built by Germania Werft in Kiel. He set out on his first patrol as commander on 5 June, heading for the North Atlantic. However, when it was realized that convoys were being re-routed to avoid a U-boat group stationed between Newfoundland and Greenland, *U-203* was sent to operate in the area of the central North Atlantic. On the 20th Mützelburg sighted the American battleship USS *Texas* inside the German-declared blockade zone just off Greenland and attempted an attack. But, after a sixteen-hour pursuit *U-203* was unable to overtake *Texas* and obtain a favourable attack position. At this time Hitler's policy was to avoid provocation actions against the US. As a result of this near-encounter Dönitz issued the following new order: 'USA warships should not be attacked even in the blockade area, since the present permission to do this does not seem to agree with the political views of the *Führer*.' Mützelburg then sighted Convoy HX133 on 23 June, south of Greenland. In the early hours of the following day he sank the Norwegian MV *Solöy*, and whilst still pursing HX-133, *U-203* encountered another convoy and sank two ships; the British MV *Kinross* and the SS *Schie*. Mützelburg then headed for home, arriving in St. Nazaire on 29 June.

On 10 July, Mützelburg set out on his second patrol and headed once again for operations in the central North Atlantic. On the 17th Convoy OB346 was sighted, but *U-203* only managed to damage one ship. Together with other boats, *U-203* began to operate off the coast of Ireland and was directed to Convoy OG69. On the 27th, Mützelburg sank the British SS *Hawkinge*, and made a further attack the following day which resulted in the sinking of the Swedish SS *Norita* and the British SS *Lapland*. Mützelburg returned to St. Nazaire on 31 July. His next patrol was short, lasting just ten days; he took *U-203* out on 20 September to the Eastern Atlantic. He was directed towards Convoy HG73 and sank three ships from the convoy before sailing into Brest. One of these ships was the British passenger ship SS *Aroceta* which was struck by a torpedo on her port side and quickly sank with the loss of forty-three crew members, four gunners and seventy-six passengers – just north of the Azores. The next patrol, his fourth, was a longer one, and he left port on 18 October to operate in the North Atlantic. A convoy was sighted on 1 November, and *U-203* sank two ships, the British SS *Empire Gemsbuck* and SS *Everoja*.

After some leave Mützelburg took *U-203* out of Brest of Christmas Day 1941, and headed for the Gibraltar area. He was one of six other boats intended for Mediterranean operations, but instead they assembled near the Azores, as *Seydlitz* Group. On 2 January 1942, the group was split up, and *U-203*, *U-84* and *U-552* were ordered to the Newfoundland Bank. On the 15th, *U-203* sank the fishing vessel MV *Catalina*, on the 17th the SS *Octavian* was sunk south of Cape Breton Island, and on the 21st he damaged the MV *North Gaspe*. He returned to Brest on 29 January. On 12 March, *U-203* left to operate in the Western Atlantic, he was ordered to patrol off the US east coast as part of Operation *Paukenschlag*. During a five-day period Mützelburg sank two ships and damaged two others, which included the British tanker *San Delfino* on 10 April and he damaged the American tanker *Harry F. Sinclair* the following day. For his next patrol, lasting from 4 June to 29 July, he was ordered to the Western Atlantic where on 26th he sank two ships by torpedo and gunfire. On the 28th he added another ship to his total when he sunk the US SS *Sam Houston*. Mützelburg then moved further south and on 9 July, sank the MV *Cape Verde* off Tobago. The Panamanian tanker the SS *Stanvac Palembang* was sunk in the same area on the 11 July.

On 28 August, Mützelburg left for operations in the Western Atlantic and headed to an area near the Azores. On 11 September, he and some of the crew were relaxing and swimming in the sea, taking it in turns diving off the conning tower and enjoying themselves, when tragedy struck. Mützelburg dived off just as the boat was hit by a big wave and he hit his head on a saddle tank and broke his neck. A doctor from *U-462* was called and arrived the next day, but Mützelburg was dead. He was buried at sea the following day. His death was announced on 15 September 1942 in the Daily Armed Forces Communiqué: '*Kapitänleutnant* Rolf Mützelburg, U-boat commander, recipient of the Knight's Cross with Oakleaves, lost his life on a war patrol. The U-boat service has lost an outstanding commander and a successful hunter. The boat continues her patrol under the command of the senior Watch Officer, *Oberleutnant zur See* Hans Seidel.'

Other awards:
15 Aug 1936: Long Service Award 4th Class
01 Jul 1941: Iron Cross 2nd Class
01 Jul 1941: Iron Cross 1st Class
01 Jul 1941: U-Boat War Badge
00.00.1942: U-Boat War Badge with Diamonds (pm)

Heinrich Günther PRIEN
Korvettenkapitän
31 ships sunk, 191,919 tons
8 ships damaged, 62,751 tons

Knight's Cross: Awarded as *Kapitänleutnant* and as commander of *U-47*, on 18 October 1939, after sinking the battleship HMS *Royal Oak* in Scapa Flow. He was the first U-boat

(Author's collection)

commander to be awarded the Knight's Cross and it was presented to him by Hitler at a very special ceremony at the Reich Chancellery in Berlin.

Knight's Cross with Oakleaves: Awarded on 20 October 1940 as *Kapitänleutnant* and as commander of *U-47*, as the 5th recipient, and the first naval officer. It was given in recognition of his continued success as a U-boat commander; he had sunk a total of 200,000 tons of ships. The Oakleaves were presented to him by Hitler on 31 October 1940 in Berlin in the Great Hall at the Reich Chancellery.

Perhaps the most famous U-boat commander of the Second World War, Günther Prien was responsible for the one of the most daring operations against the Royal Navy's base at Scapa Flow, resulting in the loss of the battleship HMS *Royal Oak*. Prien became the first U-boat commander to be awarded the Knight's Cross, and was responsible for the sinking of thirty-one ships, for a total of 191,919 shipping tons. This made him the ninth most successful U-boat commander of the Second World War.

Günther Prien was born on 16 January 1908 in Osterfeld, Thüringen, and he was one of three children. His father was a judge and just after he left the family and filed for divorce he died, leaving the young Günther and his mother in financial difficulties. His mother then moved to Leipzig, taking her children with her. In 1923, at the age of fifteen Prien decided to abandon his education and get a job, to help his mother who was living very much on the bread-line. Prien joined the Merchant Navy, spending the last of his savings on a three-month course at the Seaman's College in Finkenwärder. His career with the German Merchant Navy lasted for eight years, beginning as a cabin boy on a sailing ship. Asas the youngest member of the crew, he was given every dirty, filthy job and had to fight continually to survive among an older crew. All of this made him more determined, something he never lost.

In 1932 he was one of the millions out of work and it was a tragic accident that would change the course of his career. In the summer the *Reichsmarine* sail training ship *Niobe* capsized and sank in the Baltic, taking one-third of the new officer candidates with her. There was now an urgent need for new trainee officers, and so Prien joined the *Reichsmarine* in January 1933. As an experienced sailor, he was soon commissioned and moved ahead at an accelerated pace; he married and volunteered to join the U-boat service. Upon his graduation from U-boat school in October 1935, he served as Watch Officer onboard an experimental Type I boat, *U-26*, making a number of voyages to Spain, being promoted to *Oberleutnant zur See* in January 1937.

Prein was short, moon-faced and was often described as cocky, stubborn and impatient. He was a simple man, clear-thinking, who argued his point, according to a fellow U-boat captain. His crew, whom he drilled to the point of exhaustion, disliked him, and he was distant toward his fellow commanders. However, his temperament appealed to Dönitz, the commander-in-chief of U-boats, whose favourite commander he was. He was rated as one of six best U-boat officers in the service, and became the third and most junior officer selected to command a new boat. He was made commander of *U-47*, a Type VIIB boat built by Germania Werft in Kiel, in December 1938. In February 1939 he was promoted to *Kapitänleutnant* and during 'war games' in the Atlantic in May Prien was rated the best, the most aggressive and he had the highest recorded score.

In August 1939, he left Kiel for his first patrol as commander of *U-47*, and headed to a patrol area north-west of Cape Ortegal. On 4 September, he sighted a neutral Greek ship and let her pass, he then closed on two other ships, but when he got closer he could see they were Swedish, also neutral. The following day his First Watch Officer, Engelbert Endraß, spotted a ship. Prien ordered the boat to dive and when he was close enough he surfaced and ordered his deck gun to fire at the ship. The ship, the British freighter SS *Bosnia*, was hit several times and her crew panicked and abandoned their ship and Prien could see the survivors in the water. He took his boat closer to them and hauled them aboard, and his men made sure the lifeboats were lowered for the survivors and a supply of clean drinking water was put in each boat. Prien then ordered his boat to fire at the freighter and she sank. She was the second British ship to be sunk after the *Athenia* – and the first freighter of the war. Prien went on to sink the British SS *Rio Claro* on 6 September and the SS *Gartavon* the next day. He returned to base on 15 September.

In what is probably the most famous single naval incident of the Second World War and one of the most audacious actions of the war, Prien was ordered to attack Scapa Flow. The plan was conceived by *Kommodore* Dönitz, the commander of U-boats, together with his operations officer *Kapitänleutnant* Victor Oehrn. Prien had been chosen personally by Dönitz. On 1 October 1939, Prien stood in front of Dönitz's desk, when he tossed a folder down in front of Prien, it was the operational plans, photos, charts and tables. Dönitz told Prien to take the folder, read it and come back in two days and, 'tell me what you think?' Prien took the folder and studied them carefully and just as Dönitz had thought Prien accepted the task. The night chosen for the attack was 13/14 October, when it was hoped that a full moon would provide just the right conditions for the attempt. Prien removed his Enigma machine and his secret codes and papers, leaving them ashore and set out from Kiel for Scapa Flow on 8 October.

He arrived on the afternoon of 13 October. That previous afternoon a German reconnaissance aircraft had reported seeing an aircraft carrier, five heavy ships and ten cruisers in Scapa Flow, including the exact position of the *Royal Oak*. However, by that night the bulk of the Home Fleet had sailed from Scapa Flow. Prien was left with one target, the *Royal Oak*, which had not joined the rest of the fleet, and instead she was lying peacefully at anchor. Prien moved into position and at 01:04 on 14 October, he fired a torpedo at the battleship, he then fired three more at 01:20: all three hit their target and exploded. The effect on the ship was immediate and catastrophic; the ship was swept by fire, fumes and smoke. With all power gone and lights extinguished there was no time to issue the order to abandon ship. She capsized and sank bow first at 01:29, just twenty-five minutes after the first hit. The loss of life was massive – 836 men were killed.

HMS Royal Oak *seen here leaving Malta in 1937. She was sunk in Scapa Flow by Günther Prien on 14 October 1939. He managed to enter the harbour and fired a spread of three torpedoes at the battleship, then turned around and fired a stern torpedo. He then fired a second spread of three torpedoes and she eventually sank with the loss of 836 officers and ratings.* (Author's collection)

When Prien returned to Germany he was instantly famous. He was awarded the Knight's Cross personally by Hitler, the first sailor of the U-boat service and the second member of the *Kriegsmarine* to receive the award. Prien received the nickname, 'The Bull of Scapa Flow', and the emblem of a snorting bull was painted on the conning tower of *U-47*, and it soon became the emblem of the 7th U-boat Flotilla. Churchill called the attack 'a feat of arms' and a 'remarkable exploit of professional skill and daring'. The manner of the sinking was a huge embarrassment to the Royal Navy. The ship which had been ordered to obstruct the very passage through which *U-47* had penetrated arrived at Scapa Flow the day after the attack. As a result of an inquiry, Vice-Admiral Sir Wilfred French, commander of the Orkneys and Shetlands, was retired.

After some leave Prien was back on board *U-47* and took her out on his third patrol on 16 November 1939, for operations against British naval forces in the Orkneys. There he sank three ships before returning on 18 December where his boat underwent important repairs and wasn't ready for operational duties until March 1940. After a short patrol in which one ship was sunk on 25 March, Prien set out in early April to join the 5th U-boat group, operating near the Shetlands, as part of Operation *Hartmut*. *U-47* went to Vaagas Fjord and in the evening of 15 April was in Bygdenfjord, where British transport ships were disembarking troops. Prien positioned his boat for the attack and fired four torpedoes, but they all failed, with one going off course. Prien returned to base.

On 3 June 1940, Prien left Kiel for a U-boat pack operation. On 14th, he sank the British SS *Balmoralwood*. Prien was the tactical commander for the group and was in command of six boats, which formed a patrol line across the expected track of Convoy HX48. However, the convoy had changed course and the group was ordered to disperse. *U-47* moved to an area north-west of Ireland, where on the 21st, Prien sank the British tanker SS *San Fernando* and on the 24th, sank the Panamanian SS *Cathrine*. During the last three days of June, *U-47* sank another four ships, and whilst on his return journey Prien sank the British passenger ship SS *Arandora Star* on 2 July. She was struck by two torpedoes, and had on board 479 German internees, 734 Italian internees, 86 German POWs and 200 military guards. The master, twelve officers, 42 crew, 37 guards, 470 Italians and 243 Germans were lost.

On 27 August, Prien left Kiel once again for his ninth patrol, this time he headed west of the British Isles. On the 29th, he sank the SS *Ville de Mons* and on 4 September Prien attacked ships from Convoy OA207 north-west of Rockall and sank the SS *Titan*. On the 7th he sank a further three ships and two days later sunk the SS *Possidon* west of Barra, Hebrides. *U-47* then had a spell on weather-reporting duties and on

A propaganda postcard produced by the artist Willich. (Author's collection)

21 September attacked and damaged the SS *Elmbank* with gunfire. Prien returned to base on 25 September. His next patrol was short, only lasting nine days. It began on 14 October and during it he sank three ships and damaged another two. On his eleventh patrol he sank only one ship and damaged another three, the patrol lasted thirty-three days.

Prien then took some leave and on 20 February 1941, he left port for the eastern North Atlantic. On the 25th he sighted Convoy OB290, but was driven off by aircraft. However, Prien returned at dusk and on the 26th he sank three ships, and damaged another. Two days later *U-47* made contact with the convoy once again and sank the SS *Holmlea*. On 1 March he was promoted to *Korvettenkapitän* and from 2 March, Prien operated against Convoy OB292 for three days without success. During the night of 7/8 March, *U-47* went missing while attacking Convoy OB293. It was thought that it had been sunk by the British destroyer HMS *Wolverine* west of Ireland. To date, there is no official record of what happened to her, or Prien and his crew. During the war there as a rumour that Prien and his crew had mutinied and as a result had been sent to a labour corps on the Russian Front. After the war another rumour surfaced this time the story was that Prien had died in a concentration camp, apparently shot just before Allied troops arrived. Friends and family of Prien tried to find out if the stories were true but nothing was found, only hearsay evidence.

Other awards:
22 Jan 1937: Long Service Award 4th Class
25 Sep 1939: Iron Cross 2nd Class
17 Oct 1939: Iron Cross 1st Class
17 Oct 1939: U-Boat War Badge
00.00.1941: U-Boat War Badge with Diamonds

Gustav Wilhelm <u>Joachim</u> SCHEPKE
Kapitänleutnant
37 ships sunk, 155,882 tons
4 ships damaged, 17,229 tons

Knight's Cross: Awarded on 24 September 1940, as *Kapitänleutnant* and as commander of *U-100*, for actions in the North Sea and in the Atlantic, where he sunk seven ships in just two days when at the time he was commander of *U-19*.

Knight's Cross with Oakleaves: Awarded as *Kapitänleutnant* and whilst still Commander of *U-100* on 1 December 1940, to become the seventh recipient, and the third naval officer to be honoured with the Oakleaves. It was awarded for his continued success in the North Atlantic and the North Channel where he sank a further ten ship for a total of 44,501 tons, which included seven in one day and damaged three others. The presentation of the award was made by Hitler at the Berghof in mid-January 1941.

Joachim Schepke was born on 8 March 1912 in Flensburg, the son of a naval officer, and became the eleventh most successful U-boat commander of the Second World War after sinking thirty-seven ships for a total of 155,882 tons. He entered the *Reichsmarine* as an Officer Candidate in April 1930, and was described as handsome and debonair; he later became a committed National Socialist. He served on board the sail training ship *Niobe* and the light cruiser *Emden* as part of his basic training, and from October 1933 he served on the 'pocket battleship' *Deutschland*. He was commissioned as a *Leutnant zur See* in October 1934 and a year later Shepke attended U-boat School. In January 1936, he served as Watch Officer on *U-13* whilst attached to U-boat Flotilla '*Weddigen*' in Kiel, and nine months served as company officer with the III. *Schiffsstamabteilung* in the Baltic. He had in June been promoted to *Oberleutnant zur See* and from March 1937 he spent eighteen

months as an instructor at the Torpedo School in Flensburg, before being appointed commander of *U-3* and was promoted to *Kapitänleutnant* in June 1939.

At the outbreak of war *U-3* was a training boat but immediately became operational and left Kiel on 4 September for a brief patrol in the North Sea. On 27 September, he left Wilhelmshaven to operate in the Skagerrak. On the 30th he sank the SS *Vendia* by torpedo north-west of Hanstholm, Sweden. Later the same day Schepke stopped another ship, the SS *Gun*. Not satisfied with the ship's papers, he put a prize crew aboard. As they took over, the *Gun* attempted to ram the boat, which only just managed to take evasive action. The prize crew then set charges and scuttled the vessel. Schepke then returned to Kiel with the crew of the SS *Gun*.

On 3 January 1940, Schepke was transferred and

(Scherzer)   appointed commander of *U-19*, a Type IIB boat built by Germania Werft. He set out from Kiel for the north-east coast of Scotland, where on 9 January he sank the Norwegian SS *Manx*. He returned to port three days later. His next patrol was also a short patrol, lasting just ten days, setting off on 18 January to patrol off the north-east coast of England. On the morning of the 23rd, *U-19* sank two ships south-east of the Farne Islands, and two days later Schepke sank the Norwegian SS *Gudveig*. He returned to Wilhelmshaven on 28 January. His next patrol began on 12 February, against British naval forces in the North Sea, it was short and without success – Schepke returned to port just fourteen days later.

From 14 March, *U-19* was operating east of the Pentland Firth and off Kinnaird's Head, in search of British submarines. On the 19th Schepke sank two ships, the SS *Minsk* and the SS *Charkov*. Both were attacked at 21:35 hours and the first torpedo hit the *Charkov* in the stern and she sank within four minutes with the loss of all her crew. *Minsk* was struck in her engine room by the second torpedo and she sank within six minutes with the loss of eleven crew members. A few hours later, during the early morning of the 20th, he sank the Dutch SS *Viking* and the SS *Bothal*. For his next patrol Schepke left Kiel on 3 April, to take part in Operation *Hartmut*, part of the invasion of Denmark and Norway. Schepke was ordered to take *U-19* to off the Norwegian coast, where from the 19th it and other boats were to support German transports and naval forces landing troops and to prevent any interference by British warships. Schepke was then ordered to join the 9th U-boat Group, which was to operate east of the Shetlands. However no contact was made with the enemy and *U-19* was ordered to return to its home base.

From 19 May 1940, Schepke attended a training course and on 30 May he was named as commander of *U-100*, a Type VIIB boat built by Germania Werft in Kiel. He left Kiel on his first patrol on 9 August, to operate west of the British Isles. On the morning of the 16th he sank the MV *Empire Merchant* south of Rockall, and sank another ship, the SS *Jamaica Pioneer*, on the 25th. Schepke then spotted Convoy OA204 on the 28th, and sank four more ships, and in addition he torpedoed and damaged the British SS *Hartismere*. His second patrol lasted just fourteen days; he left on 11 September, to operate once again west of the British Isles. He soon located Convoy HX72 near Rockall, but didn't make an attack until the 21st. In just over three hours, Schepke sank seven ships, for a total of 50,340 tons.

On 17 October, during his third patrol, Schepke sighted eastbound Convoy SC7 in the North Channel. *U-100* was part of a patrol line and together with *U-46*, *U-99*, *U-101* and *U-123*, waited during the night of the 17th/18th for the convoy. The group reached the patrol line but failed to sink any ships, only managing to damage three ships. On 19 October, *U-100* encountered eastbound Convoy HX79 south-west of Rockall. Just after midnight Schepke sank two tankers, the MV *Caprella* and the British MV *Sitala*, and during the morning of the 20th he sank the SS *Loch Lomond*, a straggler from the convoy – which lost twelve ships. With all his torpedoes gone, Schepke headed home to Lorient. His next patrol began on 7 November, and lasted

A portrait of Kapitänleutnant *Schepke wearing his Knight's Cross with Oakleaves from an official Hoffmann postcard.* (Author's collection)

fourteen days. He left for the North Channel and began to operate against a westbound convoy on the 18th/19th, but had no success. During the early hours of 23 November, Schepke encountered Convoy SC11 south-east of Rockall and attacked, he sank five ships, and later that same day he sank another two ships, the British MV *Leise Maersk*, and in the evening the Dutch SS *Bussum*. He returned to Lorient on 27 November.

During his fifth patrol, which began on 2 December, Schepke sank three ships. He returned to Kiel on New Year's Day 1941. After some leave and repairs to *U-100*, Schepke left to operate in the North Atlantic on 9 March. He sighted Convoy HX112 south of Iceland and during the night of the 15th/16th he made an unsuccessful attack before being driven off on 17 March by the convoy's escorts, and was slightly damaged by depth charges. As a result Schepke was forced to surface and was almost immediately spotted by the destroyer HMS *Vanoc*, which attacked and rammed the U-boat. The ship hit the boat's conning tower and Schepke was crushed by his periscope and killed. Thirty-seven crew were also killed, only six escaping.

Other awards:
02 Oct 1936: Long Service Award 4th Class
00 Oct 1939: U-boat War Badge
27 Feb 1940: Iron Cross 2nd Class
27 Feb 1940: Iron Cross 1st Class
00.00.1941: U-boat War Badge with Diamonds

Otto <u>Adalbert</u> SCHNEE
Korvettenkapitän
23 ships sunk, 95,889 tons
3 ships damaged, 28,820 tons

(Scherzer)

Knight's Cross: Awarded on 30 August 1941 as *Oberleutnant zur See* and as commander of *U-201* for sinking eight ships for a total of 25,005 shipping tons whilst patrolling in the Atlantic.

Knight's Cross with Oakleaves: Awarded on 15 July 1942, as *Kapitänleutnant* and as commander of *U-201*, to become the 105th recipient, for further actions in the Atlantic which resulted in the sinking of a further ten ships. The award was presented by Hitler at his *'Wehrwolf'* Headquarters in the Ukraine near the town of Vinnitsa.

Adalbert Schnee was born on 31 December 1913 in Berlin and joined the *Reichsmarine* in April 1934, as an Officer Candidate. He served on the light cruiser *Emden* and other ships as part of his basic training and was commissioned as a *Leutnant zur See* in April 1937.

He served on the light cruiser *Leipzig*, taking part in the non-intervention patrols in Spanish waters from October 1936 during the Civil War. Schnee transferred to the U-boat Service in May 1937, and received his first posting as Watch Officer onboard *U-23*, under Otto Kretschmer, who was destined to become the greatest of all U-boat aces. In April 1939 Schnee was promoted to *Oberleutnant zur See* and from the outbreak of war he participated in eight war patrols with *U-23*, operating mainly around the area of Scotland and the Orkneys, during which time his boat sank seven ships.

On 31 January 1940, Schnee took command of his own U-boat, *U-6*, a small Type IIA coastal submarine built by Deutsches Werke. It was a brief command, lasting until June, but he failed to see any action. In July, he was appointed commander of *U-60*, a larger boat, a Type IIC, and he went out on his first war patrol on 30 July. He sank the Swedish SS *Nils Gorthon* from Convoy HX62 on 13 August, and returned to port five days later. On his next patrol he damaged the SS *Volendam*, a Dutch merchant ship from Convoy OB205, sailing from Liverpool to the United States. His torpedo struck the ship but failed to detonate. On 3 September he sank the British SS *Ulva* south-east of Rockall and returned to port three days later.

On 27 November, Schnee transferred to the 1st U-boat Flotilla and served as deputy commander of *U-121*. Here he learnt how to be a successful U-boat commander under the watchful eyes of *Kapitänleutnant* Karl-Ernst Schroeter. On 25 January 1941, Schnee was given command of *U-201*, a Type VIIC, the type which formed the backbone of the U-boat fleet. He left Kiel in transit for western France, and on the 2 May, he came upon the abandoned wreck of the tanker MV *Capulet*, 300 miles north-north west of Rockall. He fired a torpedo to sink the stricken ship and claimed her himself. On 8 May, he was ordered by radio to help with the attack on Convoy OB318 near Cape Farewell. Schnee sunk the SS *Gregalia* and damaged another ship the British SS *Empire Cloud*: the torpedo failed to explode when it struck the ship. *U-201* was soon driven off by depth-charge attacks from the corvette HMS *Nigella*. Schnee decided to return to base on 18 May.

In early June Schnee took *U-201* from Brest for operations in the North Atlantic, to join *Kurfürst* Group south of Iceland. However no contact was made with any convoy and Schnee joined another group. From 26 June, he was one of three boats ordered to locate Convoy HX133, which he did soon afterwards but failed to make an attack and was driven off by destroyers. He returned to his home base on 19 July. Almost four weeks later Schnee headed out on his third patrol, again in the North Atlantic. The patrol was short, lasting just eleven days, but within that time he sank four ships. On 19 August he sank the SS *Aguila*, a British passenger ship. She was attacked at 04:06 hours and was struck by two of the four torpedoes fired; the other two struck another ship. The *Aguila* was the ship of the convoy commodore Vice-Admiral Patrick E. Parker, and sank within ninety seconds. The Vice-Admiral, five naval staff officers, five gunners, fifty-four crew members and eighty-eight passengers were lost. Among the passengers on board were twenty-one women from the WRNS (Women's Royal Navy Service), who had volunteered for cipher and wireless duties in Gibraltar. None of the Wrens survived the sinking. The SS *Ciscar*, which had been struck by the other two torpedoes, sank almost immediately with the loss of nine crew members and four gunners. His next patrol was even more successful. He left for the North Atlantic once again on 14 September, and was called to an area where Convoy OG74 had been sighted, north-north east of the Azores. Schnee was forced to call off his first attack when *U-201* was spotted by a Martlet aircraft from the escort carrier

HMS *Audacity* and was later driven off by the sloop HMS *Deptford* and the corvette HMS *Arbutus*. Not to be put off, Schnee approached the convoy again on the evening of the 21st. He sank three ships, the SS *Runa*, the SS *Lissa* and the SS *Rhineland*. When contact was lost, *U-201* joined with *U-124* and they were directed towards Convoy HG73, which had left Gibraltar on 17 September. On the 27th Schnee attacked two ships, damaging one and sinking the SS *Margoreta*. With his torpedoes expended he headed back to base.

The fifth patrol began on 29 October, when Schnee took *U-201* out towards Ireland. On 5 November he joined *Störtebecker* Group, west of Spain, and waited for the convoys. By the 25th nothing had been sighted and so Schnee was ordered to form part of *Letzte Ritter* Group, together with *U-69* and *U-402*. Again no contact was made and Schnee returned to base on 9 December, disappointed. On 20 February 1942 he was promoted to *Kapitänleutnant* and the following month he left for operations in US waters. There Schnee joined a fifth wave of boats patrolling off the coast of the US, as part of Operation *Paukenschlag*. On 18 April, Schnee torpedoed a neutral Argentinean ship, 400 miles south-east of New York, it was the tanker MV *Victoria*. The crew abandoned ship, and then returned when she failed to sink: she was later towed to port. It caused a 'slight exchange of words' between Argentina and Germany. Schnee later moved south and on 21 April, he sank the SS *Bris* and two more ships the following day. He returned to Brest on 21 May.

His sixth and last patrol as commander of *U-201* began when he left port for operations in the Central Atlantic on 27 June. En route to a pre-arranged assembly point Schnee sank the British passenger ship SS *Avila Star* on 6 July. Together with five boats he began a sweep south and came upon Convoy OS33. After dark a group of ships bound for America split from the convoy, and *U-201* and *U-116* decided to pursue them. Just after midnight on 10 July, they both made an attack and both fired torpedoes at the SS *Cortona*, and both scored hits. According to the official report it was Schnee who claimed the ship. Four hours later Schnee sank the SS *Siris* and in the early hours of the 13th he claimed the SS *Sithonia*. A total of six ships were lost from the convoy, with the loss of *U-136*. The five surviving boats now began to reform their patrol line. Schnee took *U-201* to a new position where he sank the tanker SS *British Yeoman* on 15 July. Once the patrol line had passed Dakar on the 21st, the group dispersed and the boats went on to patrol independently. On the evening of the 25th, *U-201* sank the trawler HMS *Laertes* and then returned to port.

On his return to base, Schnee was posted to duties ashore, and from October 1942 was attached to the 27th U-boat Flotilla in Gotenhafen. He was later served as a staff officer, attached to the staff of the *Kriegsmarine* High Command, as an expert on the tactics of attacking convoys. In December 1944, he was promoted to *Korvettenkapitän* and in March 1945, Schnee briefly commanded *U-2511*, a Type XXI boat. But while at sea awaiting suitable targets, he received orders that in view of the imminent end of the war he was not to carry out any attacks. He survived the war and went on to become a leading figure in the U-boat Veterans Association. He was the son-in-law of *Großadmiral* Dönitz, and was one of the pallbearers at Dönitz's funeral. Schnee settled in Hamburg where he died on 4 November 1982.

Other awards:
08 Apr 1938: Long Service Award 4th Class
21 Oct 1939: Iron Cross 2nd Class
27 Nov 1939: U-boat War Badge
20 Dec 1939: Commemorative Medal for 01 Oct 1938

15 Aug 1940: Iron Cross 1st Class
00.00.1942: U-boat War Badge with Diamonds

Klaus SCHOLTZ
Fregattenkapitän
25 ships sunk, 128,190 tons

Knight's Cross: Awarded on 26 December 1941, as *Kapitänleutnant* and as commander of *U-108*, in recognition of his success in the Atlantic where he sank twelve ships for a total of 59,273 shipping tons.

Knight's Cross with Oakleaves: He became the 123rd recipient on 10 September 1942, as *Korvettenkapitän* and as commander of *U-108*, for continued actions in the Atlantic where he sank a further thirteen ships for a total of almost 68,917 shipping tons. Hitler presented him with his award at his military headquarters '*Wehrwolf*' at Vinnitsa in the Ukraine in mid-October 1942.

Klaus Scholtz was the nineteenth most successful U-boat commander of the Second World War, sinking twenty-five ships for a total of 128,190 shipping tons. He was born on 22 March 1908, in Magdeburg, and entered the *Reichsmarine* at the age of nineteen in April 1927.

Above left: (Author's collection)

Above right: Klaus Scholtz as a Cadet. (Author's collection)

On completion of his basic training, which included service on the sail training ship *Niobe* and the light cruiser *Berlin,* Scholtz was commissioned as a *Leutnant zur See* in October 1931 and appointed Watch Officer aboard the torpedo boat *GII*. In September 1932, he served as a company officer with the 5th Navy Artillery Battalion at Pillau. He was promoted in October 1933, to *Oberleutnant zur See* and to *Kapitänleutnant* in October 1936 before serving as adjutant and Watch Officer aboard the torpedo boat *G8*. In June 1937, he became commander of the torpedo boat *Jaguar*, and in April 1939 was serving as a company commander in 7th Ship Battalion in the Baltic.

In April 1940, *Kapitänleutnant* Scholtz transferred to the U-boat service, and after attending various training courses he was eventually appointed commander of *U-108*, a Type IXB boat built in Bremen. His first patrol began on 15 February 1941, when he left Wilhelmshaven to operate west of the British Isles. On the 22nd Scholtz sank the SS *Texelstorm* off the south coast of Iceland. The following day Convoy OB289 was sighted south-west of the Faroes Islands, and together with *U-95* and *U-97* they closed in on the convoy – without success. On the 28th he sighted the British merchant ship *Effna* and made an attack. She was hit amidships by a single torpedo just south of Iceland. A second torpedo missed but a third hit its target. The ship sank with the loss of the master, thirty-two crew members and one gunner. On 2 March, another convoy was sighted, and together with *U-47*, *U-70*, *U-95*, *U-99* and *U-552*, a patrol line was formed to intercept the convoy, but again without success. On the 4 March the convoy was once again located, but had been re-routed to avoid the patrol line. Scholtz returned to Lorient on 12 March. His next patrol was short but he did sink the British armed merchant cruiser HMS *Rajputana* before returning to port. He had spotted the cruiser at about 09:45 hours on 11 April, and the chase was hampered by periscope problems and by thick ice and snow. Two torpedoes were fired on 11 April but missed and another two were fired on the 12th but they also missed. A fifth was fired on 13 April but that missed too, but the sixth struck the ship in the stern and caused a fire. A seventh torpedo was fired which was intended to be the *coup de grâce* but this failed, but the next torpedo struck in the after part and caused the ship to sink by the stern. Forty-two crew members were lost and 283 survivors were later picked up by HMS *Legion* and were landed at Reykjavik.

Scholtz took *U-108* out of port for the Western Atlantic on 25 May, and was immediately called on to assist the battleship *Bismarck*. On the 24th the *Bismarck* and the heavy cruiser *Prinz Eugen* had made an attempt to enter the Atlantic via the Denmark Strait. The plan was for a group of U-boats to form a patrol line running north-west, south of Cape Farewell and once the two warships had passed through the line then the U-boats would deal with any British ships pursuing them. However, the plan was changed when *Bismarck* was damaged in the Battle of the Denmark Strait. *Bismarck* then headed for St. Nazaire and *Prinz Eugen* headed south-west. During the evening of 25 May, *Bismarck* was damaged by a torpedo from an aircraft. To assist her into the comparative safety of the Bay of Biscay, *U-74*, *U-97*, *U-98*, *U-556*, *U-109* and the outward-bound *U-48*, *U-73* and *U-108* were ordered to assemble 450 miles west of St. Nazaire. They were then ordered to form a patrol line running north-west from Cape Ortegal. However, because of bad weather the boats were not in position until the following day. On the evening of that day, 26 May, *Bismarck* was at the north-west end of the line. Any boats with torpedoes were ordered to go to her assistance but heavy seas prevented this. *Bismarck* was sunk on the morning of the 27th. *U-108*, *U-48* and *U-73* searched until the 31st, but found no survivors. Scholtz resumed his patrol, and on 2 June he sank the British SS *Michael E* in the central North Atlantic. In the early hours of the 8th *U-108* attacked and sank the British SS *Baron Nairn*, and the SS *Dirphys*. On the 10th just east of Newfoundland he sank the Norwegian SS *Christian Krohg* from Convoy OB328. On the 20th, *U-108* joined *West* Group, but it soon became clear that the convoys had been re-routed to avoid the group, so all boats were redistributed in a loose formation over a wide area in the central North Atlantic. Scholtz sank the Greek SS *Ellinico* and SS *Nicolas Pateras* on the 25th. There was little success for the next few days, and then on 1 July, *U-108* sank a weather-observation ship, the British SS *Toronto City*, and six days later returned to port.

Scholtz's next patrol began on 19 August 1941, when he took *U-108* out to operate in the Central Atlantic, but it proved to be an unsuccessful patrol. He was promoted to *Korvettenkapitän* on 1 November and on 9 December, he took his boat out to operate west of Gibraltar and enroute to join *Seeräuber* Group he sank the SS *Cassequel*. He met up with the group and waited for Convoy HG76, but once again it was an unsuccessful patrol. The convoy had not been spotted until 16 December, and *U-108* had been driven off by the convoy's destroyers. On the 17th, the convoy was sighted again, and *U-131* was sunk. Two days later Scholtz torpedoed and damaged the SS *Ruckinge* west of Lisbon. He returned to port on Christmas Day.

Scholtz and his crew enjoyed Christmas ashore before setting out on patrol on 8 January 1942, to operate off the US coast, part of Operation *Paukenschlag*. On the 8th Scholtz sank the SS *Ocean Venture* near Cape Hatteras. The crew were seen to abandon ship after she was struck amidships by two torpedoes. Twenty-nine crew members and two gunners were lost. Fourteen crew members and the master were later picked up by the destroyer USS *Roe* and were landed at Norfolk, Virginia. On the evening of the 9th he sank the SS *Tolosa*, and on the 12th he sank the Norwegian SS *Blink*. On the 16th, west of Bermuda, Scholtz sank the SS *Ramapo* and later that day he sank the British SS *Somme*, before returning to port on 4 March. He left on his seventh patrol on 30 March and headed for the Western Atlantic, a patrol that would last until 1 June. He sank the British ship SS *Modesta* on 25 April, and on 29th near Bermuda he sank the US tanker SS *Mobiloil*. He took *U-108* through the Bahama Passage and later on 5 May he sank the US SS *Afoundria*. He would claim another two ships before returning to base.

His final patrol as commander of *U-108* took him to the Caribbean. He left port on 13 July, and was called into action five days later, when Convoy OS34 was sighted. Two ships were sunk, but Scholtz's attacks were unsuccessful and *U-108* was depth-charged and driven away. By the following day *U-108* was in the area east of Trinidad, where on the 3rd Scholtz sank the tanker MV *Tricula*, and on the 7th he sank the Norwegian MV *Brenas*. On the 15th whilst on the surface *U-108* was spotted by aircraft just north-east of Georgetown and was attacked by a Hudson of 53 Squadron. *U-108* was only slightly damaged as a result. On the 20th Scholtz sank his twenty-fifth and last ship, the US tanker MV *Louisiana*. Driven off by aircraft, *U-108* left the area and headed for its home port of Lorient.

Scholtz was given a posting ashore, when he was appointed commander of the 12th U-boat Flotilla at Bordeaux on 15 October. Promoted to *Fregattenkapitän* in July 1944 he took command of the 3rd Battalion of Naval Regiment *Badermann*, which had been hastily formed from the personnel of the 12th U-boat Flotilla the following month. Scholtz fought against Allied troops in the area around Bordeaux and was captured by US forces on 11 September. He was eventually transferred to a prison camp in the United States, being released in April 1946. He later served with the *Bundesmarine* and was promoted to *Kapitän zur See* in August 1959. Appointed commander of Wilhelmshaven in March 1962, he retired from military service in March 1966. He died in the town of Bad Schwartau, Schleswig-Holstein on 1 May 1987.

Other awards:
02 Oct 1936: Long Service Award 4th Class
05 Apr 1939: Long Service Award 3rd Class
00.00.19__: Iron Cross 2nd Class
00 Apr 1941: Iron Cross 1st Class
00 Apr 1941: U-boat War Badge

Herbert Emil SCHULTZE
Korvettenkapitän
26 ships sunk, 169,709 tons
1 ship damaged, 9,456 tons

Knight's Cross: Awarded as *Kapitänleutnant* and as commander of *U-48* on 1 March 1940, after sinking sixteen ships for a total of 109, 704 shipping tons. He was presented with the Knight's Cross by Hitler during a ceremony at the Reich Chancellery in April 1940.

Knight's Cross with Oakleaves: Awarded on 12 June 1941, to become the sixth naval recipient, as *Kapitänleutnant* and as commander of *U-48* for his exploits in the North Atlantic, where he sank nine ships for a total of 53,630 shipping tons. He was presented with the award by Hitler on 29 June 1941, at *Führer* Headquarters '*Wolfschanze*' in Rastenburg, East Prussia.

(Author's collection)

Herbert 'Vaddi' Schultze was born on 24 July 1909, in Kiel and was responsible for the sinking of twenty-six ships for a total of 169,709 shipping tons which made him the eighth most successful U-boat commander of the Second World War. He was called 'Vaddi' ('Daddy') because he took good care of his crew, and was a well-liked and respected commander.

Schultze joined the *Reichsmarine* in April 1930, entering as a cadet with the 2nd Ships Division in the Baltic. From July 1930 until October 1934, he attended various training courses. He served aboard the light cruisers *Leipzig* and *Karlsruhe* together with other future U-boat aces, including Heinrich Lehmann-Willenbrock. In October 1934, he was commissioned as a *Leutnant zur See*, serving as the Second Wireless Officer on board the *Leipzig*, and from September 1935 he served in a similar capacity aboard the *Karlsruhe*. He was promoted in June 1936 to *Oberleutnant zur See*, and began his training as a U-boat commander. In January 1938, he was appointed commander of *U-2*, a training boat. On 22 April 1939, he was named as commander of *U-48*, a Type VIIB boat, which became the most successful submarine of the Second World War. The boat was attached to the 7th U-boat Flotilla, and spent the next four months training.

For his first patrol on 19 August 1939, he left Kiel for operations in the Atlantic. Schultze took *U-48* to the area north-west of Cape Ortegal where on 5 September he came upon the SS *Royal Sceptre*. He fired a shot across her bows, but she refused to stop so he fired another shot – a direct hit and the crew began to abandon ship. Schultze then torpedoed her and she sank. Soon afterwards he stopped the British SS *Browing* and fired a shot across her bows which caused the crew to abandon ship. Schultze approached the lifeboats and told the captain to re-board his ship and pick up the *Royal Sceptre* survivors – which he did. On 7 September, *U-48* was one of ten boats ordered to return to port to prepare for Atlantic operations in early October. On the 8th Schultze sank the British SS *Winkleigh*, and on the 11th he sank the British SS *Firby* by torpedo and gunfire north of Rockall. Schultze sent a message to Churchill, which said, 'I have sunk the British steamer *Firby*... Save the crew if you please. German submarine.' The message made Schultze famous in Germany and Britain. On his return to port on 17 September, he was interviewed by William L. Shirer, an American reporter, who later became famous for writing the book *The Rise and Fall of the Third Reich*.

On 4 October, Schultze left Kiel for the Atlantic, this time to take part in the first attempt at a controlled pack-operation, with four other boats. On 12th en route to the assembly point, he encountered the French tanker SS *Emile Miguet*, and sank her. A few miles away the SS *Heronspool* heard the fireing and headed towards the fight. There was an exchange gunfire between *U-48* and the *Heronspool*, and eventually *U-48* sank her. In the morning of the 13th, Schultze sank the French SS *Louisiane* from Convoy OA17 and the following day he sank the SS *Sneaton*. Of the five boats called upon to take part in the controlled wolf-pack operation, three were lost on the way, *U-40*, *U-42* and *U-45*. On 16 October, Convoy HG3 was sighted and the two remaining U-boats which included *U-48* were put into action. Contact however with the convoy was briefly lost, but soon found and three ships were sunk during the evening of the 17th, *U-48* claiming one of the ships.

His next patrol started on 20 November, when he left for the Orkneys to operate against British forces. He sank the Swedish tanker MV *Gustaf E. Reuter* on the 26th. He then moved south, attacking the westbound Convoy OB48 and sank the SS *Brandon* just before midnight on 8 December. The next day *U-48* damaged the British tanker MV *San Alberto*, and then sank the Greek SS *Germaine* on the 15th, before heading for his home port of Kiel. His fourth patrol began on 24 January 1940, when he left for a minelaying operation off Weymouth, which resulted in no ships being sunk. On completion of this operation he took *U-48* to the western entrance of the English Channel and operated off the Scilly Islands. On the 10th, he sank the Dutch SS *Burgerdijk* and on the 14th he sank the British SS *Sultan Star*, and the Dutch tanker MV *Den Haag* the following day. She was hit amidships by one torpedo, broke in two and sank 150 miles west of Ouessant. He sank the Finnish SS *Wija* on the 17th, before making an unsuccessful attack on the British warships HMS *Ark Royal* and HMS *Renown*, before returning to port on 26 February.

On 3 April, Schultze left Kiel under sealed orders to take part in Operation *Hartmut*. He was ordered to join the 5th U-boat Group, to operate north-east of the Shetlands. On the

10th, his group was ordered up to Narvik, which the Germans had to hold. Schultz was then ordered to take *U-48* to another fjord where British troops were expected to start landing. On the 13th, the situation worsened at Narvik and other boats were directed to the fjord. The next day Schultze made an attack on HMS *Warspite*, which failed due to defective torpedoes. Schultze returned to port on 20 April, and handed command of *U-48* over to *Korvettenkapitän* Rudolf Rösing due to illness stemming from a stomach and kidney disorder. Schultze spent five months in hospital recuperating. From October 1940, he took up new duties as Deputy Commander of the 7th U-boat Flotilla, based in St. Nazaire, France.

On 17 December, he returned to command *U-48*. He left for duties in the Atlantic on 20 January 1941, and headed out towards the British Isles. He sank the Greek SS *Nicolaos Angelos* on 1 February south of Iceland. Later a patrol line was ordered and more U-boats headed to the area, but inaccurate information caused the line to be formed in the wrong place and the operation was called off on the 21st. On the 24th, Schultze came upon a straggler from Convoy SLS64, the British SS *Nailsea Lass*, which he sank. He then put in at his new base at St. Nazaire. On 17 March, Schultze left port for the North Atlantic, on what would be a short patrol, but a successful one. During the early morning of the 29th he sighted Convoy HX115 south of Iceland. Here he sank three ships, the British SS *Hylton* and the SS *Germanic*, and the Belgian SS *Limbourg*. On 2 April, he also sank the British tanker SS *Beavedale*, before returning to base six days later.

His final patrol began on 22 May, and he was ordered to the North Atlantic to help the German battleships *Bismarck* and the heavy cruiser *Prinz Eugen* attempt to enter the Atlantic via the Denmark Strait. However, the plan was changed after HMS *Prince of Wales* damaged *Bismarck* during the Battle of the Denmark Strait, and a patrol line, which had been ordered, was not required, and the two German warships split up. *Bismarck* headed for St. Nazaire, and was later damaged by a torpedo on the 25th. All U-boats in her area were called upon to assist, including Schultze and *U-48*. They were ordered to form a patrol line on the 25th, and to assemble 450 miles west of St. Nazaire. This was delayed by a heavy storm, and the U-boats were not in position until the 26th. HMS *Ark Royal* was sighted by *U-556*, but she had no torpedoes left and the other boats were too far away. *Bismarck* was sunk on 27 May. A search was made for survivors and *U-48* joined the search until 31st, but no survivors were found. Schultze then took *U-48* to join *West* Group in an area north of the Azores. On moving further into the central North Atlantic, Schultze sank three more ships in the space of six days. Returning to Kiel on 21 June, Schultz was transferred and *U-48* was put on training duties, *U-48* was decommissioned in October 1943. She was the most successful U-boat of the Second World War, in terms of tonnage and number of ships sunk – sinking fifty-two ships for 307,934 shipping tons.

Schultze was appointed commander of the 3rd U-boat Flotilla on 28 July 1941, in La Rochelle. After spending time in hospital due to his old illness he became a staff officer in March 1942 with Naval Group North, and was assigned to the staff of *Admiral* Dönitz. Promoted to *Korvettenkapitän* in March 1943, he was once again briefly hospitalized in February 1944. The following month he was assigned as commander of Department II at the Naval School in Schleswig, where he remained until the end of the war.

In August 1945, he was employed by the Allies as commander of the Naval Academy at Mürwik. Now a civilian from November 1945 until October 1946, he took a job of manager of the naval facilities in Flensburg-Mürwik. He joined the *Bundesmarine* in July 1956, and served in various staff positions. He served as a staff officer with the Personnel Office; he was commander of convoy ships, teaching group leaders at the Naval Academy and was head of the volunteer adoption headquarters of the Navy until his retirement in September 1968, with the rank of *Kapitän zur See*. Schultze died on 3 June 1987 in London.

Other awards:
02 Oct 1936: Long Service Award 4th Class
20 Apr 1937: German Olympic Commemorative Medal
25 Sep 1939: Iron Cross 2nd Class
25 Oct 1939: U-boat War Badge
27 Oct 1939: Iron Cross 1st Class
15 Jul 1941: U-boat War Badge with Diamonds
24 Oct 1941: Italian War Cross with Swords
00.00.1943: U-boat Combat Clasp in Bronze

<u>Viktor</u> Hermann Otto Ludwig Paul Ferdinand SCHÜTZE
Kapitän zur See
35 ships sunk, 180,073 tons
2 ships damaged, 14,213 tons

(Author's collection)

Knight's Cross: Awarded as *Korvettenkapitän* and as commander of *U-103* on 11 December 1940, for his leadership and in recognition of his success of sinking seventeen ships in the Atlantic, for a total of 77,252 shipping tons.

Knight's Cross with Oakleaves: He became the 23rd recipient, and the seventh naval officer to win the Oakleaves on 14 July 1941, as *Korvettenkapitän* and as commander of *U-103*, for sinking eighteen ships for a total of 102,821 shipping tons. The award was presented to him personally by Hitler at his headquarters in Rastenburg, East Prussia, '*Wolfschanze*', in August 1941.

Born on 16 February 1906, in Kiel, Viktor Schütze was the fifth most successful U-boat commander of the Second World War, sinking thirty-five ships, for a total of 180,073 shipping tons. He joined the *Reichsmarine* in April 1925, and served in the Baltic with 8th Company of 2nd Ships Division. He attended the Naval College at Flensburg and served on board the sail training ship *Niobe*, and the light cruiser *Hamburg* between August 1925 and April 1928. He then attended various other courses, including torpedo training and navigation, being commissioned as a *Leutnant zur See* in October 1929. He served as Third Watch Officer aboard the torpedo boat *T-55*, and following his promotion to *Oberleutnant zur See*, in July 1931 he served as Second Watch Officer on the torpedo boat *G-10*.

Promoted to *Kapitänleutnant*, he transferred to the U-boat service in October 1935. He was appointed commander of *U-19*, a Type IIB boat, which had been commissioned in January 1936. It was a brief command, but he learnt what he needed to know about commanding a submarine. In October 1937, he was relieved of that command so he could attend destroyer training with the 3rd Destroyer Division. He returned to duty in August 1938, when he was appointed commander of the training boat *U-11*. He then served briefly as a staff officer in Kiel, before taking command of *U-25* in September 1939. He sailed on three patrols with his new boat, which began in October, when he left Wilhelmshaven for the Mediterranean. He sank the French SS *Baoulé* on the 31st, and later during an attack on a ship, the boat's torpedo hatch was damaged by blast from its own gun and Schütze had to return to base.

He left Wilhelmshaven for his second tour on 13 January 1940, for operations in the Atlantic. He sank two ships en route to the operational area, the British SS *Polzella* and the Norwegian SS *Enid* on the 17th. The next day he sank the Swedish MV *Pajola* near the Hebridean island of North Rona, and on the 22nd he sank the Norwegian SS *Songa*. Schütze then took his boat further south, patrolling west of the Bay of Biscay. He attacked Convoy OG16 on 3 February, and sank the British SS *Armanistan*, and on his return journey he sank the Danish tanker MV *Chastine Maersk* just north of the Shetlands on the 13th. He returned to his home base on 19 February, and was informed he had been promoted to *Korvettenkapitän*. For his third patrol he left port on 3 April under sealed orders to take part in Operation *Hartmut*. He was ordered to join the 1st U-boat Group, operating off Narvik. On the 10th the group attacked British destroyers leaving Vest Fjord, after they had attacked German destroyers at Narvik. The next day Schütze torpedoed two ships but the torpedoes failed to explode. On the 13th he made other attacks but again these were unsuccessful. Yet again his score had been hindered by faulty torpedoes – exasperated, Schütze returned to port on 6 May.

On 5 July 1940, at the age of thirty-six, Schütze transferred to the 2nd U-boat Flotilla and took command of *U-103*, a Type IXB boat built by AG Weserin Bremen. He left for his first patrol in his new boat on 21 September, to operate in the North Atlantic. On 6 October he sank the Norwegian tanker MV *Nina Borthen*, and just three days later he sank two more ships and damaged another. On the 13th north-east of Rockall he sank the SS *Nora* and two days later he sank the British SS *Thistlegarth*, with the loss of thirty of her crew: it was his fifth ship of the patrol. His next patrol began on 9 November, when he left for the North Channel and sighted a westbound convoy on the 20th. On the morning of the next day he sank the British SS *Daydawn* and the Greek SS *Victoria*. *U-103* was then driven off by the corvette HMS *Rhodedendron*. He sank another three ships within three days and on 8 December he sank the British passenger ship SS *Calabria* when it was struck by two torpedoes. There were no survivors; the master, 128 crew members, one gunner and 230 Indian seamen were lost. The following day he sank the British SS *Empire Jaguar* to bring his total to nineteen.

His next patrol lasted thirty-four days, and between 21 January and 24 February 1941, Schütze sank three ships and damaged a fourth. On 18 February he sank the British merchant ship *Seaforth*. She was hit by a single torpedo amidships about 300 miles south of Iceland and sank quickly. The U-boat crew observed that lifeboats were launched, but the master, forty-six crew members, two gunners and nine passengers were lost. The following day he sank the Norwegian *Benjamin Franklin* about 120 miles north of Rockall; all thirty-six crew members survived. His next patrol, however, would prove to be one of the most successful patrols of any U-boat commander of the Second World War. He left for operations in the area between the Canaries and Freetown on 1 April 1941. On the 15th, Schütze sank the Norwegian SS *Polyana*, and from early May during a ten-day period he sank six ships, which included the British SS *City of Winchester* and the SS *City of Shanghai*. On the 17th he stopped for refuelling and checked his supplies. He returned to operational duties and had immediate success. On the 20th he sank the Egyptian SS *Radames* and on the 22nd sank the tanker MV *British Grenadier*, followed by the Greek SS *Marionga* on the 24th and the Dutch SS *Wangi Wangi* the following day. He moved near to Freetown, and on 8 June sank the British SS *Elmdene*. On the 15th, he received a radio message telling him that his supply ship *Lothringen* had been captured by the cruiser HMS *Dunedin*, so Schütze decided to begin his journey home. On the way he sank the SS *Enrani* from Convoy SL76. However, this vessel was an Italian blockade-runner heading for Bordeaux and had been sunk by mistake. Schütze reached port on 12 July, after his very successful patrol in which he had sunk thirteen ships for a total of 65,172 shipping tons. Two days later he was awarded the Knight's Cross with Oakleaves. The sinking of the Italian ship *Ernani* was investigated fully by the *Kriegsmarine* after the Italian Navy protested. It was found that the *Ernani* had disguised herself as a Dutch steam ship and Schütze had not been informed of her presence and he could not have recognized the ship correctly anyway, due to her appearance having been altered. He was cleared of all blame.

On 13 August 1941, Schütze was appointed commander of the 2nd U-boat Flotilla in Kiel. In February 1943, he was named as Leader of U-boat training for the 18th, 19th, 20th, 23rd, 24th, 25th, 26th and the 27th U-boat Flotillas and was based in the Baltic. He was promoted to *Fregattenkapitän* in March 1943 and a year later was promoted to *Kapitän zur See*. Schütze ended the war as Naval Area Commander of Flensburg-Keppeln, under the new Dönitz government. Captured by British troops in May 1945, he was released from captivity in March 1946. He didn't return to naval service in post-war Germany and settled in Frankfurt am Main where he died on 23 September 1950.

Other awards:
02 Oct 1936: Long Service Award 4th Class
01 Apr 1939: Long Service Award 3rd Class
13 Nov 1939: Iron Cross 2nd Class
21 Feb 1940: Iron Cross 1st Class
21 Feb 1940: U-boat War Badge
21 Aug 1939: Spanish Naval Service Cross in White
15 Jul 1941: U-boat War Badge with Diamonds
01 Nov 1941: Italian War Cross with Swords
30 Jan 1944: War Service Cross 2nd Class with Swords
01 Sep 1944: War Service Cross 1st Class with Swords

Rolf THOMSEN
Kapitänleutnant
1 ship sunk, 7,176 tons

Knight's Cross: Awarded on 4 January 1945, as *Kapitänleutnant* and as commander of *U-1202*, for his leadership and for the sinking of the American Liberty Ship *Dan Beard* on 10 December 1944.

(Scherzer)

Knight's Cross with Oakleaves: Awarded on 29 April 1945, as *Kapitänleutnant* and as commander of *U-1202* for the sinking of two destroyers off the coast of Ireland (they were unconfirmed victories and after the war they were never proved). Thomsen is only credited with one victory even though he was awarded the Oakleaves. Nevertheless, the presentation was made in Bergen, Norway by *Kapitän zur See* Hans Rudolf Rösing on 29/30 April 1945, one of the last Oakleaves to be awarded during the war.

Rolf Thomsen was born on 6 May 1915 in Berlin, and was known for his exaggerated claims while in command of *U-1202* during the Second World War. With only one confirmed sinking to his credit, it is perhaps surprising that he was not only awarded the Knight's Cross but also the Oakleaves.

Thomsen joined the *Reichsmarine* in April 1936, and was commissioned as a *Leutnant zur See* in October 1938. He served as a naval aviator from September 1939 to April 1943. He served in several squadrons, including *Kampfgeschwader* 26 (Bomber Wing 26), the only air group in the *Luftwaffe* which was equipped with air-dropped torpedoes. He was promoted to *Oberleutnant zur See* in October 1940 and from April 1942 he served as adjutant with *Kampfgeschwader* 26. He was promoted to the rank of *Hauptmann* in the *Luftwaffe* on 1 July 1942.

In April 1943, he transferred to the U-boat service with the rank of *Kapitänleutnant* and began his training. He was appointed commander of *U-1202*, a Type VIIC boat, in January 1944, and after some delay he finally took his boat out on its first war patrol. He left for British coastal waters on 30 October and began to operate in the Irish Sea. On 19 November, he was directed towards the Bristol Channel and started his patrol off Milford Haven. It was in that area on 10 December that he attacked a convoy and claimed the 'probable' sinking of four ships, but only one, the 7,200-ton American Liberty ship *Dan Beard*, was confirmed. He then briefly returned to patrolling the Irish Sea before he had to return to his home port because of mechanical problems. It seems that as a result of his claims, even thought they would prove to be false later, he was nevertheless awarded the Knight's Cross.

On 4 March 1945, Thomsen left for operations in the Atlantic, and began to patrol south-west of Ireland. On the 21st, he claimed that he sank a destroyer and got two hits on a 'jeep' carrier, that produced sinking noises, so he said, but neither claim was ever confirmed. Ten days later he claimed that he hit two ships and both had sunk for a total of 14,000 shipping tons. These claims could not be confirmed. On 1 April, Thomsen claimed that he had sunk two corvettes and damaged another freighter. Again none could be confirmed. However because of his claims, it does seem that he was given the benefit of the doubt by Dönitz who awarded him the Oakleaves, and who personally presented him with the award.

Rolf Thomsen in the uniform of an Oberleutnant *in the* Luftwaffe *while adjutant of* Kampfgeschwader *26.* (Scherzer)

Thomsen returned to Norway on 27 April, but made no further patrols. *U-1202* was sunk in Bergen on 10 May, and was later salvaged by the Norwegian Navy.

On 3 June, Thomsen surrendered to British troops and was kept in custody until 9 February 1946. He joined the *Bundesmarine* in November 1955, and was attached to the Ministry of Defence Department VII – Naval Auxiliary Questions. From October 1962, he served as a Staff Officer with the Chief of the Command Staff of the *Bundeswehr*. In January 1966, Thomsen was promoted to *Flotillenadmiral* and appointed Head of the Working Staff of the Federal Minister in Paris, and he later became a staff officer attached to NATO. In April 1970, he was appointed Commander of the Naval Division in the North Sea, and two years later he retired. Rolf Thomsen died on 27 March 2003, in Bonn-Bad Godesberg.

Other awards:
25 Nov 1939: Iron Cross 2nd Class
01 Apr 1940: Long Service Award 4th Class
17 May 1940: Iron Cross 1st Class
14 Oct 1943: German Cross in Gold
00 Apr 1940: Narvik Campaign Shield in Gold
00 Aug 1940: Wound Badge in Black
25 Apr 1941: Operational Flying Clasp for Reconnaissance in Silver
26 Mar 1942: Operational Flying Clasp for Reconnaissance in Gold
03 Jan 1945: U-boat War Badge
00 Apr 1945: U-boat War Badge in Diamonds
00 Apr 1945: U-boat Combat Clasp in Bronze

Knight's Cross

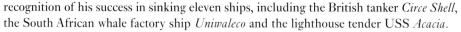

Albrecht Adolf Konrad ACHILLES
Korvettenkapitän
14 ships sunk, 64,542 tons
6 ships damaged, 41,122 tons

Knight's Cross: Awarded on 16 January 1943, as *Kapitänleutnant* and as commander of *U-181*, in recognition of his success in sinking eleven ships, including the British tanker *Circe Shell*, the South African whale factory ship *Uniwaleco* and the lighthouse tender USS *Acacia*.

Albrecht Achilles was born on 25 January 1914, in Karlsruhe, entering the *Kriegsmarine* in April 1934. He served on the battleship *Schleswig-Holstein* before attending various training courses at the Cadet Naval College at Flensburg-Mürwik in 1935, and three years later he served on board the battleship *Gneisenau* as a signals officer. Achilles was commissioned as a *Leutnant zur See* in April 1937 and was promoted to *Oberleutnant zur See* on 13 April 1939.

In April 1940, he attended a U-boat officer's course, and later joined the U-boat training battalion at Plön. In November Achilles served on *U-66* whilst it was still under construction – enabling him to familiarize himself with the boat before it became operational. In January 1941, he was appointed Watch Officer and served during three patrols, under the command of *Korvettenkapitän* Richard Zapp. He was promoted to *Kapitänleutnant* in August 1941 and on 1 January 1942, Achilles was appointed commander of *U-181*, and would complete six patrols and be credited with fourteen ships sunk for a total of 64,542 shipping tons. On 24 January *U-181* left Lorient for the Caribbean, and on the night of 18/19 February torpedoed the SS *Mokihana* and the British tanker SS *British Consul*, both of which were damaged. On 21 February Achilles sank his first ship, the British tanker MV *Circe Shell*, during an evening attack near the Port of Spain, Trinidad. On 7 March he sank the South African whale factory ship the *Uniwaleco*. She was struck by one of two torpedoes about 45 miles west of St. Vincent Passage. The ship apparently went out of control because she ran in circles and settled but did not sink. A third torpedo was fired and finished her off; she sank within three minutes after breaking in two. Eighteen crew members were lost. Achilles attacked two ships and damaged both, the Canadian passenger ship *Lady Nelson* and the British steamer *Umtata*, on 10 March. *Lady Nelson* caught fire by the stern in shallow water whilst in the harbour of Port Castries, St. Lucia, with the loss of twenty-five

(Scherzer)

crew. On the 14th Achilles sank the Canadian steamer *Sarniadoc* about 200 miles west of Guadeloupe. She was hit by a single torpedo and sank within thirty seconds after her boiler exploded, with the loss of her master and all of her crew. The next day he sank the lighthouse tender USCGC *Acacia* which was shelled by *U-181* from her deck guns and caught fire and sank by the stern about 80 miles south-west of Saint Kitts and Nevis. The survivors were rescued by USS *Overton* and landed at San Juan on 16 March.

He began his third patrol on 28 April 1942, heading for the Atlantic in the company of *U-126* and *U-128*. On 11 May they encountered the northbound Convoy SL109 about 220 miles north-west of the Cape Verde Islands. The convoy was shadowed but only *U-126* and *U-128* made attacks. The three boats continued on to waters north of Brazil and then along the Brazilian coast. By mid-June *U-181* was in the eastern Caribbean and later moved eastwards towards the harbour of Porto Limon, Costa Rica where it sank the Panamanian SS *San Pablo* tied up at the pier. Achilles then patrolled along the coast of Panama before leaving the Caribbean and later attacked a convoy off Bermuda sinking the American SS *Fairport*. He thren headed for Lorient, arriving on 7 August. In late Septmeber he headed out again on his next patrol where he carried out a reconnaissance of the Gulf of Guinea and the Congo Delta, following reports of shipping activity in those areas. From 20 October Achilles was stationed off the Congo when on the 23rd he torpedoed and dmaged the British cruiser HMS *Phoebe* off Pointe Noire. Few ships were then seen and Achilles took *U-181* north to the Gulf of Guinea in search for more targets. On the evening of 8 November he sank the American SS *West Humhaw*, 60 miles

HMS Phoebe *was assigned to the 15th Cruiser Squadron in September 1940, as part of the Home Fleet and employed in the North Atlantic on trade protection duties. In April 1941, she joined the Mediterranean Fleet at Alexandria from where she took part in the evacuation of Greece and Crete. She returned to Alexandria on 29 May with New Zealand troops evacuated from Crete, but was sent back to Crete to evacuate as many as possible of the remaining New Zealand and Australian solders before Crete capitulated. She was attacked by an Italian aircraft on 27 August 1941 and damaged while covering troop transports to the besieged Tobruk, and had to be repaired. She returned to service in May 1942 and on 23 October was struck by two torpedoes from U-161 and was seriously damaged. She was repaired and returned to active service in August 1943.* (Author's collection)

south-west of Takoradi and on the 29th he sank the Dutch steamer *Tjileboet* with the loss of the entire crew. In March 1943, during the boat's fifth patrol in the North Atlantic together with *U-174*, it met the German ship *Regensberg* and later the Italian ship *Pierto Orseolo*, and headed for the US east coast. They patrolled from east of New York up to an area south of Nova Scotia where he sank the Canadian sailing ship *Angelus* by gunfire north of Bermuda after her crew of ten had abandoned ship in a lifeboat. When the boat was found after five days by the destroyer USS *Turner*, only two survivors were found alive: the others including the master had died from exposure.

In August 1943, during his sixth patrol, Achilles had a special task to perform. He was ordered to rendezvous with the Japanese submarine *I-8* south of the Azores. Two German officers were put aboard *I-8* with radar equipment. Achilles then continued with his patrol and headed to the coast of Brazil. The boat moved north-westwards towards the Säo Francisco River, Brazil where on 26 September it sank the SS *Itapagé*. That same evening, *U-181* was attacked by a United States Navy Mariner, based at Aratu. It crash-dived and made its escape. The following day it wasn't so lucky, it was hit by depth charges and sank: there were no survivors. Achilles was posthumously promoted to *Korvettenkapitän* on 5 April 1945.

Other awards:
08 Apr 1938: Long Service Award 4th Class
15 Jul 1941: High Seas Fleet Badge
07 Aug 1941: Iron Cross 2nd Class
07 Aug 1941: U-boat War Badge
05 Apr 1942: Iron Cross 1st Class

<u>Klaus</u> Heinrich BARGSTEN
Kapitänleutnant
5 ships sunk, 22,171 tons

Knight's Cross: Awarded as *Kapitänleutnant* and as commander of *U-521*, on 30 April 1943, in recognition of sinking 22,171 shipping tons, five ships in total including one warship.

Klaus Bargsten was born in Bad Oldesloe, Schleswig-Holstein in Germany on 31 October 1911, and after completing his schooling trained as an officer in the merchant service and was later employed by North German Lloyd Steamship Company. He joined the Naval Academy at Flensburg in 1935, and was appointed an Officer Candidate with a training battalion in the Baltic Sea in April 1936. He was accepted into the Naval School at Flensburg-Mürwik in March 1937. He was commissioned as a *Leutnant zur See* in April 1938 and was serving at the Naval Training School in Neutstadt when the Second World War started.

 (Wehrkundearchiv)

Promoted to *Oberleutnant zur See* on 1 October 1939, Bargsten briefly served as a Watch Officer on board *U-6*, before being transferred to *U-99*, where he served until February 1941 under *Korvettenkapitän* Otto Kretschmer – who would become one of the most successful U-boat commanders of the war. He took part in seven patrols whilst attached to *U-99* and Kretschmer claimed a total of thirty ships for a total of 235,000 shipping tons. Bargsten was learning how to be a successful commander from one of the best!

In March 1941, he became the commander of *U-563*. His first two patrols were uneventful. His third patrol, which began on 31 July 1941, was in the North Atlantic. His boat became one of a number of U-boats which were operating around Iceland. On 12 August, *U-129* sighted a convoy and *U-563*, *U-206* and *U-567* were directed to it, but failed to find it. On 4 October, Bargsten set-out on his fourth patrol, again in the Atlantic and was directed to a convoy west of the North Channel but failed to find it. He spotted it again on the 8th but soon lost contact with it, and then on 12 October he found the convoy again but was driven away by aircraft. On the 23rd Bargsten patrolled west of Gibraltar where he sank the destroyer HMS *Cossack* south-west of Cape St. Vincent. She was struck by one of two torpedoes forward of the bridge. The explosion blew off the bow section and destroyed most of the forward section, killing the captain. Twenty-nine survivors were picked up by HMS *Legion* and HMS *Carnation*. The next morning the wrecked ship was re-boarded and the engines were repaired. The destroyer was taken in tow, but the weather worsened and prevented the salvage so the tow was abandoned and the corvette left with the skeleton crew from *Cossack*. She then sank shortly afterwards. *U-563* returned to Brest on 1 November 1941.

HMS Cossack *was struck by a single torpedo fired from* U-563 *on 23 October 1941, and the explosion blew off the bow and destroyed most of the forward part of the ship, killing her commander. The survivors were later picked up by HMS* Legion *and HMS* Carnation. Cossack *was taken in tow by the tug HMS* Thames *but whilst under tow the weather worsened and* Cossack *sank on the 27th. (Author's collection)*

On 3 June 1942, Bargsten took command of *U-521,* a Type IXC, and he left Kiel for Kristiansand on 3 October. Three days later he headed out for Canadian waters. He had been ordered to an area off Newfoundland to wait for eastbound convoys, with *U-520* and *U-522.* However, with the changing weather conditions in the Gulf of St. Lawrence, the boats were ordered south towards Halifax. He was promoted to *Kapitänleutnant* on 1 August and on 30 October *U-522* sighted Convoy SC107 and the three boats closed in. *U-520* was sunk and *U-521* was driven off the following day. In the morning of 2 November, *U-521* had a near miss when a torpedo fired by HMCS *Moosejaw* detonated close by. An hour later, east of Belle Isle, Bargsten sank the SS *Hartington* and in the morning of the 3rd, Bargsten sank the US tanker SS *Hahira,* south of Cape Farewell. On 6 November Bargsten made contact with Convoy ONS 144, together with other U-boats, and despite the fog five ships were sunk. He then made two unsuccessful attacks on the convoy and on 8 December, now out of torpedoes, returned to Lorient. On 7 January 1943, Bargsten took *U-521* out on its third patrol and headed for an area west of the Canaries. He met up with other U-boats to form the *Rochen* Group. On 28 January *U-521* sighted a small convoy, Gib No: 2, heading for Gibraltar. In the morning of 8 February Bargsten sank the British armed trawler HMS *Breden*, and by the 11th *U-521* had moved eastwards. On 25 February another convoy was spotted and Bargsten made an unsuccessful attack on the convoy. On 12 March, *U-521,* now part of *Tümmler* Group, was ordered north-west to intercept Convoy VGS6, heading for Gibraltar, but because of bad weather none of the five boats in the group could make a successful attack. On the morning of the 18th *U-521* sank the SS *Molly Pitcher* and on 26 March returned to Lorient.

On 5 May 1943, Bargsten took *U-521* out on what would be its last patrol. On 31 May it was sighted by a Norfolk-based aircraft 25 miles off Cape Hatteras. Bargsten ordered the boat to dive and it moved off. On 2 June, one of the US Navy patrol ships made contact with *U-521* and closed in. She dropped five depth charges which caused severe damage: all instruments were shattered, and the diving planes and rudder were disabled. Seawater was coming down the main hatch and Bargsten gave the order to dive. After a few seconds, *Oberleutnant* Henning reported that they were sinking, Bargsten gave the order to blow all ballast. However, before he could do anything the U-boat broke the surface and Bargsten pushed open the conning tower hatch and rushed to assess the situation. As he did the ship opened fire with its 20mm guns and shells burst all around the conning tower. Realizing that all was lost, Bargsten gave the order to abandon ship. At that moment *U-521* sank under Bargsten's feet with amazing speed and he was left floating in the ocean alone. He swam towards the nearest Allied ship and was safely helped aboard, but his entire crew of fifty-one had perished in the sea. Bargsten was transported to Norfolk, Virginia and later held in Camp Blanding in Florida until his release on 30 November 1946. He settled in Bremen after the war where he died on 25 October 2000.

Other awards:
03 Apr 1940: Long Service Award 4th Class
23 Jul 1940: Iron Cross 2nd Class
10 Aug 1940: U-boat War Badge
25 Sep 1940: Iron Cross 1st Class

Ernst Rudolf Ludwig BAUER

Korvettenkäpitan
26 ships sunk, 119,010 tons
4 ships damaged, 31,304 tons

Knight's Cross: Awarded on 16 March 1942, as *Kapitänleutnant* and as commander of *U-126*, in recognition of his considerable success in sinking almost 63,000 shipping tons, which represented sixteen ships.

Ernst Bauer was one of the most successful U-boat commanders of the war, sinking 119,010 shipping tons and was the twenty-second highest scoring U-boat ace. He was born in Fürth, Bavaria on 3 January 1914, and joined the Navy in 1935. He trained as an officer on board the light cruiser *Königsberg* from October 1936 when he was commissioned as a *Leutnant zur See*. A year later he transferred to the Torpedo School at Flensburg-Mürwik and in June 1938 he was promoted to *Oberleutnant zur See*. In August Bauer was appointed First Watch Officer aboard *U-37*, under the command of *Kapitänleutnant* Heinrich Schuch and later under *Korvettenkapitän* Werner Hartmann. On 19 August 1939, *U-37* left Wilhelmshaven for the Atlantic, but the patrol was cut short when the boat was recalled and returned to base on 15 September. On 5 October 1939, *U-37* left port to take part in the first attempt at a controlled wolf-pack operation, and it was joined by *U-42*, *U-45*, *U-46* and *U-48*. En route to their designated position, *U-37* sank the SS *Vistula* and on 12 October sank the SS *Aris* and three days later sank the SS *Vermont*. By the end of their patrol only three boats returned to port, *U-42* and *U-45* having been sunk.

(Author's collection)

In March 1941, Bauer was promoted to *Kapitänleutnant* and appointed commander of *U-126*, and left the port of Kiel on his first patrol as a U-boat commander on 5 July. His first attack was on the Gibraltar-bound Convoy OG69 on 27 July, in which he sank the British steamer *Erato*, which exploded after a direct hit, and soon afterwards he sank the SS *Inga*. Just eight days later *U-126* sank the British steamer *Robert Max* by gunfire. There followed a period of no action for the next ten days; a convoy was spotted but the U-boats were driven away by the escorts. On 14 August, Bauer torpedoed and sank the Yugoslavian SS *Sud* and returned to Lorient on 24 August 1941. He left for his second patrol on 24 September, and his first success came on 10 October when he sank the British SS *Railsea Manor* and nine days later he sank the US SS *Lehigh*. This was a risky 'kill' as America had not yet entered the war. The following day Bauer claimed another ship when he sank the British tanker *British Mariner* about 80 miles south-west of Freetown. Bauer returned to Lorient on 13 December 1941.

It was during 1942 that Bauer and *U-126* achieved their greatest victories: he sank a total of four ships in five days. On 2 March he sank the Norwegian SS *Gunny*, and on the 5th he sank the US SS *Mariana*, struck by a single torpedo off Turks Island and sinking within five minutes with the loss of twenty-eight crew. On the morning of the 7th he sank two ships, the US SS *Barbar* and SS *Cardonia*. All of his victories in March were in the Caribbean.

Towards the end of April 1942, Bauer took *U-126* on its fourth patrol, and in June sank the Norwegian tanker MV *Hoegh Giant* just off the coast of Brazil. However, targets were few and together with two other U-boats Bauer moved north in the Caribbean once again. On 15 June he sank the sailing vessel *Dutch Princess*, and the following day he sank the American merchant ships the SS *Arkansan* and SS *Kahuku* both by torpedo and gunfire. There was no more successes until 27 June when Bauer sank the Norwegian tanker *Leviv Eriksson* and two days later sank the Canadian sailing vessel *Mona Marie*. Bauer now set sail for Lorient and during the return journey he sank the large American tanker SS *Warrior*, and just two days later severely damaged the US tanker SS *Gulfbelle*. His final patrol in *U-126* began on 19 September 1942 when he left to operate in the South Atlantic. He sank the American SS *George Thatcher* on 1 November 100 miles off the west coast of Africa. On 22 November, *U-126* met up with the auxiliary cruiser *Atlantis* to take on fuel. While Bauer and much of his crew were having some hot food and coffee, the British cruiser HMS *Devonshire* was sighted. Bauer and his men ran back towards *U-126*, but the boat crash-dived before Bauer could get aboard. *Atlantis* meanwhile was disabled with a faulty engine and had no chance against the large cruiser and was soon sunk. The British, assuming the U-boat was still in the area, sped off. *U-126* surfaced and took on the survivors, who included Bauer.

On his return to Germany, Bauer was appointed Training Officer in the 17th U-boat Flotilla and in October 1944, he took command of the Flotilla. In April 1945, he was promoted to *Korvettenkapitän* and took over command of the 36th U-boat Flotilla in Warnemünde. He was wounded and admitted to the Naval Hospital at Flensburg-Mürwik where he stayed until October 1945. He joined the *Bundesmarine* in December 1955 and was for a time based in Paris as the *Bundesmarine* representative for NATO and in October 1967 he was commander of the Naval Supply School in List, Sylt. He retired in March 1972 as *Kapitän zur See*. Bauer died on 12 March 1988, in Westerland auf Sylt.

Other awards:

01 Apr 1937:   Long Service Award 4th Class
08 Nov 1939:   Iron Cross 2nd Class
08 Nov 1939:   U-boat War Badge
01 Aug 1941:   Iron Cross 1st Class
20 Apr 1944:   War Service Cross 2nd Class with Swords
01 Apr 1945:   War Service Cross 1st Class with Swords

Gerhard Otto BIGALK

Korvettenkäpitan
6 ships sunk, 32,412 tons
1 ship damaged, 8,096 tons

Knight's Cross: Awarded on 26 December 1941, as *Kapitänleutnant* and as commander of *U-751*, in recognition of his sinking of the escort carrier HMS *Audacity* five days previously. The award was presented on the same day he returned from patrol.

Gerhard Bigalk was born on 26 November 1908, in Berlin-Niederschönhausen, and during his relatively short career he sank six ships, which included the British escort carrier HMS *Audacity*. He entered the *Reichsmarine* in April 1934, and attended the Ships Gunnery School in Kiel from June of that year. He attended the Naval Academy

(Scherzer)

in Flensburg-Mürwik, attending many different training courses, from June 1935. He was commissioned as a *Leutnant zur See* in October 1936 and initially trained as an observer in the Navy's coastal service, and from February 1937 he saw service during the Spanish Civil War, making twenty-one combat flights. He was promoted to *Oberleutnant zur See* on 1 June 1938. Bigalk transferred to the U-boat arm in November 1939, with the rank of *Kapitänleutnant* and underwent his commander's training. On 2 June 1940, he was appointed commander of *U-14*, a Type IIB boat built by Deutsche Werke in Kiel. The boat operated as a training vessel whilst attached to the 24th U-boat Flotilla in the Baltic.

On 31 January 1941, Bigalk took command of *U-751*, a Type VIIC, and left Kiel for the North Atlantic on 3 June. He sank his first ship north of the Azores, the British SS *St. Lindsay* on the 14th. He then took *U-751* to join *West* Group south-east of the Newfoundland Bank. Unfortunately no convoys were sighted: only a few independent ships were seen, and a few were sunk, but none by Bigalk. He returned to port on 5 July. His second patrol began on 2 August and lasted until 8 September and proved to be unsuccessful for Bigalk. He took *U-751* out to join four other boats and although a convoy was sighted, none of the boats scored a hit. On 1 September, *U-751* together with other boats formed *Bosemüller* Group near Ireland. A convoy was sighted by *U-73*, but again contact was lost and no hits were recorded due to bad weather.

For his next patrol, Bigalk took *U-751* out on 11 October, and was directed to Convoy SC48 in the central North Atlantic. He closed in on the convoy but failed to score. Other boats were more successful, and by the end of the operation nine ships had been sunk, which included a corvette and a destroyer. Bigalk then briefly joined *Reissewolf* Group, and *U-751* was directed towards another convoy, and although contact was made, *U-751* was driven away by a US destroyer escort. Bigalk returned to St. Nazaire on 8 November, still without further success.

On 16 December, *U-751* set out for operations in the Atlantic, and soon made contact with Convoy HG76 which had sailed from Gibraltar. *Seeäuber* Group was directed to it, and *U-131* was sunk, soon other boats including *U-751* were directed to join the attack on the convoy. The ships of the convoy then decided to take a mock battle using starshell,

The 11,000-ton escort carrier, HMS Audacity *was completed in March 1939 as the German MV* Hannover. *On 7 March 1940 the* Hannover *was captured in the Mona Passage off Dominica by HMCS* Assiniboine *and prevented from being scuttled by a boarding party. The ship was first renamed* Sinbad *by the Ministry of War Transport and then* Empire Audacity. *From January to June 1941 she was converted to the first escort carrier of the Royal Navy, equipped with six Martlet aircraft and renamed HMS* Audacity *on 30 July 1941.* (Author's collection)

snowflake flares and depth charges to distract the U-boat pack while the convoy executed a major alteration of course. However, the snowflake flares lit up the sky so much that Bigalk spotted the British escort carrier HMS *Audacity* on 21 December, and decided to make an attack. He fired four torpedoes at her, but only one found its mark, detonating near the engine room. The other three passed astern. Major damage was caused to *Audacity*'s unprotected hull, but the ship was in no immediate danger of sinking. However, within a few minutes of the attack a small bulkhead in the shaft tunnel collapsed, flooding the engines which caused complete electrical failure. Unable to manoeuvre, she was an easy target. Bigalk fired two more torpedoes, both hit and exploded forward within a few seconds of each other, breaking her back. Within just twenty-five minutes *Audacity* sank. As a result, over seventy of her crew were lost.

Bigalk returned to port on 26 December. He was awarded the Knight's Cross on his return, but there was little satisfaction at his success, as the Germans had lost five U-boats, including the ace Engelbert Endraß in *U-567*. Nevertheless, Bigalk had won the Knight's Cross and celebrated with his crew. On 14 January 1942, he left for Canadian waters and headed to the Nova Scotia area. On 2 February, Bigalk attacked Convoy HX173 and damaged the Dutch tanker MV *Corilla* in difficult conditions. He had fired three torpedoes of which only one struck its target. A further attack was prevented by the tanker zigzagging and *U-751* was driven off by the escorts. On 4th Bigalk sank the British MV *Silveray* and on the 7th sank the British catapult-armed ship SS *Empire Sun*. She was sunk south of Halifax and the master, seven crew members, two gunners and one member of the RAF personnel were lost. With all torpedoes used he headed for port.

Promoted to *Korvettenkapitän* on 5 April, Bigalk took command of *U-751* on the 15th and headed for US waters, by mid-May he was patrolling off the Bahamas. On 16 May, he torpedoed and sank the SS *Nicarao* and three days later he sank the SS *Isabela*. He then patrolled in the Eastern Mediterranean but had no further success, returning to St. Nazaire on 15 June. Bigalk had now sunk six ships and damaged another, and on 17 July he left for the North Atlantic, hoping to add to his score. On the 17th *U-751* was attacked north-west off Cape Finisterre by two aircraft, a Lancaster and a Whitley, which both dropped depth charges and sank the German submarine. There were no survivors – fifty-seven men were lost.

Gerhard Bigalk, an officer of great experience, had been awarded the Knight's Cross after only sinking four ships. It was exceptional for an officer with such a limited tonnage to be given such a high award. But it does perhaps show the importance given by the German propaganda machine to sinking large ships, especially carriers.

Other awards:
02 Nov 1936: Observers' Badge
08 Apr 1938: Armed Forces Long Service Award 4th Class
01 Jun 1939: Spanish Cross in Silver with Swords
01 Jun 1939: Spanish Campaign Medal
01 Dec 1939: Commemorative Medal of 1 October 1938
30 Nov 1940: Iron Cross 2nd Class
07 Jul 1941: U-Boat War Badge
26 Dec 1941: Iron Cross 1st Class

Paul BRASACK
Kapitänleutnant
No ships sunk

Knight's Cross: Awarded on 30 October 1944, as *Kapitänleutnant* and as commander of *U-73 7* in recognition of his bravery and leadership, especially his actions against convoys when he would attack the escorting destroyers and in doing so would enable other U-boats from his own pack to attack and sink the unprotected ships of the convoys.

Paul Brasack was born in Stettin, on the Baltic Sea and now part of Poland, on 9 May 1916. He entered the *Reichsmarine* on 1 April 1937, as an Officer Candidate and served with the naval infantry in the Baltic. From July 1937 he spent his basic training aboard the training ships *Gorch Fock* and *Schlesien*, and after twelve months he attended the Naval Academy at Flensburg-Mürwik. He attended flying school from September 1939, and joined Coastal Squadron 1/706 as an Observer with the rank of *Leutnant zur See*. From July 1940, he flew with Bomber Group 126, which later became Bomber Group 28, equipped with Heinkel He 111s. In June 1941, he transferred to Franc Port, near Soissons, Northern France, where he was a Staff Officer in the IX Air Corps under the command of *Generalleutnant* Joachim Coeler. In September, Brasack was promoted to *Oberleutnant zur See* and the following month he transferred to the Advanced Training Group 28, as an observer training officer in Bomber Wing 4 '*General Wever*'.

On 1 March 1942, Brasack transferred to the U-boat service, and was assigned to the 2nd U-boat Training Division. Here he trained as a Watch Officer and underwent training as a torpedo officer and a U-boat commander. On 30 January 1943, he was appointed commander of *U-737*, a Type VIIC boat built by Schichau in Danzig. From July until January 1944, he operated in northern waters and later around the coast of Narvik – they were short patrols without success. On 16 January 1944, he left for operations and headed out towards Iceland and followed Convoy JW56A. *U-737* was now part of *Isegrim* Group, and waited for convoys in Bear Island Passage, until contact was made on the night of the 25th/26th when nine of the ten U-boats made attacks. Unfortunately, *U-737* had no success. *Isegrim* Group reformed as *Wehrwolf* Group and moved towards the Kola Inlet to wait from Convoy JW56B. Contact was made on 29th and the following day *U-737* had a near miss with the destroyer HMS *Milne*, with a torpedo exploding

(Author's collection)

in her wake. Later that same evening Brasack made an unsuccessful attack on a destroyer. He returned to port on 12 February. Between 28 February and 31 October 1944, Brasack took *U-737* out on at least ten patrols, some of which were short but all without sinking one ship.

On 6 March 1944, *U-737* was attacked and damaged by a Liberator of 120 Squadron. Depth-charges were dropped and although badly damaged Brasack managed to get his boat back to port safely, putting in at Skjomenfjord on 8 March. Promoted to *Kapitänleutnant* in July he completed his last patrol on 31 October and went on leave. In December he was recalled and appointed Training Officer with the 25th U-boat Flotilla in Travemünde, Lübeck, where he remained until the end of the war. He was captured by Allied troops on 9 March 1945, remaining in captivity until 15 August 1947.

He joined the *Bundesmarine* in October 1957, and among other positions, he was commander of the destroyer *Z-2* and for more than three years he was the Federal German naval attaché in the United States. He retired from service with the rank of *Kapitän zur See* on 30 September 1974. Brasack died in Bad Pyrmont, Lower Saxony on 11 March 2013, at the age of ninety-six.

Other awards:
28 Feb 1940: Observers' Badge
00 May 1940: Iron Cross 2nd Class
00 Nov 1940: Iron Cross 1st Class
10 Mar 1941: Combat Clasp for Bomber Pilots in Gold
24 Jun 1941: Honour Goblet of the Luftwaffe
24 Sep 1942: U-Boat War Badge
28 Oct 1944: U-Boat Combat Clasp in Bronze
24 Mar 1945: U-Boat Combat Clasp in Silver

Asmus <u>Nicolai</u> CLAUSEN
Korvettenkapitän
24 ships sunk, 74,807 tons

Knight's Cross: Awarded on 13 March 1942 as *Kapitänleutnant* and as commander of *U-129* for sinking nineteen ships for a total of 39,166 shipping tons.

Nicolai Clausen was born on 2 June 1911 in Flensburg and he joined the *Reichsmarine* as a seaman in October 1929 at the age of eighteen. He spent the next four years serving aboard torpedo boats, including *T185* and *G10*, also spending time training on board the sail training ship *Gorch Fock*. On 28 September 1935, he was transferred to the U-boat service and in April 1936, after completing his training, was assigned to *U-26*, under *Kapitänleutnant* Werner Hartmann. In March 1937 he attended the Naval Academy at Mürwik where

(Scherzer)

he received several months training as an officer and was commissioned as a *Leutnant zur See* in January 1938. In May he was attached to the 'pocket battleship' *Admiral Graf Spee*, and from September 1939 he served as commander of the minesweeper *M134*, with the rank of *Oberleutnant zur See*. In November 1939, Clausen transferred as First Watch Officer to *U-37* where he served under his former commander Werner Hartmann. He took part in three patrols, mostly in the Atlantic, and on his return from his first patrol he was personally decorated by Dönitz with the Iron Cross. From July 1940, he attended a U-boat commander's course, and in August was appointed commander of *U-142*, a training vessel. In October he took command of his own boat, *U-37*, the boat in which he had previously served under Hartmann.

On 28 November he left port for an area west of Spain. He sank the British SS *Palmella* north-west of Lisbon on 1 December, and the following day he sank the Swedish SS *Gwalia* and the British SS *Jeanne M*, both from Convoy OG46. On 19 December Clausen sank two Vichy French vessels, the fleet oiler *Rhßne* and the submarine *Sfax* (*Q182*), both by mistake seven miles off Cape Juby, Morocco. Of the officers and men on board the French submarine sixty-five were lost, only four surviving. Clausen, who had now sunk a total of seven ships, headed back to port. On 1 January 1941 he was promoted to *Kapitänleutnant* and on the 30th he took *U-37* out on his second patrol, to operate off Freetown. He sighted Convoy HG53 on 8 February and in the early hours of the 9th he attacked, sinking two British merchant ships, the SS *Estrellano* and SS *Courland*. Clausen continued to shadow the convoy and radioed its position to the bombers of Bomber Wing 40, which sank a further five ships. In the early morning of the 10th, Clausen sank the British SS *Brandenburg*, and returned to base on 18 February. His final patrol as commander of *U-37* began on 27 February, when he headed out into the North Atlantic. He sank two more ships, the SS *Mentor* on 7 March, and a fishing vessel, the Icelandic steam trawler *Petrusey*, on the 12th with the loss of ten of its crew. He arrived at his home port ten days later.

Clausen was granted leave and in early May he transferred to the 5th U-Boat Flotilla and on 22 May he took command of *U-129*, a Type IXC boat. His first patrol was short, lasting only twenty-seven days and was without success. He left for his next patrol on

27 September with orders to escort the German supply ship *Kota Pinang* on the first part of her journey. On 3 October, the *Kota Pinang* came under long-range gunfire from the cruiser HMS *Kenya* and she was hit and the captain decided to scuttle her to avoid capture. The entire crew of 119 men was picked up by *U-129* and were later put aboard a Spanish naval tug off the port of El Ferrol. Clausen returned to Lorient on 8 October.

His next patrol began on 21 October, and although it was unsuccessful in that he didn't sink any ships *U-129* was once again used as a rescue boat. Clausen had been ordered to escort the German supply ship *Python*, and once he had been refuelled he headed for his operational area. On 1 December *Python* was sunk 1,000 miles south of St. Helena and the 414 survivors, which included men from *Atlantis*, were placed in two U-boats or were being towed behind them in lifeboats. On the 5th *U-129* and *U-124* caught up with the boats and between them they took aboard the 214 men being towed. Clausen then had to travel with an overcrowded boat for 5,000 miles, arriving in Lorient on 28 December.

On 25 January 1942, *U-129* headed out towards the Caribbean, as part of *Neuland* Group, together with *U-67*, *U-156*, *U-181* and *U-502*. The plan was for the five boats to be in position by mid-February and for simultaneous attacks to be made on approaching convoys. On 20 February, *U-129* sank the Norwegian SS *Nordvangen* off the west tip of Tobago and on the 22nd sank the Canadian SS *George L. Torain* and the American SS *West Zelda*. Clausen then took *U-129* east, where he later sank a further three ships, bringing his total to nineteen ships sunk. On his return journey to Lorient, *U-129* was attacked in the Bay of Biscay by a Whitley aircraft and was damaged, Clausen finally reached Lorient and safety on 5 April.

Clausen went on leave and oversaw the repairs on *U-129* and on 1 July was transferred as commander of *U-182*, a larger Type IXD2 boat. He spent several months training

Above left: The conning tower of U-129, *1944.* (Author's collection)

Above right: U-129 *covered in ice during a patrol in the South Atlantic, 1944.* (Author's collection)

with his crew and learning about the new systems. On 9 December he left on what would be his last patrol. He headed out for the South Atlantic, where on the 29th he spotted Convoy GUS2 near the Canaries. He shadowed her for a time, but was driven off, and resumed his southward journey. On 15 January, Clausen sank the SS *Ocean Courage*, 250 miles south of the Cape Verde Islands. He then joined *U-506*, *U-509* and *U-516*, and moved through the South Atlantic as *Seehund* Group. On the 17th, *U-182* sank the British SS *Llanashe*, and from early March Clausen took his boat south and cruised between Durban and the end of the Mozambique Channel. On 10 March he sank the US SS *Richard D. Spaight*, and on 5 April sank the SS *Aloe*, being promoted to *Korvettenkapitän* the same day. On 1 May, Clausen sank the Greek SS *Adelfotis*, 600 miles west north-west of the Ascension Islands. Then on the 16th, he encountered Convoy UG-S8, but was spotted by the escorts. *U-182* was depth-charged by the destroyer USS *Mackenzie*, north-west of Madeira. Sixty-one men were killed including Clausen: there were no survivors.

Awards:
02 Oct 1936: Long Service Award 4th Class
28 Feb 1940: Iron Cross 2nd Class
18 Apr 1940: U-Boat War Badge
10 Jun 1940: Iron Cross 1st Class
15 Oct 1941: Long Service Award 3rd Class

Peter-Erich CREMER
Korvettenkapitän
6 ships sunk, 26,873 tons
2 ships damaged, 9,252 tons

Knight's Cross: Awarded as *Kapitänleutnant* and as commander of *U-333*, on 5 June 1942, in recognition of his leadership qualities and for the sinking of six ships for a total of 26,873 shipping tons.

Peter-Erich Cremer was born in Metz on 25 March 1911; his father was a respected lawyer. When the Great War ended in 1918, the Cremer family moved to Geinhausen in Hesse. He completed his schooling in 1929 and studied law for eighteen months before deciding on a naval career. He joined the *Reichsmarine* in August 1932, and spent twelve months training on board the light cruiser *Köln* before spending a few months on the 'pocket battleship' *Deutschland*. He was commissioned as a *Leutnant zur See* in January 1936, and from April served with naval artillery. Promoted to *Oberleutnant zur See* on 1 October 1937 Cremer returned to sea duties in October 1939 as Second Watch Officer aboard the destroyer *Z6 Theodor Riedel*.
   Promoted to *Kapitänleutnant* on 1 February 1940 Cremer transferred to the U-boat service on 22 August, being attached to the 1st U-boat Training Division until October when he attended the Torpedo School at Flensburg. On 29 January 1941, he took command of a training boat, *U-152*, and spent six months training as a U-boat commander. In August he was appointed commander of *U-333*, a Type VIIC boat. He took his new boat out for operations

in the North Atlantic on 27 December 1941. After passing between the Faroe Islands and the Shetlands on the 31st, Cremer sighted the SS *Algonquin*. He fired four torpedoes of which all missed and *U-333* was driven off by Allied aircraft. In the early morning of 18 January 1942 Cremer reported that he had sunk an unescorted steamer of 8,000 tons east of St. John's, Newfoundland and he reported that it was the British SS *Caledonian Monarch*. But according to Lloyd's it was impossible for the *Caledonian Monarch* to be in the same area as *U-333* – in fact it was revealed after the war that *U-588*, under the command of *Kapitänleutnant* Victor Vogel, had sunk the steamer on 7 January 1942, north-west of Lewis in the Outer Hebrides. So Cremer's victim, if any, remains unidentified. On 22 January Cremer sank the unescorted Greek SS *Vassilios A. Polemis* about 300 miles south of St. John's. She was struck on the port side by one torpedo. No distress signal could

(Scherzer)

be sent as the explosion brought down the funnel and the foremast with the aerial. Only one lifeboat was launched before the ship sank and this began to pick up survivors who had been blown overboard by the explosion or had jumped into the water when the ship began to sink. The U-boat then went alongside the lifeboat to question the survivors and then Cremer gave them a box of biscuits and forty cigarettes and left the area. The lifeboat had seventeen survivors aboard, but five died of exposure and were buried at sea, the rest being picked up by the Greek SS *Leonidas N. Condylis* and landed at Halifax on 27 January.

On 24 January, he sank the Norwegian MV *Ringstad* and on the 31st he sank a ship which he believed to be British but turned out to be the German blockade-runner *Spreewald*, off the Azores. He had fired two torpedoes, both hit amidships, causing the ship to burn furiously and slowly sink. A search was launched for survivors in which *U-333*, *U-575* and *U-123* were joined by four other boats, as well as five Luftwaffe Fw-200 Condor long-range aircraft from bases in France. Of the 152 people aboard the ship, 72 were killed. Cremer was devastated and was court-martialled. He was charged with disobedience in action, damage to military property and manslaughter. He was acquitted because, against orders, *Spreewald* was in the wrong position and not showing correct markings.

On 30 March 1942, Cremer took *U-333* out on operations in US waters. Three days into his patrol *U-333* was attacked on the surface by an aircraft, which dropped depth charges after Cremer had given the order to dive. The boat was seriously damaged but after some repairs to patch-up the leaks, Cremer decided to continue with the patrol. On the 30th he spotted the tanker MV *British Prestige*. He attacked her with two torpedoes, both missed, and as a third was prepared the ship turned towards *U-333* and rammed her, causing serious damage to the bow, conning tower, bridge and casing. Temporary repairs were again carried out, and *U-333* continued on towards Florida. On the morning of 6 May Cremer torpedoed three ships off Port Salerno, sinking the Dutch SS *Amazone* and the US tanker SS *Halsey* and damaging the US tanker SS *Java Arrow*, which later sank.

Later that same day, *U-333* was attacked with depth charges by two USN patrol craft and the destroyer USS *Vigilant*. The attacks went on for fifteen hours, and when the ships finally left Cremer surfaced only to find the destroyer USS *Dallas* nearby. She spotted the U-boat and began depth-charge attacks but inflicted no further damage to the boat and soon left the area. On the morning of the 10th, Cremer sank the SS *Clan Skene* and then headed back to port, arriving on 26 May.

There was a long period of repairs and during this time Cremer had been awarded the Knight's Cross, He was the forty-eighth member of the *Kriegsmarine* to receive the award. He celebrated with his crew who were very proud of their commander. Finally the boat was ready and on 11 August Cremer took *U-333* out and headed for the Central Atlantic. Cremer joined *Blücher* Group, which had assembled south-east of the Azores. There they waited for the convoys. On the 18th, Convoy SL118 was sighted, and *U-333* was herself spotted by a Liberator and was forced to dive. Cremer managed to avoid serious damage to *U-333* during a two-day depth-charge attack. But nevertheless he had to return to base for repairs.

On 1 September, *U-333* once again set out on patrol in the Central Atlantic, this time as part of *Iltis* Group. The boats assembled west of Lisbon from the 14th, and during this time, no ships were sighted. The group continued towards the Freetown area, being refuelled on the way. On the evening of 6 October, the corvette HMS *Crocus* had left Freetown to search for U-boats. In the early morning of the 7th she sighted *U-333* and immediately opened fire. Before Cremer could retaliate, *U-333* was rammed twice and Cremer had no choice but to dive, and he went to the bottom as *Crocus* started to drop depth charges. Eventually the attack stopped, and *U-333* was able to surface and move away unobserved. Cremer lost three men during the attack, and Cremer and two officers were wounded. The dead, who included a young *Leutnant*, were buried at sea. Cremer had a finger-long shell splinter embedded in his chest. Every breath was painful. It had to come out. He had been in terrible pain through the depth-charge attack. The chief engineer on board *U-333* was entrusted with the surgical procedure of removing the splinter – there was no doctor onboard a U-boat. Cremer's uniform was slit open and the chief engineer disinfected his hands, as far as possible, and fetched a pair of pincers from a toolbox. To dull the pain Cremer drank two mugs of French rum. Three men held their commander down while the chief took the pincers and twisted out the splinter. The procedure was a success. However, Cremer also had other wounds. He had suffered a cut on his head, a splinter in his lower left knee, one in his shoulder and he had bruising to his chest and abdomen and was suffering from cardiac weakness through loss of blood. He needed proper medical treatment – and fast. *U-333* made contact with another boat and a 'commander under instruction', *Kapitänleutnant* Lorenz Kasch who had been aboard *U-107*, took over command of *U-333*. On the way home they came under attack in the Bay of Biscay from the submarine HMS *Graph* but her torpedoes were avoided and *U-333* reached La Palice on 23 September. (HMS *Graph* was in fact a German Type VIIC U-boat which had captured by the Royal Navy on 27 August 1941. She had been commissioned as *U-570* and was attacked on her first patrol by aircraft and was forced to the surface by depth charges. The damaged boat was towed to Iceland and was eventually repairer and entered service with the Royal Navy on 19 September.)

Cremer was immediately taken to the military hospital in La Rochelle, and on 22 November was transferred to the hospital at Garmisch Partenkirchen. He remained in hospital for several weeks and then rested at home. In February 1943, he served on the staff of the Commander-in-Chief of U-boats, before returning to command *U-333* in June. He left for the North Atlantic on the 2nd and failed to locate a convoy until the 29th, when *U-333* was attacked by aircraft but managed to escape without damage. The patrol was without success and *U-333* was attacked a total of three times by air. On his next patrol Cremer took *U-333* out on 21 October as one of eight boats making up *Schill* Group. The plan was to make a one-night attack on a convoy off the north-west coast of Spain. On the 30th, aircraft found the convoy and Cremer made an attack against a destroyer but this was unsuccessful. The operation was called off, due to strong Allied air support. *U-333* was attacked by the frigate HMS *Exe* whilst at periscope depth. When the depth charges exploded the U-boat shot upwards, hitting the bottom of the frigate, which caused the periscope to snap off. *U-333* was seriously damaged but managed to get away. Somehow temporary repairs were made and Cremer resurfaced and managed to get the boat back to port – eventually. Cremer took *U-333* out for two more patrols and both were unsuccessful. When attacked from the air on 12 June 1944, Cremer's gunners managed to shoot down a RAF Sunderland flying boat.

On 11 July Cremer was promoted to *Korvettenkapitän* and transferred to the 1st U-boat Flotilla where he served as an instructor. From November 1944 until February 1945 he commanded *U-2519*, a Type XXI boat. He took this new boat out on sea trials and training duties but never took part in war patrols. In April 1945 it was damaged during a raid on Hamburg, and was scuttled in early May. With no boat Cremer and his crew together with other naval stragglers were hastily formed into a naval anti-tank battalion under Cremers' command. This battalion fought against superior British forces with only small arms and bazookas, together with troops from the *Volkssturm* and member of the Hitler Youth. In May Cremer and his battalion were ordered to Plön where *Admiral* Wilhelm Meisel, Chief of Naval Operations, informed Cremer that his battalion was now responsible for the security of the headquarters of *Großadmiral* and Reich President Dönitz.

Cremer surrendered to British troops after the fall of the Dönitz government but was released from internment a month later. He settled in Hamburg, and was often interviewed for television, including the British television documentary series *The World at War* in the early 1970s. Later he recounted his life in his books, *U-333: The Story of a U-boat Ace* and *U-boat Commander: a periscope view of the Battle of the Atlantic*. Cremer died in Hamburg on 5 July 1992.

Other Awards
02 Oct 1936: Long Service Award 4th Class
00.00.1939: Commemorative Medal of 01 Oct 1938
11 Feb 1940: Iron Cross 2nd Class
19 Oct 1940: Destroyer War Badge
10 Feb 1942: Iron Cross 1st Class
26 May 1942: U-Boat War Badge
27 Sep 1942: U-Boat Combat Clasp in Bronze
11 Nov 1942: Wound Badge in Black
00 Dec 1942: Wound Badge in Silver
27 Sep 1944: U-Boat Combat Clasp in Bronze
00.00.1945: U-Boat Combat Clasp in Silver

Kurt DOBRATZ
Kapitän zur See
4 ships sunk, 24,531 tons
1 ship damaged, 2,373 tons

Knight's Cross: Awarded on 23 January 1945 as *Kapitän zur See* and as commander of *U-1232*, in recognition of his leadership and for the sinking of four ships for a total of 24,531 shipping tons.

Kurt Dobratz was born on 9 April 1904 in Stettin and he began his naval career in March 1922. He won his commission as a *Leutnant zur See* in October 1926 and was promoted to *Oberleutnant zur See* two years later and then to *Kapitänleutnant* in July 1934. He then spent just over ten years on board the cruisers *Hamburg* and *Leipzig* and the battleships *Schleswig-Holstein* and *Hannover*. Dobratz transferred to the *Luftwaffe* in September 1935 with the rank of *Hauptmann* and was promoted to *Major* in April 1936 whilst attached to the Luftwaffe Personnel Office in the Reich Ministry where he stayed until June. In March 1937 he attended a flight training course at the pilots' school in Pütwitz.

On 15 November 1938, he was appointed *Staffelkapitän* of the 8th Squadron of Bomber Wing 255. In July 1939 he took over as commander of the II. Group of 1st Training Wing, and was at the same time Commandant of the airbase at Schwerin. In August 1940, he was transferred and appointed Adjutant of the 5th Air Fleet under *Generaloberst* Hans-Jürgen Stumpff. He was promoted to *Oberstleutnant* in December 1940, and in May 1941 took command of 1st Group of Bomber Wing 26.

On 31 March 1943, Dobratz, now an *Oberst*, was transferred to the *Kriegsmarine*, and began training as a U-boat commander. In May he was appointed *Kapitän zur See* and attended various training courses, and for a brief period served as deputy of the 24th U-boat Flotilla – a training flotilla under the command of *Fregattenkapitän* Karl-Friedrich Merten. On 8 March 1944, Dobratz was appointed commander of *U-1232*, a Type IXC-40 boat built by Deutsche Werft in Hamburg. He left for the North Atlantic on 10 November, one of four boats on weather-reporting duties. When these duties were complete, *U-1232* headed for Canadian waters. En route, the boat was slightly damaged by bad weather, and had to stop to make repairs. In early January 1945, Dobratz began to look for targets off Novia Scotia. On the 2nd he reported that he had sunk a destroyer, but this was unconfirmed, and the next day he attacked the troopship *Nieuw Amsterdam* but the torpedoes missed their target. On the 4th he sighted Convoy SH194 near Halifax. He torpedoed two ships, sinking the SS *Polarland* and damaging the tanker MV *Nipiwan Park* about four miles off Halifax. The *Nipiwan Park* was later salvaged and repaired at Pictou. On the 14th,

(Scherzer)

Dobratz attacked Convoy BX141 and torpedoed

another three ships, sinking two of them and damaging a third, the SS *Martin van Burren*, which was beached and declared a total loss. As *U-1232* dived it was attacked by the escort vessel HMS *Ethrick*, which Dobratz had previously missed with a torpedo. The boat was slightly damaged, but managed to escape further attacks, and he headed out southwards. In mid-December he headed towards the Norwegian coast, where a German patrol appeared to lead *U-1232* in. However, due to a navigation error the U-boat went on to a reef and had to be pulled off by a tug and was towed in to Marviken.

In April 1945, Dobratz was made Chief of Staff to the Commanding Admiral of U-boats, *Admiral* Hans-Georg von Friedeburg. During the last few days of the war, Dobratz succeeded von Friedeburg after he committed suicide. Dobratz surrendered to Allied forces in early May and spent nine months in captivity, being released on 26 February 1946. When he returned to Germany he studied law, eventually earning a doctorate. He settled in Bromine where he died on 21 December 1996 at the age of ninety-two.

Other awards:
01 Oct 1935: Combined Pilots' and Observers' Badge
02 Oct 1936: Long Service Award 4th to 3rd Class
00.00.1940: Iron Cross 2nd Class
15 Jun 1941: Combat Clasp for Bomber Pilots in Bronze
18 Aug 1941: Iron Cross 1st Class
27 Feb 1942: Finnish Freedom Cross 3rd Class
15 Feb 1945: U-Boat War Badge
00.00.1945: U-Boat Combat Clasp in Bronze

Wilhelm DOMMES
Fregattenkapitän
11 ships sunk, 43,964 tons
2 ships damaged, 4,010 tons

Knight's Cross: Awarded on 2 December 1942 as *Kapitänleutnant* and as commander of *U-431* in recognition of his leadership and success as a U-boat commander in sinking five ships for a total of 11,275 shipping tons.

Born in Buchberg, West Prussia on 16 April 1907, Wilhelm Dommes volunteered for the *Reichsmarine* in January 1933. On completion of his basic training, service aboard the gunnery school ship *Dracho* and the light cruisers *Karlsruhe* and *Leipzig*, he was commissioned as a *Leutnant zur See* in April 1935. From September he served as Watch Officer aboard the sail training ship *Gorch Fock*, and after his promotion to *Oberleutnant zur See* in January 1937, he transferred to the light cruiser *Nürnberg* where he served as Watch Officer and Divisional Officer until October 1938. From January 1939 until April 1940, (Author's collection)

Dommes served as Watch Officer on the battleship *Scharnhorst*, seeing action together with the battleship *Gneisenau*. He had been promoted to *Kapitänleutnant* in February and in November took part in the battle against HMS *Rawalpindi*, the British armed merchant cruiser which was sunk by the *Scharnhorst* on 23 November 1939.

In April 1940 he transferred to the U-boat service, being assigned to the U-boat School in Kiel. Here he trained as a U-boat Watch Officer and from September attended the U-boat training course for officers at the Naval Academy in Flensburg-Mürwik. From the 30 September he was attached to the training boat *U-4*, and underwent commander training. From January 1941, he served aboard *U-96* as a trainee commander under *Kapitänleutnant* Heinrich Lehmann-Willenbrock. In April he was appointed commander of *U-431*, taking part in ten war patrols. His first began on 10 July when he left Trondheim to join fifteen other boats to operate between Greenland and the Azores. On the 17th Convoy OB346 was sighted and the nearest boats formed a patrol line, but the convoy evaded it. Without success, Dommes returned to port on 11 August.

His next patrol began on 13 September when he left for the North Atlantic joining *Brandenburg* Group south-east of Greenland. On the 18th Convoy SC44 was sighted but because of radio interference no attacks could be organised. In the late evening of 2 October, *U-431* sank the British SS *Hatasu*, 600 miles east of Cape Race. Dommes returned to port on 12 October – he had broken his duck. After various patrols which lasted just a few months Dommes had added two more ships to his total. He sank the British trawler (minesweeper) HMS *Sotra* on 29 January 1942. She was struck by a single torpedo at 21:46 hours off Bardia, the ship exploded and sank almost immediately with the loss of twenty-two men. Dommes then sank the British SS *Eocne* on 20 May 1942. On 7 November he took *U-431* out on patrol and headed for the Western Mediterranean, where he joined other boats west of a line from the Balearic Islands to Algiers. In the early hours of the 10th, he sank the British destroyer HMS *Martin*, which was operating as part of Force H covering the landings during Operation Torch (the Anglo–American invasion of French North Africa), north-east of Algiers, and reported three hits on a cruiser, which blew up. She was HMS *Martin* and her 161 officers and men. Later that evening Dommes sank the Dutch destroyer HNMS *Isaac Sweers*. She had refuelled at sea from a fleet oiler of Force R and was ordered to cover the oilers until the morning and then return to the Force. At 06:16 hours on 13 November she was hit on the starboard side by a torpedo and this struck an oil tank, spreading burning oil over the ship and the water. The second torpedo hit the wardroom and officers' quarters, killing all thirteen officers sleeping there. The eighty-six survivors were picked up by HMS *Loch Oskaig*: 108 officers and men were lost.

Promoted to *Korvettenkapitän* in January 1943 he served as a staff officer attached to the Admiral of U-boats, *Konteradmiral* Hans-Georg von Friedeburg. From 21 February, Dommes took command of *U-178*, a Type IXD2 boat. He left for operations in the Indian Ocean and on 1 June torpedoed and damaged the Dutch SS *Salabangka* off Port Shepstone. On 4 July, he sank the Norwegian SS *Breiviken* and the Greek SS *Michael Livanous*, followed by her sister-ship the SS *Mary Livanous* on 11 July off Angoche, Mozambique. During the early hours of the 14th, he sank the SS *Robert Bacon* in the same area, and on the evening of the 16th he sank the British SS *City of Canton* north-east of Nacala, Mozambique. On 22 July, Dommes was ordered to rendezvous with the Italian submarine *Torelli* south-east of the Cape of Good Hope. They met on 8 August and then set out together for Penang, where *U-178* was to be overhauled before returning to operations.

Dommes relinquished his command of *U-178* to *Kapitänleutnant* Wilhelm Spahr and in January 1945 was made base commander of Singapore and chief of all *Monsun* U-boats in the Indian Ocean, whereby German and Japanese forces fought together in the only time in the war. On 29 January Dommes was promoted to *Fregattenkapitän* and was the first commander of the U-boat base, in the former British seaplane base in Penang. He ended the war as a prisoner of the British, and spent almost two and a half years in the British POW camp in Sudbury, Derby and later in Camp 200, Llanover Park, Aberganenny. Dommes was released in October 1947, and returned to Germany, settling in Hannover, where he died on 23 January 1990, at the age of eighty-two.

Other awards:
23 Jan 1937: Armed Forces Long Service Award 4th Class
29 Nov 1939: Iron Cross 2nd Class
20 Dec 1939: Commemorative Medal of 01 Oct 1938
10 Feb 1942: Iron Cross 1st Class
10 Feb 1942: U-boat War Badge
27 Jul 1942: Italian Medal for Military Valour in Bronze
29 May 1943: Italian Medal for Military Valour in Silver
30 Jan 1945: War Service Cross 2nd Class + Swords
05 Mar 1945: U-boat Combat Clasp in Bronze
20 Apr 1945: War Service Cross 1st Class + Swords

Alfred EICK
Kapitänleutnant
10 ships sunk, 67,191 tons
1 ship damaged, 3,702 tons

Knight's Cross: Awarded the Knight's Cross on 31 March 1944 as *Oberleutnant zur See* and as commander of *U-510* in recognition of his success in sinking eight ships with a total of 59,806 shipping tons.

Alfred Eick was born in Essen, Germany on 9 March 1916. After he had completed six months' service in the *Reichsarbeitsdienst* (Reich Labour Service) he entered the *Kriegsmarine* in March 1937, as an officer cadet. He first saw service with the II. *Schiffsstammabteilung* in the Baltic and like most other recruits he completed a period of training with the sail training ship *Gorch Fock*. This was followed by a period of service aboard the old battleship *Schlesien* from September 1937 until April 1938. He then attended the Naval Academy at Flensburg–Mürwik before being commissioned as a *Leutnant zur See* in August 1939. From September 1939 until November 1940, Eick served with the

(Scherzer)

minesweeping branch of the navy before transferring to the U-boat service. On completion of his training he was posted to *U-176* as Watch Officer, a Type IXC boat under the command of *Korvettenkapitän* Reiner Dierksen. He participated in two war patrols in the Atlantic, resulting in the sinking of nine ships.

Promoted to *Oberleutnant zur See* in September 1941, Eick took command of *U-510* from *Fregattenkapitän* Karl Neitzel on 22 May 1943. He took *U-510* out on his first patrol on 10 June, and headed across the Central Atlantic to the coast of Guiana, where he made contact with Convoy TJ1 on 8 July. During that same morning he torpedoed two ships, sinking the Norwegian tanker MV *B.P. Newton* and damaging the Latvian SS *Everagra*. The Norwegian tanker had a cargo of about 14,700 tons of aviation fuel. When she was struck by the torpedo her cargo was immediately ignited by the explosion and flaming fuel sprayed over the stern and bridge, destroying all lifeboats apart from one on the starboard side. The men on watch below were killed before they were able to stop the engines. Of a crew of forty-seven, twenty-three were lost. Two hours later Eick sank the US SS *Eldena*. On the 10th he sank the Latvian MV *Scandinavia* and continued with his patrol but had no further success. He returned to Lorient on 29 August.

On 3 November, he left for the Indian Ocean and headed towards the Cape Verde Islands and then further south. On 10 December, *U-510* was reported by an Ascension-based Liberator, which called up US warships. *U-510* then found itself being hunted by elements of TG 41.1 and TG 41.3 from the 11th to the 13th, but managed to escape. In January 1944, *U-510* reached the Indian Ocean, and after being refuelled Eick took his boat north, to patrol in the Gulf of Aden. On 22 April he made two attacks and sank the British tanker MV *San Alvavo* and the US tanker SS *E.G. Seubert* and damaged the Norwegian tanker MV *Erling Brövig*. The *E.G. Seubert* was struck by a single torpedo about 200 miles from Aden; the torpedo struck the ship on the post side. The explosion blew one of the after machine guns over the side and started a small fire. The engines were stopped, as the tanker settled rapidly with a list to port. Only one lifeboat could be launched before the ship suddenly capsized and sank by the stern, twelve minutes after being hit. Most of the crew jumped overboard and had to swim through oil several inches thick. One officer, two men and three armed guards, including the commanding officer, were lost.

In March, *U-510* searched for ships in the Arabian Sea. He sank the Norwegian MV *Tarifa* on 7 March, and on the 19th he sank the US SS *John A Poor* north-west of the Laccadive Islands. He sank a sailing vessel on the 24th by gunfire and three days later *U-510* sank the British whaler HMS *Maaløy*, with the loss of the entire crew of twenty-six men. Eick returned to port on 5 April. Promoted to *Kapitänleutnant* in April shortly after his return to port, he was in Batavia in the New Year, and left for the South Atlantic. On 23 February 1945, he sank the Canadian SS *Point Pleasant Park* north-west of Cape Town. He took *U-510* across the Equator on 21 March, and although his intention was to go to a Norwegian port, he put in at St. Nazaire due to lack of fuel. On 12 May, he was captured by the French authorities, being released on 26 July 1947. He settled in Germany and died at the age of ninety-nine on 12 April 2015.

Other awards:
12 Jan 1940: Iron Cross 2nd Class
19 Oct 1940: Destroyers War Badge
01 Sep 1942: U-boat War Badge
01 Aug 1943: Iron Cross 1st Class
16 Mar 1944: German Cross in Gold

Horst-Arno FENSKI
Oberleutnant zur See
9 ships sunk, 53,649 tons
3 ships damaged, 9,634 tons

Knight's Cross: Awarded the Knight's Cross on 26 November 1943 as *Oberleutnant zur See* and as commander of *U-410* for his leadership skills and for sinking six ships for a total of 39,600 shipping tons.

Horst-Arno Fenski is credited with sinking seven merchant ships and two warships, including HMS *Penelope* in February 1944. He was born on 3 November 1918, in Königsberg, Germany. He began his naval career as an Officer Candidate in October 1937. He completed the usual training aboard the sail training ship *Horst Wessel*, and the battleship *Schleswig-Holstein* from February 1938. From December 1939 until April 1940 he served aboard the battleship *Gneisenau* and participated in the ship's first combat operation on patrols between Iceland and the Faroe Islands, together with her sister-ship *Scharnhorst*.

In May 1940, Fenski was commissioned as a *Leutnant zur See*, and transferred to the U-boat service. On completion of his training he joined *U-742*, serving as First Watch Officer under the command of *Kapitänleutnant* Karl-Ernst Schroeter. He took part in four patrols in the Atlantic in which five ships were sunk and one damaged. He was given his own chance at command on 16 June 1942, when he took over the training boat *U-34*. On 2 February 1943, Fenski took command of *U-410*, a Type VIIC boat. He left port for his first war patrol as a U-boat commander on 9 February, and together with six other boats headed for operations west of Portugal. On the 12th a southbound convoy was sighted 200 miles west of Cape Finisterre, but bad weather prevented Fenski from making any attacks. By the 21st, *U-410* and the other boats headed for Gibraltar. Five boats, *U-410*, *U-103*, *U-107*, *U-445* and *U-511*, were stationed from the 28th at the approach of the Gibraltar Straits. On 4 March, the boats were directed to Convoy KMS10 but because of a strong Allied escort they were ordered further west. On the 6th Fenski sighted another convoy and torpedoed two ships, sinking the British SS *Fort Battle River* and damaging another. Promoted to *Oberleutnant zur See* on 18 March, he headed for his home base.

During his next two patrols, which lasted from 26 April until 30 August, *U-410* was depth charged by aircraft and slightly damaged, and on 20 August sank the SS *John Bell* and the SS *Richard Henderson*. On 12 September, Fenski took his boat for a patrol off the Algerian and Tunisian coasts, where on the 26th he sank the Norwegian SS *Christian Michelsen* about 30 miles east of Bona. When the torpedo struck the ship

(Wehrkundearchiv)

immediately exploded and sank in less than a minute. Forty-seven men were lost; thirty-five of them were Norwegian, including the master. Three men miraculously survived and were picked up from their raft by one of the escort ships. On the evening of the 30th Fenski sank the British SS *Fort Howe* and the British tanker SS *Empire Commerce*. His final patrol as commander of *U-410* began on 3 February 1944, when Fenski left to operate off the Italian coast, south of Rome, where there was a lot of activity after the Allied landings at Anzio on 22 January. He sank the SS *Fort St. Nicholas* on 15 February, and on the 18th sank the cruiser HMS *Penelope* in the Gulf of Gaeta. *Penelope* had taken part in the shelling of Anzio, during the invasion and on 17 February she turned towards Naples to resupply. She was ordered to return to Anzio immediately after, and began to steer a course and was zigzagging at 26 knots when Fenski sighted her. Having just missed the chance of attacking an Allied landing craft, Fenski attacked the unescorted cruiser. Though HMS *Penelope*'s high speed called for careful calculation she nonetheless provided an easy target. The ship sank within two minutes of the second torpedo exploding, going down with about 400 of her crew. Of the almost 200 survivors who managed to swim to the rescue boats, thirteen drowned before they could be dragged from the water.

In the same area on the evening of the 19th, Fensi attacked a destroyer, but missed, and the following day he sank the landing ship USS *LST-348*, before returning to port. The first torpedo ruptured the bulkheads in several compartments and tore out the deck in a length about 40ft. Lookouts had noticed an unidentified object off the port quarter, thought to be a U-boat, the ship fired one shot and this happened simultaneously with the hit of a second torpedo. The blast broke the ship in two, causing a fire which

The light cruiser HMS Penelope *which was sunk by* U-410 *on 18 February 1944 while en route to Naples. She sank immediately after being hit in the boiler room. She was returning from bombarding enemy positions during Operation Shingle, the landings at Anzio, in which she was part of the Gunfire Support Group. (Author's collection)*

lasted for two minutes and swept down over the entire stern. The order to abandon ship was given and all five rafts were launched. The commanding officer was the last to leave the ship and as the rafts paddled away the ship broke in two and sank. Four officers and twenty ratings were lost. On 11 March, *U-410* was severely damaged in an air attack by US bombers in Toulon and one member of her crew was killed. The boat was decommissioned on 22 March, and Fenski, who had been promoted, went on leave. When he returned in April, he was appointed commander of *U-371*, a Type VIIC, boat built in Kiel. Fenski left for operations on the 23rd, and during the early hours of 3 May he torpedoed and damaged the destroyer escort USS *Menges*. He then ordered his boat to surface to see the full extent of the damage to the ship. As the boat surface it was spotted by two destroyers, the USS *Pride* and USS *Joseph E. Campbell*, so Fenski submerged to try and get away. Meanwhile the two destroyers had been joined by another four ships and the hunt intensified to cover a wider area. *U-371*, which had been lying on the bottom and was forced to surface because of foul air and low batteries. Upon resurfacing she sighted the French destroyer *Sénégalais* waiting and she immediately opened fire on the U-boat. Fenski knew there was no hope against a destroyer that was so close, and he ordered his men to abandon ship and prepare to scuttle. The engineer, Ferdinand Ritschel, and a crew member went below to open ballast-tank vents and were never seen again. His final action was to fire a torpedo which struck *Sénégalais*, causing serious damage. Of his forty-nine crew, four drowned and the rest, including Fenski, were rescued from a beach by US forces.

Fenski spent two years in a prisoner-of-war camp near New York, being released on 4 May 1946 when he returned to Germany. He settled in Hamburg-Wandesbek where he died on 10 February 1965; he was only 46 years old.

Other awards:
09 Oct 1941: Long Service Award 4th Class
10 Oct 1941: Iron Cross 2nd Class
28 Oct 1941: High Seas Fleet Badge
13 Dec 1941: U-boat War Badge
28 Mar 1943: Iron Cross 1st Class

Karl FLEIGE
Kapitänleutnant
1 ship sunk, 400 tons
2 ships damaged, 7,801 tons

Knight's Cross: Awarded as *Oberleutnant zur See* and as commander of *U-18* on 18 July 1944, in recognition of his leadership and service to the U-boat arm as well as sinking one ship and damaging two others.

Karl Fleige was born on 5 September 1905, in Hildesheim, Lower Saxony, and joined the *Reichsmarine* in October 1924 as a seaman. He spent the next few years on torpedo boats and cruisers and between September 1934 a September 1936 he served aboard the sail training ship *Gorch Fock*.

(Scherzer)

In October 1937, Fleige transferred to the U-boat service and after a few months training, he was assigned in May 1938 to *U-20*, which was under the command of *Oberleutnant zur See* Karl-Heinz Moehle, a future Knight's Cross holder. He served as an *Obersteuermann* or Petty Officer and Watch Officer. In June 1940, Moehle, now a *Kapitänleutnant* took over command of *U-123* and he requested that his former Petty Officer, Fleige join him, the request was granted. Fleige spent fourteen months aboard *U-123* and took part in five war patrols in which sixteen ships were sunk.

In August 1941, Fleige was transferred to join the 5th U-boat Flotilla in Kiel; once again he was under the command of Moehle. On 1 April 1942 he was commissioned as a *Leutnant zur See* and began training as a U-boat commander, which included attendance at the Naval Academy in Flensburg. He was promoted to *Oberleutnant zur See* in October and on 3 December he was appointed commander of *U-18*, a Type IIB boat, taking over from *Oberleutnant zur See* Friedrich-Wilhelm Wissmann. He carried out seven patrols as commander of *U-18*, between 26 May 1943 and 24 July 1944. In total Fleige spent 203 days at sea but sank only one ship, the Soviet trawler (minesweeper) *TSC-11* at 21:51 hours on 29 September. The ship was hit by a torpedo which struck under the aft mast after almost two minutes and further detonations she sank very quickly by the stern about 25 miles north-west of Poti. Fifteen of her crew were lost and twenty-three were rescued. The following day he torpedoed and damaged the Soviet patrol craft *SKA-0132*. Fleige had to break off the attack because a searchlight from the coast dazzled the Germans. On 18 November he damaged another ship, the Soviet tanker *Josif Stalin*. She was struck by two torpedoes at 17:15 hours about 14 miles west-north-west of Lazarevskoje and reported the sinking of the ship after twenty minutes. However, the crew had managed to extinguish the flames aboard and the tanker continued to Tuapse where she was repaired and later returned to active service. At the end of his final patrol, he put in at Konstanza and four days later *U-18* was seriously damaged in a raid by Soviet aircraft. The Germans then evacuated the harbour on 25 August and *U-18* was scuttled.

In December 1944, Fleige was an instructor with the 24th U-boat Flotilla and later transferring to the 1st U-boat Training Division in Hamburg under the command of *Kapitän zur See* Hans-Georg Poske. On 1 April 1945 Fleige was promoted to *Kapitänleutnant* and on 4 May, a few days before the German surrender, he supervised the destruction of *U-4712*, a Type XXIII boat, one of the new so-called *Elektroboats*. Without making a single war patrol it was scuttled in Kiel, just one day after it was commissioned. Fleige surrendered the same day, and only spent a brief period in captivity, being released on 1 August 1945. He died on 16 February 1975 in Erzhausen, Gandersheim, Germany.

Other awards:
02 Oct 1936: Armed Forces Long Service Award 4th to 1st Class
00 Nov 1939: U-Boat War Badge
00 Nov 1939: Iron Cross 2nd Class
00 Dec 1939: Commemorative Medal of 01 Oct 1938
00.00.194_: Iron Cross 1st Class
08 Oct 1943: German Cross in Gold

Johann <u>Ulrich</u> Hermann FOLKERS
Kapitänleutnant
17 ships sunk, 82,873 tons

Knight's Cross: Awarded as *Kapitänleutnant* on 27 March 1943, whilst commander of *U-125* in recognition of sinking sixteen ships for a total of 78,136 shipping tons.

Ulrich Folkers was born in Kiel on 6 March 1915, and entered the *Reichsmarine* in April 1934 as a cadet. From June 1934 he spent time on board the sail training ship *Gorch Fock* and then the light cruiser *Emden*, before attending various courses at the Naval Academy. From September 1937, he served as Watch Officer with the rank of *Leutnant zur See* once again aboard the *Emden*. He was promoted to *Oberleutnant zur See* in April 1939 and from November served in a similar capacity on board the destroyer *Z8 Bruno Heinemann*.

On 27 April 1940, he transferred to the U-boat service, and attended various training courses, which included both signals and torpedo training. From July he was attached to the 1st U-boat Training Division, and from November he served as Watch Officer on board the torpedo boat *Panther*. On 15 January 1941, he was assigned to *U-37*, where he served as Watch Officer, a position he knew well, whilst under the command of *Kapitänleutnant* Nicolai Clausen. He took part in two war patrols with *U-37*, and continued with his training under Clausen. In April he took over from him as commander.

In November 1941, Folkers was promoted to *Kapitänleutnant* and at the same time was transferred and given command of *U-125*, a Type IXC boat, taking over from *Kapitänleutnant* Günter Kuhnke. He took his new boat out on patrol on 18 December. The patrol lasted sixty-eight days, and although Folkers made contact with two convoys he only sank one ship, the SS *West Ivis*, on 26 January 1942. She was struck by two torpedoes underneath the stack and in the engine room and broke in two and sank in

(Scherzer)

fourteen minutes off Cape Hatteras. The Germans observed lifeboats, but did not question them. They were never seen again: forty-five men were lost. He left port on his second patrol on 4 April, and headed for the Western Atlantic, whilst en route to the Caribbean he sank the US SS *Lammont du Pont* on the evening of 23 April. For the next two weeks *U-125* operated in the western Caribbean around Grand Cayman. During this time Folkers sunk a total of eight ships, which included the Dominican SS *San Rafael*, followed by the US SS *Tuscaloosa City* on 4 May, and he claimed two more ships two days later. On 9 May he sank the Canadian tanker MV *Calgarolite* and on the 14th sank the Honduran SS *Comayagua*. He then continued along the western tip of Cuba where on the 18th he sank two more ships, the US tanker MV *Mercury Sun* and the US SS *Williams J. Salmon*. With his torpedoes almost used up, he began the return journey, arriving in Lorient on 13 June 1942.

His next patrol began in late July and he headed for Freetown and then to the Cape Verde Islands where *U-125* was refuelled. On 1 September 1942, he sank the British SS *Ilorin*, but then had to wait until the 23rd for more success, when he sank the British SS *Bryère* south-west of Freetown. Folkers then torpedoed and sank three more ships, the SS *Baron Ogilvy*, SS *Empire Arocet* and SS *Kumsang*, south-west of Monrovia. The *Kumsang*, a British passenger ship, was struck on the port side amidships in the engine room by a single torpedo. When the ship settled on an even keel, the crew and eight gunners began to abandon ship in eleven of the twelve lifeboats, Only four of the boats got clear as the water rushing into the engine room prevented men on watch below to secure the engines and the vessel was still making headway of about 4 knots when the boats were launched. Many survivors had to jump overboard and swim to several rafts. After about fifteen minutes after being torpedoed the ship sank, rapidly after breaking in two. Remarkably only four crew members were lost and 110 men were rescued. His final victim of this patrol was the British SS *Glendere*, sunk on 8 October. He reached his home port on 6 November. He left on his fourth patrol on 9 December and headed again for the waters of the Caribbean. It was a long patrol, lasting seventy-three days, chasing convoys without any success. He met up with three other boats and they chased a large convoy for three days. By the end of the chase seven tankers had been sunk, none by *U-125*. Another operation against a convoy was cancelled due to strong Allied air cover and Folkers frustrated and disappointed headed for home.

However, Folkers had by this time been responsible for the sinking of sixteen ships and was awarded the Knight's Cross. On 13 April 1943, he left for the North Atlantic, and joined *Specht* Group north-east of Newfoundland. On the 19th another group joined them and by 1 May the two groups waited in an arc formation just off Newfoundland for Convoy SC128. However, due to bad weather the convoy passed through the patrol line and contact was lost. On 4 May a new convoy was sighted; Convoy ONS5, delayed by the bad weather. On the 6th Folkers spotted the British SS *Lorient* and fired a torpedo. She sank south of Cape Farewell, with the loss of the entire crew. Then shortly afterwards a British destroyer rammed *U-125*, but the boat managed to get away. However, *U-125* was soon located by the destroyer HMS *Vidette* and was attacked with depth charges, Hedgehog bombs and gunfire. *U-125* was sunk, and fifty-four men died: there were no survivors.

Other awards:
01 Nov 1936: Bulgarian Order for Military Service 4th Class with Crown
00.00.1936: Officers Cross of the Romanian Order of the Star with Crown
08 Apr 1938: Armed Forces Long Service Award 4th Class
15 Jan 1940: Iron Cross 2nd Class
26 Mar 1941: Iron Cross 1st Class
26 Mar 1941: U-boat War Badge

Hans-Joachim FÖRSTER
Oberleutnant zur See
4 ships sunk, 14,621 tons

Knight's Cross: Awarded as *Oberleutnant zur See* and as commander of *U-480* on 18 October 1944, for the sinking of two merchant ships and two warships, to become the 266th *Kriegsmarine* and the 130th U-boat recipient.

Born on 20 February 1920 in Groß-Köris, Teltow, Hans-Joachim Förster joined the *Kriegsmarine* in October 1938. In September 1939, he was assigned to the 4th Company of the 3rd Naval Petty Officers Training Battalion. From December 1940 he was attached to the destroyer and torpedo boat base at Swinmünde. In April 1941 he was commissioned as a *Leutnant zur See*, and from June served aboard the destroyer *Z29* as Third Watch Officer, and later as Second Watch Officer.

In July 1942, he transferred to the U-boat service and began his training. From December he served on *U-380* as First Watch Officer, under the command of *Kapitänleutnant* Josef Röther, taking part in three war patrols in the Mediterranean. Promoted to *Oberleutnant zur See* in April 1943, he began training as a U-boat commander the following month. In October, he was appointed commander of *U-480*, a Type VIIC boat built in Kiel. He supervised the crew's training and oversaw the loading of supplies and torpedoes before taking out his boat for sea trials in May 1944.

Förster took *U-40* out on its first war patrol on 7 June 1944, when he left Arendal, Norway to operate north-west of the British Isles. His orders were later changed and he headed towards the English Channel. On 13 June, *U-480* shot down a Catalina flying boat of 162 Squadron of the Royal Canadian Air Force. In early July Förster was ordered, together with *U-243* and *U-678*, to pass through the western Channel, en route to the invasion area. The (Scherzer)

boats were recalled and ordered to wait for further instructions, but both *U-243* and *U-678* were sunk and Förster only just managed to get *U-480* away safely and put in at Brest on 7 July.

On 3 August, Förster took *U-480* out and headed once again towards the English Channel, where on the 18th he made an unsuccessful attack on a convoy. On the 21st he sank the Canadian corvette HMCS *Alberni* by torpedo. The ship was on patrol east of the channel to the Normandy beaches when she was struck on the port side aft of the engine room and sank by the stern within around thirty seconds about 25 miles south-east of St. Catherine's Point, Isle of Wight. Four officers and fifty-five ratings were lost. On the 22nd the British minesweeper HMS *Loyalty* was sunk when it was struck by a Gnat acoustic torpedo and sank by the stern within ten minutes south-east of the Isle of Wight. The commander and nineteen ratings were lost; the survivors were picked up after a few hours by two landing ships. The following day Förster torpedoed and damaged the British SS *Fort Yale* which sank 17 miles south-east of St. Catherine's Point with the loss of just one man. Then after sinking a straggler from Convoy FTM74 on the 25th, *U-480* was hunted for seven hours but managed to escape, due to Förster's skill as a commander and its special Alberich[1] coating. *U-480* then headed for Trondheim, Norway where it arrived on 4 October.

After some leave Förster took *U-480* out of Trondheim and headed for British coastal waters on 6 January 1945. On 24 February, *U-480* was at the western entrance to the English Channel when it encountered Convoy BTC78. Förster torpedoed the SS *Oriskany* and she sank between the Scillies and Land's End. Now the British started to hunt for *U-480*. They soon found it, and it was sunk. There were no survivors: forty-eight men were dead. It was assumed that *U-480* had been destroyed south-east of the Scilly Isles by the frigates HMS *Duckworth* and HMS *Rowley* shortly after sinking the SS *Oriskany*. However in 1998, a U-boat wreck was discovered some 20 miles south-west of the Isle of Wight and 300 miles from the position of HMS *Duckworth* and *Rowley*'s action. It has become clear that *U-480* was in fact sunk when it entered a secret minefield 'Brazier D2', some time between 29 January and 20 February 1945. Then in 2010 a diving team found the wreck of *U-1208* who they believed had in fact sunk the SS *Oriskany*.

Other awards:
01 Feb 1941: Minesweepers Badge
17 Feb 1942: Iron Cross 2nd Class
00.00.1942: Iron Cross 1st Class
18 May 1943: U-Boat War Badge
12 Sep 1944: German Cross in Gold

---

1 *U-480* was an experimental boat, considered the first stealth submarine and was equipped with a special rubber coating (codename *Alberich*, after the German mythological character who had the ability to become invisible) which made it difficult for the British to locate using their sonar, known as ASDIC.

Siegfried von FORSTNER

Korvettenkapitän
15 ships sunk, 71,036 tons
3 ships damaged, 28,682 tons

(Scherzer)

Knight's Cross: On 9 February 1943, as *Kapitänleutnant* and as commander of *U-402*, in recognition of sinking seven ships and damaging two others, to become the 80th U-boat commander and the 149th *Kriegsmarine* recipient.

Siegfried von Forstner was the son of an aristocratic Prussian family whose men had served for generations as Army and Navy officers. He was born on 19 September 1910 in Hannover, he had three brothers, his younger brother Wolfgang-Friedrich would also become a U-boat commander, his other two brothers, Ernst Richard and Hans Dietrich were Army officers. Wolfgang, however, would be the only brother to survive the Second World War. Their great-grandfather and grandfather had been army officers, and their father was a *General* who had won the *Pour le mérite* (the 'Blue Max').

Forstner entered the *Reichsmarine* in April 1930 as an Officer Candidate and spent the next four years training. He served for almost eighteen months aboard the light cruiser *Emden* before being admitted to the Naval Academy at Flensburg. From June 1932 until November 1934 he attended various training courses which included navigation, gunnery, torpedo and officer training. From November 1934 he served on the 'pocket battleship' *Admiral Scheer* as a *Leutnant*, and from April 1936 he was attached to the staff of the Commanding Admiral of the Baltic Sea. Promoted to *Oberleutnant zur See* in May 1936, and was assigned to the light cruiser *Nürnberg* as Artillery Technical Officer from August 1937. He took part in the non-intervention patrols during the Spanish Civil War, and during the early stages of the Second World War when the ship was used to lay defensive minefields Forstner remained onboard until January 1940, apart from a brief secondment to the 'pocket battleship' *Deutschland* from August to September 1938.

He was promoted to *Kapitänleutnant* in May 1939 and transferred to the U-boat service in April 1940. On completion of his training he took command of *U-59*, used from October 1940 as a training vessel, part of the 22nd U-boat Flotilla at Gotenhafen. In April 1941, he was appointed commander of *U-402*, a Type VIIC boat built by Danziger Werft. After completion of the standard sea trials the boat was ready for its first war patrol. *U-402* left Kiel on 26 October for an area south of Iceland. Forstner was ordered to remain in the area, together with three other U-boats to support the *Admiral Scheer*. However, the operation did not take place and Forstner was ordered west to join *Störtebecker* Group in the central North Atlantic and hunt for convoys. Although a number were spotted Forstner failed to sink anything and arrived at St. Nazaire on 9 December.

His next patrol lasted thirty days; he left port on 11 January 1942 for the area around Gibraltar. On the 16th he torpedoed and damaged the British troopship the MV *Llangibby Castle*. On 13 April, during his third patrol, he sank the British SS *Empire Progress*: she was struck by one of two torpedoes south of Cape Race. The torpedo was a dud but the ship stopped nevertheless and was missed by a third torpedo. Seven minutes later a fourth struck the ship and caused her to sink within eight minutes. The master, seven crew and four gunners were lost. He then sank the Soviet SS *Ashkhabad* on the 30th, in shallow water near Cape Lookout, North Carolina. On 2 May he sank the armed patrol yacht USS *Cythera* west of Cape Clear. Forstner had been stalking the ship for over two hours and he fired three torpedoes of which one struck the ship dead centre and the ship immediately split in two and the forward half rose steeply out of the water. The ship sank very quickly and at least two of her depth charges exploded underwater. Of her seventy-one crew only two survived. His next patrol began on 16 June, when he took *U-402* out for operations off the US east coast. On 14 July the boat was spotted by aircraft off Cape Hatteras and was damaged by depth charges but managed to escape, and returned to port.

After minor repairs Forstner took *U-402* out on 4 October, for operations in the North Atlantic, where he joined *Panther* Group west of Ireland. On the 16th, the twelve boats of this group and ten from *Wotan* Group were ordered to attack Convoy ON137. However, the weather was bad and contact was soon lost. Boats from *Wotan* Group left for home on the 18th, when a gale developed and the following day the operation was called off. *U-402* and the other boats from *Panther* Group formed a new patrol line on the 24th, 400 miles east of Newfoundland. On the 30th Convoy SC107 was sighted south of Cape Race and was attacked. Several attacks were made before *U-402* claimed success. On 2 November Forstner closed with the convoy and sunk four ships, the British SS *Dalcroy*, the Greek SS *Rinos*, and the British SS *Empire Leopard* and SS *Empire Antelope*. *U-402* also damaged the SS *Empire Sunrise*, later sunk by *U-84*. The U-boats were eventually driven off by Liberators and made for their home port.

On 14 January 1943, Forstner left for the North Atlantic, and *U-402* joined *Landsknecht* Group west of Ireland. It wasn't until the beginning of February that the group was able to begin attacks. On the 7th, Forstner made several attacks and he sank five ships, which included the British SS *Toward*, the American tanker SS *Robert E. Hopkins* and the Greek SS *Kalliopi*. He also damaged the Norwegian tanker MV *Daghild*, which was later sunk by *U-608* whilst under the command of *Kapitänleutnant* Rolf Struckmeier (holder of the German Cross in Gold). He then sank the American troop transport ship USS *Henry R. Mallory* about 600 miles south-south-west of Iceland. She began to list after thirty minutes or so, and two of her lifeboats had been destroyed by the initial explosion, a third could not be launched and two more on either side capsized in the rough seas. Only three boats with 175 men cleared the ship, many others jumped into the water and tried in vain to reach the rafts. None of the other ships in the convoy had noticed that the troop transporter had been hit. The 222 survivors were found four hours later – 272 men were lost. During the early hours of 8 February *U-402* sank the British SS *Newton Ash*. With all his torpedoes gone Forstner headed for home, arriving at La Pallice on 23 February.

Promoted to *Korvettenkapitän* on 12 April 1943 he began his seventh patrol on the 21st when he joined *Ansel 1* group, forming a patrol line east of Newfoundland. A convoy was located, and several attacks were made which caused the convoy to split into several groups. By 5 May, late in the afternoon fog came down and the operation was abandoned. Twelve ships had been sunk and six U-boats had been lost. *U-402* had made no attacks. On the 7th, the U-boat groups were ordered east of Newfoundland to operate against two eastbound convoys. On the 11th, a convoy was sighted and Forstner made an attack and sank two ships, the British SS *Antigone* and the Norwegian SS *Grado* north-west of the Azores. Another convoy was located on the 12th, but the boats were driven off. When the escort carrier HMS *Biter* arrived to join the escort the operation was called off and Forstner refuelled for the journey home.

On 4 September, Forstner left for the Atlantic, his eighth patrol. *U-402* was one of fourteen boats that had set out to form a patrol line just off Iceland. They were joined by six other boats, and waited to intercept a convoy. The boats remained submerged and there was radio silence, secrecy had to be maintained if they were to prevent their presence becoming known to the Allies. However, on the 19th, *U-341*, which should have been submerged was spotted on the surface, and was sunk by a Canadian aircraft. The next day, the U-boats closed in on the convoys, but on the night of 21st/22nd fog came down, and when it lifted an Allied aircraft was spotted and the boats on the surface had to fight it out. *U-373* was attacked by a Liberator, and *U-402* arrived to help. The aircraft came in for a strafing attack and fire was exchanged until *U-402* went in to fog. Further attacks were made on the convoy and more ships were sunk, although *U-402* was again unsuccessful. On the 17th, *U-402* joined the newly-formed *Rossbach* Group in the central North Atlantic, to operate against Convoy ON203. On 1 October, *Rossbach* Group moved northwards to intercept ONS19 and then from the 3rd went east to intercept Convoy ON204. Neither convoy was found. Now short of fuel various U-boats, including Forstner and *U-402* headed south to refuel. It was always risky to stop and refuel as the boats were under constant threat of attack by destroyers and by aircraft. However, *U-402* was refuelled successfully and left the area. On the 13th, she was sighted by an Avenger aircraft. Unable to use his homing torpedo whilst *U-402* remained on the surface, the pilot called for assistance. The arrival of a US Wildcat aircraft caused Forstner to decide to dive – that was a mistake. As the boat dived the pilot took his chance and dropped his torpedo: it was a direct hit and *U-402* was destroyed. There were no survivors: fifty men were killed.

Forstner's wife Anna-Maria made distinctive red pom-poms for the crew of *U-402* to wear on their caps. Forstner and his wife saved their home in Hamburg from burning during air-raids in August 1932, by staying on the roof and extinguishing incendiary bombs.

Other awards:
02 Oct 1936: Armed Forces Long Service Award 4th Class
20 Dec 1939: Commemorative Medal of 01 Oct 1938
18 Feb 1942: Iron Cross 2nd Class
07 Aug 1942: Iron Cross 1st Class
07 Aug 1942 U-boat War Badge

Rudolf <u>Heinz</u> FRANKE
Kapitänleutnant
4 ships sunk, 13,935 tons

Knight's Cross: Awarded on 30 November 1943 to become the 107th U-boat commander to be awarded the Knight's Cross as *Kapitänleutnant* and as commander of *U-262*, in recognition of his success in sinking four ships for a total of 13,935 shipping tons.

Heinz Franke was a Berliner, born on 30 November 1915, and he began his career as an Officer Candidate with the *Kriegsmarine* in April 1936. After attending the usual training courses he was assigned to the battleship *Gneisenau* as a *Leutnant zur See*, where he served as the Anti-aircraft Officer from December 1938. He was aboard *Gneisenau* during her sea trials and when war broke out in September 1939. On the 4th, the day after the British declaration of war, *Gneisenau* was attacked by fourteen Wellington bombers – they failed to hit the ship. Franke also took part during the ship's first operation together with her sister-ship *Scharnhorst*, during the invasion of Denmark and Norway.

In October 1940 Franke was promoted to *Oberleutnant zur See* and transferred to the U-boat service and on completion of further training he was assigned to *U-84* as First Watch Officer. He took part in two war patrols from April 1941, whilst under the command of *Kapitänleutnant* Horst Uphoff. On 16 January 1942, Franke took command of the training boat *U-148* until October. He then took command of *U-262*, a Type VIIC boat, and left for his first patrol on 5 November 1942. He left Narvik for the North Atlantic, and was directed to Convoy ONS144 which was sighted on the 15th. Three days later Franke sank HNoMS *Montbretia*, a Norwegian corvette. She was hit in the starboard bow by one of three torpedoes. The impact caused an explosion which opened a large

hole in the bow, and the ammunition of the 4in gun also exploded, which killed three men. The roof of the Asdic (sonar) deck came down, the bridge was distorted and the bulkheads in the wheelhouse were stoved in, killing the helmsman. The order was given to abandon ship. Then the second torpedo struck on the port side in the boiler room, breaking the ship in two and caused it to quickly sink. Of seventy officers and men, a total of forty-seven were lost. The operation against the convoy lasted for five days, ending on the 21st because of fog. On 9 December, he sank the SS *Ocean Crusader* east of Newfoundland. She had been struck by two torpedoes whilst on her maiden voyage. The sea was very rough and although a distress signal was sent there were no survivors – fifty men were lost.

On the night of 5/6 February 1943, during his second patrol, Franke sank the Polish steamship *Zagloba*. *U-262* was located soon after and was

(Wehrkundearchiv)

damaged during a depth-charge attack by the destroyers HMS *Beverley* and *Vimy*. She was further damaged during another attack by the French corvette *Lobélia*. Franke then headed for his home port, arriving in La Pallice on 15 February. After some repairs *U-262* was ready to leave port once again, and left for Canadian waters on 27 March. Franke was ordered to carry out Special Task 'Magpie'. The plan was for *U-262* to pick up German POWs, who would escape from Camp 70 and rendezvous with his boat at North Point, Prince Edward Island. However, all did not go to plan. Franke found himself being hunted by Allied ships and then encountered areas of surface ice and the boat became stuck. Franke decided to break free, submerged and then proceeded to his destination. After sixteen hours an attempt was made to surface but by this failed due to thick ice. He then moved ahead, blowing his tanks the boat rose and burst through the ice. The U-boat had been badly damaged by the ice and the armament had been rendered almost useless. He reached his destination on the correct date but had to dive due to aircraft in the area. He did manage to surface several times but the planned escape by the POWs had been called off. He was promoted to *Kapitänleutnant* on 1 April and soon after *U-262* was ordered back to port – returning to La Pallice on 25 May.

On 24 July, *U-262* left for the Central Atlantic, and on the fourth day *U-262* and *U-760* were spotted by Allied aircraft but managed to escape. On 8 August *U-262* was sighted again on the surface by two aircraft from the escort carrier USS *Card*, an Avenger and a Wildcat. The fighter made an attack, but the Avenger aircraft was seriously damaged by anti-aircraft fire and its radioman was killed. The Wildcat fighter made another attack and then that was shot down and crashed into the sea. The pilot was never found. Franke later made an unsuccessful at attack on USS *Card* and headed for home.

In October 1943, during his fifth patrol, Franke attacked Convoys MKS28 and SLI38 together with seven other boats, off the north-west coast of Spain. On 31 October, Franke sank the Norwegian steamer *Hallfried*. A destroyer was also attacked using an acoustic torpedo designed to home in on propeller noise. The detonations were heard as were the sounds of the sinking vessels breaking up, but no losses were recorded by the Allies and the destroyer was never identified. On 9 November Franke made an attack on a destroyer, again using an acoustic torpedo, but the results were the same as before, inconclusive. On the 28th *U-262* made another attack on Convoys MKS31 and SKI40 – three torpedoes were fired and all three were heard to explode but there was never any confirmation of ships sunk.

From February 1944, *Kapitänleutnant* Franke was attached to the Naval Ship Building Commission, part of the *Kriegsmarine* High Command (*Oberkommando der Kriegsmarine*). In May he was assigned to the Staff of Naval Group Command West, and from July was assigned to the Navy's *Kleinkampfverband*, serving as head of training and instruction. In April 1945, Franke was placed in command of a Type XXI boat, *U-2502*. These were huge boats, having a displacement of almost 1,800 tons, and travelled at 16 knots with a range of 11,150 nautical miles. They were armed with four 30mm anti-aircraft guns and carried twenty-three torpedoes. If enough had been produced in time they could almost certainly have swung the Battle of the Atlantic in favour of Germany.

Franke sailed from Horten in Norway to England to surrender his boat during Operation Deadlight in May 1945, never having had the opportunity to take his boat into action. He was released from captivity on 17 November 1945. He later entered the West German Navy, the *Bundesmarine*, rising to the rank of *Fregattenkapitän* in September 1967. He retired in March 1972, and he died on 5 April 2003, in Sasbach, western Baden-Württemberg at the age of eighty-seven.

Other awards:
23 Feb 1940: Iron Cross 2nd Class
03 Apr 1940: Armed Forces Long Service Award 4th Class
21 Nov 1941: U-boat War Badge
16 May 1942: High Seas Fleet Badge
12 Dec 1942: Iron Cross 1st Class
23 Mar 1944: Cuff title '*Afrika*.'
24 Jan 1945: U-boat Combat Clasp in Bronze

Wilhelm August FRANKEN
Korvettenkapitän
4 ships sunk, 12,887 tons
2 ships damaged, 17,565 tons

Knight's Cross: Awarded as *Kapitänleutnant* and as commander of *U-565* on 30 April 1943, in recognition of his leadership and skill as a U-boat commander which included the sinking of four ships and damaging another two.

Wilhelm Franken was born on 11 September 1914 in Schildesche, Bielefeld, in the region North-Rhine Westphalia just after the start of the First World War. He entered the *Kriegsmarine* as an Officer Candidate in April 1935 and was attached to the 4th Company of the II. *Schiffsstamabteilung*. Franken completed several training course, including service aboard the sail training ship *Gorch Fock* and the light cruiser *Karlsruhe*. From June 1937, he attended training courses at the Naval Academy in Flensburg and from October he served aboard the destroyer *Z6 Theodor Riedel*.

In March 1938, he served in the 3rd Company of the 2nd Naval Artillery Battalion, and was commissioned as a *Leutnant zur See* the following month. From October 1938 until September 1939 he was attached to the Danube Flotilla as an gunnery officer, and was promoted to *Oberleutnant zur See* in October. Franken then served as a divisional officer aboard the battleship *Scharnhorst*. In October 1940, he transferred to the U-boat service, and on completion of his training he was assigned as First Watch Officer to *U-331*, under *Oberleutnant zur See* Hans-Diedrich von Tiesenhausen. He took part in three war patrols with Tiesenhausen and during their third patrol *U-331* sank the British battleship HMS *Barham*.

In March 1942, on completion of a commander's course, Franken was appointed commander of *U-565*, a Type VIIC boat. Promoted to *Kapitänleutnant* on 1 April, his

(Scherzer)

first war patrol as commander began on ten days later, when he left for the Eastern Mediterranean. On the 23rd, whilst operating against the supply ships on their way to Tobruk he torpedoed and sank the British SS *Kirkland*, part of Convoy TA36. She was struck about 35 miles east-north-east of Sidi Barrani. The ship developed a list and then stopped. It was then hit by two more torpedoes and sunk with the loss of only one crew member. During his next four patrols he had no success, and was attacked by a Blenheim aircraft on 2 June, but managed to escape any damage. On 29 October he made an unsuccessful attack against the aircraft carrier HMS *Furious*, reporting four hits but these were never confirmed. He returned to his home base at La Spezia on 13 November. His next patrol was in the Western Mediterranean, and whilst patrolling off the Algerian coast he torpedoed and sank the destroyer HMS *Partridge*. On 22 November, Franken made contact with Convoy KMF5 and attacked the SS *Cameronia*, but only damaged her. On 24 February 1943, during his next patrol, again off the coast of Algeria, he damaged the US merchant ship *Nathanael Greene*. This vessel was later hit by an aircraft torpedo and was towed into harbour but was later declared a total loss. On the 27th, he torpedoed and damaged the tanker MV *Seminole* and returned to La Spezia on 5 March. On 8 April, Franken left for the Western Mediterranean and took *U-565* out to engage Convoy U-G57. On the 20th, he sank the US SS *Michigan* and the French troop transport *Sidi-Bel-Abbès*, which was struck by at least two torpedoes about 60 miles west of Oran and sank with the loss of over 610 men, mainly Senegalese soldiers. There were 520 survivors who were later picked up and taken to port. During his next two patrols he claimed a hit on a southbound convoy near Salerno but this was never confirmed.

From October 1943, he served as a staff officer with the Commanding Admiral of U-boat, *Admiral* Hans-Georg von Friedeburg. On 13 January 1945, a fire broke out on the naval accommodation ship *Daressalam* in Kiel harbour. Franken had been on board and was one of the three former U-boat officers killed. Franken was buried with full military honours and was buried in the Kiel Military Cemetery, and lies in block VII, grave 366. He was posthumously promoted to *Korvettenkapitän* which was backdated to 1 January 1945.

Other awards:
04 Apr 1939: Long Service Award 4th Class
14 Apr 1940: Iron Cross 2nd Class
31 May 1940: Commemorative Medal of 01 Oct 1938
15 Oct 1941: U-Boat War Badge
28 Jan 1942: Iron Cross 1st Class
28 Jan 1942: High Seas Fleet Badge
30 Mar 1942: Italian War Cross with Swords
29 May 1943: Italian Bravery Medal in Bronze

<u>Fritz</u> Hermann Günter FRAUENHEIM
Fregattenkapitän
18 ships sunk, 78,248 tons
2 ships damaged 15,655 tons

(Scherzer)

Knight's Cross: Awarded on 29 August 1940, as *Kapitänleutnant* and as commander of *U-101* for sinking eleven ships for a total of 51,375 shipping tons, and for damaging the British cruiser HMS *Belfast*.

Fritz Frauenheim was born on 9 March 1912, in Friedenau, Tempelhof-Schöneburg in Berlin. He joined the *Reichsmarine* in April 1930 as a cadet and from July 1930 until September 1935, he underwent basic training which included gunnery, communications, signal training, as well as attending the coastal artillery school and the torpedo school at Flensburg. From June 1934 he served aboard the light cruiser *Karlsruhe*, and in October was commissioned as a *Leutnant zur See*. On 1 May 1936, he served as Watch Officer aboard *U-25*, and began to rise rapidly through the ranks, being promoted to *Oberleutnant zur See* in June.

It appears that he spent some time with the German forces supporting the Spanish Nationalists during the Spanish Civil War. Although his exact role is unknown, it can be assumed he took part in these actions because he was awarded the Spanish Cross in June 1939. Frauenheim was commissioned as a *Leutnant zur See* in October 1934 and by April 1939 he had been promoted to *Kapitänleutnant*.

In October 1937, he was appointed commander of *U-21*, a Type IIB boat built by GermaniaWerft in Kiel. His first war patrol was against British naval forces, and began on 9 September 1939. On the 22nd, he attacked a destroyer off Berwick-upon-Tweed but the torpedo misfired. He returned to Kiel on 1 October. He left port again for the Firth of Forth on 22 October, to take part in minelaying operations. He laid mines off the entrance to Rosyth on 4 November, and the British cruiser HMS *Belfast* detonated one of these mines and was damaged, and was out of action for over two years. Two other ships set off the mines and were sunk, the netlayer HMS *Bayonet* and the British SS *Royal Archer*. His next patrol, although short, was successful, he sank the SS *Arcturus* off Peterhead and the Finnish steamer *Mercator* about 12 miles south-east of Buchan Ness with the loss of just one member of her crew on 1 December, returning to Kiel just four days later. During his last patrol of the year he sank the Swedish SS *Mars* and SS *Carl Henckel*. Both were struck at the same time on 21 December and sank within about ninety seconds with the total loss of twenty-eight men.

In March 1940, Frauenheim was transferred and took command of *U-101*. He took the boat out for its sea trials in April, and the following month left Kiel for its first war patrol. He headed for the western entrance of the English Channel, together with *U-29*, but because of the thick fog they had no success. He were then ordered to join *Rösing* Group, and with five other U-boats was now under the tactical command of *Kapitänleutnant* Hans Rösing. They were ordered to assemble just west of Cape Ortegal on 12 June, and wait for Convoy US3, which included the RMS *Queen Mary* and two other large liners, carrying 26,000 troops from Australia and New Zealand. The convoy was escorted by HMS *Hood*, an aircraft carrier and some cruisers. However when the convoy had failed to appear by

HMS Belfast, *a light cruiser, built in Belfast in 1939. She struck a magnetic mine laid on 4 November 1939 by* U-21 *near May Island, Firth of Forth. The explosion broke the back of the ship causing extensive damage, and injuring twenty-one crew members. She was taken in tow to Rosyth for repairs, and then onto Plymouth where she remained until December 1942. She was finally decommissioned in 1963, and is now on display on the River Thames.* (Author's collection)

17 June, the *Rösing* Group was disbanded. Frauenheim continued to patrol west of the English Channel and later moved just west of the Bay of Biscay. On the 30 May he sank the British SS *Stanhall* and the following day he sank the British SS *Orangemoor*, and on 2 June he claimed the SS *Polycarp* south of Land's End. *U-101* then sailed west of Vigo, where Frauenheim sank the Greek SS *Mount Hymettus* by gunfire on the 11th and torpedoed and sank the British SS *Earlspark* the next day. On the morning of the 14th, he sank the Greek SS *Antonis Georgandis*, and two days later he sank the British MV *Wellington Star* (13,212 tons), by torpedo north-west of Cape Finisterre. Frauenheim returned to port on 25 June, he had sunk a total of seven ships, and his personal tally was now eleven ships sunk and two damaged.

His next patrol took him to the North Channel where he sank two more ships. He sank the British SS *Ampleforth* on 19 August and the Finnish SS *Elle* on the 28th. On 1 September, Frauenheim torpedoed and damaged the Greek SS *Efploia*. *U-101* then briefly joined other boats in an operation against Convoy SC2, but this was unsuccessful. Frauenheim put in at Lorient on 16 September and a few days later he was presented with the Knight's Cross. After some well-deserved leave, he left port for his fourth patrol with *U-101* and headed once again for the Channel. On 12 October he sank a straggler from Convoy HX77, the Canadian SS *Saint Malo*, which was hit amidships by a single torpedo, broke in two and sank within thirty minutes, with the loss of twenty-eight. On the 17th Convoy SC7 was sighted and together with *U-46*, *U-99*, *U-100* and *U-123*, they formed a patrol line to await the convoy. On the evening of the 18th the convoy reached the line, and numerous attacks were made during the night of the 18th/19th. Frauenheim torpedoed and damaged the SS *Blairspey*. During the early hours of the 19th *U-101* sunk two ships, the SS *Assyrian* and the SS *Soesterberg*. With all torpedoes used, Frauenheim headed for Lorient.

In November Frauenheim was transferred and appointed as instructor with the 2nd U-boat Training Division. He went onto hold a number of staff positions before taking command of the 23rd U-boat Flotilla in the Mediterranean in September 1941. On 29 May, he took command of the 29th U-boat Flotilla, remaining in the Mediterranean. Promoted to *Korvettenkapitän* in March 1943, he joined the staff of the Commanding Admiral of U-boats in August. In February 1944, he transferred to the staff of the Admiral of Small Battle Units, and was promoted to *Fregattenkapitän* in December and later becoming Chief of Staff, where he remained until the end of the war.

He surrendered to the Allies on 8 May 1945, and was released from captivity in January 1946. He later worked for Mobil Oil Company in West Germany. He was a member of the board and head of the Department of Naval Transportation and Pipelines when he became ill and died on 28 September 1969 in Hamburg.

Other awards:
02 Oct 1936: Long Service Award 4th Class
06 Jun 1939: Spanish Cross in Bronze
02 Oct 1939: Iron Cross 2nd Class
07 Nov 1939: Iron Cross 1st Class
00 Dec 1939: U-Boat War Badge
20 Dec 1939: Commemorative Medal of 01 Oct 1938
01 Nov 1941: Italian War Cross with Swords
23 Nov 1944: German Cross in Gold
00.00.1945: U-Boat Combat Clasp in Bronze

Harald Franz Wilhelm GELHAUS
Kapitänleutnant
19 ships sunk, 100,373 tons
1 ship damaged, 10,068 tons

Knight's Cross: Awarded on 26 March 1943 as *Kapitänleutnant* and as commander of *U-107* in recognition of sinking eighteen ships for a total of 87,962 shipping tons.

Born in Gottingen, Lower Saxony on 24 July 1915, Harald Gelhaus entered the *Kriegsmarine* as an Officer Candidate in April 1935. He was assigned to the II. *Schiffsstammdivision* in the Baltic from June 1935, and then attended various training courses which included service aboard the light cruiser *Emden*. In April 1938 he was commissioned as a *Leutnant zur See* and the following month was assigned to the battleship *Gneisenau* as adjutant and then later as Signals Officer. Gelhaus was promoted to *Oberleutnant zur See* in October 1939, and transferred to the U-boat service the same month. After the completion of his training he was assigned to *U-103* as First Watch Officer, under the command of *Kapitänleutnant* Victor Schütze. He took part in three war patrols during which time *U-103* sank twenty-one ships.

On 31 March 1941, Gelhaus was appointed commander of *U-143*, a Type IID, which had been a training boat since September 1940. She became operational in April, and was attached to the 3rd U-Boat Flotilla. Gelhaus took *U-143* out on its first war patrol on

19 April but was unsuccessful. However during his third patrol whilst en route to the operational area he sighted the Norwegian tanker *Inger* and torpedoed and sunk her about 30 miles north-west of the Butt of Lewis, Scotland, with the loss of nine of her crew. In September *U-143* returned to training duties. On 1 December, he took command of *U-107*, succeeding *Korvettenkapitän* Günter Hessler. On 10 December he left port for the area west of Gibraltar, joining *Seeräuber* Group, which was directed to attack Convoy HG76. The convoy moved south along the Moroccan coast but wasn't located until the 16th. Whilst shadowing the convoy *U-107* was driven off by the corvette HMS *Pentstemon*.

(Author's collection)

On 7 January 1942, Gelhaus left to operate in the western North Atlantic. *U-107* was part of the first wave of five boats of Operation *Paukenschlag*, the surprise attack on the east coast of the United States by U-boats. The first attacks on shipping were made on the 13th. On the 31st Gelhaus torpedoed and sank the British tanker MV *San Aradio* north of Bermuda. She was struck in the bow by two torpedoes and caught fire. A *coup de grâce* torpedo struck the engine room two hours later which caused the tanker to break in two and sink. The master, thirty-seven of the crew and three gunners were lost. On 6 February he sank the US SS *Major Wheeler* which was hit on the starboard side below the after mast by a torpedo while steaming on a non-evasive course in good weather about 130 miles east-south-east of Cape Hatteras. The ship sank within two minutes by the stern, and there were no survivors. On the 21st he torpedoed and damaged the Norwegian tanker the MV *Edga*, returning to port on 7 March. He was promoted to *Kapitänleutnant* on 1 April and during his next patrol he sank the SS *Western Head* on 29 April, and for the next three weeks operated in the Caribbean, between Cuba and the Yucatan. On 1 June, Gelhaus sank the SS *Bushranger*, on the 7th he sank the Honduran SS *Castilla* and two days later he also sank the SS *Suwied* south of the western tip of Cuba, and on 10th he sank the US SS *Merrimack*. He returned to Lorient on 11 July. It had been a successful patrol; he had sunk a total of six ships.

His next patrol took him to the Freetown area and on 15 August he joined *Iltis* Group. On the 16th Convoy SL119 was sighted west of Lisbon, but the boats were driven off by the escorts. On the morning of 3 September, *U-107* sank two ships off the Portuguese coast. *Itlis* Group was joined by three more boats and on the 9th they began a southerly sweep towards the Cape Verde Islands. They patrolled in an area south-west of the Canaries until the 24th, when the group dispersed. Gelhaus then took *U-107* back to the Freetown area, where he sank the British passenger ship SS *Andalucia Star* on 7 October. The ship had been hit by two torpedoes on the port side while steaming on a non-evasive course about 200 miles south-west of Freetown. She was carrying over 250 passengers and crew, but miraculously only four were lost. When the commander of *U-333*, Peter Cremer, was seriously wounded in an engagement with HMS *Crocus* on the 7th, Gelhaus was ordered to rendezvous with *U-333* because he had a commander 'under instruction' aboard and he was put aboard *U-333* to take command and get the boat back to port with its wounded commander.

Gelhaus left for operations in the North Atlantic on 30 January 1943, and joined *Hartherz* Group west of the Bay of Biscay. Here they were ready to intercept convoys but none were located and within a few days the group was disbanded. Gelhaus was ordered to take *U-107* south off the coast of Portugal, the German High Command feared an Allied invasion of Portugal, and more boats were sent. On the 12th a convoy was sighted, and the boats waiting west of Portugal were ordered to intercept. However, the convoy had a strong air escort and the U-boats stayed submerged and were unable to make attacks. With the fear of the Allied invasion of Portugal now passed, *U-107* and other boats formed a new group north-east of the Azores. Here they searched for more ships but without success. On the 21st boats with enough fuel were ordered to Gibraltar and en route Gelhaus sank the British MV *Roxborough Castle*. When they reached the coast of Gibraltar they were under constant Allied air attack. On 5 March, Gelhaus managed to close in on Convoy KMS10, but was driven off by a Catalina flying boat. On the 12th Convoy OS44 was sighted and *U-107* closed in and sank four ships on the night of the 12th/13th west of Vigo. *U-107* returned to port on 25 March and the next day Gelhaus was informed he had been awarded the Knight's Cross.

After leave and celebrations Gelhaus took *U-107* out for the Newfoundland area on 24 April. Early on 1 May he sank the British MV *Port Victor* and joined *Amsel 1* Group just east of Newfoundland. Here they formed a patrol line and waited for the convoys. Attacks were made and the convoy dispersed into several smaller escorted groups. In the late afternoon the fog came down and contact was lost with the convoys. Twelve ships were sunk and six U-boats were lost. From the 8th *Amsel 1* and *2* Groups reformed together with *Elbe* Group east of Newfoundland to await more convoys. Attacks were made on Convoy SC129, but the U-boats were driven off. Some boats had been damaged and *U-186* was sunk. When the escort carrier HMS *Biter* arrived to join the convoy the operation ended. *U-107* left the group and returned to Lorient on 26 May.

From 7 June, Gelhaus was attached to the Operations Staff of the *Kriegsmarine*, and in February 1944 he was appointed Training Officer for the 22nd and 27th U-Boat Flotillas. On 21 December, he was transferred to the Baltic area where he served as U-boat Operations Chief attached to the Staff of *Admiral* Theodor Burchadi, the Commander of the Baltic Sea and of the 9th Security Division. Gelhaus spent the last few weeks of the war as a staff officer attached to the Naval High Command North. He surrendered to Allied troops in Sylt, northern Germany on 5 May 1945, spending just three weeks in captivity. He died on 2 December 1997 in Bochum, Westphalia.

Other awards:
05 Apr 1939: Long Service Award 4th Class
31 Oct 1940: Iron Cross 2nd Class
13 Dec 1940: U-Boat War Badge
24 Feb 1941: Iron Cross 1st Class
01 Sep 1944: War Service Cross 2nd Class with Swords
01 Oct 1944: U-Boat Combat Clasp in Bronze

Gustav Julius <u>Werner</u> HARTENSTEIN
Korvettenkapitän
19 ships sunk, 97,489 tons
4 ships damaged, 20,001 tons

Knight's Cross: Awarded on 17 September 1942 as *Korvettenkapitän* and as commander of *U-156* in recognition of his success in sinking seventeen ships for a total of 73,049 shipping tons.

(Scherzer)

Werner Hartenstein was born on 27 February 1908, in Plauen, Saxony, situated near the border of Bavaria and Czechoslovakia. Hartenstein joined the *Reichsmarine* in April 1928, and was assigned to the Baltic Sea area in January 1930. He attended various training courses at the Naval Academy at Flensburg, gaining practical experience aboard the light cruiser *Köln* from October 1931. He was commissioned as a *Leutnant zur See* a year later, and promoted to *Oberleutnant zur See* in September 1934. In September 1936, Hartenstein was assigned to the torpedo boat *Greif* as First Watch Officer. He later went on to command his own torpedo boat during the navy's non-intervention patrols during the Spanish Civil War.

At the beginning of the Second World War, Hartenstein, now a *Kapitänleutnant*, was commander of the torpedo boat *Jaguar*, and completed sixty-five patrols during the first years of the war. In March 1941 he transferred to the U-boat service, and after completing his training was appointed commander of *U-156*, a Type IXC boat built by AG Weser in Bremen. On 19 January 1942, Hartenstein took *U-156* out of Lorient to operate in the Caribbean area, as part of *Neuland* Group. The plan was for five U-boats to be in position by mid-February and to attack together various ports and oil installations. On the morning of 16 February, Hartenstein torpedoed three tankers off Saint Nicolaas, Aruba. He damaged the British tanker *Pedernales* and the US tanker *Arkansas* before sinking the British SS *Oranjested*. In the evening Hartenstein made an attempted night bombardment of the Shell Lago oil terminal. However the wooden plug or tompion had not been removed from the boat's gun before it fired, which resulted in the gun barrel splitting and the Second Watch Officer was injured and a crewman killed. On the 20th, the US SS *Delplata* was sunk west of Martinique, and after several attacks on the morning of the 25th the British tanker the SS *La Carriere* was sunk, south of Puerto Rico. With his torpedoes used but the gun temporarily repaired, Hartenstein sank two more ships off Cabrera, Dominican Republic. It was reported that when he sank the US SS *Oregan* on the 18th, the crew were machine-gunned whilst they were in the water. But this was never substantiated as most survivors denied it ever happened.

On 22 April 1942, Hartenstein left for the Western Atlantic, and began to patrol east of the Caribbean. On 13 May, *U-156* sank the Dutch MV *Koenjit* and the British SS *City of Melbourne* by torpedo and gunfire in the evening of the same day. On the 15th the Yugoslavian SS *Kupa* and the Norwegian MV *Siljestand* were sunk and on the 17th the

British SS *Barrdale* was also sunk and the US SS *Quaker City* the following day. He was promoted to *Korvettenkapitän* on the 19th and the following day Hartenstein received orders to move westward towards Martinique. It had been reported that Port de France was under surveillance by US naval forces and the Vichy French feared that French naval and merchant ships in the harbour might be seized. On the 21st Hartenstein sank the SS *Presidente Trujillo* from the Dominican Republic. She was struck by a torpedo just after leaving Fort de France and sank within four minutes with the loss of twenty-four. Then just four days later he torpedoed and damaged the American destroyer USS *Blakeley*. On the 29th, he sank the British SS *Norman Prince* about 70 miles west of Martinque. She was hit on the starboard side amidships in the engine room by a single torpedo, which caused an explosion which threw up a tremendous amount of water and debris, blowing the starboard lifeboat away. Sixteen crew members were lost and thirty-three managed to get away from the ship and were later rescued. Hartenstein decided to leave the area: his crew were suffering from stress, the boat had been submerged for over a week and Hartenstein knew he had to surface soon, for the sake of the crew's sanity. When fear of an attack passed he surfaced.

On 1 June he sank the Brazilian SS *Alegrete* and on the 3rd sank the British sailing vessel *Lillian* by gunfire south of Bridgetown, Barbados. He began the journey home on the 24th and on that day sank the SS *Willimantic* again by gunfire. His last torpedo had started its motor running whilst still in the tube and had to be jettisoned. The attack continued and Hartenstein had to use his guns. During the initial attack the senior radio officer was killed, and after the second salvo the radio shack was destroyed killing, another officer. With the order to abandon ship the lifeboats were lowered and the crew scrambled into them. When Hartenstein noticed this he broke off the attack and headed towards the lifeboats. He ordered the captain aboard *U-156* as a prisoner. The ship was checked for any sign of life and then the U-boat withdrew. Once the lifeboats were away from the ship, the shelling continued until the ship sank. It was a successful patrol and he had sunk eleven ships for a total of 44,385 shipping tons, damaging two others. He reached Lorient on 7 July.

For his fourth patrol Hartenstein left for the South Atlantic on 20 August, together with *U-68*, *U-172* and *U-504* as *Eisbär* Group. Convoy SL119 was sighted on the 25th, and *Eisbär* Group was ordered to intercept. However the convoy course changed and the U-boats were ordered south. During this time Hartenstein sank the US merchant steamer *Clan MacWhirter* north-north-west of Maderia. From early September *Eisbär* Group was broken up and *U-156* operated independently. On the 12th Hartenstein sank the troopship *Laconia* north-east of the Ascension Islands. The ship carried 2,732 people, including 463 officers and crew, 286 service passengers, 80 civilians, 1,800 Italian POWs and 103 Polish soldiers guarding the Italians. When *U-156* surfaced, Hartenstein heard the survivors calling out in Italian and he realized what had happened and decided to risk a rescue. He broadcast the location of the sinking and undertook not to attack any rescue vessels. Three other U-boats were ordered to the scene to help pick up survivors, while *U-156* itself picked up 193. Dönitz requested that the Italian submarine *Capellini* join the rescue operation, and he also asked for Vichy French warships to be sent from Dakar. On 13 September Hartenstein had a large white 6ft-square sheet sewn with a red cross. On the 16th, when an aircraft was sighted, the flag was spread over the boat's deck gun for the aircraft to see. A message was sent to the aircraft and the situation

The British troop transport Laconia *was sunk by* U-156 *on 12 September 1942 with the loss of 1,619 people. She had been requisitioned by the Royal Navy on 5 September 1939, as an armed merchant cruiser. On 1 October 1941, she was transferred to the Ministry of Transport and used as a troopship.* (Author's collection)

was explained. The aircraft then left, but another Liberator appeared and dropped its bombs, which missed the boat. Hartenstein then cut the line of the boats he was towing as the aircraft came in for a second attack. This time the bombs destroyed one lifeboat and overturned another. Hartenstein took his boat close to the lifeboats, and put fifty-five British survivors and fifty-five Italians who had been onboard *U-156* into the lifeboats. The French naval vessels and the *Capellini* took on board the remaining survivors from the other U-boats – around 1,100 people were saved. However, one of the lifeboats wasn't picked up until 21 October and only four of the original fifty-one men had survived.

On 17 September, Hartenstein sank the British SS *Quebec City* and returned to Lorient on 16 November. On 8 March 1943, whilst patrolling east of the Caribbean, *U-156* was located by a US Naval Catalina, Coming from behind some clouds, the aircraft took the U-boat completely by surprise – some of the crew were sunbathing on the deck. From 100ft four bombs were dropped: it was a direct hit. The U-boat broke into three parts and sank immediately: there were no survivors.

Other awards:
02 Oct 1936: Long Service Award 4th Class
06 Jun 1939: Spanish Cross in Bronze
16 Nov 1939: Iron Cross 2nd Class
01 Apr 1940: Long Service Award 3rd Class
27 Apr 1940: Iron Cross 1st Class
24 Dec 1940: Destroyers War Badge
02 Feb 1942: German Cross in Gold
17 Mar 1942: U-Boat Badge

Ferdinand Adam <u>Ernst</u> HECHLER
Korvettenkapitän
4 ships sunk, 13,804 tons
1 ship damaged, 1,400 tons

(Wehrkundearchiv)

Knight's Cross: Awarded as *Korvettenkapitän* and as commander of *U-870* on 21 January 1945, for his leadership and success during his varied career in the *Luftwaffe* and *Kriegsmarine*.

Ernst Hechler was born on 21 November 1907, in Lauterbach, Hesse-Nassau, Prussia. He joined the *Reichsmarine* in April 1929, and underwent basic training in the 4th Company, II. *Schiffsstammdivision* in the Baltic Sea. He was transferred to the sail training ship *Niobe* in July as a Naval Cadet. In October he transferred to the Naval Academy at Flensburg-Mürwik before his six month stay on board the light cruiser *Emden*. At this time the cruiser was under the command of Lothar von Arnauld de la Perière, who had been a U-boat commander during the First World War. Hechler sailed on *Emden*'s third training cruise, which took him and her crew to Madeira, Saint Thomas, New Orleans, Kingston Jamaica, Charlestown and back to Germany, returning to Wilhelmshaven in May 1930.

Hechler was commissioned as a *Leutnant zur See* in October 1933, and was serving aboard the light cruiser *Königsberg* when he was promoted to *Oberleutnant zur See* in September 1934. In April 1935, he was released from what was now the *Kriegsmarine*, at his own request, to join the newly-formed *Luftwaffe*. His naval rank was re-designated *Oberleutnant*. After completing various training courses he was attached to Coastal Reconnaissance and was for a time appointed as a *Staffelkapitän* (Squadron Leader) with the rank of *Hauptmann* from March 1937. In August 1939, he was appointed Operations Officer in the headquarters of the 9th Air Division. Just over a year later he took command of the 2nd Squadron of 126th Bomber Group. In December 1940 the unit was re-designated 2nd Squadron of 128th Bomber Wing. From September 1940 until March 1941, Hechler flew a total of sixty-two combat missions flying the Heinkel He 111. He was then assigned to various staff positions and was promoted to *Major.i.G* (General Staff) on 1 September 1941.

On 1 July 1943, Hechler changed his mind again and requested to be transferred back to the *Kriegsmarine*, this was accepted and re-entered with the rank of *Korvettenkapitän*. He requested to enter the U-boat service, and after a number of training courses he was attached to the 24th U-boat Flotilla in Bremen. With his training complete he was named as the new commander of *U-870*, a Type IXC-40 submarine. From 3 January to 2 February 1944, he underwent construction training and took his new boat out on her sea trials, which were a success. He officially took command on 4 February, and in November he took *U-870* out on her first war patrol. He headed for the North Atlantic.

His first assignment was to perform weather-reporting duties, as part of the information-gathering preparations for the German offensive in the Ardennes. With this assignment complete he headed for the Gibraltar area. On 20 December, he made contact with a large convoy of twenty-one ships, and he torpedoed two ships east-north-east of the Azores. He sank the landing ship USS *LST-359*, and damaged the destroyer USS *Fogg*, which was towed into port with a damaged stern. Hechler operated west of Gibraltar for three weeks. On 3 January 1945, he torpedoed and damaged the SS *Henry Miller*, about 22 miles south-west of Cape Spartel. The torpedo struck the bulkheads and a fire broke out, but when the holds filled with water it extinguished the flames. The ship started to list to port and drifted away from the convoy, but the crew remained on board. The engines were restarted and the master took a skeleton crew aboard and headed for Gibraltar. Twenty-five crew, twenty-four armed guards and one passenger were later picked up in two lifeboats. The ship reached Gibraltar on 4 January 1945 and was declared a total loss after the war she was towed to Spain and scrapped. Six days later he sank the French patrol craft FFL *L'Enjoue*, and the following day he torpedoed and damaged the British SS *Blackheath* west of Gibraltar. She ran aground two miles south of Cape Spartel but broke up under tow and was declared a total loss. He returned to Norway and put in at Kristiansand on 20 February, and a week later he arrived at Flensburg, where he served as Operations Officer on the staff of the Commander of U-boats until the end of the war.

Hechler surrendered to British troops at Flensburg as part of the Dönitz government in May 1945. He lived quietly in retirement until his death in Alzey, Germany on 23 October 1965.

Other awards:
21 Nov 1935: Pilot and Observers Badge
02 Oct 1936: Long Service Award 4th Class
23 May 1940: Iron Cross 2nd Class
25 Oct 1940: Iron Cross 1st Class
15 Mar 1941: Combat Clasp for Bomber Pilots in Silver
15 Jul 1941: Combat Clasp for Bomber Pilots in Gold
27 Feb 1945: U-Boat Badge
27 Feb 1945: U-Boat Combat Clasp in Bronze

<u>Hans</u> Otto Joachim Heinrich HEIDTMANN
Kapitänleutnant
7 ships sunk, 18,988 tons

Knight's Cross: Awarded on 12 April 1943 as *Kapitänleutnant* and as Commander of *U-559* in recognition of his leadership and for sinking seven ships.

Hans Heidtmann was born on 8 August 1914, at the railway station in Gleschendorf, in the city of Lübeck, Schleswig-Holstein. He entered the *Reichsmarine* at the age of nineteen in April 1934, being assigned to the 4th Company of the 2nd Standing Ships Division

in the Baltic. From June 1934 until January 1938, he completed his basic training, serving on the sail training ship *Gorch Fock*, the light cruiser *Emden* and aboard the 'pocket battleship' *Deutschland*. He attended the Naval Academy from March 1936 and was commissioned as a *Leutnant zur See* the following year. In September 1938, he served as First Watch Officer (commander in training) on *U-33*, and was promoted to *Oberleutnant zur See* in April 1939. From January 1940 he was attached to the 1st U-boat Training Flotilla whilst serving, at the same time as First Officer on *U-14*, under the command of *Oberleutnant zur See* Herbert Wohlforth.

On 7 July 1940, Heidtmann was appointed commander of *U-2*, a training boat, attached to the 21st Flotilla at Pillau. From September he took command of another training boat, *U-14*, stationed in the Baltic. In February 1941, he was appointed commander of *U-559*, a Type VIIC boat built by Blohm und Voss of Hamburg. With her sea trials over and the crew fully trained he took his new boat out on his first war patrol. He left port on 4 June 1941, and headed for the North Atlantic, where he was ordered to sail to the Denmark Strait, to support the 'pocket battleship' *Lützow* (ex-*Deutschland*). But when the breakout failed *U-559* returned to normal duties. Heidtmann was then ordered to operate in loose formation and search for convoys but there was no sign of any, they had been re-routed. His next patrol began on 26 July, and although contact was made with various convoys, he failed to sink any ships. Then on 17 August, Convoy OG71 was sighted and Heidtmann torpedoed and sank the British steamer *Alva*. He was promoted to *Kapitänleutnant* in October and the following month during his fourth patrol he sank the sloop HMAS *Parramatta* off Bardia. She was hit amidships by a single torpedo, which caused an explosion in the magazine. The ship was torn apart and rapidly rolled to starboard and sank. About thirty survivors, including two officers, clung to a raft that floated between the debris but they were never seen again. A total of 138 crew members were lost, including all the officers.

On 8 December, Heidtmann took *U-559* out for operations, but had no success until the evening of the 23rd, when he sank the British SS *Shuntien* near Tobruk. The ship was carrying seventy crew members, eighteen gunners and 850–1,100 prisoners-of-war. The torpedo struck and blew off the stern, killing the captain, four officers and the chief steward. Her bow rose in the air and she sank within five minutes and the crew having been unable to launch the lifeboats. Approximately forty-seven crew were picked up by HMS *Salvia* but all were later lost when she was sunk by *U-568* the next day. Around 700 men died. Then in the same area on 26th he sank the Polish steamer *Warszawa*. She did not sink and was finished off at dusk after firing a torpedo at the damaged ship, which struck the stern: twenty-three men were lost but 445 were saved. Heidtmann didn't have any more success until 10 June 1942, during his seventh war patrol. He was operating against supply shipping in the Eastern Mediterranean where

U-559 encountered Convoy AT49. On 10 June, he torpedoed two ships, sinking the Norwegian tanker MV *Athene*, with the loss of half the crew, and he damaged the British fleet oiler *Brambleleaf*.

On 29 September, Heidtmann left for what would be his final patrol of the war. On 30 October, *U-559* came under attack by the destroyers HMS *Dulverton*, *Hurworth*, *Pakenham* and *Petard* and a Wellesley of 47 Squadron. Altogether 288 depth charges were dropped and *U-559* was forced to surface. The crew abandoned the boat, and a specially trained party boarded her. Unfortunately the leader of the boarding party, Lieutenant F.A.B. Fasson, who was trying to recover the German Enigma cipher machine, went down with the boat when she sank. Of *U-559*'s crew, eight men were lost, and thirty-seven, including Heidtmann, were taken prisoner. Heidtmann was first taken to Egypt and then on to a POW camp in Canada and eventually ending up in England in May 1946. He was released twelve months later and returned to Germany.

In January 1958, Heidtmann joined the *Bundesmarine*, and in May 1964 became commander of the Naval Command in Wilhelmshaven. From April 1965 he was commander of freight ships in Brake and from April 1968 until his retirement in September 1972, he was Head of the Department of Merchant Shipping in Hamburg, with the rank of *Kapitän zur See*. Hans Heidtmann died in Hamburg on 5 April 1976.

Other awards:
08 Apr 1938: Long Service Award 4th Class
06 Jun 1939: Spanish Cross in Bronze with Swords
26 Nov 1939: U-boat Badge
27 Nov 1939: Iron Cross 2nd Class
23 Sep 1941: Iron Cross 1st Class

<u>Hans-Jürgen</u> Karl Ferdinand HELLRIEGEL
Kapitänleutnant
4 ships sunk, 11,175 tons
2 ships damaged, 17,179 tons

Knight's Cross: Awarded on 3 February 1944 as *Kapitänleutnant* and as commander of *U-543* for his leadership, extreme bravery and for sinking four ships and damaging another two.

Born in Berlin-Wilmersdorf on 16 June 1917, Hans-Jürgen Hellriegel entered the *Reichsmarine* in April 1936. His training began on the sail training ship *Gorch Fock* in June, and in September he was assigned to the light cruiser *Emden*. He attended various other training courses until he was commissioned as a *Leutnant zur See* in October 1938.

In April 1939, Hellriegel joined the U-boat service, and after further training was assigned to *U-46* as the Second Watch Officer. He took part in six patrols whilst under the command of *Kapitänleutnant* Herbert Sohler, until May 1940 and *Kapitänleutnant* Engelbert Endraß. Hellriegel was promoted to *Oberleutnant zur See* on 1 October and in March 1941, took command of *U-140*, a training boat attached to the 22nd

(Scherzer)

U-boat Flotilla. A year later he took command of *U-96*, succeeding the very successful Heinrich Lehmann-Willenbrock. He left for his first patrol on 23 April heading for the western North Atlantic. He took part in operations together with *U-94*, *U-124*, *U-406*, *U-569* and *U-590* in a planned operation as *Hecht* Group, in the area of the Newfoundland Bank. On 11 May, the group of boats sighted Convoy ONS92. Attacks were made and ships were sunk but none by Hellriegel. During the next few weeks and months various convoys were sighted, and a number of ships were sunk, but again none by *U-96*. Hellriegel's inexperience as a new commander showed, but it was only his first operational patrol. He did, however, sink a Soviet submarine on 21 July with the loss of eight of its crew.

He left for his second patrol on 24 August, and headed for the Atlantic. From the 31st, *U-96* was with *Stier* Group, and from 4 September the group combined with *Vorwärts* Group to form a long patrol line west of Ireland, to wait for more convoys. On the 10th contact was made with Convoy ON127, and Hellriegel sank the Belgian SS *Elisabeth van Belgie* together with the Norwegian tanker MV *Sveve*. *U-96* fired four torpedoes, of which three hit their target, with the British tanker MV *F.J. Wolfe* being only damaged. The SS *Elisabeth von Belgie* was hit in number three hold, and the ship began to break in two and later sank with the loss of just one crew member. The MV *Sveve* was hit on the port side, and the explosion destroyed the steering gear. Within four minutes the main tank and the pump room flooded. Twenty minutes later the thirty-seven crew and two gunners abandoned ship in four lifeboats. They were all picked up safely. Attacks against the convoy continued until the 14th, and all the participating U-boats fired at least one torpedo each, and seven ships were sunk – five by *U-96*. He was refuelled north-west of the Azores on the 17th, and then joined a new patrol line east of Newfoundland. Soon another convoy was sighted; it was made up of steamers from the Great Lakes, going to England. Late on the 25th, Hellriegel torpedoed and damaged the British passenger ship SS *New York* in the central Atlantic. She was sunk soon afterwards by *U-91*. Hellriegel headed back to his home port of St. Nazaire, arriving on 5 October. He took part in one more patrol with *U-96* which was unsuccessful, and lasted for forty-four days, ending in Königsberg on 8 February 1943.

U-96 was taken off operations, and went on to training duties attached to the 24th U-boat Flotilla at Memel. On 21 April, Hellriegel, now newly promoted to *Kapitänleutnant* took command of *U-543*, a Type IXC-40 boat built by Deutsche Werft. On 9 November, he took his new boat out into the North Atlantic. Together with a number of other boats they waited in positions west of the British Isles. In early December they assembled west of the North Channel and searched for Convoy ONS24 but failed to make contact due to bad weather, even German aircraft failed to locate it. On 3 January 1944, Hellriegel made an unsuccessful attack on a destroyer east of Cape Race. *U-543* returned to its base in Lorient on 24 January. Hellriegel left for operations in the Central Atlantic on 28 March. On the 19 April he managed to escape the attentions of the US escort carrier USS *Tripoli*. From mid-May, *U-543* operated west of Freetown and in the Gulf of Guinea without success. On 2 July, whilst on his return journey, *U-543* was spotted by an Avenger aircraft from the escort carrier USS *Wake Island*. The aircraft made two depth-charge attacks, and *U-543* was sunk south-west of Tenerife, Spain. There were no survivors: fifty-eight men were lost.

Other awards:
03 Apr 1940: Long Service Award 4th Class
24 Jun 1940: U-boat Badge
26 Apr 1940: Iron Cross 2nd Class
03 Jul 1940: Iron Cross 1st Class

Hans-Georg Adolf HESS
Oberleutnant zur See der Reserve
6 ships sunk, 9,474 tons

Knight's Cross: Awarded on 11 February 1945 as *Oberleutnant zur See der Reserve* and as commander of *U-995* for sinking four ships and in recognition of his extreme bravery.

A Berliner, Hans-Georg Hess was born in Germany's capital city on 6 May 1923, and volunteered to join the *Kriegsmarine* in April 1940, at the age of sixteen. He was initially assigned to surface vessels and served for two years on minesweepers, before being transferred to the U-boat service in April 1942. He was at first assigned to the 1st U-boat Training Division at the U-boat Officer Training School from June. He was commissioned as a *Leutnant zur See* in March 1943, and in December Hess was made Watch Officer aboard *U-466*, under the command of *Kapitänleutnant* Gerhard Thäter. He took part in four war patrols, all of them in the North Atlantic, but no ships were sunk. During his last patrol with Thäter, *U-466* broke into the Mediterranean, but was caught in Toulon during the Allied invasion of the south of France. They managed to get away and made their way back to Germany.

Hess, now promoted to *Oberleutnant zur See*, spent the next few months training as a U-boat commander, and on 4 July 1944, was appointed commander of *U-995*, a Type

(Author's collection)

VIIC-41 boat built by Blohm und Voss in Hamburg. He took his new boat out on his first war patrol on 14 October, leaving Skjomenfjord, Narvik for operations against Allied convoys. He was part of *Panther* Group, which formed a patrol line in Bear Island Passage. Unsuccessful attacks were made against destroyers escorting the convoy. Hess returned to port on 11 November. During his second patrol, *U-995* was part of *Stock* Group during operations west of Bear Island Passage. Here Hess sunk the Soviet SS *Proletarij* on 5 December. She had been struck on the port side by a single torpedo about 15 miles north of Tsyp-Navolok Cape. The crew, ten gunners and thirteen passengers abandoned ship, but many drowned or froze to death after their lifeboat capsized upon launch. Others died of exposure after swimming to the rafts. In all, twenty-nine men were lost. He had no further success and put in at Bogenbucht on the 9th. He left for his next patrol just two days later and on 21st he picked up a survivor from a Soviet fishing vessel that had just been sunk. On the 16th Hess sunk his a vessel, the Soviet SS *RT-52 Som* with the loss of thirty-one of her crew. She was unescorted and *U-995* fired a torpedo and she sank within less than a minute. In early January 1945, *U-995* was briefly with *Stier* Group which again proved unsuccessful, and soon headed for home.

En route to Kola Inlet, on 9 February, Hess took *U-995* into Kirkenes harbour, where he fired a torpedo, narrowly missing the Norwegian SS *Idefjord* tied up at the wharf. He left the harbour unnoticed and joined *U-293*, *U-318* and *U-992* waiting off Kola Inlet for Convoy JW64. It was only *U-992* that had any success, when it torpedoed the corvette HMS *Denbigh Castle*, which was badly damaged and later capsized. On the 14th the boats waited for another convoy but were driven off by a large force of British and Soviet vessels. On 2 March, Hess torpedoed and sank the Soviet sub-chaser *BO-224* north-north-east of Kola Inlet. He returned to Narvik on 6 March. A week later he took *U-995* out for its fifth patrol and again was ordered to the area of the Kola Inlet, where he was joined by *U-313* and *U-992*. On the 17th *Hagen* Group joined the three boats and they formed two patrol lines. On the morning of the 20th the convoy passed through the first line and Hess torpedoed the US merchant ship *Horace Bushnell* and claimed two hits on two other ships. The *Horace Bushnell* was beached and declared a total loss. On the 21st, the boats attempted to make attacks against the escort carriers HMS *Campania* and *Trumpeter* but were unsuccessful. *U-995* put in at Harstad on 25 March. The following day Hess was ordered to sail *U-995* to Trondheim where on 8 May he surrendered to the Allies and the boat was decommissioned. (*U-995* entered service on 1 December 1952 with the Royal Norwegian Navy as the *Kaura*.)

Hess spent the next twelve months in Norwegian captivity, being released in June 1946. He returned to Germany and settled in Hannover where he eventually became a lawyer. Hess died on 20 March 2008, in Wunsdorf-Idensen at the age of eighty-four and is buried at the village cemetery.

Other awards:

00 Aug 1941:	Minesweepers Badge
00 Sep 1941:	Iron Cross 2nd Class
00 Jul 1943:	U-boat Badge
00 Aug 1943:	Wound Badge in Black
00 Nov 1944:	Iron Cross 1st Class

Günther Wilhelm HESSLER
Fregattenkapitän
21 ships sunk, 118,822 tons

Knight's Cross: Awarded on 24 June 1941, as *Kapitänleutnant* and as commander of *U-107*, in recognition for the sinking of eighteen ships for a total of 105,181 shipping tons. It was presented to him by his father-in-law, *Vizeadmiral* Karl Dönitz, on 11 September 1941.

Günter Hessler was the twenty-first most successful U-boat commander of the Second World War he sank twenty-one ships for a total of 118,822 shipping tons. Hessler was born on 14 June 1909, in Beerfeld, Brandenburg and joined the *Reichsmarine* in April 1927. He underwent his basic training in the 8th Company of 2nd Standing Ship Division in Stralsund, in the Baltic Sea. In July 1927, he transferred to the sail training ship *Niobe*, and after more than sixteen months aboard the light cruiser *Berlin* he was commissioned as a *Leutnant zur See* in October 1931, and by July 1933 he had been promoted to *Oberleutnant zur See*. From September 1934, he served as Third Watch Officer aboard the torpedo boat *Greif*.

In October 1936, he was promoted to *Kapitänleutnant* and transferred as First Watch Officer on the *Aviso Grille*, Hitler's state yacht, and in March 1938 transferred to the battleship *Gneisenau*. In November 1937, he married the daughter of the Commander-in-Chief of U-boats Karl Dönitz. They had two sons, Peter and Klaus, and a daughter, Ute.

Above left: (Scherzer)

Above right: *Günther Hessler as a cadet in 1927.* (Author's collection)

On 27 March 1939, Hessler took command of the torpedo boat *Falke*, and was assigned to the 5th Torpedo Boat Flotilla, remaining in this position until 8 January 1940. At the outbreak of war *Falke* had been tasked with laying defensive minefields, escort duty and security duties in the North Sea. On 1 April 1940, Hessler transferred to the U-boat service and spent the next six months training. On 8 October, he was appointed commander of *U-107*, a Type IXB boat built by AG Weser in Bremen. His first patrol began on 24 January 1941, when he left Kiel to operate in the North Atlantic. On 3 February, south of Iceland Hessler sighted Convoy OB279. During the early hours of the 3rd, he sank the British SS *Empire Citizen*. She was struck below the bridge by one torpedo south of Reykjavik. She sank slowly on an even keel and the crew abandoned ship. Another torpedo struck and the ship sank more quickly, with the loss of its master, sixty-four crew, one gunner and twelve passengers. Later that evening he torpedoed the ocean boarding vessel HMS *Crispin*, north-north-west of Rockall. She was struck in the engine room and sank the following day with the loss of twenty lives, including her commander. On the 6th Hessler sank the Canadian SS *Maplecourt*, with the loss of thirty-eight of her crew, before joining other boats south-east to form a patrol line to wait for Convoy OB287. However, the convoy failed to show and the operation was called off. He sank the British ocean boarding vessel HMS *Manistee* on the 23rd, before starting his journey back to Lorient.

Hessler left for the Central Atlantic on 29 March, to operate in the Freetown area and on the evening of 8 April he attacked the southbound Convoy OG57, south-east of the Azores, and sank the British SS *Eskdene* and the SS *Helena Margareta*. During the next two days he sank four ships for a total of 20,332 shipping tons, which included the British tanker MV *Duffield* which was hit by two torpedoes west-south-west of Madeira. The tanker caught fire, developed a list and stopped, but within a few minutes the flames went out and the crew managed to get her under way again. Hessler ordered two more torpedoes to be fired which struck the ship amidships and in the bow, but it was only the fifth torpedo which caused her to break up and sink in flames, with the loss of twenty-five men. On the 21st, west-south-west of the Canaries Hessler sank the British SS *Calchas*, and on the 30th he sank the British MV *Lassell* south-west of the Cape Verde Islands. He then moved south to replenish with fuel and torpedoes. Once he reached the Freetown area, he began to increase his success rate. He sank the Dutch tanker MV *Marisa* on the 16 May and the British SS *Piako* on the 18th, the SS *Colonial* on the 27th, the Greek SS *Papalemos* on the 28th, the British SS *Sire* on the 31st, the British MV *Alfred Jones* on 1 June, and the British passenger ship SS *Adda* on the 8th. Hessler then moved westwards towards another replenishment area near St. Paul Rocks, where on the 13th he sank the Greek SS *Pandias*. He was supposed to have been refuelled by the supply ship *Lothringen* on 18 June but this had been captured by HMS *Dunedin* three days before. Without further supplies of fuel, food and torpedoes, Hessler had little choice but to head for his home port. This patrol was the most successful by a U-boat during the Second World War. On his return to Lorient on 2 July he was informed that he had been awarded the Knight's Cross. It was later presented to him by his father-in-law *Vizeadmiral* Dönitz.

On 6 September, Hessler left for the Central Atlantic where he joined several other boats to form a patrol line. On the 21st Convoy SL87 was sighted and attacks were made over a period of three days, when seven ships were sunk, three of them by Hessler. One of the ships was the British SS *John Holt* which had on board the convoy commodore who survived the sinking. The operation continued south and the area was searched but no more contact was made.

There were no more successes for Hessler and he returned to Lorient on 11 November. He had been promoted to *Korvettenkapitän* in September and from 24 November was attached to the staff of the Admiral Commanding U-boats (until January 1943 this was *Admiral* Dönitz), serving as an aide de camp until the end of the war. It's possible to conclude that he was transferred on the personal request of Dönitz; perhaps he was acting on a request made by his daughter. He was promoted to the rank of *Fregattenkapitän* on 18 December 1944.

Hessler spent just over a year in Allied captivity, and he testified at the Nuremberg trials on behalf of his father-in-law. In 1947, Hessler was commissioned to write *The U-Boat War in the Atlantic*, a definitive account of the German U-boat offensive. He completed the three-volume work in 1951. Hessler died in Bochum, Laer, in the Ruhr area of Germany on 4 April 1968.

Other awards:
02 Oct 1936: Long Service Award 4th Class
05 Apr 1939: Long Service Award 3rd Class
18 Nov 1939: Iron Cross 2nd Class
01 Mar 1941: Iron Cross 1st Class
03 Jul 1941: U-boat Badge
09 Nov 1944: German Cross in Gold

Günther HEYDEMANN
Kapitänleutnant
8 ships sunk, 36,010 tons
1 ship damaged, 12,910 tons

Knight's Cross: Awarded as *Kapitänleutnant* and as commander of *U-575* on 3 July 1943, in recognition of his success in sinking eight ships for a total of 36,010 tons.

Günther Heydemann was born on 11 January 1914 in Greifswald in north-east Germany, in Mecklenburg, only 50 miles from the Polish border. Heydemann joined the *Reichsmarine* in April 1933, and was initially attached to an infantry battalion in the Baltic. From June he began his training, he served on the sail training ship *Gorch Fock*, and from September he served aboard the light cruiser *Karlsruhe*. He was attached to the Naval Academy at Flensburg for ten months before being assigned to the Coastal Artillery School in May 1936. In October he was commissioned as a *Leutnant zur See* and from May 1937, was a platoon leader with the 3rd Ships or Training Division in the North Sea, and later served in the Baltic.

(Scherzer)

From March 1939, now an *Oberleutnant zur See*, Heydemann served on the battleship *Schleswig-Holstein*. On 25 August the battleship sailed into New Harbour in Gdansk on an apparent courtesy visit. There, on 1 September, she fired the opening shots of the Second World War, and Heydemann had a 'front row seat'. He served on the *Schleswig-Holstein* until April 1940, when he was transferred to the U-boat service. With his training complete, he was assigned as First Watch Officer or commander in training to *U-69*, under the watchful eye of *Kapitänleutnant* Jost Metzler. He participated in two patrols during which four ships were sunk and one was damaged.

On 2 April 1941, Heydemann was promoted to *Kapitänleutnant* and was named as commander of *U-575* on 27 May. He took his new boat out of Trondheim for his first patrol on 8 September and headed for the North Atlantic. He was directed to the eastbound Convoy SC42 but contact was soon lost due to poor visibility. Heydemann joined *Brandenburg* Group south-east of Greenland and on the 18th they sighted Convoy SC44, but because of radio interference an organised attack was not possible. A new patrol line was ordered south-east of Cape Farewell, but with no further convoys sighted it was dispersed. Heydemann took *U-575* south and continued his patrol until 2 October when he attacked a group of four ships in the central North Atlantic with three torpedoes, sinking the Dutch MV *Tuva*. He then headed for St. Nazaire, his new base, arriving on the 9th.

In early November, *U-575* left for the North Atlantic and headed to an area off Newfoundland, joining *U-43*, *U-105*, *U-372*, *U-434* and *U-574* to form *Steuben* Group. However, no contact was made with any convoys and the group was soon dispersed. Some boats including *U-575* headed towards Gibraltar, but when they arrived in the operational area they found strong anti-submarine patrols at the entrance of the Straits, forcing them to remain submerged and unable to make an attack. The boats waited for orders but it was soon decided that attacks on the convoys should cease. Heydemann put in at Vigo and was refuelled, he headed back to St. Nazaire. He then took part in two more patrols from 14 January to 14 May 1942. He sank the US SS *Robin Hood* on 16 April, but had no further success and then headed south-east of Cape Cod and then for his home port. On 10 June, he left for the Caribbean area, and together with various other boats was directed to Convoy HG84. The boats formed the patrol line *Endrass*, but only one boat, *U-552*, was successful, sinking five ships. The operation ended on the 16th, because of good calm weather and good visibility – not good for U-boat attacks. After being refuelled Heydemann torpedoed and ssnk the US merchant steamer *Norlandia* north-east of Cabo Samaná, Dominica. He then took *U-575* away from the Caribbean and early on the 9th sank the British SS *Empire Explorer* by torpedo and gunfire. He then sailed to an area east of Trinidad and Tobago, where on the 18th he attacked three ships, sinking the British sailing vessels *Glacier* and *Comrade* and damaging the tanker SS *San Gaspar*. He returned to St. Nazaire on 7 August.

On 16 September, Heydemann left for the North Atlantic and joined *Luchs* Group west of Ireland. On the 29th a convoy was sighted, and although *Luchs* Group was ordered to intercept it, nothing was located. On 3 October Convoy HX209 was spotted, but bad weather delayed the boats and they were unable to make an attack and together with a strong air escort they had no choice but to keep their distance, and two days later the operation was called off, and some of the boats left the group. From the 8th, the remaining boats were formed into *Panther* Group, and on the 11th another convoy was sighted, and seven boats from *Panther* were ordered to intercept it. On the 16th, Convoy ONS137 was sighted as it passed through the southern section of the patrol line and eleven boats were ordered to attack it. The remaining boats of the group formed a new smaller group – *Puma* Group – and together with *U-575* were ordered southwards to seek Convoy ONS138. On the 22nd *Puma* Group sighted Convoy ONS139 in the central North Atlantic and were ordered to attack, but they were unable to catch the convoy and the attack was broken off. *Puma* Group moved westwards until 24th, when *U-606* reported two destroyers seen moving north-west at high speed so they headed away and made contact with another convoy but were again driven off. Despite the difficulty in making attacks, six ships were sunk, but none by Heydemann. On the 29th, however, he attacked and sank the British passenger ship MV *Abosso*, firing four torpedoes but only one hit. Fifteen minutes later he fired a *coup de grâce* which struck the ship causing her to sink within thirty-five minutes. The master, 150 crew members, eighteen gunners and 193 passengers were lost. Heydemann returned to Lorient on 8 November.

He left for the Gibraltar area on 17 December and joined *Delphin* Group to operate against US–Mediterranean convoys carrying supplies for the Allied armies in North Africa. However, no contact was made with any convoys and the boats were ordered towards Brazil instead. On 7 January 1943, the *Delphin* boats were ordered south to form a patrol line ahead of a newly-sighted convoy. It was spotted on the 8th, and the following day Heydemann claimed one tanker sunk and two others damaged, possibly the MV *Norvik* and the MV *Minister Wedel*. On the 16th, *U-575* was refuelled and was still attached to *Delphin* group when Heydemann took it south of the Azores. The group moved westwards to wait for Convoy UGS4. On the evening of the 25th, Heydemann torpedoed and sank the US SS *City of Flint*, a straggler from UGS4. When nothing more materialized the group moved eastwards. *U-575* had no more success and Heydemann decided to head for St. Nazaire, arriving on 18 February.

On 22 April, *U-575* left port on its next patrol and joined *Amsel 1* Group east of Newfoundland, and became part of a patrol line ahead of the south-west-bound Convoy ONS5. Attacks were made and the convoy split up, and on 5 May fog came down and contact was lost. The following morning contact was established once again, but only briefly, nevertheless twelve ships were sunk, but none by Heydemann. Contact was made again on the 12th, but with the arrival of the escort carrier HMS *Biter* the operation was called off. From the 24th Dönitz temporarily halted operations against convoys in the North Atlantic. (This was a period known as 'Black May' when the German U-boat service suffered heavy casualties and with fewer Allied ships being sunk; it proved to be a turning point in the Battle of the Atlantic.) Heydemann returned to St. Nazaire on 11 Jun: it would be his last patrol as a U-boat commander. On 30 July, after some leave Heydemann was transferred to the 23rd U-boat Flotilla in Danzig where he took up duties as the new Ballistic Leader. From 23 February 1945, he was part of the 25th U-boat Flotilla as its training officer in Travenmünde. In June he ran the Naval Service Station in Neustadt, working with the Allies until October 1945.

Heydemann became a businessman after the war and later settled in Hamburg-Wedel, where he died on 2 January 1986.

Other awards:
01 Apr 1937: Long Service Award 4th Class
17 Sep 1939: Iron Cross 2nd Class
12 Apr 1941: Iron Cross 1st Class
12 Apr 1941: U-Boat Badge

Ulrich HEYSE
Korvettenkapitän
12 ships sunk, 83,639 tons

Knight's Cross: Awarded on 21 January 1943 as *Kapitänleutnant* and as commander of *U-128* in recognition of his outstanding leadership and for the sinking of twelve ships for a total of 83,639 shipping tons.

Ulrich Heyse was born on 20 September 1906 in Berlin-Friedenau and joined the *Reichsmarine* in October 1933, being assigned to the 6th Company of 3rd Ships Training Division in the Baltic. From January 1934 he attended various training courses, which included attendance at the Ships' Gunnery School in Kiel, the Coastal Artillery School at Wilhelmshaven, and torpedo training at Flensburg. He also spent time aboard the light cruisers *Leipzig* and *Köln*, before being commissioned as a *Leutnant zur See* in June 1936.

In September he was assigned as radio officer aboard the light cruiser *Emden*, and from May 1937 he was an instructor at the 2nd Naval Non-commissioned Officer Training Battalion. Promoted to *Oberleutnant zur See* in October he transferred as an instructor to the Torpedo School in December. In October 1938 Heyse was appointed

First Watch Officer on the *Z6 Theodor Riedel*, a Type 1934A class destroyer, and in April 1939 was promoted to *Kapitänleutnant*. At the beginning of the Second World War the ship laid minefields in the North Sea. Heyse was still aboard during the opening stages of the Norwegian campaign when the destroyer was responsible for transporting troops to the Trondheim area in early April 1940. In June Heyse took part in minelaying operations off the coast of France, before transferring to the U-boat service the following month. After attending various training courses Heyse was assigned to the staff of the 2nd U-boat Flotilla in Lorient, France.

On 12 May 1941, Heyse was appointed commander of *U-128*, a Type IXC boat built by AG Weser in Bremen. After his general formalization training and the conclusion of sea trials, *U-128* was finally ready for operations.

(Author's collection)

On 9 December, *U-128* left Kiel and went

round the north of Scotland, arriving at its new base of Lorient on Christmas Eve. On 8 January 1942, Heyse took *U-128* out on its first war patrol, heading for the Western Atlantic. He operated between Bermuda and the coast of Florida, where he sank two US tankers off Cape Canaveral, the SS *Pan Massachusetts* on the 19th, and the SS *Cities Service Empire* on the 22nd. On 5 March just east of the Great Aloaco Islands, Heyse sank a third tanker, the Norwegian MV *O.A. Knudsen*. He left for his second patrol on 25 April, heading for the Central Atlantic. Together with three other boats, he encountered Convoy SL109 and shadowed it for several hours before attacking. *U-128* was the only boat to have any success – Heyse sank the British SS *Denpark* on the 14th He then continued to patrol alone, heading for the area east of the Caribbean. There on 8 June, he sank the Norwegian tanker MV *South Africa*, and on the 21st sank the US SS *West Ira* near Barbados, followed by the Norwegian tanker MV *Andrea Brövig* and the US SS *Polybius* on the 23rd and 27th respectively. On the 28th Heyse took *U-128* south and torpedoed and damaged the British SS *Steel Engineer*. He rerurned to port after a very successful patrol in which he had sunk five ships for a total of 35,620 shipping tons.

His next patrol took him to the Freetown area, arriving in early October 1942. Heyse patrolled south-west of Freetown until early November and encountered very few ships and had no success. He then moved south-west of the Cape Verde Islands, where he sank the Norwegian MV *Maloja* on the evening of the 8th, the British tanker SS *Cerinthus*. She was struck by one of three torpedoes about 180 miles south-west from the Cape Verde Islands. The tanker stopped after the first hit and was shortly after struck by a second torpedo which missed, but twenty minutes later another one struck the ship in the engine room but had little effect. Heyse then the surfaced and fired all his guns until the tanker capsized and sank. Twenty men were lost. He then sank the British SS *Start Point* on the afternoon of the 10th. During the last week of November and the first week of December Heyse spent patrolling near St. Paul Rocks, where he sank the British MV *Teesbank* on the morning of 5 December. He then joined a patrol line running from St. Paul Rocks to an area north of Natal, Brazil. Seven ships were sunk but none by *U-128*. Heyse decided to head for home, and began the return journey, reaching Lorient on 15 January 1943.

Heyse now spent the remainder of the war on land. From March he served as an instructor with the 2nd U-boat Training Division. Promoted to *Korvettenkapitän* in April, he took over officer training in the 1st U-boat Training Flotilla in December. In January 1944, he was appointed commander of the 1st Department of the 1st U-boat Flotilla and at the same time between February a March 1945 he was commander of the 1st Training Division in Hamburg-Finkenwärder. From 3 March until the German surrender in May he served as commander of 32nd U-boat Flotilla in Hamburg. He didn't rejoin the navy after the war and lived in Flensburg until his death on 19 November 1970. Heyse was the first U-boat commander to sink a ship in the Bahamas area during the Second World War.

Other awards:
01 Nov 1936: Order for 'Military Service' 5th Class
04 Oct 1937: Long Service Award 4th Class
11 Feb 1940: Iron Cross 2nd Class
19 Oct 1940: Destroyer War Badge
24 Mar 1942: Iron Cross 1st Class
24 Mar 1942: U-Boat Badge

<u>Otto</u> Christian ITES
Kapitänleutnant
15 ships sunk, 76,882 tons
1 ship damaged, 8,022 tons

Knight's Cross: Awarded as *Oberleutnant zur See* and as commander of *U-94* on 28 March 1942 for outstanding leadership and for the sinking of eight ships for a total of 46,602 shipping tons.

Otto Ites was born on 5 February 1918 in Norden, Lower Saxony, he joined the *Kriegsmarine* in April 1936 as an Officer Candidate. He first saw service in the Baltic with naval infantry, and from June began his basic training. He served aboard the battleship *Schelsien*, attended various courses at the Naval Academy in Flensburg and then served aboard the torpedo boats *Kondor* and *Albatros* in mid-1938. In October he was commissioned as a *Leutnant zur See* and began training at the U-boat School.

In April 1939 he was appointed as Second Watch Officer aboard *U-51* and later with *U-48*. In October 1940 he was promoted to *Oberleutnant zur See*, and from 10 November served as First Watch Officer aboard *U-48*, under the command of *Kapitänleutnant* Heinrich Bleichrodt. As First Watch Officer, he was basically a 'commander in training', and who could want for a better mentor than Bleichrodt, who sank twenty-five ships and was a recipient of the Knight's Cross with Oakleaves. He took part in two patrols in which nine ships were sunk and one was damaged.

On 31 March 1941, Itles was named as commander of *U-146*, a Type IID boat built by Deutsche Werke in Kiel. From April until early June *U-146* was put on training duties, part of the 22nd U-boat Flotilla. However, in mid-June she was briefly made operational under Ites and left Kiel on the 17th to operate north of the Shetlands, where during the early hours of

the 18th Ites sunk the Finnish SS *Pluto*, north-west of the Butt of Lewis. He returned to Kiel on 14 July.

On 27 August Ites was named commander of *U-94*, a Type VIIC boat built by Germania Werft in Kiel. He left port on his first patrol in his new vessel on 2 September and en route to join a group south-east of Greenland he sank three stragglers from Convoy ON14. He sank the British SS *Newbury* on the 15th, which was hit by one torpedo and sank off Cape Farewell. Although the crew abandoned ship in lifeboats, the master and thirty-eight crew together with six gunners were never found. He also sank the Greek SS *Pegasus* and the British SS *Empire Eland*. From the 18th, *U-94* was part of *Brandenburg* and a number of ships were sunk by the group but none by *U-94*. The group was dispersed on the 26th and whilst on his return journey Ites sank the SS *San Florentino*, a British tanker (12,842 tons) on 1 October. Ites returned arrived back in Kiel on 15 October.

(Scherzer)

During his third patrol, which began on 12 February 1942, Ites took *U-94* into Canadian waters. On the 21st a convoy was sighted about 600 miles north-east of Cape Race. Together with four other boats *U-94* was directed to the convoy. En route Ites sank the British SS *Empire Hail* in the early hours of the 24th east of Newfoundland. When the operation ended *U-94* moved to an area south of Nova Scotia. On 9 March Ites sank the Brazilian SS *Cayrü* and two days later sank the Norwegian SS *Hvosleff*. During the return journey *U-94* was directed towards Convoy ON77, and on the morning of the 25th Ites attacked and damaged the British tanker MV *Imperial Transport*. He arrived at St. Naziare on 2 April.

On 4 May, *U-94* left for operations in the North Atlantic where she joined five other boats to take part in a planned group-operation *Hecht* near the Newfoundland Bank. On the 11th a convoy was located and attacked by the U-boat group. *U-94* sank the Panamanian tanker *Cocle*, and on the 13th sank the British SS *Batra* and SS *Tolken*. Contact with the convoy was soon lost afterwards, and was not regained. Further patrols were made by the group and although another convoy was sighted the boats were soon driven off by a large number of escort ships. On 8 June, *U-124* sighted Convoy ONS100 and sank the French corvette *Mimose* but then contact was lost because of bad weather. On the 10th contact was made once again and Ites attacked and sank two ships, the British SS *Empire Clough* and SS *Ramsay*. The following day he torpedoed and sank a straggler from Convoy ONS100, the British SS *Pontypridd*. She had been struck by a torpedo fired from *U-569* and Ites finished the ship off. On the 16th Ites sighted another convoy. The group attacked but both *U-94* and *U-590* were damaged during depth-charges attacks. The operation was broken off on the 18th and the boats began their journey home.

On 3 August, Ites took *U-94* out for operations in the Caribbean, and during an operation against Convoy TAW15 near the eastern tip of Haiti was spotted on the surface by a USN Catalina flying boat. Ites ordered the boat to immediately dive, but resurfaced after depth charges were dropped by the aircraft. A flare was dropped which revealed the boat's position to HMCS *Oakville*, a Canadian corvette. *U-94* was attacked by gunfire and depth-charges and the corvette rammed the U-boat three times. After the third time the order was given to abandon ship. *Oakville* sent a boarding party and two of *U-94*'s crew who resisted were shot. Twenty-one survivors were rescued by USS *Lea* and another five by *Oakville*. Ites was among them.

Ites was eventually taken to a POW camp, Camp Crossville in Tennessee where on 1 April 1943 he was informed he had been promoted to *Kapitänleutnant*. He remained in Allied captivity until 1 May 1946. He entered the University of Bonn and submitted a dissertation in October 1950 at the medical faculty. He later joined the *Bundesmarine* and as a *Fregattenkapitän* he commanded the destroyer *Z2*, formerly USS *Ringgold*, from November 1960 to September 1962. He was promoted to *Kapitän zur See* in December 1964 and in October 1968 he was appointed commander of the Naval Locating School, and at the same time he was Garrison Leader in Bremerhaven. In April 1975 he was made Naval Office Chief with the rank of *Konteradmiral*. Ites retired from the Navy on 30 September 1977, and settled in his hometown of Norden, where he died on 2 February 1982. He had a twin brother, Rudolf, an *Oberleutnant zur See* and as commander of *U-709*. He was killed in action on 1 March 1944, when his boat was sunk by depth charges.

Other awards:
27 Oct 1939: Iron Cross 2nd Class
21 Dec 1939: U-Boat Badge
25 Feb 1940: Iron Cross 1st Class
03 Apr 1940: Long Service Award 4th Class

Günter JAHN
Korvettenkapitän
5 ships sunk, 27,572 tons
2 ships damaged, 14,180 tons

Knight's Cross: Awarded on 30 April 1943 as *Korvettenkapitän* and as commander of *U-596* for sinking five ships for a total of 27,572 shipping tons.

Günther Jahn was born in Hamburg on 27 September 1910, and he entered the *Reichsmarine* as an Officer Candidate in April 1931. He first served on the light cruiser *Karlsruhe* until January 1933, and spent the next four years on various training courses. He was commissioned as a *Leutnant zur See* in April 1935 and promoted to *Oberleutnant zur See* in January 1937. From August 1938 he served aboard the light cruiser *Nürnberg* as Watch Officer. He saw action during the opening stages of the Second World War when the cruiser was used to lay defensive minefields off the German coast. He was promoted to *Kapitänleutnant* in September 1939 and took part in escort offensive minelaying in the North Sea, until the ships was torpedoed and damaged by a British submarine in December. From then on she was used as a training ship in the Baltic. Jahn continued to serve aboard the ship until March 1941, when he transferred to the U-boat service.

With his basic training complete, Jahn was assigned to *U-98* in August 1941 as Watch

Officer, but this was cancelled at the last minute and from October he commanded *U-596*. He left on his first patrol on 8 August 1942, heading for the North Atlantic. *U-596* was one of a number of boats which joined an operation against Convoy SC94 to form a new patrol line *Lohrs*, 60 miles west of the North Channel. En route Jahn torpedoed and sank a straggler from Convoy SC95, the Swedish MV *Suecia*. The *Lohrs* patrol line was formed on the 17th west of Scotland. On the 21st the group moved northwards and the following day sighted Convoy ONS122. Although contact was at first lost, nine boats from the group did make attacks. But fog came down and the operation was called off. In late August the *Lohrs* Group moved to a new position and on 6 September they formed a new patrol line, 400 miles north-east of Cape Race. On the 20th Jahn made an attack and sank the British SS

(Scherzer)

Empire Hartebeeste. More ships were sighted by Jahn, but he had no further success. The operation finally ended on the 25th and *U-596* returned to St. Nazaire.

On the 4 November, Jahn headed out for the Mediterranean to join other boats operating against Allied shipping that were taking part in the landings in North Africa. The operation was short, ending on the 15th. During the next five months Jahn took *U-596* out on another four patrols, and damaged two ships on 9 March 1943, the SS *Fort Norman* and the SS *Empire Standard*, both from Convoy KMS10. On the 7 January he torpedoed and sank the British landing craft HMS *LCI 162*, his only success during this time. From 25 March, he made various attacks on convoys off the Algerian coast, but all were unsuccessful. However, on the 30th he attacked Convoy ET16, and sank two ships, the Norwegian tanker MV *Hallanger* and the British SS *Fort á la Corne*.

On 1 August Jahn was appointed commander of the 29th U-boat Flotilla, stationed in Toulon, southern France, and he also was responsible for the U-boats operating in Marseille and Salamis. He was promoted to *Korvettenkapitän* in October 1943. The Flotilla was disbanded in September 1944, and Jahn fell into French captivity when France was liberated and spent almost two years in prison. He was released in July 1946, returning to Germany. He never rejoined the navy and worked as a civilian until his retirement. He died in Krailling, Starnberg, Upper Bavaria on 12 April 1992.

Other awards:
02 Oct 1936: Long Service Award 4th Class
18 Oct 1939: Iron Cross 2nd Class
03 Mar 1942: High Seas Fleet Badge
06 Oct 1942: Iron Cross 1st Class
06 Oct 1942: U-Boat Badge

Hans JENISCH
Kapitänleutnant
17 ships sunk, 110,139 tons
3 ships damaged, 22,749 tons

Knight's Cross: Awarded on 7 October 1940 as *Oberleutnant zur See* and as commander of *U-32* for sinking fifteen ships for a total of 63,185 shipping tons and for damaging another three during five war patrols.

Hans Jenisch was born on 19 October 1913, in Gerdauen, East Prussia, and was responsible for sinking seventeen ships during the Second World War, and he became the fifteenth U-boat recipient of the Knight's Cross. He entered the *Reichsmarine* in 1933, at the age of nineteen, and served for ten months aboard the 'pocket battleship' *Deutschland* as part of his training. He was commissioned as a

(Scherzer)

Leutnant zur See in October 1936, and in May the following year had decided to begin training as a U-boat commander. From January 1938 he served as Watch Officer on *U-32*, under the command of *Kapitänleutnant* Paul Büchel. As Watch Officer he was basically a commander in training, taking part in two patrols during the Spanish Civil War between February and May 1938. Jenisch was promoted to *Oberleutnant zur See* in June 1938 and during the first half of 1939, *U-32* took part in tactical exercise in the Baltic and from July acted as a temporary replacement for *U-36* at the U-boat School at Neustadt. From 30 August 1939, *U-32* was in the Baltic, at the start of the Polish campaign but was recalled when it became apparent that three Polish destroyers had escaped the German blockade. From 5 September, Jenisch took part in minelaying operations, with *U-32*, in the British Channel. On 18 September *U-32* sank the SS *Kensington Court* by gunfire: the crew abandoned ship and were later picked up by two Sunderland flying boats. On 30th, *U-32* went into Kiel for repairs. Jenisch took part in one more patrol as Watch Officer, and from February 1940 he took over as commander of *U-32*.

On 26 February 1940, he took *U-32* out of Wilhelmshaven for a minelaying operation off Liverpool. On 2 March Jenisch fired three torpedoes at the SS *Belpamela* but they exploded prematurely, but later that morning he sank the Swedish merchant ship *Lagaholm* by gunfire. He then took *U-32* through the North Channel into the Irish Sea and laid eight mines off Liverpool. His next patrol lasted for just two weeks and he failed to sight a single ship. He returned to Wilhelmshaven on 13 May for further repairs. On 3 June he left port for another patrol, passing north of the Shetlands and down the west coast of Scotland. He joined a group of six boats under the command of Günther Prien. They formed a patrol line to intercept Convoy HX48, but no contact was made. With the group broken up, Jenisch took *U-32* to the western approaches of the English Channel, and during the evening of the 18th he sank three ships, the Norwegian *Attair* and two Spanish trawlers, the *Salvora* and the *Nuevo-Ons*. On the 19th he also claimed the Yugoslavian SS *Labud*, sunk south-west of Fastnet Rock, and three days later he sank the Norwegian tanker MV *Eli Knudsen*. He returned to port on 1 July.

Jenisch and his crew had some well-deserved leave, whilst *U-32* had a refit and repairs were made to her diesel engines. On 15 August she was ready and left Wilhelmshaven for operations in the Atlantic. On the morning of the 30th Jenisch attacked three ships. The SS *Mill Hill* was hit in the stern by a single torpedo and sank with a heavy list in a few short minutes. The master and all of her 33-man crew were lost. The SS *Chelsea* was struck amidships but initially remained afloat. She eventually sank with the loss of twenty-four of her crew. The MV *Norne* was struck just forward of her engine room and sank in less than a minute after the boiler exploded. The next day Jenisch encountered the British Dakar Task Force and fired a torpedo at the British light cruiser HMS *Fiji*, which was damaged and five of her crew were killed. She managed to get to the Clyde under her own power. *U-32* put in at Lorient on 8 September. During his next patrol Jenisch joined other boats operating against Convoy HX72 on 21 September. He torpedoed and damaged the British SS *Collegian* the following day. However, *U-32* was spotted on the surface by HMS *Lowestoft* and was fired upon, and when Jenisch dived contact was made and depth charges were dropped but they were set too deep and Jenisch managed to escape westwards and out of danger. Early on the 25th Jenisch sank the British SS *Mabriton*, and the next day he torpedoed and damaged the British SS *Corrientes*, and then sank the Norwegian MV *Tancred*. That same day he sank the British SS *Darcoila* with a single torpedo about 500 miles west of Ireland. She sank within five minutes after an explosion in the boiler room and the master, thirty-five of her crew and one gunner were lost. On the 28th, Jenisch sank the British SS *Empire Ocelot* by torpedo and gunfire and on the 29th he sank the SS *Bassa* in the same area. Apparently Jenisch recorded in his logbook that he and his crew watched as the survivors made it to the lifeboats, but tragically they were never seen again. The master, forty-seven crew and two gunners were lost. Jenisch then took *U-32* west into the central North Atlantic and on 30 September he sank the Dutch SS *Haulerwijk*, south-east of Cape Farewell. He missed the ship with a torpedo but after following her for eight hours she was sunk by gunfire. On 2 October, Jenisch sank the British SS *Kayeson* south of Reykjavik. *U-32* arrived at its home base on 6 October.

On 24 October, Jenisch took *U-32* out on weather-boat duties west of the British Isles. In the early hours of the 26th an aircraft from Bomber Wing 40 had severely damaged the British passenger liner the SS *Empress of Britain* (42,348 tons), setting her on fire. All U-boats in the area were ordered to pursue. On the 28th Jenisch caught up with the liner and fired three torpedoes from only 600 yards away, and then left the scene because of the threat of escort ships. The liner was hit by two of the torpedoes and sank north-west of Aran Island, with the loss of 118 lives. She was the largest ship ever sunk by a U-boat. On 30 October, Jensich attacked the SS *Balzac*; he fired a torpedo which missed. The *Balzac*, believing that she was being shelled, called for assistance and the destroyers HMS *Harvester* and *Highlander* were sent to help. Jenisch continued to follow *Balzac* and after a few hours *Harvester* made contact with *U-32* and attacked with depth charges. At one point *Highlander* dropped fourteen depth charges, and *U-32* was seriously damaged. Jenisch had to surface and *U-32* was unable to dive again and was incapable of attacking the destroyers. They opened fire as the boat's crew began to abandon ship. Nine men were lost and thirty-three

The Empress of Britain *was used as a troop transport in 1940, and on 26 October she was hit by two 250kg bombs from a German Fw-200 Kondor aircraft, piloted by* Oberleutnant *Bernhard Jope (Knight's Cross with Oakleaves holder) and caught fire. Most of her crew managed to abandon ship, including 205 passengers, military personnel and their families, leaving only a skeleton crew on board. The ship was then taken in tow and was being escorted by two warships and had air cover. On 28 October she was struck by two torpedoes fired from* U-32 *and sank north-west of Bloody Foreland, County Donegal, the largest ship sunk by a U-boat in the Second World War.* (Author's collection)

including Jenisch were picked up. He went into British captivity where on 1 November 1940 he was promoted to *Kapitänleutnant* and remained a prisoner until June 1947.

In October 1956, Jenisch joined the *Bundesmarine* with the rank of *Korvettenkapitän*. He spent the next two years training new recruits, and in November 1958 he transferred to the Ministry of defence and was further promoted. From December 1960 he commanded the frigate *Hipper*, and in March 1963 was promoted to *Kapitän zur See*. He was later appointed Chief of Staff and Leader of the Operational Department of the Naval Command in NATO. From October 1966 he was Training Commander at the Naval Command Academy in Hamburg. He retired in March 1972 and settled in Kiel where he died on 29 April 1982.

Other awards:
00.00.1937: Long Service Award 4th Class
00.00.1939: Iron Cross 2nd Class
00 Oct 1940: Iron Cross 1st Class
00 Oct 1940: U-Boat Badge

Ernst Friedrich Franz KALS
Kapitän zur See
20 ships sunk, 145,656 tons
1 ship damaged, 6,986 tons

Knight's Cross: Awarded on 1 September 1942, as *Korvettenkapitän* and as commander of *U-130* in recognition of sinking fifteen ships for a total of 99,907 shipping tons. The award was presented by *Konteradmiral* Hans-Georg von Friedeburg at Lorient in late September 1942.

(Scherzer)

Ernst Kals was the sixteenth most successful U-boat commander of the Second World War, sinking twenty ships for a total of 145,656 shipping tons. He was born in Glauchau, Saxony on 2 August 1905, and he volunteered for the *Reichsmarine* in March 1924. From April 1925 he served aboard the sail training ship *Niobe* and later on the light cruiser *Berlin*. He attended the Torpedo School at Flensburg in May 1927, before being assigned to the battleship *Schlesien* from January 1928. Kals was commissioned as a *Leutnant zur See* in October and by July 1930 was serving as a Platoon Leader with the 4th Naval Artillery Battalion in Cuxhaven as an *Oberleutnant zur See*. In September 1933 he was appointed adjutant with the 6th Naval Artillery Battalion and the following year he was serving aboard the light cruiser *Köln* again as an adjutant. Promoted to *Kapitänleutnant* in April 1935, and from

September was attached to the light cruiser *Emden* as an gunnery officer. From October 1937, he was serving on board the 'pocket battleship' *Admiral Scheer* as Third Watch Officer, and then aboard the light cruiser *Leipzig* from April 1939. In August he was promoted to *Korvettenkapitän* before being transferred to the U-boat service in October 1940.

Kals was initially attached to the 1st U-boat Training Division, and then transferred to serve briefly as First Watch Officer on board *U-37*. On 11 June 1941 he took command of *U-130*, a Type IXC boat built by AG Weser in Bremen. Kals left port on 1 December, in transit to a new base in western France. During the journey he made contact with Convoy SC57, and on the evening of the 10th sank three ships, the British SS *Kurdistan* and SS *Kirnwood* and the Brazilian SS *Star of Luxor*. He arrived at Lorient on 15 December. His second patrol began on the 27th when he headed out to the Western Atlantic where *U-130* was part of the first wave of Operation *Paukenschlag* – the targeting of shipping along the coast of America. On 12 January 1942, *U-130* was spotted by an Allied aircraft, and two depth charges were dropped but the boat escaped without damage. The following morning Kals sank two ships south of Cape Breton Island, the Norwegian SS *Frisco* and the Panamanian SS *Friar Rock* with the loss of thirty-one crew members. Kals had to break-off an attack on a third ship when *U-130* was chased away by a US destroyer. *U-130* lay on the bottom for a while and then left the area. On the 21st Kals sank the Norwegian tanker MV *Alexander Höegh* east of New York. He went onto sink two more tankers off the US coast – the Norwegian MV *Varanger* on the 25th and the US SS *Francis E. Powell* on the 27th. Later that same day he torpedoed and damaged the tanker SS *Halo* off Cape Hatteras. He returned to Lorient on 25 February.

For his next patrol, he left for operations in the Caribbean on 24 March 1942 and within a short time came across a convoy. He sank the Norwegian merchant ship the MV *Grenager* on 11 April. Kals then sank the American tanker SS *Esso Boston* on the following day about 300 miles north-east of St. Martins. *U-130* was then ordered to bombard the oil installations at Bullen Bay in Curaçao. The boat approached and began firing at the Shell oil depot at 03:00 hours on the 19th, but the U-boat was driven off by shore batteries after firing only twelve rounds. With slight damage Kals took the boat back to port. During his next patrol, this time in the Atlantic, Kals and *U-130* were operating against Convoy SL115 and almost sank the sloop HMS *Lulworth* on 14 July. On the 25th he attacked the Norwegian tanker the MV *Tankexpress* and sank her south-west of the Cape Verde Islands, then just two days later he sank the British SS *Elmwood*. After being refuelled *U-130* sank the British MV *Danmark* on the 30th and the Norwegian tanker SS *Malmanger* on the 9 August. Kals was having great success and the 11th he sank the Norwegian tanker SS *Mirlo* north-west of St. Pauls Rock, followed on the 25th by the British SS *Viking Star* and the day after that the SS *Beechwood*. He ended what had been a very successful patrol on 12 September when he returned to Lorient. Soon after returning to port he was informed he had been awarded the Knight's Cross.

He left for operations in the Central Atlantic on 29 October. He sailed *U-130* south, when news of the Allied landings in North Africa came in early November. When he arrived off the Moroccan coast, on the 12th, he took *U-130* towards Fedala where he noticed twenty ships, including an aircraft carrier and a cruiser. With five torpedoes Kals sank three US troop transports from Convoy UGF1 – the USS *Edward Rutledge*, *Tasker H. Bliss* and *Hugh L. Scott*. The area soon became dangerous for U-boats as the escorts and destroyers closed in on their positions. Kals quickly took *U-130* off northwards, close inshore, and escaped.

He soon joined *Westwall* Group and on the 26th they moved west of the Azores to intercept new convoys beyond the range of land-based aircraft. During the night of 6/7 December, four ships were sunk, none however by *U-130*. On the 12th, the group began to move east and soon broke up shortly after being refuelled, and took up new positions west of Portugal. After almost a week of no contacts, Kals headed for his home port.

When Kals reached base he was given leave and in early January 1943, was named as commander of the 2nd U-boat Flotilla. He was promoted to *Fregattenkapitän* in June and in August was made chief of the submarine base at Lorient, whilst also being flotilla commander. In November he was appointed Chief of Staff to the Sea Commander Lorient, and whilst visiting a naval company he was seriously wounded by a mine. He eventually recovered and returned to duty, and was promoted to *Kapitän zur See* in September 1944. He spent the remainder of the war in this position and surrendered to French troops on 10 May 1945, remaining in Allied captivity until 20 January 1948. Kals returned to Germany and settled in Emden, Lower Saxony. He died on 8 November 1979.

Other awards:
02 Oct 1936: Long Service Award 4th to 3rd Class
18 Dec 1939: Iron Cross 2nd Class
18 Dec 1941: Iron Cross 1st Class
18 Dec 1941: U-Boat Badge
30 Jan 1944: War Service Cross 2nd Class with Swords

Otto Friedrich <u>Gerd</u> KELBLING

Kapitänleutnant
15 ships sunk, 51,295 tons
3 ships damaged, 6,530 tons

(Scherzer)

Knight's Cross: Awarded on 18 August 1943 as *Kapitänleutnant* and as commander of *U-593* for the sinking of ten ships for a total of 36,686 shipping tons, and for damaging another four, of which two were later declared total losses.

Born on 12 June 1915 in Bad Salzbrunn, Lower Silesia, now in south-western Poland, Gerd Kelbling entered the *Reichsmarine* in April 1934. He was initially assigned to the 4th Company of 2nd Ships Training Division in the Baltic Sea, and spent time on the sail training ship *Gorch Fock* and the light cruiser *Karlsruhe*, before attending the Naval Academy at Flensburg from March 1936. In April 1937 he was commissioned as a *Leutnant zur See*, and assigned to the minesweeper *M132* where he served as Second Watch Officer and later as First Watch Officer. In September 1938, Kelbling was transferred to the minesweeper *M146* where he served as adjutant. In April 1939 he was promoted to *Oberleutnant zur See* and assigned as Leader of River Auxiliary Minesweepers as part of the Danube River Flotilla. From November he was commander of the minesweeper *M89* and from August 1940 commanded the minesweeper *M6*, and took part in minesweeping and escort duties in the North Sea.

In January 1941 Kelbling transferred to the U-boat service, and he began his training as a commander in August, aboard *U-557*. Promoted to *Kapitänleutnant* soon afterwards he was given his own command of *U-593*, a Type VIIC boat in October. With its sea trials complete, Kelbling took *U-593* out on its first war patrol on 2 March 1942. He headed for the Atlantic and *U-593* was one of seven boats carrying out operations west of the Faroes and the Hebrides as part of Hitler's orders to repel an expected invasion of Norway. However this operation was discontinued in March and Kelbling continued to search for convoys. On the 18th *U-507* sighted Convoy ONS76, and *U-593* was one of three boats directed to the area but could not close in time. On the morning of the 27th, *U-593* surfaced and in doing so was spotted by two British destroyers of a naval force heading to raid St. Nazaire. Kelbling ordered the boat to dive and the destroyer HMS *Tynedale* closed and made a depth-charge attack, *U-593* was driven to the surface but then managed to dive again and escaped.

On 1 May, during his second patrol, Kelbling sighted a convoy 80 miles north-west of Cape Sable. *U-593* and three other boats were directed toward the convoy, but contact was lost, the boats split up and the operation was called off. On the 14th *U-593* torpedoed and damaged the SS *Stavros* east-north-east of Atlantic City. Then on the afternoon of the 25th Kelbling sighted the tanker MV *Persephone*, and torpedoed and sank her just east of the Narmegat Light, New Jersey. Kelbling put in at St. Nazaire on 18 June. On 22 July, Kelbling took *U-593* on patrol and headed for the North Atlantic. There he joined *Steinbrinck* Group and on the 5th *U-593* sighted Convoy SC94 and called up other boats to join them. The convoy was pursued for sometime by the group and they sank eleven ships from the convoy. *U-593* torpedoed and sank the Dutch SS *Spar* on 5 August east of Newfoundland. The patrol ended on 19 August.

Kelbling was ordered to take his boat from St. Nazaire on 3 October and sail her to her new base at La Spezia. On 2 November *U-593* left its new base and began its fourth patrol, heading out for the western Mediterranean. On the 8th the landings in North Africa began and the boats operated against the invasion and supply shipping. But *U-593* failed to sink any ships and returned to port on the 16th. From 29 November until early March 1943, *U-593* carried out two more patrols but these were both unsuccessful and there is little information on either. On 13 March *U-593* left for the eastern Mediterranean and made some successful attacks on the convoys. On the 18th, off Derna, Libya, Kelbling sank two ships, the British SS *Dafila* and SS *Kaying*. The patrol ended on the 21st.

From 25 March until 8 August 1943 Kelbling took his boat on another four war patrols and sank a further six ships and damaged two others. One of these ships was carrying nearly 300 Canadian troops. On 5 July Kelbling fired two spreads of two torpedoes and one of the torpedoes struck the British MV *Devis*. She wasn't just carrying troops but also had on board landing craft for Operation Husky, the invasion of Sicily. Fifty-two soldiers were lost as were the landing craft. A total of twenty-four crewmen, twenty-one gunners and 237 soldiers were picked up by HMS *Cleveland*. On 15 September Kelbling took *U-593* out from Toulon for operations in the Salerno bridgehead. He attacked invasion shipping in the Tyrrhenian Sea south of Salerno and on the 21st sank the US SS *William W. Gerhard* and on the 25th sank the minesweeper USS *Skill*. During his next patrol Kelbling sank the French SS *Mont Viso* on 3 November, north-west of Cherchel.

On 1 December, *U-593* left for the Algerian coast and on the 12th sighted Convoy KMS34. She attacked the convoy, sinking the destroyer HMS *Tynedale* north-east of Bougie. From the crew of 155, seventy-three were lost. A search began for the boat but it was not found. In the afternoon Kelbling sank another British destroyer HMS *Holcombe*. Another search was made for *U-593* which lasted ten hours, the boat was found soon after midnight by a Leigh Light Wellington. The aircraft was damaged by flak and left the area. The search continued, however, for another twelve hours before *U-593* was again located by the destroyer USS *Wainwright*. Together with the destroyer HMS *Calpe* depth-charge attacks were made and *U-593* had to surface and came under fire from both warships. Kelbling soon gave the order to abandon and scuttle the boat, which went down as an American boarding party came alongside. The entire crew of *U-593* survived and were taken to North Africa.

On 13 December 1943, Kelbling was transferred to a POW camp in England and was later transferred to one in Canada. He was released on 20 September 1947 and returned to Germany. Kelbling was well regarded by his crew who stated to Allied interrogators that although he was a strict disciplinarian on board he was always fair and gave praise when it was due. His officers spoke of his unusual skill as a U-boat commander. Kelbling died in Ammersee, Upper Bavaria on 9 June 2005, just three days before his ninetieth birthday.

Other awards:
08 Apr 1938: Long Service Award 4th Class
31 May 1940: Iron Cross 2nd Class
29 Aug 1940: Iron Cross 1st Class
03 Dec 1940: Minesweepers Badge
30 Mar 1942: U-Boat Badge

Eitel-Friedrich KENTRAT

Korvettenkapitän
8 ships sunk, 43,358 tons
2 ships damaged, 11,525 tons

Knight's Cross: Awarded on 31 December 1941 as *Kapitänleutnant* and as commander of *U-74* for sinking five ships for a total of 25,619 shipping tons, and for damaging another two.

Eitel-Friedrich Kentrat was born on 11 September 1906, in Stahlheim (now known as Amnéville) in north-east France. He volunteered to join the Coastal Defence Department of the *Reichsmarine* in October 1925. In March 1927 and for the next eighteen months he spent training aboard the sail training ship *Niobe*, and from January 1930 he attended the Naval School at Flensburg before being assigned to the survey vessel *Meteor* for navigation training. Kentrat was commissioned as a *Leutnant zur See* on 1 October 1932, and then served aboard the battleship *Hessen* with the rank of *Oberleutnant zur See* and from October 1935 on the heavy cruiser *Deutschland* as adjutant, and later as Signals Officer with the rank of *Kapitänleutnant*.

From May 1938, Kentrat served as a company leader with the I. *Schiffsstammabteilung*, and from early September 1939 he was briefly attached to the Navy Department Office in Hamburg, before serving as Watch Officer on board the battleship *Scharnhorst* until October. He then transferred to the U-boat service, attending various training courses before being assigned as First Watch Officer onboard *U-25*, under the command of *Kapitänleutnant* Viktor Schütze in January 1940. He took part in one war patrol with *U-25*, from 13 January until 19 February, during which six ships were sunk. He attended a commanders' training course and in May 1940 was appointed commander of *U-8*, a Type IIB boat built by Germania Werft in Kiel. It was to be a brief command. Kentrat took out his new boat from Kiel to operate west

(Scherzer)

of the Orkney Islands on 19 May. However, on 4 June he suffered a serious injury after a freak accident on board and the boat had to stop in Esbjerg, Denmark where Kentrat spent over three months recovering in hospital.

Finally fit for duty, Kentrat took command of *U-74*, a Type VIIB boat, on 31 October 1940, and after training duties he took his new boat out on his first war patrol as commander. He left port on 5 March 1941, to operate south of Iceland. On the night of the 8th/9th a convoy was sighted but Kentrat was unable to make an attack. On the 11th he was directed towards the westbound Convoy HX112, but only *U-99* had any success. The other boats, including *U-74*, were driven off by the escorts. More convoys were sighted on the 19th by German aircraft but the boats failed to locate them. Finally the U-boats were able to intercept a convoy on the evening of 2 April, and from then until the early morning of the 3rd seven boats made attacks, sinking eleven ships and damaging another. Kentrat sank the Greek *Leonides Z. Cambanis* and torpedoed and damaged the British armed merchant cruiser HMS *Worcestershire*, both west of Rockall. Kentrat put in at his new base at St. Nazaire on 11 April.

His next patrol began on 8 May, when *U-74* left to operate in the North Atlantic, where it was, from 13th, part of a patrol group south-east of Greenland. Over the next three days boats from the group sank nine ships but *U-74* had no success. During a depth-charge attack *U-74* had been damaged and on 25th Kentrat decided to make for home. However, together with other boats *U-74* was ordered to assist the *Bismarck*. On the 24th the battleships *Bismarck* and the heavy cruiser *Prinz Eugen* attempted to enter the Atlantic via the Denmark Strait. The idea was that the U-boats would form a patrol line and protect the two battleships and would deal with any British vessels that were seen to shadow the two battleships. However, the plan was changed when the *Bismarck* was damaged during the Battle of the Denmark Strait by HMS *Prince of Wales* on 24 May. *Bismarck* would make for St. Nazaire and *Prinz Eugen* would head to the south-west. On the evening of the 25th *Bismarck* was damaged by a torpedo attack. Eight U-boats, including *U-74* were then ordered to assist *Bismarck* into the comparative shelter of the

Bay of Biscay. They assembled on the 25th, 450 miles west of St. Nazaire and were then ordered to form a patrol line running north-west from Cape Ortegal. This was delayed until the 26th because of bad weather. Boats that still had torpedoes were ordered to assist *Bismarck* but heavy seas prevented them from locating the battleship. *Bismarck* was sunk on the morning of the 27th. Kentrat arrived at the scene of the sinking but was unable to make an attack against British ships because of the bad weather. HMS *Devonshire*, which had stopped to pick up survivors, sighted the periscope of *U-74* and left the scene after only picking up 110 men. *U-74* picked up only three men. Over 2,000 German sailors were lost. *U-74* then returned to base on 30 May.

Kentrat took *U-74* out on his third patrol from Lorient on 5 July, and headed for the central North Atlantic. No convoys were sighted until the 17th, and the patrol line was avoided by the convoy on the 19th and another was formed on the 20th, with *U-74* and twelve other boats. This was also unsuccessful. Kentrat then took part in another failed operation against Convoy SL80 between the 24th and 26th. On 1 August, Convoy SL81 was located south-west of Ireland, but the boats were prevented from making any attacks by a strong escort presence. During the early morning of the 5th Kentrat made an attack in the convoy and torpedoed and damaged the British SS *Kumasian* west of Ireland. *U-74* returned to St. Nazaire on 12 August. During his next patrol which began on 8 September, Kentrat sank the Canadian corvette HMCS *Levis* during the morning of the 19th, and the following day he sank the British catapult-armed merchant ship *Empire Burton*, both east of Cape Farewell. His next patrol, still in the North Atlantic lasted from 22 October until 11 November when as part of *Reissewolf* Group he was directed towards Convoy ON28, 500 miles west of Ireland. Only *U-74* and *U-77* were successful, Kentrat torpedoed and sank the British merchant ship *Nottingham* on the 7th. At about 22:34 hours, *U-74* sighted the unescorted *Nottingham*, which was on her maiden voyage. She was hit in the stern by the torpedo and tried to ram *U-74* but was unsuccessful. She managed to avoid two more torpedoes fired by Kentrat but was hit by a third at 23:00 hours and sank. The crew were seen to abandon ship in lifeboats, but they were never seen again. Sixty-two men were lost.

On 23 March 1942, Kentrat transferred to the staff of the 2nd Admiral of U-boats, *Kapitän zur See* Hans-Georg von Friedeburg. He remained in this position until 11 September when he was named as commander of *U-196*, a Type IXD2 boat built by AG Weserin Bremen. He was promoted to *Korvettenkapitän* in January 1943, and after initial training of his crew and sea trials, he took his new command out on its first patrol on 13 March 1943. *U-196* passed through the South Atlantic and reached the area near Cape Town at the end of April, but had no success. Kentrat then took *U-196* around the Cape and on 11 May he torpedoed and sank the British SS *Nailsea Meadow*. Kentrat then began a patrol off the coast of South Africa until mid-June when he headed for a pre-arranged point where the boat was replenished. After being refuelled by the German supply ship *Charlotte Schliemann*, which had been sent from Japan, *U-196* returned eastwards and from 8 July was operating off the Mozambique Channel. On 2 August Kentrat torpedoed and damaged the British steamer the SS *City of Oran*, 50 miles east of Memba. The boat then moved south and on 14th was spotted by a Ventura aircraft, from the South African Air Force, off the coast of Natal. The aircraft dropped five depth charges but caused no damage. There then followed a three-day hunt for the U-boat. *U-196* was attacked twice by a Ventura on the 15th but again no damage was caused. Kentrat managed to sail *U-196* out of danger and on 20th he successfully rendezvoused with *U-181*, 300 miles south-south-west of Madagascar and passed current code keys which *U-181* had received from *U-197* on the 19th. While the boats were together they received a signal that *U-197* had been attacked by aircraft and was unable to submerge. So Kentrat together with *U-181*, under the command of *Korvettenkapitän* Wolfgang Lüth, moved to meet the stricken boat. However, after a search they found no trace of the U-boat. They gave up and on the 24th headed for home. Kentrat finally reached Bordeaux on 23 October after 225 days, which must be the longest single operational patrol by a U-boat in the Second World War.

On 16 March 1944, Kentrat left for operations in the Indian Ocean, taking *U-196* through the Central Atlantic and on 23 April was located by destroyers and came under attack. The boat escaped without damage. *U-196* passed Cape Town and moved into the Indian Ocean, and sailed north where Kentrat torpedoed and sank the British SS *Shahzada* on 9 July. It was Kentrat's only success of this patrol. He returned to port at Penang, Malaysia on 10 August. From September 1944 until the end of the war Kentrat served in several staff positions in Penang and from October in Tokyo, Japan. From 28 March 1945 Kentrat served as base commander at Kobe and was an assistant to the German Naval Attaché in Tokyo.

He surrendered to the Americans in June 1945 and was imprisoned until 1 October 1947 when he returned to Germany, via the US troopship *General Black*. Kentrat died on 9 January 1974 in Bad Schwartau, Ostholstein.

Other awards:
02 Oct 1936: Long Service Award 4th Class
01 Oct 1937: Long Service award 3rd Class
13 Apr 1941: Iron Cross 2nd Class
13 Apr 1941: Iron Cross 1st Class
13 Apr 1941: U-Boat Badge
20 Sep 1944: U-Boat Combat Clasp in Bronze

Johannes Siegfried KOITSCHKA

Kapitänleutnant
2 ships sunk, 2,181 tons
2 ships damaged, 17,754 tons

Knight's Cross: Awarded on 27 January 1944, as *Oberleutnant zur See* and as commander of *U-616* in recognition of his leadership and skills as a commander and for sinking two ships.

Siegfried Koitschka was born in Siebitz, Bautzen, Germany on 6 August 1917. He entered the *Reichsmarine* at the age of nineteen in April 1937. He joined as an Officer Candidate and was initially assigned to the 3rd Company of the II. *Schiffsstammdivision* in the Baltic. From June he saw service in the sail training ship *Gorch Fock* and the light cruiser *Emden* before being assigned to the Naval School at Flensburg in April 1938.

(Scherzer)

In April 1939 he was transferred to the heavy cruiser *Admiral Hipper* where he served until September. On 23 August, Koitschka was commissioned as a *Leutnant zur See* and continued with his basic training. In July 1940 he transferred to the U-boat service and was attached to the 1st U-boat Training Division until October when he was briefly assigned to a training unit in Plön. From December he served as Second Watch Officer aboard *U-552*, whilst under the command of *Korvettenkapitän* Erich Topp. He participated in a total of six patrols with Topp during which time a total of thirteen ships was sunk, for a total of 75,085 shipping tons, which included the first US ship sunk by a German U-boat in the Second World War, the destroyer USS *Reuben James*. He had been promoted to *Oberleutnant zur See* in August 1941, and from December until January 1942 he spent training as a U-boat commander – serving aboard a boat commanded by someone like Topp, who became a top U-boat ace, was a good start.

On 16 January 1942 he took command of *U-7*, a Type IIB U-boat which had from May 1940 been used as a training vessel. In October, with his training complete, Koitschka took over the command of *U-616*, a Type VIIC boat built by Blohm und Voss of Hamburg. He took his new boat out on his first patrol as commander on 6 February 1943, leaving Kiel for operations in the Atlantic. Koitschka soon joined *Burggraf* Group, formed on the 26th in the central North Atlantic, north of the Azores. The boats swept westwards and joined *Wildfang* Group stationed to the north. The two groups formed a long patrol line from 4 March and waited for Convoy SC121 to pass. In stormy weather and heavy seas, attacks began on the convoy. In the afternoon of the 10th Koitschka made an unsuccessful attack on a ship. Soon after the operation against SC121 ended on the 11th, *U-616* was refuelled by *U-119* north of the Azores and was then directed towards Convoy HX229. Koitschka made two more unsuccessful attacks against the destroyers and on the 17th attacked a corvette but again without success. *U-616* left the area early due to being out of torpedoes and arrived at her new base at St. Nazaire on 26 March. From 19 April until 18 September 1943, Koitschka took part in three short patrols in the Mediterranean area where he missed an opportunity to sink an escort but claimed another ship but this was unconfirmed.

On 3 October, Koitschka took *U-616* out from Toulon and sailed for the Salerno area where on the 9th he torpedoed and sank the destroyer USS *Buck*. She was struck by an acoustic torpedo just off the Salerno beachhead about 50 miles south of Capri, Italy. The destroyer had picked up a radar contact when the torpedo struck the starboard bow. The explosion ignited the forward magazines as two explosions occurred almost simultaneously, blew off the bow and wrecked the navigating bridge, killing the commander and all four officers on watch. The crew tried to set the depth charges on safe but the destroyer sank within just four minutes of being hit. No distress signal was sent and the convoy didn't notice the ship's loss until the following morning. USS *Gleaves* picked up sixty-four survivors and four bodies, but four later died after being rescued. A total of 168 men were lost. On the 11th he sank the British landing craft HMS *LCT-553*, and he claimed another but this is unconfirmed. He returned to port on 15 October. From 20 November Koitschka took *U-616* out on another three patrols and claimed another three ships sunk but all of these are unconfirmed. On 30 April 1944, *U-616* left for the Mediterranean and by early May was in contact with Convoy UGS40, and was promoted to *Kapitänleutnant* on the 15th. *U-616* and *U-967* attempted to close but were prevented by bad weather. During the night of the 13th/14th Koitschka torpedoed and damaged two ships from Convoy GUS39, the British tankers MV *G.S. Walden* and SS *Fort Fidler*. Then the destroyers

Gleaves, *Nields* and *Macomb* were joined at the scene by other US destroyers, as well as aircraft of 36 Squadron. Early on the 14th USS *Hilary P. Jones* damaged *U-616* during a depth-charge attack. The other destroyers hunted for her all that day but found nothing. A Wellington bomber made a clear radar contact at nightfall, catching *U-616* on the surface. It dived and was again depth-charged but contact was lost. At dawn a 10-mile oil slick was seen. The hunt continued for another day and again *U-616* was seen on the surface at midnight on the 15th, but the boat dived and markers were dropped. The searching ships closed in, and contact was made by the destroyer USS *Macomb* just before midnight on the 16th. She caught *U-616* in a searchlight and fired six rounds before she submerged. More depth-charge attacks were made and *U-616* surfaced and immediately came under fire. Koitschka had no choice but to order abandon ship and the boat was scuttled, and it sank in five minutes. Koitschka and all of his forty-seven crew were picked up by the USS *Ellyson*. The three-day hunt for *U-616* was the longest one for a single U-boat carried out during the Second World War. Koitschka spent the remainder of the war in captivity in Camp MS Cain in the United States. He was released on 1 June 1946 and returned to Germany.

Years later Koitschka and his wife were invited every year to the annual reunion of the USS *Ellyson* and USS *Rodman*. He and his wife were well liked and were highly respected by their neighbours in their small farming community. Koitschka died in Lohra, Hessen on 17 May 2002. He was eighty-four, and was remembered for his excellent sense of humour.

Other awards:
03 Apr 1941: Long Service Award 4th Class
08 May 1941: Iron Cross 2nd Class
08 May 1941: U-Boat Badge
07 Oct 1941: Iron Cross 1st Class
19 Nov 1943: German Cross in Gold

<u>Claus</u> Theodor Friedrich Otto KORTH

Korvettenkapitän
15 ships sunk, 73,015 tons
1 ship damaged, 4,996 tons

Knight's Cross: Awarded as *Kapitänleutnant* and as commander of *U-93* on 29 May 1941, in recognition of his leadership and in sinking fourteen ships for a total of 66,780 shipping tons during sixteen war patrols.

Claus Korth was born on 7 November 1911 in Berlin and he joined the *Reichsmarine* in April 1932, being assigned to the II. *Schiffsstammdivision* in the Baltic. He attended the usual training courses from July 1932, which included service aboard the light cruiser *Köln*. From April 1935 Korth served aboard the 'pocket battleship' *Deutschland*, and in January 1936 he was commissioned as a *Leutnant zur See*. In June he served

(Author's collection)

as Watch Officer with U-boat Flotilla *Saltzwedel* and from January 1937 he served as Watch Officer aboard *U-31*. In October Korth was promoted to *Oberleutnant zur See*, and continued with his training.

On 29 December 1938 Korth was appointed commander of *U-57*, a Type IIC Boat, which was used as a training boat until August 1939 when it became operational. On 25 October 1939, Korth took *U-57* out on patrol operating against British naval forces in the area of the Orkneys, returning to Kiel on 5 November. His second patrol began on 12 November in the North Hinder area, in the southern North Sea. On 17th he sank the Lithuanian SS *Kaunas* and later on the 19th he also sank the British SS *Stanbrook* in the same area. She was struck by a single torpedo and broke in two and sank quickly west-north-west of the North Hinder Lightship. During a later patrol he sank the Estonian SS *Mina* on the 13 December, off the coast of England for the loss of seventeen of her crew. On 16 January 1940, during his seventh patrol during a minelaying operation Korth sank the Norwegian SS *Miranda* with a single torpedo about 30 miles north-west of Peterhead. The explosion broke the keel of the ship which caused her to sink within five minutes, and fourteen of her crew were lost. *U-57* went onto lay mines off Invergordon and four days later the British accommodation ship HMS *Durham Castle* struck one these mines and sank. Korth took *U-57* to Wilhelmshaven on 25 January.

On 8 February Korth left to operate against British naval forces in the Shetlands area. Early on the 14th Korth sank the MV *Gretafield*, a tanker from Convoy HX18. On the evening of the 21st he torpedoed and damaged the SS *Loch Maddy* from Convoy HX19. His next patrol took *U-57* east of the Pentland Firth where he sank the SS *Svinta* on 21 March. This vessel had already been damaged in a bombing attack by German aircraft the previous day. In the evening of the 25th, in the same area, Korth sank the British tanker MV *Daghestan*.

His next patrol began on 4 April when he took *U-57* out of Kiel under sealed orders to take part in Operation *Hartmut*, part of the German invasion of Denmark and Norway. His orders were opened on the 6th and the boats in the area were ordered just off the Norwegian coast, where from the 9th they were to support German transports and naval forces landing troops and to defend them against British warships. Korth was then ordered to join the 6th U-boat group, which was to operate east of the Orkneys from the 9th, and *U-57*'s patrol ended on the 7 May when Korth returned to Kiel.

On 30 July 1940, now a *Kapitänleutnant*, Korth took command of *U-93*, a Type VIIC built by Germania Werft. He left on his first war patrol with his new boat on 5 October to operate west of Britain. On the 14th Korth torpedoed and sank the British SS *Hurunui* from Convoy OB227, south-west of the Faroes. On the 16th he made contact with Convoy OB228 and in the early hours of the following day Korth sank the Norwegian SS *Dokka* and the British SS *Uskbridge*. During his next patrol Korth failed to score and after only twenty-two days at sea he put in at Lorient. On 11 January 1941, Korth took *U-93* out of port to operate west of the North Channel and Ireland. Although many convoys were spotted by German aircraft the co-operation between the aircraft and the U-boats wasn't good and as a result most U-boats failed to make contact with any convoys. However, the aircraft were more successful in their attacks and sank seven ships. During the early hours of the 29th Korth sighted Convoy SC19 south of Rockall. He torpedoed and sank three ships, the British SS *King Robert*, the British tanker SS *W.B. Walker* (10,468 tons) and the Greek SS *Alkaterini*. Korth also sank the British SS *Dione II* on 4 February, with the loss of thirty of her crew. On his return journey *U-93* was attacked by a Whitley aircraft and was damaged. Korth arrived safely into Lorient on 14 February.

Korth left for the North Atlantic on 3 May and joined up with *U-94*, *U-98* and *U-556* on the 11th to form a patrol group south-east of Greenland. Two days later they were joined by *U-74*, *U-97*, *U-109* and *U-111*. The group moved to the south-west on the 15th and formed a new patrol line. On the 19th Convoy HX126 was sighted and the boats closed in. On the night of the 21st/22nd Korth sank the Dutch tanker MV *Elusa* east of Cape Farewell. On the 24th some of the boats were ordered to form a patrol line south of Cape Farewell, ahead of the fleeing *Bismarck*, in the hope of sinking some of her pursuers after she had passed through their line. However, the plan was cancelled when the *Bismarck* changed course and headed towards St. Nazaire. In late May *U-93* and *U-94* left the group and moved near Greenland for refuelling by the German supply ship *Belchen*. On 3 June, *Belchen* was attacked by two British cruisers and sunk and *U-93* picked up forty-nine survivors and instead of joining a new group Korth decided to return to port with his exhausted and shocked passengers and headed for St. Nazaire, arriving on 10 June. During his final patrol with *U-93* he headed for operations in the Central Atlantic but these were all unsuccessful. He made several patrols together with other boats from 22 July until 16 August when they were called off. He returned to port on 21 August.

From 1 October 1941 Korth served as aide-de-camp to the *2. Admiral der U-Boote*, *Konteradmiral* Hans-Georg von Friedeburg. In June 1942 he was appointed training officer to the 27th U-Boat Flotilla under the command of *Fregattenkapitän* Werner Hartmann and from October 1942 under *Korvettenkapitän* Erich Topp and was located at Gotenhafen. In January 1944 Korth was promoted to *Korvettenkapitän* and From March until the end of the war he was attached to the Torpedo Trial Institute in North Eckernförde, where he worked on the further development of torpedoes and was one of the military representatives. However, by April 1945, with the advance of the Red Army, the work of the Institution came to a standstill and munitions and staff were moved north to escape the Soviet advance. Korth was captured by the Western Allies and held until November 1945.

In November 1955 Korth joined the *Bundesmarine* where he was for nearly four years the head of the Torpedo Trial Station. He retired in March 1970 with the rank of *Kapitän zur See*. He lived in Kiel until his death on 24 January 1988.

Other awards:
02 Oct 1936: Long Service Award 4th Class
06 Jun 1939: Spanish Cross in Bronze
05 Nov 1939: U-Boat Badge
22 Nov 1939: Iron Cross 2nd Class
26 Jan 1940: Iron Cross 1st Class
20 Apr 1944: War Service Cross 2nd Class with Swords

Hans-Werner KRAUS
Kapitänleutnant
8 ships sunk, 12,702 tons
2 ships damaged, 9,336 tons

(Scherzer)

Knight's Cross: Awarded on 19 June 1942 as *Kapitänleutnant* and as commander of *U-83* for his leadership skills and for sinking five ships and damaging another two during eight war patrols.

Born on 1 July 1915 in Beulwitz, Saale, Hans-Werner Kraus joined the *Reichsmarine* in April 1934 as an Officer Candidate with the II. *Schiffsstammdivision* in the Baltic. From June 1934 until October 1939 Kraus attended various courses as part of his basic training. This included attendance at the Naval Academy at Flensburg where he underwent tactical navigation and officer training, practical training aboard the sail training ship *Gorch Fock* and the light cruiser *Königsberg*. Kraus was commissioned as a *Leutnant zur See* in April 1937 and promoted to *Oberleutnant zur See* in April 1939.

From October 1939 he attended the U-boat School and then continued his training at the naval Academy, training to be a Watch Officer. On 2 January 1940 Kraus was made First Watch Officer aboard *U-47*, under the command of *Kapitänleutnant* Günther Prien. He participated in five war patrols and during this time *U-47* sank a total of nineteen ships and damaged another three. He left *U-47* in November and attended a U-boat commander's course before being appointed commander of *U-83* in February 1941. *U-83* was a Type VIIB boat built by Flenderwerft in Lübeck, and Kraus left Kiel for the Atlantic on his first patrol as commander on 26 July 1941. He was en route to his operational area in the central North Atlantic when he was ordered to intercept Convoy SL81. Together with three other boats a total of five ships were sunk – none by Kraus. From September *U-83* was part of *Bosemüller* Group and patrolled an area west of Ireland. On 1 October a convoy was sighted by *U-73* and *Bosemüller* Group was ordered to intercept, but bad weather prevented them from making contact. Another convoy was sighted but again contact could not be made and by the 4th, the whole operation was called off. Kraus returned disappointed to port on 9 September.

On 28 September, Kraus left for an area west of Ireland, and was directed to the southbound Convoy OG75. Contact was soon lost due to bad weather. On the 12th Kraus sank the Portuguese SS *Corte Real*. From the 17th *U-83* was part of *Breslau* Group, and together with *U-71* and *U-204* waited for the northbound Convoy HG75 from Gibraltar. On the 21st Kraus sighted a British naval task force off the coast of Gibraltar and he fired four torpedoes at two aircraft carriers, HMS *Eagle* and *Furious*, but they all missed. During the early hours of the 26th Kraus attacked HMS *Ariguani*, a British fighter catapult ship, and she was seriously damaged. The patrol ended on 31 October and the following day Kraus was promoted to *Kapitänleutnant*. From 11 December 1941 until April 1942 Kraus took *U-83* out on four patrols in the Mediterranean, and although he claimed to have torpedoed a steamer and a corvette off the Egyptian coast on 14 February, they have never been confirmed. On the 17th he torpedoed and damaged the British the MV *Crista* north of Bardia.

During his seventh patrol, which began on 4 May 1942, Kraus headed to the Eastern Mediterranean where he attacked a steamer on the 15th, but his torpedo missed. On the 28th, *U-83* was to have taken part in the German-Italian amphibious assault in the Gulf of Bomba, Cyrenaica but the boat had technical problems and had to be withdrawn from the operation, and returned to its base. His next patrol, which began on 4 June, took Kraus off the coast of Palestine. During the early hours of the 8th, he sank the Palestinian sailing ship *Esther* off Sidon and the Egyptian SS *Said*, both by gunfire. The next day he sank another Palestinian sailing ship, *Typhoon*, also by gunfire, and on the 13th he claimed the British patrol craft HMS *Farouk*. On 17 August during his final patrol as commander of *U-83* he sank the Canadian troopship SS *Princess Marguerite*. The ship was struck by two of four torpedoes and sank north-west of Port Said. Five crew members and fifty-three troops were lost. The master, 119 crew members and 945 troops were picked up by HMS *Hero* and HMS *Kelvin*.

After a period of service with a warship construction training division, Kraus was appointed commander of *U-199*, a Type IXD2 boat built by AG Weser, Bremen, on 28 November 1942. He left for operations in the South Atlantic on 13 May 1943, and whilst patrolling off the coast of Brazil *U-199* was sighted by a Brazilian aircraft but managed to escape. On the 27th, Kraus attacked the SS *Charles Willson Peale* which managed to evade a torpedo and reached Rio safely. On 3 July *U-199* was spotted again by two Brazilian aircraft, and was attacked. The aircraft was shot down and the crew lost. Kraus then sank the Brazilian sailing ship *Changri-La* on the 4th by gunfire. On the morning of 24th he sank the British SS *Henzada* approximately 100 miles south-west of Rio. Then on the 31st *U-199* was sighted on the surface by a US naval Mariner and had to dive. The aircraft dropped six depth charges, *U-199* had to surface and was so badly damaged that she was unable to submerge. More aircraft arrived, and a Brazilian Hudson made strafing attacks on the boat, a Brazilian Catalina made another attack and *U-199* was sunk. Eleven crewmen and Kraus were rescued, but fifty of the crew were lost.

Kraus arrived at Fort Hunt, a POW camp, on 18 August 1943, and was transferred in September 1943 to Crossville and then on 27 January 1944, he was sent to Papago Park. Kraus escaped from the camp on the night of 23/24 December, and a week later Kraus, together with another prisoner Helmut Drescher, had travelled 43 miles. However, Drescher had suffered an injury and they both had to surrender. They were returned to Papago Park. In February 1946 Kraus was sent to Camp Shanks, New York and then to a compound in the British zone of Germany near Münster, before being released on 22 May. Hans-Werner Kraus died in Wangen im Allgäu south-east of Baden-Württemberg, Germany on 25 May 1990.

Other awards:
00.00.193_: Golden Hitler Youth Badge
08 Apr 1938: Long Service Award 4th Class
29 Apr 1940: U-Boat War Badge
08 Jul 1940: Iron Cross 2nd Class
28 Sep 1940: Iron Cross 1st Class
18 Mar 1942: Italian Medal for Military Valour in Bronze

Günther Paul KRECH
Kapitänleutnant
19 ships sunk, 100,771 tons
2 ships damaged, 15,070 tons

Knight's Cross: Awarded on 17 September 1942 as *Kapitänleutnant* and as commander of *U-558* for the sinking of fourteen ships for a total of 66,526 shipping tons and for damaging two ships during eight war patrols.

Günther Krech was born on 21 September 1914 in Wilhelmshaven and entered the *Reichsmarine* in April 1933 as a cadet. His training was typical of any recruit and he served aboard the sail training ship *Gorch Fock* and the light cruiser *Karlsruhe* before entering the Naval Academy in Flensburg. Like Reinhard Hardegen and several other officers who would go on to become successful U-boat commanders, he was seconded to the Luftwaffe. From September 1936 until February 1939, he served in various staff positions, which included service with coastal artillery and at one point he served in the Luftwaffe High Command.

Krech was commissioned as a *Leutnant zur See* on 1 October 1936 and in eighteen months he had been promoted to *Oberleutnant zur See*. He attended torpedo school on his return to the *Kriegsmarine* and entered the U-boat service in November 1939. From March 1940 he briefly spent time training aboard *U-5* as a Watch Officer. He received his first combat experience from May when he was appointed First Watch Officer on *U-100* under *Kapitänleutnant* Joachim Schepke. He left the boat in November 1940 and after attending commander training whilst attached to the 24th U-boat Flotilla he took command of *U-558* in February 1941. He was promoted to *Kapitänleutnant* on 13 March.

On 1 June, Krech took *U-558*, a Type VIIC boat, out of Kiel for operations in the

North Atlantic. He joined *West* Group south-east of the Newfoundland Bank but no convoys were located and only one ship was sunk by *U-108*. Without success, Krech returned to Kiel on 7 August. His third patrol began on 25 August, and Krech took *U-558* to the Atlantic. On the 26th the southbound Convoy OS4 was sighted west of Ireland, and in the afternoon of the 28th he sank the British MV *Otaoi*, with the loss of thirteen crew members. Other convoys were sighted but Krech had no further success, and returned to Brest on 16 September. Krech left for the Atlantic on 11 October and in the evening of the 15th he sank the Canadian merchant ship *Vancouver Island*. At 21:54 hours the ship was spotted by *U-558*. Krech fired three torpedoes from about 200 metres, hitting the ship with two of them. The vessel was struck in the fore part and amidships and stopped but did not sink. Because Krech wanted to continue his search for

(Scherzer)

convoys he fired two more torpedoes, hitting the ship aft and causing her to sink fast by the stern. The master, sixty-four crew members, eight gunners and thirty-two passengers were lost. During the early hours of the 17th about 600 miles west of Rockall, Krech sank three ships the British SS *W.C. Teagle* and two Norwegian steamers *Erviken* and *Rym*. It was also presumed that *U-558* sank a corvette of the escort, HMS *Gladiolus*, but this cannot be confirmed. With all torpedoes used Krech returned to Brest on 25 October.

The next patrol was short because *U-558* was attacked by an aircraft and was damaged and returned to base. On 10 February 1942, Krech left once again for the North Atlantic and was directed to the westbound Convoy ONS67. The convoy was attacked on the morning of the 24th; three ships were hit by *U-558*, the British tankers MV *Anadara*, which was damaged and SS *Inverauder* and the Norwegian tanker MV *Eidanger* were sunk. During his next patrol, which began on 12 April, Krech headed for the coastal waters of the US. On 12 May he sunk the British armed trawler HMS *Bedfordshire* off Cape Lookout, North Carolina. There were no survivors, but four bodies later washed up on the beach at Ocracioke Island. Krech then took *U-558* southwards and on the 18th sank the Dutch SS *Fauna* near the Bahamas. Then three days later he sunk the Canadian SS *Troisdoc* west of Jamaica. On the 23rd he torpedoed and damaged the American tanker SS *William Boyce Thompson* and on the 25th he sank the US SS *Beatrice* by gunfire south-east of Kingston. This was followed by the sinking of the US Army transport ship *Jack*, just south of Haiti, two days later. The torpedo struck *Jack* on the starboard side and the explosion ripped open a large hole in the hull, blew the hatch covers off, stopped the engines, and damaged the radio. The ship quickly sank within four minutes. Of a crew of sixty, thirty-seven were lost including the master. He sank one more ship, on 1 June, the Dutch SS *Triton*, before reaching Brest on 21st.

On his next patrol Krech headed for the Caribbean, arriving in mid-August. He attacked a straggler from Convoy TAW15 on the 25th, and she was sunk with the loss of thirteen of her crew. By September *U-558* was in the eastern Caribbean and on the 13th sank the Dutch SS *Suriname*, the British MV *Empire Lugard* and the Norwegian tanker MV *Vilja* west of Grenada. Krech left the area and continued his patrol, on the 16th he sighted the US SS *Commercial Trader* and fired two torpedoes. She was hit and sank within two minutes, bow first. Two officers, five men and three armed guards died. The patrol ended in Brest on 16 October. There was time for leave before his next patrol which began on 9 January 1943, when Krech left for the Central Atlantic and where on the 23rd *U-558* joined *Delphin* Group. Towards the end of January the group headed for an area north-west of the Canaries and then towards Gibraltar. On 7 February a small coastal convoy was sighted and five boats from *Delphin* Group closed in. But the operation was cancelled due to a strong air escort. The group then headed westwards for four days and were directed towards another convoy. During the evening of the 23rd Krech torpedoed and sank the British tanker SS *Empire Norsemann*, 500 miles south of the Azores. Other convoys were later sighted but no more ships were sunk by Krech due to bad weather and strong Allied air cover. He headed home and reached Brest on 29th.

On 8 May, *U-558* left for the Atlantic and was from the 18th part of *Oder* Group and was hunting for Convoy HX238. The convoy was sighted on the 22nd but because of the risk of aircraft attacks the group kept away. However they were spotted by the Allied air escorts and many boats were attacked and damaged. On the 23rd the operation was terminated. During the next few weeks two patrol lines were formed in the areas near the Azores and east of Bermuda. The boats waited for the convoys to appear but none were sighted and the boats were again attacked by Allied aircraft. From 16 to 22 June, the U-boats waited for two convoys to pass the patrol line, having seen nothing during that time they moved eastwards and halted 200 miles south-west of the Azores. By the 29th it was obvious that the convoys had bypassed the lines. The operation was called off.

On 15 July *U-558* was attacked by a Wellington bomber but the aircraft was driven off and the boat dived to escape. Its position had, however, been reported and two days later whilst on the surface it was attacked by air and was damaged. On the 20th, while on its return journey *U-558* was sunk north-north-east of Cape Ortegal after depth-charge attacks by a Liberator of 19 Squadron and a Halifax of 58 Squadron. Of *U-558*'s crew, forty-five men were lost. There were only five survivors: Krech, his chief engineer *Leutnant zur See* Jürgen Scheller, *Obermaschinist* Ernst Kelch, *Matrosenobergefreiter* Martin Kaiser and *Matrose* Kurt Wagner. They were picked up by HMCS *Athabascan* on 25 July, all suffering from exposure.

Krech spent the next three years in British captivity, being released in 1946. He returned to Germany and entered civilian life. During his time in British captivity he was interrogated and a report stated that *Kapitänleutnant* Krech was cool, efficient, serious and a commander who was greatly respected by his men. The four men who survived the sinking of *U-558* said that they were in no doubt that their survival was due mainly to the attitude and humour of their commander. Krech died in Wuppertal, North-Rhine-Westphalia on 3 June 2000. He was eighty-five years old.

Other awards:
02 Nov 1936: Long Service Award 4th Class
00.00.1940: Iron Cross 2nd Class
09 May 1940: The Return of Memel Commemorative Medal
03 Sep 1940: Commemorative Medal of 01 Oct 1938
26 Sep 1940: Iron Cross 1st Class
26 Sep 1940: U-Boat War Badge

Günter KUHNKE
Korvettenkapitän
13 ships sunk, 56,272 tons
2 ships damaged, 10,067 tons

Knight's Cross: Awarded on 19 September 1940 as *Korvettenkapitän* and as commander of *U-28* for sinking twelve ships and damaging one for a total of 54,306 shipping tons.

Günter Kuhnke was born on 7 September 1912 in Elbing and entered the *Reichsmarine* as an Officer Candidate in April 1931. His basic training began in June when he was assigned to the sail training ship *Niobe* and from October he served on the light cruiser *Karlsruhe* for almost eighteen months. In November 1934 he was assigned to the 'pocket battleship' *Admiral Scheer*, and was commissioned as a *Leutnant zur See* in April 1935. From September Kuhnke began his training with the U-boat service with torpedo training at the Naval Academy in Flensburg. From August 1936 until June 1938, he was assigned to

Flotilla *Saltzwedel*, based in Kiel which later became known as the 2nd Training Flotilla. In January 1937 he had been promoted to *Oberleutnant zur See*, and in October 1938 was named as commander of *U-28*, a Type VIIA boat built by AG Weser.

In August 1939, Kuhnke took *U-28* out from Wilhelmshaven and headed for the Atlantic to operate west of the British Isles. While at sea Germany invaded Poland and the Second World War began. On 14 September he sank the British MV *Vancouver City* in the Celtic Sea south-west of Ireland, with the loss of three of her crew. Kuhnke was promoted to *Kapitänleutnant* on 1 October 1939, and during his second patrol where he operated in the Bristol Channel he sank the Dutch tanker MV *Sliedrecht* on 17 November. Kuhnke ordered her crew to abandon ship

(Scherzer)

and he then sank her with a torpedo at 02:00 hours. Five crew members in one lifeboat were picked up safely by a British trawler but another with twenty-six crew onboard was never seen again. On 25th he attacked the northbound Convoy SL8B and sank the British SS *Royston Grange*. He then laid mines off Swansea on 5 December and the British SS *Protesilaus* sunk when she hit one of his mines on 21 January 1940. His next patrol began on 18 February when he left for operations in the English Channel where he laid mines off Portsmouth. On 9 March he claimed the Greek SS *P. Margaronis* south-west of Land's End when she struck one of his mines, then on the 11th he sank the Dutch tanker MV *Eulota* south-west of the Scillies. He returned to base on 23 March.

U-28 was taken to Trondheim in late May for repairs and left for the Atlantic on 8 June as part of a pack-operation made up of six boats, commanded by Günther Prien. They formed a patrol line south-west of Ireland from the 12th, to intercept Convoy HX48. But no contact was made and the group was broken up. In the area of the Fastnet, Kuhnke sank three ships, the Finnish merchant the SS *Sarmatia* on the 18th, the Greek SS *Adamandois Georgandis* on the 19th and on the 21st the British Special Service Ship HMS *Cape Howe*, disguised as SS *Prunella*. She was struck by two torpedoes on the starboard side. The explosion blew out the hatches, put the Asdic and steering gear out of order and killed two crewmen. A *coup de grâce* was fired after an hour which caused the ship to slowly sink. Fifty-seven crew members were lost and forty were saved. Kuhnke returned to Wilhelmshaven. During his next patrol he took *U-28* to the west coast of Scotland where on 27 August he sank the Norwegian SS *Eva* by torpedo and gunfire just west of the Outer Hebrides. The following day Kuhnke sank the British SS *Kyno*. In early September, whilst patrolling in the Atlantic, a convoy was sighted but bad weather with very high winds prevented an attack being made. On 9th he did sink the British SS *Mardinian* south-west of Barra. On the 11th *U-28* attacked Convoy OA210 south-west of Rockall and damaged the British SS *Harpenden* and sank the Dutch SS *Maas*. Kuhnke put in at his new base at Lorient on 17 September.

After some well-deserved leave Kuhnke took *U-28* out to operate as a weather boat west of the British Isles on 12 October. A convoy was spotted on the night of the 16th/17th and four other boats were directed against it, but without success. During the early hours of the 26th Kuhnke torpedoed and damaged the British SS *Matina*. The abandoned wreck was later sunk by *U-31* on the 29th. On 26 October a Kondor aircraft from Bomber Wing 40 bombed the liner SS *Empress of Britain* and set her on fire. *U-28*, *U-31* and *U-32* were ordered to pursue, and on the 28th *U-32* sank the liner with two torpedoes. Kuhnke returned to Wilhelmshaven on 15 November 1940. Soon after returning Kuhnke relinquished his command and *U-28* went on to become a training boat, she was decommissioned in August 1944.

In March 1941, Kuhnke took command of *U-125*, a Type IXC Boat, and after her sea trials he left for operations in the Central Atlantic on 12 August. He operated together with two other boats west of the Azores and later towards the Cape Verde Islands and then into the Freetown area, but during this time no convoys were located. He returned to base in Lorient on 5 November. On 15 January 1942, Kuhnke was appointed commander of the 10th U-boat Flotilla at Lorient. He was promoted to *Korvettenkapitän* in March 1943, and assumed command of the 33rd U-Boat Flotilla at Flensburg in October 1944. He surrendered to British forces together with members of the Dönitz government in mid-May 1945, remaining in captivity until April 1946.

He entered the *Bundesmarine* in November 1955, and was from January 1957 a Naval Training Administrator with the rank of *Fregattenkapitän*. From July 1959 he commanded the destroyer *Z-2* (formerly USS *Ringgold*), and in November 1960 he served as a Staff Officer with the Naval High Command until October 1962. In October 1964 he became Deputy Commander of the Naval Fleet and was promoted to *Konteradmiral* in March 1966. From April 1966 until his retirement in September 1972 he served as Chief of the Naval Office. He died on 11 October 1990 in Schortens a town in Lower Saxony, Germany.

Other awards:
02 Oct 1936: Long Service Award 4th Class
29 Sep 1939: Iron Cross 2nd Class
01 Oct 1939: Iron Cross 1st Class
01 Oct 1939: U-Boot War Badge
30 Jan 1944: War Service Cross 2nd Class with Swords

Herbert Otto KUPPISCH
Kapitänleutnant
16 ships sunk, 82,108 tons

Knight's Cross: Awarded as a *Kapitänleutnant* on 14 May 1941 as commander of *U-94* in recognition of his success in sinking fourteen ships for a total of 71,262 shipping tons.

Herbert Kuppisch was born in Hamburg on 10 December 1909, and he joined the *Reichsmarine* in October 1933, and became one of the few naval officers who spent his entire career in

U-boats. From January 1934 he began his basic training he attended the Naval Gunnery School, the Naval Signals School and the Coastal Artillery School. He later served aboard the light cruisers *Leipzig* and *Königsberg*. He was commissioned as a *Leutnant zur See* in January 1936 and in December he attended the Torpedo School at Mürwik.

From May 1937 he was briefly attached to *U-29* as Second Watch Officer, the following month he attended a commander's course and in October was promoted to *Oberleutnant zur See*. For the next fifteen months he was attached to *U-9* and *U-23* where he served as Second Watch Officer, continuing his training as a U-boat commander. In February 1939 he took command of *U-58*, a Type IIC Boat, built by Deutsche Werke in Kiel. On 25 August he took *U-58* out of Wilhelmshaven and headed for the North Sea. When war broke out on 3 September, *U-58* was one of five boats in a north-east–south-west patrol line south-west of Norway. Kuppisch was ordered to return to base on the 9th.

(Scherzer)

From 23 October until 5 December 1939, Kuppisch took *U-58* out on two patrols, one around the area of the Orkney Islands and the other was a minelaying operation off Lowestoft. He had been promoted to *Kapitänleutnant* on 1 November 1939. On 27 December *U-58* left port to patrol off the north-east coast of Scotland and where on 1 January 1940 Kuppisch sank the Swedish SS *Lars Magnus Trozelli* and then a little further south he sank another Swedish vessel, the SS *Svareton*, from Convoy HN6. During his next patrol he sank the Estonian SS *Reet* in the northern region of the North Sea on 3 February, there were no survivors. On 31 March Kuppisch left port to take part in Operation *Hartmut*, the codename for the submarine operation during the German invasion of Denmark and Norway. He was ordered to join the 6th U-boat Group, which was to operate in the Pentland Firth and east of the Orkneys. Kuppisch had no success during this patrol and returned to Kiel on 3 May. During his seventh patrol which began on 27 May, Kuppisch sank the British boom defence ship HMS *Astronomer* on 1 June north-north-west of Kinnairds Head. After the sinking *U-58* was hunted by various naval vessels for forty-three hours but escaped. He headed back to Kiel, arriving on 17 June.

On 10 August 1940, now a *Kapitänleutnant*, Kuppisch took command of *U-94*, a Type VIIC boat built by Germania Werft of Kiel. He took his new boat out on its first war patrol on 20 November and headed towards the North Channel. A convoy was sighted on 1 December and five boats together with *U-94* shadowed the convoy and during the night of the 1st/2nd eight ships were sunk, but none by *U-94*. However on the afternoon of the 2nd Kuppisch attacked and sank the British SS *Stirlingshire* and later that same evening sank another British ship, the SS *Wilhelmina*. The convoy then scattered and the operation was terminated. On the 11th Kuppisch sighted the British SS *Empire Statesman*. He fired two torpedoes and she sank with loss of all hands. He then put in at his new base at Lorient on 31 December.

On 9 January 1941 Kuppisch left port to operate in the North Channel once again, soon after midnight on 19th he sank the British SS *Florian*. In the early hours of the 29th a convoy was sighted by *U-94*, and Kuppisch sank the SS *West Wales* and the next day he sank another British ship, SS *Rushpool*, south-east of Rockall. He returned to Lorient on 19 February. During his next patrol, his third with *U-94*, he encountered Convoy SC26 near Iceland and during the evening of 3 April Kuppisch sank the British SS *Harbledown*, then on the 6th he sank the Norwegian tanker MV *Lincoln Ellsworth* south-west of Reykjavik. His fourth patrol began on 29 April, with operations in the North Atlantic against Convoy OB318 south of Iceland. On the 7 May he attacked two ships, the British SS *Ixion* and the Norwegian SS *Eastern Star* and sank both of them. *U-94* was then detected and attacked by two destroyers. Kuppisch managed to escape the depth-charge attacks after four hours, and *U-94* left the area slightly damaged. On the 19th another convoy was sighted and on the morning of the 20th Kuppisch sank two more ships, the British SS *Norman Monarch* and in the evening the Norwegian tanker the MV *John P Pedersen*, both south-south-east of Cape Farewell. On the 24th *U-94* together with *U-43*, *U-46*, *U-66*, *U-93*, *U-111* and *U-557* was ordered to form a patrol line south of Cape Farewell, ahead of the fleeing *Bismarck*, in the hope of sinking some of her pursuers, but the plan was cancelled when it was decided that *Bismarck* would head for St. Nazaire. The patrol ended on 4 June when Kuppisch returned *U-94* to base. The next patrol, his last as commander of *U-94*, began on 12 July when Kuppisch headed out for the Central Atlantic. He joined three other boats and although they located a convoy they failed to sink any ships. They continued south past Morocco but no convoys were located. They were joined by other boats between Gibraltar and the Azores from 6 August, and a convoy was located but the boats were driven off before any attack could be made. The operation against the convoy was called off on the 16th and *U-94* returned to port five days later.

From September 1941 Kuppisch served on the Staff of the Commander of U-boats, in the Operations Department. On 29 December he transferred to the naval Operations Office where he remained until June 1943 when he briefly took command of *U-516*. On 6 July 1943, he took command of *U-847*, a Type IXD2 boat, and left Kiel for operations in the Atlantic, but *U-847* was damaged by pack ice in the Denmark Strait and he returned to base on the 20th. Nine days later Kuppisch took the newly repaired boat out for the Indian Ocean. *U-847* was ordered to serve as a U-tanker, following the loss of two tankers. On 19th August Kuppisch successful refuelled various boats returning from US waters. On completion of the operation, Kuppisch radioed to headquarters and his transmission was intercepted and *U-847* was sighted on the surface by three aircraft of VC-1 from the escort carrier USS *Card*. On 30 August the boat was forced to submerge by strafing attacks. One of the aircraft then dropped a homing torpedo and *U-847* was destroyed. There were no survivors; sixty-three men were dead.

Other awards:
04 Oct 1937: Long Service Award 4th Class
05 Dec 1939: Iron Cross 2nd Class
20 Dec 1939: Commemorative Medal of 01 Oct 1938
04 May 1940: Iron Cross 1st Class
04 May 1940: U-Boat War Badge

Hans LEHMANN
Oberleutnant zur See der Reserve
2 ships sunk, 1,708 tons
1 ship damaged, 4,287 tons

Knight's Cross: Awarded on 7 May 1945 as *Oberleutnant zur See der Reserve* and as commander of *U-997* in recognition of his leadership and achievements as a *Kriegsmarine* officer which included the sinking of two ships.

Hans Lehmann was born on 24 September 1915 in Brunsbüttelkoog, a small town in Schleswig-Holstein, northern Germany, which lies on the mouth of the River Elbe. Lehmann was recruited into the *Kriegsmarine* in November 1938, at the age of twenty-three. He was attached to the 1st Heavy Artillery Regiment until April 1939 when he transferred to 1st Minesweepers

(Scherzer)

Flotilla and served on the minesweeper *M3*. In December he attended a petty officer's training course, which included service aboard the heavy cruiser *Admiral Hipper* from February until April 1940. In July 1940 he was made commander of the German trawler *VP-402*, an auxiliary ship. Used as small minesweepers, they would sail ahead of other vessels through minefields to detonate any mines in their path – it was a difficult and dangerous job, and many such ships were destroyed during the Second World War. In March 1941 Lehmann was commissioned as a *Leutnant zur See*, and in November took command of *VP-407*.

In August 1942 Lehmann transferred to the U-boat service and began to train as a U-boat commander. In March 1943 he was promoted to *Oberleutnant zur See* and from June served as First Watch Officer aboard *U-454*, whilst under the command of *Kapitänleutnant* Burkhard Hackländer, although he didn't participate in any war patrols. In July he was named as commander of *U-997*, a Type VIIC-41 boat built by Blohm und Voss in Hamburg. The boat was completed in September 1943 and Lehmann took her through her sea trails and on board training of her crew. On 25 May 1944 *U-997* left Bogenbucht on her first war patrol. It was brief and there are no details of this patrol in the archives. Lehmann arrived back in port on 22 June. On 6 August *U-997* left on her second patrol as part of *Trutz* Group. On the 21st the group made contact with the eastbound Convoy JW59 and *U-344* sank the escort ship HMS *Kite*. On the 22nd the boats were attacked by aircraft and surface vessels. *U-997* was attacked by Swordfish and Martlets from the escort carriers HMS *Vindex* and *Striker*, and also from a Soviet Catalina. Lehmann was forced to order the boat to dive. During the early hours of the 24th *U-997* attacked two destroyers north of Vardø without success. Lehmann put in at Narvik on 2 September. His next patrol was brief and began on 13 September, when *U-997* was part of *Grimm* Group. No convoys were seen and the group avoided any problems. Lehmann put in at Bogenbucht on 2 October.

Lehmann then took *U-997* out on another patrol as part of *Panther* Group on 14 October and searched for convoys. On the night of the 26th/27th a convoy passed through the patrol line of *Panther* Group and attacks were made, but all were unsuccessful. Lehmann returned to Narvik on 9 November. During his next patrol Lehmann torpedoed and sank the Soviet sub-chaser *BO-229* on 7 December. He made an attack against the Soviet destroyer *Zhivuchiy* on the 9th but this was unsuccessful. On the 21st Lehmann sank the auxiliary patrol craft *Resitel'nyj* in Kola Fjord by gunfire. *U-997* returned to Narvik on 26 December. The next patrol was short, cut short due to carbon monoxide poisoning because of a defective *schnorkel* (device that allows a submarine to operate submerged while taking in air from the surface) and one of the crew went overboard. On 12 March 1945, Lehmann took *U-997* out on operations with *Hagen* Group in Bear Island Passage. Eventually a convoy was sighted and it passed through the *Hagen* patrol line and by the 21st two ships from the convoy had been sunk, but neither by *U-997*. Lehmann returned to port on 24th.

On 17 April 1945, Lehmann left from Kola Inlet and was soon joined by other boats to await Convoy JW66. On the 22nd Lehmann made several attacks on Soviet coastal Convoy PK9 off Mola Inlet. During the morning Lehmann missed the Soviet destroyer *Karl Libknecht* and the patrol craft *BO-225*, then a little later he torpedoed two ships, the Norwegian SS *Idefjord* which was damaged and the Soviet SS *Onega* which was sunk. In late April whilst still in the Kola Inlet area *U-997* was driven off by Allied and Soviet forces. Lehmann returned to Narvik on 30 April.

Lehmann was in Narvik when the war ended and was taken prisoner by British forces on 19 May. *U-997* was one of 116 boats disposed of by the Royal Navy in Operation Deadlight. In December 1945 she was towed from Loch Ryan out through the North Channel and was sunk by aircraft on 11 December. After his release from captivity Lehmann settled into civilian life and lived in Maschen near Hamburg until his death on 25 November 1981.

Other awards:
00.00.1940: Iron Cross 2nd Class
00.00.1940: Minesweepers Badge
27 May 1942: Iron Cross 1st Class
17 Jun 1942: High Seas Fleet Badge
27 May 1943: U-Boat War Badge
28 Dec 1944: German Cross in Gold
00 Mar 1945: U-Boat Combat Clasp in Silver

Fritz-Julius LEMP
Kapitänleutnant
20 ships sunk, 96,639 tons
4 ships damaged, 45,417 tons

Knight's Cross: Awarded on 14 August 1940, as *Kapitänleutnant* and as commander of *U-30* for sinking sixteen ships for a total of 79,862 shipping tons, and for damaging another two, to become the 9th U-boat recipient of the award.

Fritz-Julius Lemp was born on 19 February 1913 in Tsingtau, a German colony in China. He joined the *Reichsmarine* as a cadet in April 1931 and served aboard the light cruiser

Karlsruhe for the next four years, where he gained valuable practical experience of being at sea. He was commissioned as a *Leutnant zur See* in April 1935 and began training as a U-boat commander, serving aboard *U-28* in November 1936. The following year Lemp was promoted to *Oberleutnant zur See* and continued his training aboard under the watchful eye of *Kapitänleutnant* Günter Kuhnke.

(Author's collection)

In November 1938 he was appointed commander of *U-30*, a Type VIIA boat, and after his sea trials he left Wilhelmshaven for his first patrol on 22 August 1939, to operate west of the British Isles. On 3 September, the first day of the war with Britain *Kapitänleutnant* Lemp became the central figure of one of the most controversial incidents of the Battle of the Atlantic. He had spotted a large blacked-out ship zigzagging at high speed, and he presumed she was an armed merchant cruiser – a converted liner fitted with deck guns – passenger liners were not supposed to zigzag. He then fired a torpedo at the liner without warning. She was struck on the port side in the engine room, and Lemp soon realized that he had sunk the British passenger liner *Athenia*. This was in contravention of Hitler's order that passenger liners should not be attacked, sailing alone or in a convoy. Most of the 315 crew and 1,103 passengers abandoned ship in twenty-six lifeboats. However, nineteen crew and ninety-three passengers (twenty-eight of whom were US citizens) were lost. Many of them died when one lifeboat, carrying fifty-two female passengers and children, in the darkness came in contact with the propeller of the Norwegian merchant ship *Knute Nelson* and capsized – only eight women survived. Altogether 112 crew members, women and children lost their lives, and 1,306 were rescued. The sinking was of great propaganda value to the British and the Germans denied all knowledge; even the daily war report was altered. When Lemp returned to Wilhelmshaven he was ordered immediately to Berlin to report to *Admiral* Dönitz, the Commander of U-boats, to explain his actions. He told the admiral that he had sunk the *Athenia* by mistake. The commander of the *Kriegsmarine*, *Großadmiral* Raeder, was informed of the incident and he in turn informed Hitler. Raeder decided not to court-martial Lemp and he was sworn to secrecy, and the log of *U-30* was altered to support the official denials. It wasn't until the Nuremberg Trials after the war that the truth was known.

In September Lemp was promoted to *Kapitänleutnant* and on 23 December, with the incident behind him, he left Wilhelmshaven on a minelaying operation off Liverpool. En route on the 28th, he sank the British trawler HMS *Barbara Robertson*, serving at the time as an auxiliary patrol craft, by gunfire. Later the same day Lemp torpedoed and damaged the British battleship HMS *Barham* (31,100 tons), which was eventually sunk by *U-331* off Alexandria on 25 November 1941. Lemp continued with his orders and laid mines near the Bar lightship on 6 January 1940 and these mines sank four ships and damaged another. The British tanker SS *El Oso* struck a mine and sank on 11 January, the British SS *Gracia* was damaged on 16 January and the following day the SS *Cainross* was sunk. On 7 February his mines claimed the British passenger ship the MV *Munster* and on 9th the British SS *Chagres* was sunk. Lemp returned to port on 17 February.

The British passenger ship Athenia *was torpedoed without warning by* U-30 *on 3 September 1939, the first ship to be sunk by a U-boat in the Second World War. One torpedo struck her on the port side in the engine room, causing the ship to sink at 10:00 hours on 4 September. Most of the 315 crew members and 1,103 passengers abandoned ship in twenty-six lifeboats. But nineteen crew members and ninety-three passengers were lost. Many of them died when one lifeboat carrying fifty-two female passengers and three sailors came into contact with the propeller of the Norwegian MV* Knute Nelson *and capsized.* (Author's collection)

The next patrol began on 11 March, initially off Trondheim when a British submarine was engaged but it wasn't sunk and the operation soon ended. On 3 April Lemp took *U-30* out on its next patrol under sealed orders to take part in Operation *Hartmut*, the naval operation during the German invasion of Denmark and Norway. His orders were opened on the 6th which confirmed *U-30* was to help with the support of the German transports and naval landing forces during the invasion.

On 8 June, Lemp took *U-30* out on its next patrol which was a wolf-pack operation in the Atlantic. Together with six other boats they made up a group which was commanded by Günther Prien. They formed a patrol line south-west of Ireland to intercept convoys. However, the group was broken up on the 17th when it became clear that the convoys had moved away. On the 20th Lemp sank the British SS *Otterpool* and on the 22nd he sank the Norwegian MV *Randsfjord* from Convoy HX49 and on the 28th he also sank the British SS *Llanarth* west-south-west of Brest. In the early hours of 1 July Lemp sank the British SS *Beignon* south-west of the Scillies, He then went on to sink another two ships, the Egyptian SS *Angele Mabro* on the 6th and the British SS *Ellaroy* on the 21st. He returned to Lorient on 24 July. On 5 August *U-30* left to operate west of the British Isles and Lemp claimed two more ships: the Swiss merchant vessel the MV *Canton* was sunk on 9th and the British SS *Clan Macphee* was sunk on the 16th.

In November Lemp was transferred and appointed commander of *U-110*, a Type IXB boat built by AG Weser of Bremen. With the usual familiarisation training and sea trials complete, he took his new boat out on patrol on 9 March 1941. He left Kiel for the North Atlantic and headed north-west of the North Channel and during the evening of the 15th sighted a convoy. Soon after midnight he fired a torpedo and damaged the British tanker MV *Erodana* but missed another ship. As a result of this attack *U-110* was hunted by destroyers but managed to escape. On the 20th Lemp was directed to another convoy and he damaged another ship, the Norwegian merchant the SS *Siremalm*, south-west of Reykjavik on the 23rd. When the ship failed to sink *U-110* surfaced and prepared to sink the ship with the deck guns but the muzzle tompion was not removed and the gun barrel exploded, damaging the periscope. She was later sunk by *U-201* on 27 September 1941. Lemp had no choice but to return to base.

U-110 left for operations on 15 April and headed for the North Atlantic together with two other U-boats and some Italian submarines, operating just west of Ireland. A convoy was sighted on the 22nd and 23rd, but Lemp was unable to make an attack until the 26th when he torpedoed and sank the British SS *Andre Moyrant*, which was struck on the starboard side near the engine room by one torpedo. The ship had been dispersed from Convoy SL68 on 21 March, went to Bermuda and then proceeded to England, alone because the vessel was too slow to join a transatlantic convoy. The crew had encountered great difficulties in launching the lifeboats in the dark of the night and the heavy swell caused the lifeboats to drift away. The ship sank in less than four minutes; only a few survivors managed to escape the suction of the sinking ship. The master, twenty-five crew and two gunners were lost.

On the morning of 8 May he approached another convoy and the next morning he sank two ships east of Cape Farewell, the SS *Esmond* and the SS *Bengore Head*. *U-110* was then attacked by depth-charges by the corvette HMS *Aubretia* and Lemp was forced to surface and as he did, the destroyer HMS *Bulldog* stopped near to the boat and prepared to launch a boarding party. Lemp had ordered the crew to abandon ship and set scuttling charges but these failed to detonate. Another destroyer was seen, HMS *Broadway*, apparently intent on ramming *U-110*. She was ordered not to but couldn't stop in time and struck *U-110* a glancing blow, causing serious damage to herself. The order was given for *Aubretia* to pick up the German survivors and *Bulldog*'s party board the boat intent on seizing any documents. The transfer of material from *U-110* to *Bulldog* took several trips and several hours to complete. A tow line from *Bulldog* was attached to *U-110* but this was slipped when a lookout reported a periscope. Half an hour later the line was re-secured and *Bulldog* headed for Iceland but on the morning of the 9th *U-110* sank. *Bulldog* set out for Scapa Flow and began to interrogate her prisoners and examine what they had captured. They realized what they had was of great significance – apart from an Enigma machine, ready to send a signal, there were marked charts, codebooks and cipher documents. When all of this material finally reached England, together with what had already been captured, the result was to have a lasting and decisive effect on the outcome of the U-boat war.

What became of Lemp? One story says that after leaving the boat he swam back when he realized that the scuttling charges had failed and that he had been shot by a member of the British boarding party. Another more likely one is that Lemp, realizing the terrible consequences of the Allies capturing what was on board *U-110*, committed suicide by allowing himself to drown. His body was not recovered.

Other awards:
02 Oct 1936: Long Service Award 4th Class
06 Sep 1939: Spanish Cross in Bronze without Swords
27 Sep 1939: Iron Cross 2nd Class
18 Jan 1940: Iron Cross 1st Class
18 Jan 1940: U-Boat War Badge

Siegfried Ernst Günther Hans LÜDDEN
Korvettenkapitän
9 ships sunk, 50,915 tons
1 ship damaged, 9.977 tons

Knight's Cross: Awarded on 11 February 1944, as *Kapitänleutnant* and as commander of *U-188*, for the sinking of seven ships for a total of 47,117 shipping tons and for damaging another.

Siegfried Lüdden was born on 20 May 1916 in Neubrandenburg, a city in the south-east of Mecklenburg-Vorpommern, Germany, and he entered the *Kriegsmarine* as an Officer Candidate at the age of nineteen. He was initially attached to the 2nd Company of an infantry training unit in the Baltic and from June 1936 he underwent basic training, serving aboard the battleship *Schlesien* and attended the Naval Academy at Flensburg. He was commissioned as a *Leutnant zur See* in October 1938 and then transferred briefly to the *Luftwaffe* where he served in the East Baltic Coastal Command, returning to the *Kriegsmarine* in April 1940.

He joined the U-boat service in August and began training as a U-boat commander, serving aboard the training boat *U-141* as a Watch Officer. In October he was promoted to *Oberleutnant zur See* and from November served as an adjutant to various U-boat flotillas, before being assigned as a Watch Officer to *U-129* under the command of *Kapitänleutnant* Nicolai Clausen. He took part in three war patrols during which seven ships were sunk for a total of 25,613 shipping tons. From May 1942 he continued with his training to become a U-boat commander. On 5 August he was finally appointed as commander of *U-188*, a Type IXC-40 boat built in Bremen by AG Weser.

He left Kiel on his first war patrol as a commander on 4 March 1943, heading for the North Atlantic. He joined *Seeteufel* Group on the 21st south of Iceland where they

formed a patrol line to await the convoys. By the 26th there were joined by *Seewolf* Group, forming a line running 800 miles southwards from Cape Farewell. But because of bad weather the operation was called off on the 30th. From 6 April, now a *Kapitänleutnant*, Lüdden joined *Adler* Group south of Greenland. A convoy was sighted on the 7th but wasn't engaged due to weather. On the morning of the 11th Lüdden sighted the British destroyer HMS *Beverley* and attacked, firing two torpedoes which struck her and she quickly sank. One hundred and fifty men were lost: HMS *Clover* picked up just five survivors. On 9 April, HMS *Beverley* had been seriously damaged in a collision with another ship and took station in the rear of the convoy, until she was torpedoed some thirty hours later. The operation against the convoys ended on the 13th and *U-188* left the group and headed for her new

(Scherzer)

base at Lorient. En route *U-188* was attacked by an aircraft and Lüdden and a crewman were wounded. The boat put in at Lorient on 4 May.

His next patrol began on 30 June when *U-188* headed for the Indian Ocean, as part of *Monsun* Group, with eight other boats. En route to the refuelling rendezvous *U-506*, *U-509* and *U-514* were sunk. Lüdden finally entered the Indian Ocean at the end of July. On 11 September the *Monsun* boats met the German supply ship *Brake* south of Mauritius and were refuelled once again. The five remaining boats then headed for their own individual area of operations. Lüdden took *U-188* north and patrolled off the coast of Somaliland. On 21st he sank the American SS *Cornelia P. Spencer*, 350 miles east of Mogadishu. He later unsuccessfully attacked a convoy near the Gulf of Oman, and then on 5 October he torpedoed and damaged the Norwegian tanker the MV *Britannia* north of Muscat. Lüdden completed his patrol down the west coast of India and put in at Penang on 30th. In December *U-188* went to Singapore where she was loaded with raw materials, which included rubber, tungsten and 500kg of quinine. The boat returned to Penang to prepare for her return journey home.

On 8 January 1944, Lüdden left port on his next patrol and again headed for operations in the Indian Ocean. On the 20th he sank the British SS *Fort Buckingham*. The ship was struck by two torpedoes north-west of the Maldive Islands and sank within ten minutes. The master, thirty crew and seven gunners were lost. Six survivors were later picked up by the British ship *Moorby*. Lüdden then had a run of success, sinking five ships in ten days. He sank three British ships, the SS *Fort la Maune* on the 25th and the SS *Samouri* and the passenger ship SS *Surada* on the 26th. The *Surada* was hit by two torpedoes, broke in two and sank in less than twenty minutes. All of the 103 passengers and crew were picked up by the British merchant ship *Darro* and were landed at Aden on 29th. In the Gulf of Aden he sank the Greek SS *Olga E. Embiricos* the same day along with the Chinese SS *Chung Cheung*.

A rare photograph showing the interior of U-188. (Author's collection)

On the 9th Lüdden sank the Norwegian SS *Viva* and some reports state that Lüdden went on to sink three sailing vessels by gunfire on the 12th, but this has never been confirmed. In late February Lüdden took *U-188* south to refuel. On 11 March Lüdden was refuelled by the supply ship *Brake* and shortly after that the weather deteriorated and *U-188* and *U-532* moved south-west. Later that morning an aircraft appeared and the boats had to dive to escape. When *U-188* surfaced twenty minutes later other aircraft appeared and the destroyer HMS *Roebuck* proceeded to engage the *Brake* with gunfire and sunk her in less than an hour. Lüdden kept *U-188* submerged and the destroyer eventually left the area. The crew from *Brake* were later picked up by *U-168*. Lüdden now began his journey back to France and was the only *Monsun* boat to arrive home on schedule and one of only three boats which reached France with its load of raw materials. Lüdden arrived at Bordeaux on 19 June.

From September 1944 Lüdden was assigned to the 1st U-boat Training Department where he stayed until November when he was attached to the Office of the Commanding Admiral of U-boats where he became head of Department 3 – Artillery and Navigation. He stayed in this position until his death in an accident while aboard a ship near Kiel on 13 January 1945. He was posthumously promoted to the rank of *Korvettenkapitän* five days later.

Other awards:
20 Dec 1939: Commemorative Medal of 01 Oct 1938
18 Dec 1941: Iron Cross 2nd Class
29 Dec 1941: U-Boat War Badge
08 Apr 1942: Iron Cross 1st Class
27 Sep 1944: U-Boat Combat Clasp in Bronze

<u>Karl-Heinz</u> Gerhard Albin MARBACH

Kapitänleutnant
No ships sunk

Knight's Cross: Awarded on 22 July 1944, as *Oberleutnant zur See* in recognition of his gallantry and aggressiveness during attacks and for his leadership qualities during seven war patrols whilst commander of *U-953*.

Karl-Heinz Marbach was born on 5 July 1917 in Kolberg a city in West Pomeranian Voivodeship, now part of Poland. Marbach entered the *Kriegsmarine* as an Officer Candidate and was assigned to an infantry unit in the Baltic Sea area. From June 1937 he served aboard the sail training ship *Horst Wessel* and from September he served on the light cruiser *Emden* before spending six month attending the Naval Academy at Flensburg. He then attended various courses which included officer, navigation and torpedo training before serving on the light cruisers *Leipzig* and *Nürnberg* between April and September 1939. He had been commissioned as a *Leutnant zur See* in August 1939 and spent most of the Polish campaign aboard the *Leipzig* laying mines. From 30 September he was employed as an auxiliary officer with Naval Command and in October was transferred to the battleship *Gneisenau* where he served until June 1940.

Marbach then transferred to the U-boat service and after his initial training was attached to *U-101* as the Second Watch Officer in May 1941. He was promoted to *Oberleutnant zur See* in September 1941, and was appointed First Watch Officer in January 1942, during which time he had briefly taken over as commander. He served under the U-boat aces *Fregattenkapitän* Fritz Frauenheim and his successor *Korvettenkapitän* Ernst Mengersen, and gained valuable experience from both of them. By now, however, *U-101* was a training boat and no longer took part in war patrols. In April Marbach left the boat to attend training at the U-boat Commanders' School.

From May until June 1942, Marbach took command of *U-28*, a Type VIIA boat that was used as a training boat from November 1940. In July he took command of *U-29* another training vessel and he remained training until November 1942 when he was appointed commander of *U-953*, a Type VIIC boat built by Blohm und Voss of Hamburg. He left Kiel on his first war

(Author's collection)

patrol for the Atlantic on 13 May 1943, and joined other boats that were waiting west of the Azores for convoys. A patrol line was formed during the night of the 30th/31st but nothing was sighted. However, on 4 June the boats were attacked by aircraft but no boats were hit. The group then moved 600 miles to the north to be refuelled and with the refuelling complete they reformed a patrol line on 15th east of Bermuda. The boats waited for the convoys until the 27th when they halted some 200 miles south-west of the Azores – by the 29th they realized the convoys had bypassed their lines. The boats were later attacked by air again and on 9 July *U-953* was attacked by a USAF Liberator. The boat was shaken but not damaged, although one crewman was killed and two wounded. Marbach returned to base, arriving at La Pallice on 22nd.

U-953 was then converted to a Flak (anti-aircraft)-boat, together with six other boats. This increased the gun armament of the boat but reduced its fuel-carrying capacity and therefore made it unsuitable for long-range operations. In October *U-953* left for operations and headed to an area west of the Bay of Biscay, to give protection against aircraft for outgoing and returning boats. During this patrol *U-953* was only partially successful as a Flak-boat and although she protected various other boats that sank some targets *U-953* failed to sink any ships herself. By 17 November Marbach had returned *U-953* to La Pallice. The Flak-boat experiment was not a success and *U-953* was restored to its original state and returned to normal duties.

Between 26 December 1943 and 22 July 1944, Marbach took *U-953* out on four war patrols. He joined *Borkum* Group west of Ireland but failed to find any convoys. On the 11th Marbach claimed a hit on the corvette HMCS *Lunenburg* but this was never confirmed. On 6 June *U-953* left Brest as part of eight U-boats ordered to go to the area north of Cherbourg, enter the English Channel and inflict what losses they could on the invasion forces. This was a very difficult and dangerous task, considering the concentration of air and surface forces they would be facing. On the morning of the 8th Marbach fired four torpedoes at destroyers that were entering the western entrance of the Channel, which detonated near the ships but caused no damage. Later during his final patrol, on the morning of 5 July Marbach attacked a convoy and claimed to have sunk the SS *Glendinnig* and claimed a hit on a second ship. But neither of these claims was confirmed. After returning to Brest on 22 July, Marbach went to Berlin to receive his Knight's Cross from *Kapitän zur See* Hans-Rudolf Rösing during a special ceremony.

Promoted to *Kapitänleutnant* on 1 September he returned to duty a few days later being assigned to *U-3014*, a Type XXI boat which had this type of boat come two years earlier; it may have won the war in the Atlantic for the Germans. These boats had much better crew facilities, were much quieter underwater and were fitted with a freezer for foodstuffs and a shower. They also had a hydraulic torpedo-reloading system that enabled the commander to reload all six tubes in less than ten minutes. However, Marbach never got a chance to take out his new boat on a war patrol as it was never ready for combat. On 3 May, with the Allies very close to its base in Neustadt, Marbach ordered the boat scuttled to prevent her falling into Allied hands. Marbach was taken prisoner and remained in Allied captivity until his release on 21 February 1948.

After the war Marbach joined the *Bundesmarine* and retired as a *Korvettenkapitän*, he later wrote a book, *Von Kolberg über La Rochelle nach Berlin* ('From Kolberg via La Rochelle to Berlin'), detailing his wartime experience in U-boats. He died on 27 September 1995 in Bonn, Germany.

Other awards:
14 Apr 1940: Iron Cross 2nd Class
01 Apr 1941: Long Service Award 4th Class
22 Jul 1941: High Seas Fleet War Badge
09 Sep 1941: U-Boat War Badge
21 Nov 1943: Iron Cross 1st Class
26 Nov 1944: U-Boat Combat Clasp in Bronze

Friedrich Wilhelm Karl MARKWORTH
Kapitänleutnant
13 ships sunk, 74,067 tons
3 ships damaged, 10,236 tons

Knight's Cross: Awarded as *Kapitänleutnant* on 8 July 1943, as commander of *U-66* for the sinking of twelve ships for a total of 74,091 shipping tons, and for damaging another two.

Friedrich Markworth was born in Wolfenbüttel a town in Lower Saxony, Germany on 14 February 1915, entering the *Reichsmarine* as an Officer Candidate with the 4th Company of an infantry training unit in the Baltic in April 1934. From June he was assigned aboard the sail training ship *Gorch Fock* and the light cruiser *Emden* and later attended the Naval Academy at Flensburg until early 1936. He continued his training, attending the Infantry Artillery School at Wilhelmshaven and saw service on the light cruiser *Königsberg*. He was commissioned in April 1937 and promoted to *Oberleutnant zur See* in April 1939. At the beginning of the Second World War Markworth was serving aboard the heavy cruiser *Blücher* and later took part in the invasion of Norway.

In December 1940 he transferred to the U-boat service and underwent his basic training and was in February 1941 assigned to *U-103* as Watch Officer. He took part in two war patrols and served with two highly able commanders *Kapitänleutnant* Victor Schütze and *Kapitänleutnant* Werner Winter who both became Knight's Cross holders, with Schütze gaining the Oakleaves. He then spent the next six months training to become a commander himself. Finally on 1 June 1942 he was appointed commander of *U-66*, a Type IXC boat built by AG Weser of Bremen.

(Scherzer)

Markworth left for the eastern Caribbean area on 23 June and on 9 July sank the Yugoslavian SS *Triglav* at 20:42 hours about 1,000 miles north-east of the Leeward Islands. She wasn't being escorted and was hit forward and aft by two torpedoes from *U-66* and sank quickly after her boiler exploded. The crew abandoned ship in two lifeboats and the master was questioned by the Germans before *U-66* left the area. Nineteen survivors were picked up by the Spanish merchant ship *Iciar* and were landed at Gibraltar on 28 July. Twenty-three of her crew and one gunner were lost. On the 26th Markworth sighted another ship, the Brazilian steamer *Tamandaré* which he sunk north-east of Tobago and on the 28th he sank the British SS *Weirbank*. On 6 August Markworth claimed to have sunk the Polish MV *Rozewie* east of Barbados but this was unconfirmed. By the end of August Markworth was thinking of his return journey when on 29th he sank the American SS *Topa Topa*, the Panamanian MV *Sir Huon* and the American SS *West Lashaway*. On the 30th he sank the British SS *Winamac* carrying 12,500 tons of oil. She was struck in the engine room by one of two torpedoes and burst into flames and quickly sank. Thirty of her crew were lost. Markworth was promoted to *Kapitänleutnant* on 14 August and before the patrol was over he had sunk the Swedish MV *Peiping* on 9 September. *U-66* refuelled and returned to base on 29 September.

On 9 November Markworth took out *U-66* for a patrol in the Western Atlantic but the next evening the boat was attacked and damaged by an Allied aircraft and had to return to base. She was repaired and left port on 6 January 1943, this time on a special mission. He had an agent aboard and on the 20th he landed the agent at Rio Ora in Spanish territory. It was reported later that an agent and two members of the boat's crew had been captured. On the 28th *U-66* joined *Rochen* Group and started the search for convoys. On the 28th Markworth sank the French trawler the *Joseph*

Elise by gunfire east of Las Palmas. On 21 February a convoy was sighted and the group spent five days chasing it, as a result three ships were sunk, but none by *U-66*. On the 27th Markworth sunk the British SS *St. Margaret* and her captain was taken aboard. Then after refuelling the boats of *Rochen* Group formed a north–south patrol line and began a sweep towards the Canaries. A small convoy was sighted on the 11th but was travelling too fast. Another convoy was intercepted and although the weather conditions were good only four ships were sunk none by *U-66*. Markworth headed for port, arriving in Lorient on 24 March.

The next patrol began on 27 April and *U-66* headed out for operations in the Western Atlantic. On 9 June she attacked two north bound tankers but missed. On the 10th Markworth sank the American turbine tanker *Esso Gettysburg*. She was struck by two torpedoes which hit the port side and blew oil 100ft into the air and disabled the steering gear. Seconds later the second torpedo struck the engine room, causing an immediate fire. The flames spread 100ft on both sides, while smoke rose over 1,000ft in the air. The crew tried to launch the lifeboats but failed because of the intense flames and smoke. Only fifteen of the seventy-two crew managed to escape the burning ship and survived. On 2 July Markwork sank another American turbine tanker the *Bloody Marsh* by torpedo and gunfire. The torpedo struck the engine room and the ship began to slowly sink. Only three crew members were lost and seventy-four managed to get to the lifeboats and safety. Further south, on the 22nd Markworth attacked another tanker, the American *Cherry Valley*, seriously damaging her. She was struck by two torpedoes which ripped open the starboard and centre tanks. The engine and steering gear weren't damaged and the tanker tried to escape. *U-66* surfaced to stop the vessel with gunfire, but the tanker was armed with one 5in and one 3in gun and eight 20mm guns and managed to fend off the U-boat. During the journey home, *U-66* was refuelled by *U-117*, but during the refuelling procedure the two boats were sighted by an Allied aircraft and attacked. A strafing attack killed three men and wounded another eight. *U-66* dived and the aircraft dropped two depth charges which missed. In a further attack Markworth was seriously wounded by a bullet and the First Watch Officer was also wounded. Assistance was requested and *U-117* rendezvoused with *U-66* and put aboard a relief commander, *Oberleutnant zur See* Paul Frerks. On the morning of the 7 August, *U-117* began to refuel *U-66* and during this procedure the two boats were attacked again by Allied aircraft. *U-117* was seriously damaged but *U-66* managed to escape having been refuelled. Markworth reached port on 1 September and Markworth and the First Officer were taken to hospital. On 19 October Markworth was assigned as a training officer with the 23rd U-boat Flotilla in Danzig, where he remained until the end of the war. Markworth settled into civilian life and later settled in Detmold-Dortmund, Germany where he died on 13 January 1994.

Other awards:
08 Apr 1938: Long Service Award 4th Class
24 Apr 1940: Iron Cross 2nd Class
13 Jul 1941: U-Boat War Badge
10 Nov 1942: Iron Cross 1st Class
27 Mar 1943: High Seas Fleet War Badge
00 Aug 1943: Wound Badge in Silver

Wilhelm Hugo <u>August</u> MAUS
Kapitänleutnant
9 ships sunk, 62,761 tons
1 ship damaged, 6,840 tons

(Scherzer)

Knight's Cross: Awarded as *Kapitänleutnant* and as commander of *U-185* on 21 September 1943, in recognition of his leadership and for sinking nine ships for a total of 62,761 shipping tons and for damaging another.

August Maus was born on 7 February 1915, in Wuppertal a city in North Rhine-Westphalia, Germany and he joined the *Reichsmarine* in April 1934 as a Cadet. He was assigned to the 2nd Company of the 2nd Shipyard Division in the Baltic Sea for basic infantry training. He then saw service aboard the sail training ship *Gorch Fock* and from September 1934 served on the light cruiser *Emden* before being assigned to the Naval Academy at Flensburg in June 1935. From 31 March until 29 July 1936 Maus attended various training courses before being assigned aboard the light cruiser *Nürnberg* from September. He was commissioned as a *Leutnant zur See* in April 1937 and was later involved in coastal security patrols during the Spanish Civil War whilst onboard the *Nürnberg*. From March to June 1939 Maus served as adjutant to the 1st Shipyard Regiment and was then assigned as education officer on the battleship *Schleswig-Holstein*, having been promoted to *Oberleutnant zur See* in April 1939. On 1 September 1939, whilst still aboard the *Schleswig-Holstein*, he witnessed the shelling of the Polish base at Danzig's Westerplatte, which marked the start of the German invasion of Poland and the beginning of the Second World War.

In October he transferred to the U-boat service and began his training, and was assigned to *U-68* as a First Watch Officer in February 1941. He took part in two war patrols whilst under the command of *Korvettenkapitän* Karl-Friedrich Merten, during which time *U-68* was responsible for the sinking of four ships in the North and Central Atlantic. From December he was assigned to various training courses, which included navigation, torpedo, artillery and as commander training. On 12 June 1942, now a *Kapitänleutnant*, Maus was appointed commander of *U-185*, a Type IXC-40, built by AG Weser in Bremen.

Maus left Kiel on his first war patrol to operate in the Central Atlantic on 27 October 1942. On 8 November news reached Maus of the Allied landings in North Africa; all available U-boats were ordered to go at high speed to the area west of Gibraltar, where they assembled as *Westwall* Group. The boats then began to carry out patrols looking for Allied shipping. On the 27th the boats formed a north-south patrol line and moved west towards and then past the Azores. During the early hours of the 7th Maus sank the British merchant ship *Peter Maersk*. She was struck by two torpedoes and when she failed to sink she was finished off with a third and then a fourth torpedo. There were no survivors. Apparently the crew had managed to send a distress signal before abandoning ship in the lifeboats, but the survivors were never found and probably perished in the bad weather. No further convoys were sighted and so the boats were refuelled and moved east and then took up positions near Portugal but found nothing. Maus took *U-185* into Lorient on 1 January 1943.

He left for operations in the Greater Antilles area on 8 February and on the 10th encountered Convoy KG123 at the southern end of the Windward Channel. Maus then sank the American tanker SS *Virginia Sinclair* and the American SS *James Sprunt*. *U-185* was then attacked by a Mariner flying boat and was damaged but the crew were able to make repairs. The boat returned to patrol south of Cuba and had no further success until 6 April, when Maus sighted the SS *John Sevier*. *U-185* put in at Bordeaux on 3 May. The next patrol began on 9 June when Maus took *U-185* for operations off the coast of Brazil, part of five outward-bound boats. On the 13th the group was attacked by a Sunderland flying boat, and one of the boats was damaged during the attack but the aircraft was shot down. The damaged boat, *U-564*, began to return to Brest and was escorted by *U-185*. On the 14th the two boats were attacked by aircraft. One made a depth-charge attack and *U-564* was severely damaged. Maus was ordered to tow the boat back to port but this failed, so *U-185* picked up the commander and seventeen other survivors from the stricken boat, who were later put aboard the German destroyers *Z24* and *Z25*.

On 7 July *U-185* encountered Convoy BT18 and torpedoed and sank four ships in two attacks. Maus sank the American SS *James Robertson*, the tanker SS *Thomas Sinnickson*, the SS *William Boyce Thompson* and damaged the SS *S.B. Hunter*. He continued his patrol off Brazil and on 1 August sank a straggler from Convoy TJ2, the Brazilian SS *Bagé*. She was hit on the port side by one torpedo and was sunk by gunfire off the Rio Real Estuary. She had been ordered out of the convoy for making too much smoke. The master, nineteen crew and eight passengers were lost. On the 6th Maus sank the British SS *Fort Halkett* 600 miles east-south-east of Recife, Brazil. *U-185* was then to rendezvous with the badly-damaged *U-604* and take on its crew and scuttle the boat. *U-604* reached the position first but Allied air activity was such that a new meeting place was arranged, 400 miles north-east, to which *U-172* was ordered to go as well.

The three boats met on 11 August and whilst stores and food were being transferred from *U-604* they were attacked by a US Liberator. *U-172* dived but the other two boats remained on the surface and opened fire on the aircraft, which made two unsuccessful bombing attacks. On its third run it was shot down by *U-185*. The crew from *U-604* were then transferred to *U-185* and *U-172* which had resurfaced soon after the failed air attack. *U-604* was then quickly scuttled. Maus now decided to head for home. On the 24th she was sighted on the surface by a Wildcat and Avenger aircraft from the escort carrier USS *Core*. They attacked *U-185* and dropped depth charges, which caused *U-185* to turn sharply to port, with thick smoke coming from the conning tower. Two more aircraft arrived and made further attacks. Maus knew it was impossible to escape as *U-185*'s battery compartment was flooding and producing poisonous chlorine gas from the wet batteries, so the order to abandon ship was given. *U-604*'s commander, *Kapitänleutnant* Horst Höltring, went to the torpedo room where he found two badly-wounded members of his crew, unable to move. They pleaded with their commander to be shot and Höltring obliged and then promptly shot himself. From *U-185*'s crew twenty-nine men were lost. Maus was one of the survivors and he spent almost three years in American captivity. After being held in a POW camp in Crossville, Tennessee, he was transferred to the camp at Papago Park, Arizona on 27 January 1944. On 12 February, he was one of five U-boat commanders to escape, but he was recaptured in Tucson together with Friedrich

Guggenberger. On the night of 23/24 December 1944 he took part in the digging of an escape tunnel through which twenty-five POWs escaped, but he wasn't one of the escapees as an injury prevented him. Following his transfer to Camp Shanks, New York in February 1946, Maus was then held in the British zone of Germany until his release later that year. He became a successful businessman in Hamburg, where he died on 28 September 1996.

Other awards:
01 Apr 1938: Long Service Award 4th Class
06 Oct 1939: Iron Cross 2nd Class
05 Jun 1940: Spanish Cross in Bronze
09 Nov 1942: High Seas Fleet War Badge
26 Dec 1942: U-Boat War Badge
05 May 1943: Iron Cross 1st Class
00.00.1944: U-Boat Combat Clasp in Bronze

Waldemar MEHL
Korvettenkapitän
9 ships sunk, 42,451 tons
4 ships damaged, 28,072 tons

Knight's Cross: Awarded on 28 March 1944, as commander of *U-371* with the rank of *Kapitänleutnant* in recognition for the sinking of nine ships for a total of 42,451 tons and including the damage of four ships. Although his success seems low compared to other commanders, the U-boat losses in the Mediterranean were high and Mehl's successes, although low in tonnage, were considerable when you take into consideration that his total included the sinking of three warships.

Waldemar Mehl was born on 7 September 1914 in Grävenwiesbach, Usingen and entered the *Reichsmarine* with a Naval Infantry division in the Baltic in April 1933. He served aboard the sail training ship *Gorch Fock* and later on the light cruiser *Karlsruhe*. Mehl continued with his training, attending various courses and in early 1935 he served aboard the light cruiser *Köln*. Commissioned as a *Leutnant zur See* in October 1936, he served as a radio officer aboard the *Köln* and the light cruiser *Nürnberg* and the battleship *Schleswig-Holstein* until December 1939. Mehl was promoted to *Oberleutnant zur See* in June 1938, and from April 1940 he served briefly as Commandant of District Wesermünde and was then appointed Naval Signals Officer at Narvik from October. In January 1941 he was promoted to *Kapitänleutnant* and served as a signals officer (Scherzer)

at Bergen. In April he transferred to the U-boat service and was appointed commander of *U-62* in November and took command of *U-72* a month later, as part of his training and without experiencing any war patrols.

On 25 May 1942, Mehl took command of *U-371*, a Type VIIC boat built in Kiel and sailed from Salamis, Cyprus on his first patrol in July. He took part in five war patrols before he experienced success. On 7 January 1943, during his sixth war patrol whilst operating in the Western Mediterranean he sank the British trawler HMS *Jura* about 35 miles east-north-east of Algiers, Algeria. On the same day he damaged the British troopship *Ville de Strasbourg*. On 14 February, he left La Spezia for operations and torpedoed and sank the British SS *Fintra* on the 23rd, about 30 miles east-north-east of Algiers. The torpedo struck the port quarter and the magazine of the stern gun exploded and this shattered the poop deck, killing five gunners and four crew members. The remaining crew had no time to launch the lifeboats and jumped overboard to escape. They were later picked up and were landed at Algiers later that day. On 28 February he torpedoed and damaged the US steamer *Daniel Carroll* before returning to port on 3 March.

During his next two patrols which were short, lasting only thirty-three days and nine days respectively, he sank one ship and damaged two others. On 7 August, during his next patrol he sank the British steamer *Contractor* about 75 miles south-west of Sardina. The master and four crew members were lost. On 7 October he left for operations and in the early hours of the 11th he sank the British fleet minesweeper HMS *Hythe*, which was escorting Convoy MKS-*27*. She was struck on the port side below the bridge by a Gnat acoustic torpedo, broke in two and sank in about four minutes north of Bougie, Algeria, with the loss of sixty-two crew. On the 13th he sank the American destroyer USS *Bristol* which was escorting a small convoy to Oran, Algeria. The ship broke in two and had to be abandoned: five officers and forty-seven ratings were lost. Two days later Mehl sank the American SS *James Russell Lowell* off Cape de Fer, Algeria. He fired four torpedoes, the first struck the ship on the rudder, the second on the port side at No. 3 hold and blew off the hatch cover and a third torpedo hit at No. 1 hold and again blew off the hatch and it began to flood. The fourth torpedo missed. The crew abandoned ship and were later rescued. Although the ship was later towed to Colla in Algeria she was later declared a total loss. Mehl was unsuccessful during his next two patrols, but it could have been different had he not missed two large destroyers which he attacked on 1 February 1944.

On 17 March, Mehl sunk the Dutch troop transport MV *Dempo* about 30 miles north-north-east of Bougie. The crew abandoned ship almost immediately and this action saved the lives of all of the 333 men aboard. A few hours later Mehl fired another torpedo to finish off the ship and it sank. Later the same day he sank the US steamer *Maiden Creek* about 30 miles north-north-east of Bougie and she settled by the stern after the hit. A few minutes later three more torpedoes were fired and two hits were heard aboard the U-boat. Most of the crew abandoned ship safely, but eight men were lost. The survivors were later picked up and the badly damaged ship was towed by a British escort vessel to Bougie on the morning of 18 March where she was declared a total loss.

After being awarded the Knight's Cross for his successes he was taken off combat duties and assigned as a staff officer to the 1st Admiral for U-boats in the Aegean, *Vizeadmiral* Werner Lange. He ended the war as a *Korvettenkapitän* on the Operations Staff of the Commander-in-Chief of the *Kriegsmarine*, *Großadmiral* Karl Dönitz. Mehl surrendered to Allied troops in May 1945 and after the war he settled in Wiesbaden where he died on 29 March 1996.

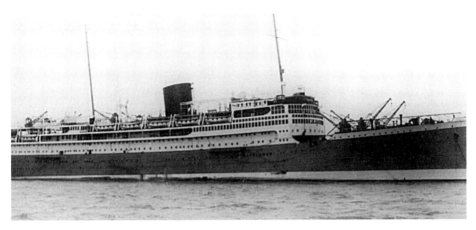

The Dutch passenger ship Dempo, *requisitioned as a troop transport ship and converted in Liverpool. She was sunk by* U-371 *about 30 miles north-north-east of Bougie on 17 March 1944. At 17,024 tons, she was one of the largest ships sunk in the Second World War.* (Author's collection)

Other awards:
31 Mar 1937: Long Service Award 4th Class
06 Jun 1939: Spanish Cross in Bronze
30 Apr 1940: Iron Cross 2nd Class
26 Oct 1940: Iron Cross 1st Class
22 Sep 1942: U-Boat War Badge
19 Nov 1943: German Cross in Gold
10 Mar 1945: U-Boat Combat Clasp in Silver

Ernst Karl August MENGERSEN
Korvettenkapitän
13 ships sunk, 68,316 tons
3 ships damaged, 20,159 tons

Knight's Cross: Awarded on 18 November 1941, as *Korvettenkapitän* and as commander of *U-101* for sinking ten ships for a total of 44,968 shipping tons and for damaging one ship.

Ernst Mengersen was born in Bremke a village in the Gemeinde Gleichen in southern Lower Saxony, Germany on 30 June 1912. He joined the *Reichsmarine* as a naval officer and was assigned to the 4th Company of the 2nd Shipyard Division stationed in the Baltic Sea. From June 1933, he received his basic training, which included time aboard the sail training ship *Gorch Fock* and aboard the light cruiser *Karlsruhe*. After completing an Ensign

(Scherzer)

training course at the Naval College he also attended a navigation course. He was commissioned as a *Leutnant zur See* on 1 June 1936 and from December he served on the U-boat tender *Saar* as First Watch Officer and Radio Officer (the *Saar* was the first purpose-built U-boat tender of the *Kriegsmarine* and served throughout the Second World War).

On 14 October 1937, Mengersen served as adjutant and Signals Officer aboard the 'pocket battleship' *Admiral Scheer* and later took part in the non-combatant security patrols during the Spanish Civil War. It was during this time he was promoted to *Oberleutnant zur See*. In April 1939, he transferred to the 6th Torpedo Boat Flotilla, where he was appointed adjutant and Third Watch Officer to *Kapitänleutnant* Helmut Neuss, commander of the torpedo boat *Tiger*. From June he trained as a U-boat commander, and in July was serving aboard *U-33* as Second Watch Officer. In September he transferred to *U-54* as First Watch Officer – a commander in waiting. On 24 November Mengersen took command of his own boat, *U-18*, a Type IIB boat built by Germania Werft in Kiel. On 8 January 1940, he took *U-18* out on his first war patrol to operate in the North Sea between the Orkneys and Norway. On the 23rd he sank his first ship, the Norwegian SS *Bisp*, with the loss of her entire crew. Mengersen remained with *U-18* until September when he was transferred to the 1st U-boat Flotilla where he continued to train as a commander. In October he was promoted to *Kapitänleutnant* and given command of *U-101*, a Type VIIB boat built in Kiel in 1939. He took his new command out on patrol to operate west of the British Isles in November and torpedoed and sank the British steamer *Aracataca* on the 30th. She was initially struck by two torpedoes but didn't sink until she was hit by a third about 230 miles west of Rockall. The engine room had been hit by the third torpedo and the ship sank after the boiler exploded. Thirty-six men were lost. Mengersen then attacked another Steamer, this time from Convoy HX90 about 340 miles west of Bloody Foreland, the ship was the SS *Loch Ranza* and she suffered minor damage and escaped any further attacks. On the 2 December he sank the British MV *Appalachee* and MV *Lady Glanely*. During the attacks on the convoy between 1 and 3 December a total of ten ships were sunk and two were damaged. Mengersen had sunk four.

During his next patrol he sank the British SS *Belcrest* on 14 February 1941, with the loss of the entire crew. In the early hours of the 17th he sank the SS *Gairsoppa*, another British merchant ship. She was struck on the starboard side just behind the bridge in No. 2 hold by a single torpedo about 300 miles south-west of Galway Bay, Ireland. The ship caught fire and because of the heavy seas the crew decided to abandon ship. The survivors managed to launch three lifeboats before the ship sank. However, two of the boats were never seen again. On 24 March, Mengersen took *U-101* on another patrol to operate west of Ireland. On the 31st Convoy OB302 was located by air reconnaissance and various other boats were directed to the area, but failed to make contact. On 2 April *U-101* was part of a patrol line, but failed to sink any ships. For Mengersen it was a disappointing patrol and headed back to his new base at Lorient. His next patrol started well but was again disappointing. In early May he sank the British SS *Trecarrell* in the central North Atlantic and on the 9th, in the same area, he sank the British SS *Trevarrack* from Convoy OB329. During the latter stages of June Mengersen participated in operations in the central North Atlantic against Convoy OB336 and from the 29th operated against Convoy HX133 south-east of Greenland. A total of nine ships were sunk but none by Mengersen.

In October Mengersen left for the central North Atlantic where *U-101* was ordered to join a new group. On the 18th he sank the British destroyer HMS *Broadwater* south of Iceland. She was hit by a single torpedo on the starboard side forward of the bridge and lost her entire bow. Three other ships were ordered to help but their rescue attempts were unsuccessful, since due to the bad weather the lifeboats became more and more waterlogged. Some of the crew of the destroyer remained on board, thinking the ship could be saved. However it soon became apparent that the back of the ship had been broken and she was beyond salvage. HMS *Angle* rescued sixty survivors and HMS *St. Apollo* stood by the abandoned wreck of HMS *Broadwater* until she sank. Five officers and forty ratings were lost. Mengersen now joined other boats which had been operating against Convoy SC48 to form *Reissewolf* Group 450 miles south-east of Greenland. On the 22nd contact was made but the boats were repeatedly driven off by the escorts and with the shortage of fuel the U-boats were forced to break off and the operation was aborted. Mengersen then took *U-101* back to Kiel, arriving on 16 November.

On 30 January 1942, Mengersen took command of *U-607*, a Type VIIC boat built in Hamburg by Blohm und Voss. It was a brand-new boat and her sea trials took six months to complete. Finally on 13 July Mengersen took *U-607* out on her first war patrol, leaving Kristiansand for the North Atlantic. He joined *Wolf* Group during its attack on Convoy ON113. On the 26th he torpedoed and damaged the British MV *Empire Rainbow*, about 300 miles east of Cape Race. But contact was soon lost with the convoy and the boats of *Wolf* Group moved south to refuel. On 2 August another convoy was sighted and two days later Mengersen sank the Belgian SS *Belgian Soldier* with the loss of twenty-one men. Rough seas and fog brought the operation to an end. Mengersen decided to take the opportunity to refuel and headed for port, arriving at St. Nazaire on the 11th.

For his next patrol Mengersen took *U-607* into the North Atlantic and was directed to join boats of *Pfeil* and *Lohs* Groups in their attack on Convoy SC100. As the boats closed in on the convoy, so did the weather, and the operation was called off. When the weather cleared the U-boats made their attacks and were very successful, but *U-607* failed to hit any ships, and a disappointed Mengersen left the area. He headed for a new position, heading south towards the Azores where he refuelled. He then joined other boats and formed a patrol line to await a new convoy just east of Newfoundland. It wasn't long before the convoy was sighted and the boats moved in. On 14 October Mengersen fired two torpedoes and hit the Greek SS *Nellie* which sank within twelve minutes with the loss of thirty-two crew members. Soon after the attack *U-607* was spotted on the surface by the destroyer HMS *Viscount* and during the depth-charge attack was slightly damaged. Mengersen decided to head for St. Nazaire and check the damage. With minor repairs completed Mengersen left St. Nazaire for the Atlantic on 2 January 1943 and joined *Falke* Group and the boats formed a patrol line 500 miles west of Ireland. No convoys were sighted because of bad weather. But on 24th Mengersen sank the Norwegian tanker MV *Kollbjörg*, part of Convoy HX223. She broke in two just aft of amidships when an enormous breaker swept across the foredeck during a hurricane. The two parts drifted away from each other and on the 26th Mengersen fired a torpedo at the forepart of *Kolbjörg* and it capsized but didn't sink. He tried to sink her with gunfire, but had problems with the deck gun. Mengersen could only claim one ship damaged and moved south-west towards Newfoundland. On 15 February *U-607* attacked a straggler from Convoy ON165, the US tanker MV *Atlantic Sun*. She was struck by two torpedoes on the port side about 150 miles off Cape Race. The first torpedo split the ship in half and the other blew a large hole in the bow. The forward section sank in less than twenty minutes a third torpedo was fired at the other half of the ship and it sank. Only one survivor was picked up from a crew of sixty-eight. Mengersen then headed for his home port, arriving safely on 9 March.

In April 1943, Mengersen was transferred and attached to the 17th U-boat Flotilla, taking over as head of training in June. From the 15 June until February 1945 he served as Chief of the 20th U-boat Flotilla stationed in Pillau. He was promoted to *Korvettenkapitän* in December 1944 and from 31 March 1945, served as tactics commander with the 25th U-boat Flotilla. From 1 April until the surrender in May he served as Acting Chief of the 15th U-boat Flotilla in Kristiansand where he was captured. He was soon released and returned to Germany on 20 February 1946. He didn't rejoin the Navy and settled in Dortmund where he died on 6 November 1995.

Other awards:
27 Jan 1940: Iron Cross 2nd Class
10 Dec 1940: Iron Cross 1st Class
01 Apr 1937: Long service Award 4th Class
25 Feb 1940: U-Boat War Badge
23 Oct 1940: Spanish Cross in Bronze with Swords
01 Sep 1944: War Service Cross 2nd Class with Swords
00.00.1944: U-Boat Combat Clasp in Bronze
30 Jan 1945: War Service Cross 1st Class with Swords

<u>Jost</u> Anton METZLER
Korvettenkapitän
11 ships sunk, 56,318 tons
1 ship damaged, 4,887 tons

(Author's collection)

Knight's Cross: Awarded on 28 July 1941, as *Korvettenkapitän* and as commander of *U-69* for sinking eleven ships for a total of 56,318 shipping tons and for damaging one ship.

Jost Metzler was born on 26 February 1909, in Altshausen, Württemberg and joined the *Reichsmarine* as an Officer Candidate in October 1933. He was initially assigned to an infantry unit in the Baltic and from April 1934 began his basic training. He served aboard the light cruiser *Königsberg* as part of his training and attended the Naval Academy at Flensburg. On completion of his training he was commissioned as a *Leutnant zur See* and served as Watch Officer on various torpedo boats and minesweepers. In September 1937, he was promoted to *Oberleutnant zur See* and assigned to the 2nd Minesweeper Flotilla. Promoted to *Kapitänleutnant* in October 1939, and in April 1940, after thirteen patrols on the *Aviso Grille*, which had previously been Hitler's official yacht, he transferred to the U-boat service.

Metzler was appointed commander of *U-69*, a Type VIIC boat built by Germania Werft in Kiel. His first war patrol began on 10 February 1941, when he took his new boat out from Kiel and headed for the North Sea and south of the Shetlands and into the Eastern Atlantic. He sank the British MV *Siamese Prince* on the 17th to claim his first 'victory'. Two days later he torpedoed and sank the British SS *Empire Blanda*, a straggler from Convoy HX107, south of Iceland. The Germans observed how the crew abandoned ship in lifeboats, but no survivors were ever found. The master and sixty-seven crew members were lost. On the 19th a German aircraft sighted the westbound Convoy OB287, but because of inaccurate information the convoy was not found by the U-boats. On the 21st *U-69* was attacked twice by depth charges by a Sunderland aircraft, but escaped undamaged. Convoy OB288 was sighted on the 23rd south of Iceland and Metzler attacked, he sank the British SS *Marslew*. She was struck by a single torpedo on the starboard side amidships in the boiler room, about 265 miles west-north-west of Rockall at 23:39 hours. The explosion that followed caused her to break in two and she sank after thirty minutes. The master and twelve crew men were lost. Shortly after the sinking *U-69* suffered a series of prolonged depth-charge attacks but escaped undamaged. Metzler decided to put in at Loreint on 1 March.

His next patrol began on 30 March, and he headed for the Atlantic where he sank the British SS *Coultarn* from Convoy OB302 south-west of Iceland. On 2 April, *U-69* joined a patrol line and contact was soon made with Convoy SC26 and Metzler torpedoed the British SS *Thirby*, loaded with 7,600 tons of maize and heading for Hull, England when she was hit. It was presumed she had been sunk but she was later refloated and repaired. However, she was later sunk by *U-109* on 23 January 1942. In May Metzler took *U-69* out on another patrol and headed for the Central Atlantic, to operate off the west coast of Africa. On the 19th, he came across a ship that was later identified as the American SS *Robin Moor*. He approached her cautiously and signalled to her for identification. When she replied '*Robin Moor*', Metzler became suspicious, especially when he could find no ship of that name in Lloyd's Register. Later, when it became light he noticed the name on the side of the ship was *Exmoor*, listed in Lloyd's as a 5,000-ton US ship. The captain came across to *U-69* with the ships' papers and cargo manifest. He claimed that the ship had only been bought by America in the last few weeks and that the name hadn't yet been changed from *Exmoor* to *Robin Moor*. Metzler, however, claimed he saw 'radio apparatus' and 'guns' on the manifest and believed that this ship was 'a neutral carrying contraband' and was, he felt, a legitimate target. Despite the explicit orders from Hitler and Dönitz to avoid any contact with American ships, Metzler decided to sink her. After the crew had abandoned ship in lifeboats, he sank her with a single torpedo and thirty rounds from the deck gun. *Robin Moor* was the first US ship to be sunk by a U-boat during the Second World War. On the same day he sank the British SS *Tewkesbury* by torpedo and gunfire. During the night of 25/26 May, Metzler laid seven mines off Lagos and on the 31st he sank the British MV *Sangara*. She was lying at anchor in the roads of Accra and sank by the stern in 33ft of water. On 4 June the British dredger *Robert Hughes* struck a mine which had been laid by Metzler and sunk at the entrance of Lagos harbour. *U-69* now moved north and was due to be refuelled from the supply ship *Lothringen* on the 19th but *Lothringen* had been sunk on the 15th by the cruiser HMS *Dunedin*. So now short of fuel, Metzler took *U-69* north and headed for Las Palmas and hopefully a refuelling ship. During the early hours of the 27th, about 300 miles south-west of the Canaries he encountered Convoy SL76. Metzler sank two ships, the SS *Empire Ability* and shortly after the British SS *River Lugar*, which was struck by a torpedo and broke in two and sank within seconds. The master, thirty-four crew members, four gunners and one passenger were lost. During the night of the 28th/29th, *U-69* entered Las Palmas harbour and was replenished and refuelled by the German supply ship the MV *Charlotte Schliemann*. Metzler continued north and on 4 July sank the SS *Robert L. Holt* by gunfire, north-west of the Canaries, with the loss of the entire crew.

On 21 August Metzler left port for operations in the Atlantic, his last patrol with *U-69*. Within three days Metzler became very ill and the First Officer, *Oberleutnant zur See* Hans-Jürgen Auffermann had to take command. The patrol was cancelled and *U-69* returned to port and Metzler was taken to hospital with a serious kidney infection. His career as a U-boat commander was over; with an infection that could flare up at any time he couldn't risk going to sea for long periods of time. A successful and promising career was over. He returned to duty in November and was reassigned to the staff of the 25th U-boat Flotilla where he became an instructor. In February 1943, took command of *U-847*, which was a training boat. On 16 September he was promoted to *Korvettenkapitän* and became deputy commander of the 5th U-boat Flotilla, a training unit based in Kiel under the command of *Korvettenkapitän* Karl-Heinz Moehe. In October he was transferred to Danzig as the new commander of the 19th U-boat Flotilla. Here he was primarily responsible for the training of new U-boat commanders. He surrendered to Allied troops in April 1945 and was briefly interned. In 1954 he wrote his memoirs, entitled, *'The Laughing Cow': The Story of U-69*. The title was derived from the time when *U-69* was assigned to the 7th U-boat Flotilla and the crew were instructed to paint Günther Prien's snorting bull insignia on the U-boat's conning tower. However no illustrations was provided and so *U-69's* First Watch officer, Auffermann instructed a shipyard worker to copy the head of the laughing cow which appeared on the package of a popular French dairy product instead – which caused great amusement. Jost Metzler died in Bavendorf-Ravensburg, Baden-Württemberg on 29 September 1975.

Other awards:
21 Dec 1939: Iron Cross 2nd Class
02 Mar 1941: Iron Cross 1st Class
04 Oct 1937: Long Service Award 4th Class
20 Dec 1939: Commemorative Medal of 01 Oct 1938
12 Apr 1941: U-Boat War Badge

Karl-Heinz MOEHLE
Korvettenkapitän
21 ships sunk, 92,086 tons

Knight's Cross: Awarded on 26 February 1941 as *Kapitänleutnant* and as commander of *U-123* to become the 24th U-boat commander to receive the Knight's Cross for his leadership and in sinking sixteen ships for a total of 64,020 tons.

Karl-Heinz Moehle was born on 31 July 1910 in Norden, Lower Saxony, a small town on the North Sea coast of East Frisia. He entered the *Reichsmarine* in April 1930, at the age of nineteen and received his initial training aboard the battleship *Schleswig-Holstein*. In October 1934 he was commissioned as a *Leutnant zur See*, and in March 1939 he transferred to the U-boat service. He began his training in Kiel where he served as a Watch Officer and in June was promoted to *Oberleutnant zur See*. He continued with his training and in December was appointed Watch Officer on *U-5*, a training boat at Neustadt. In October 1937, he took command of his first boat, *U-20*, a Type IIB, attached to U-boat Flotilla '*Lohs*' a training unit in Kiel.

Moehle was promoted to *Kapitänleutnant* in April 1939 and with the outbreak of the Second World War in September he took *U-20* out on his first war patrol. He left Wilhelmshaven to patrol off the southern coast of Norway. He returned to

(Author's collection)

Kiel on the 20th without sinking a ship. On 18 November *U-20* left port for a minelaying operation and on 29th a British merchant ship struck one of his mines and sank, and later on 10 December another British ship, the SS *Willowpool*, also hit one of his mines and was lost. The day before he had torpedoed and sunk the Danish SS *Magnus* about 40 miles north-north-east of Peterhead. She sank within ninety seconds with the loss of all but one member of her crew. On 13 January 1940, during his last patrol with *U-20*, he sank the Swedish SS *Sylvia*, with the loss of the entire crew.

Moehle now spent the next five months on land, familiarizing himself with the plans and construction of his new command, *U-123*, a Type IXB boat built by AG Weser of Bremen. He left Kiel with his new boat on 21 September, and headed out into the Atlantic where he had been assigned to weather-reporting duties. In fact Moehle was soon ordered to join other boats in the area in the search of convoys. On 6 October *U-20* sank the British SS *Benlawers*, north-east of St. Johns, then on the 10th Moehle sank a straggler from Convoy SC6, the SS *Graigwen*. On the 17th *U-48* sighted another convoy and a patrol line was formed by *U-46*, *U-99*, *U-100*, *U-101* and *U-123*. The convoy crossed the line on the 18th, and during the night Moehle sank four ships, the Dutch SS *Boekelo* and the British SS *Sedgepool*, SS *Shekatika* and SS *Clintonia*. With her torpedoes expended *U-123* headed for home.

On 14 November, *U-123* left Lorient to operate west of the British Isles. During the early hours of the 22nd Moehle sank the British SS *Cree* south-west of Rockall. The following day he took *U-123* west to close in on Convoy OB244 and sank five ships. The steamer *Oakcrest*, a straggler, was struck on the starboard side below the bridge by a single torpedo and immediately developed a heavy list until she capsized and sank. A total of thirty-five crew were lost. At 07:12 hours he sank the SS *King Idwal* followed about an hour later by SS *Tymeric*, hit by a stern torpedo and she sank in flames after seventeen minutes with the loss of seventy-one crew. At 09:14 he sank the fifth ship from the convoy, the Swedish SS *Anten*, struck by a single torpedo. The crew abandoned ship and were later picked up by HMS *Sandwich* and were landed safely at Liverpool on the 27th. The wreck sank two days later. Moehle had tried to finish off the ship, but *U-123* collided with an object, either a wreck or debris. Both periscopes and the conning tower were damaged and Moehle was forced to break off his patrol and return to Lorient.

With *U-123* repaired, which took longer than Moehle had anticipated, he finally left to operate in the North Atlantic on 14 January 1941. He sank the Norwegian SS *Vespasian* on the 24th; she was struck by a single torpedo about 290 miles west-south-west of Rockall. On 4 February he spotted a straggler from Convoy SC20, the SS *Empire Engineer*. Moehle fired one torpedo which struck the ship in the bow and she sank in less than four minutes, with the loss of the entire crew. After moving eastwards Moehle attacked and sank another British ship, the SS *Holystone* from Convoy OB284 on the 15th: again there were no survivors. On the 24th he came across the Dutch SS *Grootekerk*, which was steaming on a zigzag course. However, after a chase of nine hours the ship suddenly turned and slowed down, which gave Moehle the opportunity to attack. His first torpedoed missed but a second torpedo struck *Grootekerk* amidships. she stopped and was hit by another torpedo. Moehle waited for a few minutes and then fired the a final torpedo which struck close to the area where the crew was lowering the lifeboats. The ship capsized and sank after twelve minutes west of Rockall. There were no survivors.

During his last patrol as commander of *U-123*, Moehle sank the Swedish merchant ship *Venezuela* on 17 April south-south-west of Rockall. She had been spotted at 04:30 hours and Moehle decided to attack her because she was not following the routes for neutral vessels. She was struck amidships and after observing the crew had abandoned ship in the lifeboats, Moehle fired another torpedo which struck the ship in the hold in the engine room but she still did not sink. So another torpedo was fired which was a dud. When the U-boat surfaced two hours later after reloading the torpedo tubes the ship was no longer visible: she had finally gone down. Moehle then left the area and joined a patrol line which failed to locate any more convoys.

From June 1941 until the end of the war Moehle was the commander both of the 5th U-boat Training Flotilla and the U-boat base at Kiel, with the rank of *Korvettenkapitän* from March 1943. He surrendered to Allied forces in May 1945, and was arrested in 1946 and charged for his part in the sinking of the passenger liner RMS *Laconia* in September 1942 in which 1,658 people died. Moehle was found guilty and sentenced to five years' imprisonment, being released on 9 November 1949. Moehle gave evidence at the Nuremberg Trials against Dönitz. He told the court falsely whilst under oath that Dönitz had wanted and requested that U-boat commanders' murder shipwrecked crews to prevent them from manning other ships. It seems that the relatively light sentence he received of five years was perhaps down to a deal in return for his 'anti-Dönitz' testimony. He also claimed at his trial that he did not issue the *Laconia* Order but had in fact interpreted it to be a subtle order from Dönitz.

Little is known about his activities after his release from prison, apart from he settled in Ahrensburg, Schleswig-Holstein where he died on 17 November 1996 at the age of eighty-six.

Other awards:
23 Sep 1939: Iron Cross 2nd Class
24 Oct 1940: Iron Cross 1st Class
02 Oct 1936: Long Service Award 4th Class
17 Oct 1939: U-Boat War Badge
20 Dec 1939: Commemorative Medal of 01 Oct 1938
01 Nov 1941: Italian War Cross with Swords
01 Sep 1944: War Service Cross 2nd Class with Swords
30 Jan 1945: War Service Cross 1st Class with Swords
01 May 1945: German Cross in Gold

Helmut August Wilhelm MÖHLMANN
Korvettenkapitän
7 ships sunk, 47,169 tons
1 ship damaged, 11,394 tons

Knight's Cross: Awarded as *Kapitänleutnant* and as commander of *U-571* on 16 April 1943, for the sinking of seven ships for a total of 47,169 shipping tons.

Helmut Möhlmann was born on 25 June 1913 in Kiel, and joined the *Reichsmarine* as a naval cadet in April 1933. He began his training aboard the sail training ship *Gorch Fock* and the light cruiser *Karlsruhe* before attending the Naval Academy at Flensburg.

He attended various training courses before being assigned to the light cruiser *Nürnberg* from December 1935. He was commissioned as a *Leutnant zur See* in October 1936 and from February 1938 served on the torpedo boat *Luchs* as First Watch Officer. In June he was promoted to *Oberleutnant zur See* and in April 1940 was transferred to the U-boat service. From June he was attached to the 24th U-boat Flotilla where he began his training as a U-boat commander.

On 19 December 1940, he was appointed commander of *U-143*, a Type IID boat, which was assigned as a training vessel attached to the 22nd U-boat Training Flotilla. In March 1941 he briefly took command of *U-52*, standing in until another commander could be found. Although he didn't take the U-boat out on a war patrol he gained command experience. In April 1941, Möhlmann was promoted to *Kapitänleutnant* and on 22 May took command of *U-571*, a Type VIIC boat built in Hamburg by Blohm und Voss. The boat had only been commissioned the day he took command and his first task was to

(Scherzer)

oversee the training of the crew and to supervise the boat's sea trials. Finally on 18 August, *U-571* was ready for its first patrol. He left Trondheim for northern waters, patrolling off the coast of Kola from the 23rd, and on the 26th he torpedoed and damaged the Soviet submarine depot ship *Marija Uljanova*. She was struck on the starboard side and then hit with a coup de grâce but refused to sink. *U-571* was chased off by destroyers which later returned to pick up the survivors who had been blown overboard by the explosion. Two hours after being hit the stern of the *Marija Uljanova* broke off, but the vessel remained afloat and was taken in tow to Uritskij, but she was later declared a total loss. Möhlmann returned to port happy that his first patrol had been a success.

His second patrol began on 22 October with *U-571* part of *Stosstrupp* Group in the North Atlantic. On the 31st, the boats were directed to Convoy OS10, sighted north-north-east of the Azores. However contact was lost and the attack was abandoned. On 8 November Möhlmann was ordered to join *Raubritter* Group, in a new patrol line south-east of Cape Farewell, and another convoy was soon located. Again contact was lost and the operation was called off. A disappointed Möhlmann headed for La Pallice. His next patrol also proved unsuccessful and no convoys were located. However, his next patrol would prove to be more successful. He left for the North Atlantic on 10 March 1942, heading for the Newfoundland area. On the 29th he sank the British SS *Hertford*. She was unescorted and was struck by two torpedoes about 200 miles south of Halifax. On 6 April he sank the Norwegian tanker MV *Koll* east of Cape Hatteras. She was struck on the port side. The explosions killed two men on watch below. When the thirty-three survivors abandoned ship in three lifeboats, *U-571* came alongside the boats and asked questions about their cargo and destination. Möhlmann then ordered fresh water and biscuit to be handed out, and then he ordered the ship to be sunk using the deck guns. On the 14th, *U-571* sank the US SS *Margaret* about 45 miles east of Cape Hatteras; she was struck by a single torpedo and quickly sank within five minutes after a boiler explosion. Some survivors were seen to leave the ship in a lifeboat and several rafts, but none of the eight officers and twenty-one crew members were was ever found.

During his next patrol Möhlmann headed for US waters and whilst en route *U-571* was directed towards the northbound Convoy HG84. Together with various other boats they formed a patrol line and as a result of the operation five boats were sunk, all by *U-552*. The operation ended on 16 June due to calm weather and good visibility – unfavourable conditions for U-boat attacks. He sank the British SS *Umtata* on 7 July north-west of Key West in the Florida Strait while under tow. She had been damaged by a torpedo from *U-181* on 10 March, and was being towed into port by a tug. The next day Möhlmann sank the US tanker MV *J.A. Moffett Jr.*, three miles south-west of Tennessee Reef on the Florida Keys. She was struck by two torpedoes on her port side and the crew began to abandon ship. As the lifeboats were being launched, one of the master's arms got caught in the falls and was amputated. He died of loss of blood. Thirty minutes after the first attack *U-571* surfaced and began shelling the ship with the deck guns. The ship was later towed back to Key West and declared a total loss. On 9 July Möhlmann sank the Honduran SS *Nicholas Cuneo* with the loss of one crew member. He went on to attack the US tanker MV *Pennsylvania Sun* on 15th; she was sunk by a single torpedo about 125 miles west of Key West. The torpedo struck amidships on the port side and blew away the port wing of the bridge, killing two crew members. The remainder of the crew abandoned ship and were later picked up by USS *Dahlgren* and taken to Key West the same day. However, the *Pennsylvania Sun* failed to sink and was the next day, escorted whilst under her own power, port and she later returned to service. Möhlmann returned to La Pallice on 7 August. He completed another three war patrols with *U-571* but failed to increase his score. He was transferred in May 1943, and attended a course at the Naval Academy before serving as a staff officer with the Commander-in-Chief of U-boats in September.

From December 1944 until the end of the war he commanded the 14th U-boat Flotilla at Narvik, Norway, where he surrendered to British troops in May 1945, and spent four months in captivity. After the war he entered the *Bundesmarine* as a *Korvettenkapitän* in July 1960. From August 1962 he served as a Staff Officer to the Commander of North Sea Forces in NATO, and from November 1969 he was Military Attaché of the German Embassy in Rio de Janeiro, Brazil. He retired with the rank of *Fregattenkapitän* in March 1970. Möhlmann died in Prien am Chiemsee, Bavaria on 12 April 1977.

Other awards:
16 Nov 1939: Iron Cross 2nd Class
01 Dec 1941: Iron Cross 1st Class
02 Apr 1937: Long Service Award 4th Class
06 Jun 1939: Spanish Cross in Bronze
26 Oct 1939: Return of Memel Commemorative Medal
20 Apr 1941: Destroyers War Badge
01 Dec 1941: U-Boat War Badge
20 Apr 1944: War Service Cross 2nd Class with Swords
16 Sep 1944: U-Boat Combat Clasp in Bronze

Günther Reinhold MÜLLER-STÖCKHEIM
Korvettenkapitän (pm)
13 ships sunk, 72,138 tons
5 ships damaged, 29,726 tons

Knight's Cross: Awarded as *Kapitänleutnant* on 27 November 1942 and as commander of *U-67*, in recognition of the sinking of twelve ships for a total of 67,441 shipping tons and for damaging another four ships.

Günther Müller-Stockheim was born on 17 December 1913, in Klein Stöckheim, a district in the south of Braunschweig on the Oder River. He entered the *Reichsmarine* as a cadet in April 1934, and was assigned to an infantry training unit in the Baltic. His basic training began with assignment to the sail training ship *Gorch Fock* and from September

(Scherzer)

he served aboard the light cruiser *Emden*. In April 1937, he was commissioned as a *Leutnant zur See* and served aboard the battleship *Schlesien* until April 1938. After attending the Naval Academy in Flensburg, Müller-Stockheim was promoted to *Oberleutnant zur See* in April 1939.

In April 1940 he transferred to the U-boat service and had to endure six months of intensive training before he was assigned to *U-123* as Watch Officer, whilst under the command of *Kapitänleutnant* Karl-Heinz Moehle, a future U-boat ace. He took part in four patrols in which twelve ships were sunk and he learnt much from Moehle. In July 1941, he finally got his own U-boat, *U-67*, a Type IXC boat which had up until then only been used for training, but that was about to change. On 1 September Müller-Stockheim was promoted to *Kapitänleutnant* and two weeks later he took *U-67* from Lorient and headed for the Central Atlantic and his first patrol as commander of a U-boat. He was to operate as one of four boats in the Freetown area. On the 21st Convoy SL87 was sighted south-west of the Canaries, and the boats closed in. On the 24th *U-67* sank the British SS *St. Cair II*, struck by a single torpedo with the loss of thirteen men. *U-67* later took part in more operations near the Cape Verde Islands but had no success.

On 26 November 1941, Müller-Stockheim headed for the coast of Spain and Portugal, and together with other boats made up *Seeräuber* Group. They formed a patrol line and waited for Convoy HG76 to leave for England. The operation lasted until the night of 23rd, during which time *U-67* made several attacks but was driven off every time. Three ships were sunk as well as the British warships HMS *Stanley* and HMS *Audacity* but five U-boats were lost. A disappointed Müller-Stockheim returned to port on the 26th. He left for the Caribbean area on 19 January 1942, hoping that a new year would bring some luck. *U-67* was part of the *Neuland* Group together with five other boats. The plan was for the five boats to be in position by mid-February and for simultaneous attacks to be made on ports and oil installations. On the morning of 16 February Müller-Stockheim sighted a ship and attacked: she was the Dutch SS *Rafaela*. She was struck amidships by a single torpedo but was left only damaged, returning to service a few months later. On the morning of the 16th *U-67* was attacked by a Douglas A-20 Havoc aircraft of the USAF 59th Bomber Squadron, but the attack was unsuccessful and *U-67* escaped without damage. During the evening *U-67* joined up with *U-502* to bombard the oil-storage installations at Aruba, but the attack was thwarted due to a blackout and enemy vessels. Müller-Stockheim decided to take his boat further west and on the 21st sank the Norwegian tanker MV *Kongsgaard*. She was struck by a single torpedo on the port side between the bridge and the poop deck. The cargo caught fire and it became difficult for the crew to launch the lifeboats. The master and seven survivors were later rescued, but thirty-seven men lost their lives. On 14 March, while moving out of the eastern Caribbean *U-67* sank the Panamanian tanker MV *Penelope*. She sank in less than fifteen minutes with the loss of two crew members, about 170 miles west of Dominica.

His next patrol began on 20 May, when *U-67* left port and headed for US waters. Initially patrolling the coast of Florida, where on 16 June she sank the Nicaraguan SS *Managua*. On the 20th in the Gulf of Mexico Müller-Stockheim sighted another ship, the Norwegian tanker MV *Nortind*, part of Convoy HX223. She was hit by two torpedoes but managed to escape any further attacks by *U-67*. Two days later she was struck by two torpedoes from *U-358*, caught fire, split in two and sank, there were no survivors. In the same area Müller-Stockheim sank the American SS *Rawleigh Warner*, with a cargo of 38,909 barrels of gasoline which burst into flames and engulfed the entire length of the ship with the loss of the entire crew. On the 29th he sank the British SS *Empire Mica* south-west of Cape St. George, Florida. She was struck by two torpedoes and sank immediately with the loss of thirty-three crew members. East of New Orleans Müller-Stockheim sank the Norwegian MV *Bayard* on 6 July. She was struck by one torpedo and the explosion destroyed the deck house, stern gun, aerial and three vehicles stored on No. 5 hatch cover and killed two gunners. The survivors, many of whom were injured, abandoned ship in both port lifeboats while the ship slowly developed a list to port. Eleven crew members were lost. The next day *U-67* torpedoed the US tanker SS *Paul H. Hardwood*. She was seriously damaged but was later repaired and returned to service. Before the patrol was over *U-67* sank two more ships, the US tankers SS *Benjamin Brewster* on the 10th and SS *R.W. Gallagher* on the 13th. Müller-Stockheim returned to Lorient on 8 August.

On 16 September *U-67* left port and headed to the Caribbean coast to join other boats in further operations against Allied convoys. The first operation however was called off due to strong Allied air cover. However, *U-67* managed to sink the Norwegian MV *Primero* on 25 October. She was struck by one of two torpedoes fired and was hit in the starboard side in the engine room. The crew abandoned ship and all but two of them survived. But during the chase *Primero* had struck *U-67* a glancing blow, causing damage to the upper deck spare torpedo containers on the port side. One seaman was severely injured and later died, being buried at sea. On 8 November whilst patrolling east of the Windward Islands Müller-Stockheim attacked and damaged the British SS *Capo Olmo*. On the 9th *U-67* sighted the unescorted Norwegian SS *Nidarland*, she was torpedoed and sank within eight minutes with the loss of one crew member. On the 15th the British MV *King Arthur* was sunk west of Trinidad, and three days later the Norwegian MV *Tortugas* was sunk east of Barbados. With all of his torpedoes gone, Müller-Stockheim damaged the British MV *Empire Glade* by gunfire. After being refuelled *U-67* reached Lorient on 21 December.

In early March 1943, with minor repairs completed, *U-67* was ready for her new patrol. She headed for the Central Atlantic where Müller-Stockheim had been ordered to join four other boats and form a patrol line from 13 March. The eastbound Convoy UGS6 had left New York on the 5th and was sighted by *U-130* which attacked the convoy but was soon sunk. With a calm sea a strong escort and good visibility, it wasn't a good time for the U-boats. On the 17th the operation was cancelled and *U-67*, *U-123*, *U-159*, *U-167*, *U-172*, *U-513* and *U-515* moved south and formed a new patrol line, *Seeräuber* Group, south of the Canaries to intercept the southbound Convoy RS3. It was soon sighted and two ships were sunk on the 28th and another on the 29th. *U-67* was damaged by one of the escort ships and was unable to take any further part in the operation and so returned to Lorient.

On 10 May, *U-67* left port to operate in an area 300 to 600 miles north-east of the Caribbean. After being at sea for ten weeks, Müller-Stockheim had no success and was short of fuel. On 16 July, desperate to find a refuelling boat and to replenish his supplies *U-67* surfaced. Whilst searching for a supply ship she was spotted by an Avenger aircraft from the escort carrier USS *Core* 850 miles west-south-west of the Azores. The aircraft approached behind the clouds and dropped four depth-bombs. It was a direct hit, the bow of *U-67* rose out of the sea, and disappeared with oil and wreckage spread across the surface. Only three survivors, one officer and two ratings, were picked up by the destroyer USS *McCormick*. Forty-eight men were lost, including Müller-Stockheim who was promoted posthumously on 1 July 1943 to the rank of *Korvettenkapitän*.

Other awards:
08 Apr 1938: Long Service Award 4th Class
01 Mar 1941: Iron Cross 2nd Class
01 May 1941: Iron Cross 1st Class
04 May 1941: U-Boat War Badge

Karl NEITZEL
Kapitän zur See
5 ships sunk, 28,496 tons
7 ships damaged, 49,587 tons

Knight's Cross: Awarded on 27 March 1943 as *Korvettenkapitän* and as commander of *U-510* for the sinking of five ships for a total of 28,496 shipping tons and for damaging another seven in just three war patrols.

Karl Neitzel was born in Kolberg, Pommern on 30 January 1901, and entered the Kaiser's Navy in July 1917 as a Cadet. He served in torpedo boats during the latter stages of the First World War, but left the Navy when the war was over. He rejoined the Navy in 1923, now the *Reichsmarine* and was commissioned as a *Leutnant zur See* in October 1927 and was promoted to *Oberleutnant zur See* in July 1929. He served in minesweepers from 1931 to 1936, and was promoted to *Kapitänleutnant* on 1 April 1935. From February 1938 he served as a Training Officer on the Staff of the Admiral Commanding the Baltic Sea. Promoted to *Korvettenkapitän* in April 1939, he was appointed commander of the 1st Minesweeper Flotilla in December and was responsible for minesweeping operations and escort service in the North Sea.

(Scherzer)

In February 1941, Neitzel transferred to the U-boat service and began his training. He became one of the oldest commanders of a U-boat when he took command of *U-510*, a Type IXC boat, in November. He left Kiel for his first patrol on 7 July and headed for the Western Atlantic. On 2 August, he sank his first ship the Uruguayan SS *Maldonado*, which he had sighted about 250 miles south-south-east of Bermuda. He had misidentified the Uruguayan flag as the Greek one and had assumed that she was heading for New York with a full load – 7,000 tons of tinned meat, hides, wool and fats. He fired two shots across her bow with the deck gun and ordered the *Maldonado* to stop. All forty-nine crew members abandoned ship in four lifeboats. Neitzel then fired two torpedoes and the ship broke in two and quickly sank. He continued with his patrol off the coast of the Caribbean where on the 10th he torpedoed and damaged the British tanker MV *Alexia*, and on the 19th he sank the British MV *Cressington Court* north-east of Belém, Brazil. The master and seven crew members were lost. On the 18th Neitzel made an unsuccessful attack on a steamer, and then left the area, and a few days later he received orders to rendezvous with *U-155*, which had been damaged during an Allied air attack and was unable to submerge. Sometime on 7 September, *U-155* was met by two other U-boats and was boarded by some engineers who attempted to fix the problem, but failed. Neitzel was ordered to tow the damaged U-boat back to Lorient, arriving on the 13th.

During his next patrol, which began on 14 October, Neitzel took *U-510* out to the Central Atlantic where on 31st he attacked and damaged the Norwegian SS *Alaska*. It was the only success of the patrol. On 24 November *U-510* was attacked but only slightly damaged, although it was enough damage to convince Neitzel to head for his home port, arriving safely at Lorient in mid-December. On 16 January 1943, Neitzel took *U-510* out once again, now fully repaired, and headed for the Cape Verde Islands, crossing the Atlantic during February and towards the Caribbean. The boat moved south and began patrolling off the coast of Guiana from early March. On the 8th he encountered Convoy BT6, about 70 miles north of Cayenne and during the night he attacked. The following day he sank the British MV *Kelvinbank*, the US SS *James K. Polk* and SS *Thomas Ruffin* (both were seriously damaged and later declared total losses), and damaging the US SS *George G. Meade*, SS *Tabitha Brown*, SS *Mark Hanna*, SS *James Smith* and SS *Joseph Rodman Drake*.

Neitzel was promoted to *Fregattenkapitän* in April 1943, and the following month he left the U-boat service. He later became the deputy commander of the 25th U-boat Flotilla in Libau, with the rank of *Kapitän zur See*, and took over as commander of the 2nd U-boat Training Division in January 1944. For the last three months of the war he served as commander of Naval Grenadier Regiment 7, and after the surrender he spent about seven months in Allied captivity. He was released in January 1946 and later settled in Kiel, where he died on 13 November 1966. Neitzel was one of the highest-ranking officers to come from the U-boat service in the Second World War.

Other awards:
02 Oct 1936: Long Service Award 4th to 2nd Class
00.00.191_: Iron Cross 2nd Class
10 Jan 1940: Bar to the Iron Cross 2nd Class
23 Mar 1940: Iron Cross 1st Class
00.00.1940: Minesweepers War Badge
00 Dec 1942: U-Boat War Badge

<u>Victor</u> Otto OEHRN
Fregattenkapitän
24 ships sunk, 104,785 tons
1 ship damaged, 9,494 tons

Knight's Cross: Awarded on 21 October 1940, as *Kapitänleutnant* and as commander of *U-37* for sinking twenty-four ships and damaging one for a total of 104,785 shipping tons in eighty-one days during four war patrols.

(Scherzer)

Victor Oehrn was born in Gadebey, the Caucasus, now part of Azerbaijan, on 21 October 1907. His father had been an executive in the Siemens Corporation whilst working at a factory when Victor was born. The young Victor grew up among Russians, Armenians, Georgians and Tatars. After the Revolution in Russia of 1917, his father was put on a list of the local 'bourgeois', to be disposed of in one way or another, so the Oehrn family was forced to move and eventually ended up in Berlin in 1921. It was quite an experience for a fourteen-year-old, and Victor could already speak English, French and was fluent in Russian – he would become one of only four Russian interpreters in the *Kriegsmarine*.

Oehrn joined the *Reichsmarine* as an Officer Candidate in April 1927. He finished his formal training in 1930 and then served for eighteen months on the light cruiser *Königsberg*, being commissioned as a *Leutnant zur See* in September 1931. During this time he was trained in minesweeping, torpedoes, signals, naval artillery and navigation. His reports stated that he was a proven leader with good leadership skills. In March 1933 he was training new recruits himself and in July was promoted to *Oberleutnant zur See* while serving as training officer on the light cruiser *Karlsruhe*. He was asked if he wanted to join the U-boat service in early 1935, but said no – perhaps he wanted his own command of a minesweeper. But then in October he was chosen to command *U-14*. He officially took command in January 1936, *U-14* was a Type IIB boat and he took her out into Spanish waters during the Civil War from July until September 1936. He was promoted to *Kapitänleutnant* in October 1936, and twelve months later he surrendered his command. From October 1937, Oehrn was attached to the Commanding Admiral in the Baltic, and spent the next few months training officers. In August 1939, he was assigned to the staff of Karl Dönitz, commander of U-boats.

On 6 May 1940, Oehrn was appointed commander of a Type IXA boat, *U-37*, built in Bremen and launched in May 1938. His first patrol began on 15th when he left Wilhelmshaven to operate north-west of Finisterre. On the 19th he sank the Swedish MV *Erik Frisell*, and moved south where on the 22nd he attacked the British MV *Dunster Grange* south of Ireland. He fired four torpedoes: the first passed underneath the ship without detonating and the second detonated prematurely, alerting the crew who were then able to evade the next two torpedoes. Oehrn ordered the attack to continue using the deck guns, but after only a short time, with accurate return fire from *Dunster Grange*, *U-37* was forced to give up the attack. During the early hours of the 24th Oehrn sank the Greek SS *Kyma*, about 175 miles off Cape Clear. He continued to his operational area where he sank a further eight ships in only seven days, sinking the British SS *Sheaf Mead* and the Argentinean SS *Uruguay* on the 27th. She was about 160 miles west of Cape Villano when *U-37* surfaced and stopped her. She had neutral markings and Oehrn examined her paperwork. The ship had been bound for Belgium, but due to the German invasion had been ordered to Ireland. The papers were not signed and Oehrn found this suspicious and decided to sink the vessel. He ordered the crew off, sent a boarding party from *U-37* to board her with charges. After about thirty minutes the boarding party returned to the U-boat and there was a large explosion and the ship sank. On the 28th, Oehrn sank the French passenger ship *Brazza* and the French sailing ship *Julien*, just west of Cape Finisterre. The following day he sank the French merchant ship *Marie Jose* with a single torpedo north-west of Vigo. She sank slowly after fifteen minutes and her crew were picked up by a Spanish fishing boat. The same day Oehrn also sank the British tanker MV *Telena* by gunfire. Her cargo of crude oil caught fire and her crew were forced to abandon ship. The *Telena* was later salvaged by the Portuguese and employed by them as the MV *Gerona*. His last two victims of this patrol were the Greek SS *Ioanna* and the Finnish SS *Snabb* sank on 3 June, 280 miles north of Cape Finisterre.

Korvettenkapitän *Victor Oehrn (right) talking with* Korvettenkapitän *Victor Schütze* (Author's collection)

On 1 August, Oehrn took *U-37* out of Wilhelmshaven in transit to western France to a new base at Lorient. He sank the British MV *Upwey Grange* during the journey. In the next patrol he took *U-37* west to operate off the British Isles. On 23 August he sank the Norwegian SS *Keret* and later the same day he claimed the British SS *Seven Leigh*. She was struck by a torpedo south of Iceland. She had been spotted the day before and had been hunted, during which time Oehrn had spotted the *Keret*. She was finished off by *U-37*'s deck guns, and two lifeboats that were still alongside the ship were hit by the shrapnel from the exploding shells and most of the occupants of the boats were killed. On the 24th Oehrn sank the British SS *Brookwood* south of Iceland. That same evening *U-37* attacked Convoy SC1 and sank a sloop of the escort, HMS *Penzance*, and five hours later sank the British SS *Blairmore*. On the 25th, he sank the SS *Yewcrest*, another British ship, by gunfire south-west of Ireland. She sank in flames after about four hours with the loss of only one member of the crew. Oehrn was almost ready to return to port when he sighted another target, the Greek SS *Theodoros T*. She was sunk by a single torpedo and gunfire. *U-37* finally reached Lorient on 30 August.

His next patrol began on 24 September when he left for the west coast of the British Isles. He sank the Egyptian SS *Georges Mabro* on the 27th, and the next day he came across the abandoned wreck of the British SS *Corrientes*, which had been torpedoed on the 26th by *U-32* but had remained afloat. She had been struck in the engine room and was eventually sunk by gunfire. Whilst operating as a weather-boat west of Ireland on the 30th, Oehrn sank two more ships, the SS *Samala* and the SS *Heminge*, a straggler from Convoy OB220. On 6 October he also sank the British tanker SS *British General*. She was struck below her bridge by one torpedo about 550 miles west of Valentia Island. Shortly after stopping she was struck again by a second torpedo which hit the aft section of the ship but still she did not sink. Oehrn attempted to finish her off with the deck guns but she refused to sink. He took the decision to fire two more torpedoes at the ship, knowing the crew were still aboard. At 20:00 hours on the 7th she finally sank, with the loss of forty-seven crew members. During the return journey *U-37* sank the British SS *Stangrant* from Convoy HX77, north-east of Rockall on the evening of the 13th. Eight crew members were lost and the remainder were rescued by a Sunderland flying boat. *U-37* returned to Lorient on the 22nd.

At Lorient he was met by Dönitz. Oehrn formed the crew into ranks and awaited an inspection by the commander of U-boats. The crew looked scruffy and dirty and Oehrn had a month's beard growth and wished he had time for a wash. Dönitz greeted the crew and smiled at Oehrn and said, 'A successful patrol, Oehrn?' 'Moderately so Herr *Admiral*' was the reply. Then Dönitz in a loud voice exclaimed, '*Kapitänleutnant* Oehrn, in the name of the *Führer*, I award you the Knight's Cross of the Iron Cross.' Dönitz then proceeded to tell Oehrn that he was relieved of his command with immediate effect and *U-37* would be commanded by his First Watch Officer, *Oberleutnant zur See* Nicolai Clausen. Oehrn was to serve as 1st Staff Officer to Dönitz. Oehrn remained silent he was in shock – he had just lost his boat. He was now to be responsible for the operations and administration of all U-boats between Gibraltar and Suez. Oehrn told Dönitz he was delighted with his new appointment and thanked the Admiral.

In September 1941, Oehrn was promoted to *Korvettenkapitän* and in November he was transferred and took command of the U-boast in the Mediterranean area. It was seen as a promotion and should have been given to an officer of a much higher rank, but Dönitz had every faith in Oehrn. If Oehrn had remained as 1st Staff Officer to Dönitz, he would have been in the thick of the planning and execution of Operation *Paukenschlag*, the U-boat campaign off the coast of the United States. But he felt he was now on the sidelines and in charge of a campaign that was neither important nor profitable. In February 1942 he was transferred once again it seems that the Commander-in-Chief of the *Kriegsmarine*, *Großadmiral* Erich Raeder, did not agree with the assignment of Oehrn and overrode the decision made by Dönitz. Oehrn had now been appointed 1st Officer on the staff of the Admiral in command of U-boats in Italy. Oehrn couldn't wait to take up his new post because he had to spend the next few months training his successor *Kapitan zur See* Leo Kreisch. The two men did not get along at all; Kreisch treated Oehrn like a junior aide. In June Tobruk fell to the Allies, and Oehrn decided to move his operations headquarters from Rome to Libya so he could supervise U-boat attacks on the expected convoys during the evacuation of ships from Tobruk. He flew out of Rome on a Ju 88 with *Generalfeldmarschall* Albert Kesselring and his staff. In the heady days after Tobruk, Oehrn lost all claim to the position of Chief of U-boats in Italy; he was relieved of all of his duties and transferred to the staff of Kesselring. Here he became almost a liaison officer; he had lost all authority and had no staff, except for a small radio detachment. He therefore kept himself busy and made himself a close advisor to Kesselring. He had become one of his staff officers – the only *Kriegsmarine* officer.

In July he was finally given some orders. *Vizeadmiral* Eberhard Weichold, head of the German Naval Command in Italy, told him that Rommel was preparing to attack across the Nile. Oehrn was informed that he was to go to Rommel to assist him. So Oehrn set off across the desert with his driver to find Rommel. He had been given command of a torpedo boat squadron, but it was 600 miles away. He left Kesselring's headquarters on 13 July. Neither he nor his driver knew where they were going and very soon they were lost. Oehrn told his driver to stop near a small hill and Oehrn got out the car and climbed to the top and saw helmets on the other side – it wasn't Rommel's men, they were British. Before he could turn round and run he was hit by a bullet in the shoulder and then three more in the same shoulder. He tried to run but a fifth shot hit him in the leg and knocked him down. His driver had his hands up in surrender. The wounds that Oehrn sustained were serious; they would kill him had he not been captured. He had a shattered left shoulder, a splintered left leg and multiple internal injuries. He was taken by ambulance to a British hospital in Alexandria, 60 miles away. He was lucky to survive the journey. He was taken into surgery immediately and woke up the next morning in a recovery ward, wracked with pain and encased in plaster and a prisoner of war.

He remained in hospital for months and it wasn't until April 1943 that his casts came off. His joints, frozen at first, began to free up, first his fingers, then his arm, then his shoulder and leg. Towards the end of spring he began to walk. By May he learnt that Rommel's *Afrika Korps* had surrendered. Later he learnt that there was to be a prisoner exchange, but only the really serious wounded would be exchanged and the rest would be sent to Canada or Australia. He decided to take action in order to secure his release. He began to starve himself and within a few weeks looked very pale and gaunt. He was seen by the repatriation committee who to his relief chose him as one of the prisoners to be exchanged. He then went around the hospital telling his friends that he was to be released. However, he was later taken off the list and his place was taken by another wounded prisoner. It seems that the doctors at the hospital didn't think he was as bad as he was making out: it could have been that while telling his friends around the hospital he wasn't using his stick and this gave the wrong impression. Oehrn was then moved from the hospital to a POW camp near the Bitter Lakes on the Suez Canal where he stayed until October. He was then told that he would be repatriated to Germany after all, and returned to his homeland via Port Said, Barcelona and Marseilles.

From April 1944, he served as an officer on special duties and from June was made head of U-boats in the area around Normandy during the Allied invasion. He was responsible for the organisation of all U-boats that were left, and supervised their movements to secure areas of the Norwegian coast and the Baltic Sea. In August he was promoted to *Fregattenkapitän* and appointed staff officer attached to the Operations Department of the *Kriegsmarine*. He surrendered to the Allies in May 1945 and was dismissed from the *Kriegsmarine* in August. He settled in Bonn, Germany with his wife and he died at the age of ninety on 26 December 1997. His wife died a year later. They are buried together at the Rüngsdorf Cemetery in Bonn.

Other awards:
02 Oct 1936: Long Service Award 4th Class
05 Apr 1939: Long Service Award 3rd Class
20 Dec 1939: Commemorative Medal for 01 Oct 1938
27 Jan 1940: Iron Cross 2nd Class
10 Jun 1940: Iron Cross 1st Class
00 Sep 1940: U-Boat War Badge
02 Nov 1941: Italian War Cross with Swords
00.00.1941: Italian Bravery Medal in Silver
00.00.1944: U-Boat Combat Clasp in Silver

Jürgen Dieter Gustav Alexander OESTEN
Korvettenkapitän
19 ships sunk, 101,744 tons
4 ships damaged, 51,668 tons

Knight's Cross: Awarded on 26 March 1941, as *Kapitänleutnant* and as commander of *U-106* for sinking eleven ships for a total of 57,640 shipping tons and for damaging three other ships.

Jürgen Oesten was born in Berlin on 24 October 1913, and was brought up within the city's artistic community. His father was a local sculptor and both parents were tolerant people but they disliked the newly-powerful National Socialist Party and its leader Adolf Hitler.

Oesten joined the *Reichsmarine* at the age of nineteen as a Cadet and was assigned to an infantry training division in the Baltic. Following standard basic training he spent just over a year on the 'pocket battleship' *Admiral Graf Spee* and then the light cruiser *Karlsruhe*. He was commissioned as a *Leutnant zur See* in October 1936 and transferred to the U-boat service the following year. In October 1937 he was served as Watch Officer on board *U-20* under *Kapitänleutnant* Karl-Heinz Moehle. Oesten was promoted to *Oberleutnant zur See* in June 1938, and on 12 August 1939, was appointed commander of *U-61*, a Type IIC boat built in Kiel. He left port on his first war patrol in October and headed out to the Norwegian coast looking for convoys but without success. On 28 November Oesten took part in a minelaying operation off the north-east coast of England. His only success was to damage the British SS *Gryferale*. His third patrol was another minelaying operation, this time in the Firth of Forth. He had no success and *U-61* returned to Kiel on 18 December.

During his next patrol he sank the Norwegian SS *Sydfold* south of the Orkney Islands. In February Oesten took *U-61* to operate in the northern North Sea between Bergen and the Shetlands, against British naval forces. On the 18th, Oetsen sank the Panamanian SS *El Sonadar* a east of the Shetlands, and observed her sinking in less than a minute. Later the same morning he sank the Norwegian MV *Sangstad*. She sank within fifteen minutes with the loss of all but six of her crew. He made three more patrols between April and August 1940, sinking two ships, the Dutch SS *Alwaki* and the British tanker, *Scottish Minstrel*.

On 24 September Oesten transferred to and took command of *U-106*, a Type IXB boat built by AG Weser of Bremen. The boat had only been commissioned in July and Oesten was her first commander. With her sea trials over and her crew keen to leave port and begin their first war patrol, Oesten received orders

(Scherzer)

to sail. He left Kiel on 4 January 1941, for an area north-west of the North Channel. He sank the British MV *Zealandic* whilst *U-106* was operating as a weather-boat. On 29th he sighted the eastbound Convoy SC19 and sank the Egyptian SS *Sesostris* during the morning. He then put in at Lorient on 10 February. Just over two weeks later Oesten took *U-106* out on another patrol, into the Central Atlantic and then headed south. In March he was promoted to *Kapitänleutnant* and on the 11th he sank the British merchant ship, the SS *Memnon*. She was hit on the starboard side underneath the aft mast by a single torpedo. The explosion blew the hatch covers off and threw some of the ore carried as cargo over the deck and buckled the plates. The ship sank by the stern after about fifteen minutes after being hit by a second torpedo. *U-106* surfaced astern of the sinking vessel to question survivors. She had lost four crew members. From the 15th, *U-106* operated together with *U-105* in the area of the Cape Verde Islands. On the afternoon of the 16th *U-106* sank the Dutch MV *Almkerk* which had been part of Convoy SL68. The ship was hit near the bridge by a torpedo, and she sank by the stern about fifteen minutes after her crew had abandoned ship in two lifeboats. During the evening of the 17th Oesten sank the Dutch SS *Tapanieli* and the British SS *Audalusian*, both west of Dakar. During the night of the 19th/20th Oetsen attacked and damaged the battleship HMS *Malaya* and the Dutch SS *Meerkerk*. Both *U-105* and *U-106* refuelled before proceeding to Rio de Janeiro to meet the German blockade-runner *Lech* and escort her up through the South Atlantic. Oesten then left *U-105* to operate alone just off the coast of the Cape Verde Islands, where on 30 May he sank the British MV *Silveryew*. The following day he sank the British SS *Clan Macdougall* with a single torpedo north of the Cape Verde Islands, with the loss of two crew members. Finally this very long patrol ended on 17 June, when *U-106* reached Lorient. After almost a two-month delay Oesten took *U-106* out on another patrol. He left for the North Atlantic and headed for an area west of the North Channel to join other boats. Within a short time a convoy was sighted and eight ships were sunk but none by *U-106*. Oesten returned to port on 11 September. However during the return journey he sank the British SS *Sacramento Valley*. She was struck on the port side amidships in the engine room by one torpedo, and she quickly sank.

On 22 October, Oesten was transferred and appointed commander of the 9th U-boat Flotilla at Brest, France. Five months later he was transferred again when he was made Staff Officer to *Admiral* Hubert Schmundt, the commander of U-boats in northern waters. From January 1943 he served as staff officer to the Leader of U-boats in Norway, *Kapitän zur See* Hans Rudolf Peters. In July he returned to U-boats when he was named as the commander of *U-861*, a Type IXD2 boat built in Bremen. The first war patrol began on 20 April 1944, leaving Kiel and heading to the South Atlantic. He began patrolling off the coast of Brazil but failed to make contact with his target, the American transport ship USS *William A. Mann*, which had left Rio on 2 July, carrying the first contingent of the Brazilian Expeditionary Force to Italy. On the 20th, he did sink the troopship *Vital d'Oliveira* with the loss of 100 men. Four days later Oesten sank the American SS *William Gaston*, hit on the starboard side by a torpedo about 150 miles off Florianopolis, Brazil. Oesten was then ordered to head for the southern tip of Africa, where he operated together with *U-862* in the area of Cape Town. Early on 20 August Oesten sank the British SS *Berkshire* about 400 miles east-south-east of Durban. Eight crew members were lost. On the evening of the same day he attacked Convoy DN68 and damaged the British tanker MV *Daronia*. Oesten then took *U-861* up through the Mozambique Channel and on 5 September he sank the Greek SS *Ioannis Fafalios*, hit on the starboard side amidships about 250 miles east of Mombasa, Kenya. The ship sank within four minutes in rough seas and seven of her twenty-nine crew were lost. He put in at Penang on 23 September.

In November Oesten was ordered back to Europe and he headed for Trondheim, Norway, where he arrived on 19 April 1945, after stopping three times for fuel and supplies. During the voyage he had been promoted to *Korvettenkapitän*. Upon arriving at Trondheim, which was under Allied control, he surrendered himself, his crew and *U-861* to the British. She was one of 116 boats disposed of by the Royal Navy as part of Operation Deadlight – the codename given to the operation to scuttle German submarines that had surrendered to the Allies. A British officer asked Oesten to take his boat from Trondheim to Ireland, but he refused. The officer wasn't sure what to say, Oesten was a large man, 6ft in height with sharp features which made him look like a Viking. So the British officer said that if Oesten and his crew did this they would then be repatriated to Germany on completion of the task. Oesten and various other commanders eventually agreed, taking Oesten's lead. He was more than happy to do this one thing if it meant the chance for his officers and crew to return to Germany within a few days. The boats were duly delivered. As Oesten and the other boats sailed into the harbour in Ireland, escorted by British destroyers, he flashed a message, 'Thank you for the escort'. The reply, 'It was a pleasure' was received. When he got off his boat Oesten was arrested and imprisoned. The agreement had not been honoured; the officer had been overruled by his superiors.

Oesten was sent to a small POW camp first of all, a camp of just two huts and a barbed wire fence. He met there another U-boat commander – Theodor Petersen. Both men were then transferred to London – to the London District Cage in Kensington for questioning. All U-boat officers captured by the Royal Navy passed through the London Cage. Oesten remembers giving nothing away and couldn't recall anything unpleasant. After his interrogation was complete he was sent, together with Petersen to an internment camp. Camp 18 at Featherstone Park located on the banks of the South Tyne in Northumberland. It was a large camp of several thousand prisoners, officers and men. Oesten was a nervous wreck when he arrived at the camp: the experience of war had left him emotionally exhausted. He could deal with Germany's defeat as he hated the Nazis. He finally left Camp 18 in March 1947, he left a very different man, he felt refreshed and looked forward to a new Germany without Hitler.

Jürgen Oesten died peacefully, according to his family on 5 August 2010, at the age of ninety-six. He was buried at sea after a service at a chapel in Hamburg-Ohlsdorf.

Other awards:
03 Dec 1939: Iron Cross 2nd Class
27 Feb 1940: Iron Cross 1st Class
31 Mar 1937: Long Service Award 4th Class
06 Jun 1939: Spanish Cross in Bronze
20 Dec 1939: Commemorative Medal for 01 Oct 1938
11 Jan 1940: U-Boat War Badge

Adolf Cornelius PIENING

Korvettenkapitän
26 ships sunk, 140,449 tons
1 ship damaged, 6,736 tons

Knight's Cross: Awarded as *Kapitänleutant* and as commander of *U-155* on 13 August 1942, in recognition of sinking nineteen ships for a total of 93,180 shipping tons.

Adolf Piening was born on 16 September 1910 in Süderende on the island of Föhr in the district of Nordfriesland, Schleswig-Holstein in Germany. He entered the *Reichsmarine* in April 1930 and was initially assigned to the sail training ship *Niobe* and later he saw service aboard the light cruiser *Emden*. In October 1934, Piening was commissioned as a *Leutnant zur See* whilst serving aboard the 'pocket battleship' *Deutschland*, before spending a few years on

(Scherzer)

torpedo boats and minesweepers. In June 1936 he was promoted to *Oberleutnant zur See* and served as Second Watch Officer aboard the torpedo boat *Tiger*. In January 1938 he was appointed commander of the minesweeper *M72* and was promoted to *Kapitänleutnant* on 1 April 1939.

On 31 October 1940, Piening transferred to the U-boat service, and following the obligatory training he was assigned to *U-48*. This was a fortunate assignment as *U-48* was commanded by one of the greatest aces, Heinrich Bleichrodt. In fact *U-48* went on to become the most successful U-boat of the Second World War. On 23 August 1941, Piening was given his own command, *U-155*, a Type IXC boat built in Bremen. She was a brand-new boat and Piening had to supervise her through the usual sea trials before, on 7 February 1942, he took her out on her first war patrol. He left Kiel for the Western Atlantic and on the 21st he sighted Convoy ONS67, 600 miles north-east of Cape Race. The following morning Piening attacked the convoy, sinking the British tanker MV *Adellen* and the Norwegian MV *Sama*. He then moved to an area south of Nova Scotia and from 6 March *U-155* operated off the US coast. On the 7th Piening sank the Brazilian SS *Arabutan* east of Cape Hatteras. She sank within thirteen minutes with the loss of just one crew member. On the 10th Piening lost one of his officers who fell overboard during a violent storm. He decided therefore to return to port and put in at Lorient on the 27th.

On 24 April he took *U-155* out to the Western Atlantic where on 14 May he sank the Belgian MV *Brabant*. She was struck on the starboard side between the foremast and the bridge while steaming about 25 miles east-north-east of Los Testigos Islands, Venezuela. Nineteen crew and gunners were lost. On the 17th he sank the British tanker MV *San Victorio* south-west of Grenada and in the same area a few hours later he also sank the US MV *Challenger*. On the 20th he sank the Panamanian tanker SS *Sylvan Arrow* from Convoy OT1, south-west of Grenada. *U-155* was then driven off by the American destroyer USS *Upshur*. Piening then took his boat south and sank another Panamanian ship, the SS *Watsonville*, off Kingston, St. Vincent on the 24th. In late May, during his journey back he sank two ships east of the Windward Islands the Dutch SS *Poseidon* and the Norwegian SS *Baghdad*. He reached Lorient on 14 June. For his next patrol he returned to the Western Atlantic where on 28th he sank the Brazilian SS *Barbacena*. She was struck by two torpedoes and sank in less than twenty minutes, about 230 miles east of Barbados. Later that same evening he sank the Brazilian SS *Piave* by gunfire about 400 miles east of Grenada. During the next four days Piening sank four more ships in the same area. He sank the Norwegian SS *Bill* on the evening of the 29th. She sank after being hit by a single torpedo within eight minutes with the loss of only one crew member. The following evening he sank the US SS *Cranford*. The torpedo struck on the starboard side between No. 2 and No. 3 holds. Her cargo of 6,600 tons of chrome ore helped to sink her within three minutes. Eleven crew members died, including the master. *U-155* surfaced and the survivors were questioned and asked if they needed help. Two injured survivors were treated aboard the U-boat and water, supplies and directions to land were given before *U-155* left the area. The survivors were later picked up by the Spanish tanker *Castillo Alemenara* and were landed at Curaçao a few days later. On 1 August the Dutch SS *Kentar* was sunk by two torpedoes and later the same evening Piening also sank the British SS *Clan Macnaughton*, struck by two torpedoes and which sank within fifteen minutes, with the loss of five of her crew. Piening then took *U-155* to the northern coast of South America where he sank four ships in six days. He sank the British SS *Empire Arnold*, hit by two torpedoes while steaming on a zigzag course about 500 miles east of Trinidad. The first torpedo hit No. 4 hold and the second hit the engine room, killing six men. The chief engineer standing on deck was killed by falling debris. No distress signal was sent because the wireless set had been destroyed. The U-boat surfaced and questioned the survivors, taking the master aboard. (He was later landed at Lorient and taken to a POW camp.) Apparently when Piening apologised for sinking the ship, a senior officer on one of the lifeboats remarked that it was, 'a bad business' and he wished it was all over. Piening replied, 'So do I'. The next day Piening sunk the Dutch merchant MV *Draco* about 420 miles east of Tobago and on the 10th he sank the British tanker MV *San Emiliano*. The following day he sank the Dutch MV *Strabo* by gunfire about 110 miles north-north-east of Paramaribo, Suriname. The crew immediately abandoned ship in two lifeboats, whereupon *U-155* closed in and fired twenty rounds until the ship caught fire. On the 16th *U-155* was sighted on the surface by a Hudson aircraft of 53 Squadron and attacked with depth charges, but escaped. On the 19th the boat was again attacked when she was bombed by a Douglas B18 aircraft resulting in one of her crew being lost overboard. The next day she was damaged during another attack and unable to submerge. She met up with another boat and repairs were made but she was still unable to dive. Piening asked to be escorted back to port and arrived in Lorient on 15 September.

After major repairs Piening took *U-155* out on the 7 November and headed for operations in the Atlantic. The following day news was received of the Allied landings in North Africa and *U-155* was ordered to go at high speed to an area near Gibraltar. Numerous boats including *U-155* assembled as *Westwall* Group and began to carry out east-west patrols in an area to the west of Gibraltar and bounded by Cape St. Vincent in the north and Casablanca in the south. During the early morning of the 15th Piening sank the British escort carrier HMS *Avenger*. He also sank the troop transport ship *Ettrick* and damaged the cargo transport ship

USS *Almaack* in a single attack. Over 600 lives were lost in the sinking of HMS *Avenger*. On the 20th *U-155* was refuelled south-east of the Azores and three days later Piening asked for permission to move further west after being constantly harassed by aircraft. He rejoined *Westwall* Group which had moved west from the 21st for the same reason. From the 27th the *Westwall* boats formed a north-south patrol line and continued west towards and then past the Azores. On the evening of 6 December Piening sank the Dutch SS *Serooskerk* from Convoy ON149. She was struck by one torpedo at around 22:00 hours while 400 miles west-north-west of the Azores. Nearly two hours later another torpedo was fired and struck the ship in the stern and she sank within two minutes. All of her 108 crew were lost. With no more convoys sighted, Piening and *U-155* returned to Lorient.

On 8 February 1943, he left for the Florida Straits and then to the Gulf of Mexico but had no success. On 1 April he was promoted to *Korvettenkapitän* and the next day he sank the Norwegian SS *Lysefjord*. Two days later he sank the US tanker SS *Gulfstate* just east of Key West. Piening then returned to Lorient on the 30th. The next patrol, Piening's sixth as commander of *U-155*, was short because the boat was damaged and five of his crew were wounded when the boat was attacked by four De Havilland Mosquito aircraft. One of the aircraft was hit by deck-gun fire and had to break off the attack. The seventh patrol was short too, and no ships were sunk. During his next patrol, he sailed towards the coast of Brazil where on 24 September 1943; he sank the Norwegian MV *Siranger* about 300 miles north of Fortaleza. He had no further success and returned to port on 1 January 1944. It was his last patrol.

On 10 March, Piening was transferred and appointed commander of the 7th U-boat Flotilla in St. Nazaire. He remained in this post until Germany's surrender on 8 May 1945. After the war he spent more than two years in Allied captivity being released in January 1948. He joined the *Bundesmarine* in April 1956, where he served for thirteen years, rising to the rank of *Kapitän zur See* in April 1960. He retired in March 1969 and settled in Kiel where he died on 15 May 1984. Piening was noted during the war for his famous 'Piening Route', which he devised as a means to evade Allied aircraft in the Bay of Biscay. The route was very successful and saved many boats during its short life. It was stopped when the Allied forced the neutral Spanish government to drive the U-boats out of their waters.

Other awards:
02 Oct 1936: Long Service Award 4th Class
06 Jun 1939: Spanish Cross in Bronze with Swords
22 Nov 1939: Iron Cross 2nd Class
27 Jun 1940: Iron Cross 1st Class
00.00.1941: Minesweepers Badge
28 Mar 1942: U-Boat War Badge

<u>Gustav</u> Artur Eduard Johann POEL
Kapitänleutant
5 ships sunk, 35,625 tons

Knight's Cross: Awarded on 21 March 1944, as *Kapitänleutnant* and as commander of *U-413* for sinking five ships which included the British troop transport ship MV *Warwick Castle*, for a total of 35,625 shipping tons.

(Scherzer)

Gustav Poel was born in Hamburg on 2 August 1917, and joined the *Reichsmarine* as an Officer Candidate in April 1936. After service aboard the sail training ship *Gorch Fock* and the light cruiser *Emden*, he spent six months on the torpedo boat *Tiger*, seeing action in the Spanish Civil War. In October 1938 Poel was commissioned as a *Leutnant zur See* and transferred to the U-boat service. After the usual training courses he was assigned, for a brief period, as Second Watch Officer aboard *U-27*, under the command of *Kapitänleutnant* Johannes Franz. From June 1939 he served in a similar capacity aboard *U-37*, under the command of *Kapitänleutnant* Heinrich Schuch (June–September 1939), *Korvettenkapitän* Werner Hartmann (September 1939–May 1940) and *Kapitänleutnant* Victor Oehrn (May–June 1940). During this time he participated in five war patrols during which time a total of twenty-nine ships were sunk. From June 1940 Poel served in various staff positions, first at Kiel on the staff of the Commander-in-Chief of U-boats, during which time he was promoted to *Oberleutnant zur See*. Then from October he transferred to the staff of the Submarine Command Liaison with the Italian Navy, at Bordeaux. In June 1941 Poel was appointed tactical instructor at the 25th Training Flotilla, and from January 1942 he served as a staff officer with the flotilla.

In May he transferred and supervised the training and preparation of *U-413*, a Type VIIC built by Danziger Werft. With its sea trials complete, on 28 October Poel took the boat out of Marviken, Norway on its first war patrol and headed for the North Atlantic. Whilst out on patrol he heard the news of the Allied landings in North Africa and all boats with sufficient fuel were ordered to proceed at high speed towards Gibraltar. En route Poel encountered Convoy MKF1 west of Lisbon, and on 14 November he torpedoed and sank the British troopship the MV *Warwick Castle*. She was struck by two torpedoes about 200 miles north-west of Cape Espichel, Portugal. She sank within an hour with the loss of ninety-six men. Poel then took *U-413* to join *Westwall* Group, stationed off Gibraltar. On the 19th *U-413* was attacked and badly damaged by a Hudson aircraft. Poel decided to head for port, arriving at Brest on 25 November.

After repairs Poel took *U-413* out again on patrol on 27 December, heading out to the North Atlantic to join *Jaguar* Group in an area north-east of Newfoundland. Once all the boats were together they waited for Convoy HX233 which passed just out of range. On 19 January, Poel was informed that he had been promoted to *Kapitänleutnant* and on the 22nd the group sighted Convoy SC117, and Poel sank a straggler, the Greek SS *Mount Mycale*. She was struck by two torpedoes about 170 miles east of Belle Isle. On 1 February, *U-413* was refuelled and then joined *Pfeil* Group in the central North Atlantic. On the 4th the eastbound Convoy SC118 was sighted by *U-187* as it passed through the centre of *Pfeil* Group's patrol line. On the evening of the 5th Poel sank the US SS *West Portal*. She was struck by a single torpedo just forward of the bridge and immediately took on a list.

Poel had fired a spread of four torpedoes and the zigzagging ship had been struck by the third torpedo. The next torpedo missed but she was hit by the second and sank within a few minutes. The crew of *U-413* watched as the thirty-two crew and twenty-five armed guards and eight officers abandoned ship in lifeboats, but they were never seen again. With the operation at an end Poel headed for Brest.

On 29 March, Poel took *U-413* out on another patrol and headed for the North Atlantic once again. He joined *Meise* Group and a patrol line was formed on 14 April and they intercepted Convoy SC126 but contact was soon lost. On the 21st a new convoy was sighted but that was lost in fog. The operation was called off. Poel then sailed his own course and on the 25th he made an unsuccessful attack on a ship. On the 28th a new patrol line was formed from the newly-formed *Star* Group east of Cape Farewell, to await another convoy. The following day attacks were made by only two boats due to bad weather, and on 1 May the pursuit of the convoy was called off. During the next five days *U-413*, still part of *Star* Group, joined the hunt for Convoy SC128 which was thought to be heading north-eastwards. However the weather was bad and most boats lost contact with the convoy. On the morning of the 6th the operation was once again called off. Six boats had been lost and twelve ships had been sunk, but none by Poel. After being refuelled *U-413* joined *Donau 2* Group, and during the night of the 18th/19th, Convoy SC130 was located south-east of Greenland. The convoy had continuous air cover and low cloud made shadowing almost impossible. The operation was abandoned on the 20th, with no ships sunk and three boats lost: *U-258*, *U-381* and *U-954*, the latter having in her crew Dönitz's second son Peter. On 21 April, Poel sank the British SS *Wanstead* from Convoy ONS3, which was struck by one torpedo south-east of Cape Farewell. Two crew members were lost. The surviving boats from *Donau 2* moved south-westwards to intercept another convoy, but it was never found. The search was called off on the 23rd and the next day all operations against North Atlantic convoys ceased. The *Donau* groups were dissolved. Poel began the journey home, arriving at Brest on 13 June.

On 4 September he left for operations but the patrol ended two weeks after *U-413* developed a defect and had to return to Brest. His next patrol began on 2 October, when Poel took *U-413* to the North Atlantic and headed towards Iceland as part of *Schlieffen* Group. *U-413* had been fitted with intermediate-wave receivers covering the 100- to 200-metre band and fitted with direction-finding attachments. Together with *U-631*, the boats were ordered to report changes of course by the convoys. In the search for Convoy ONS20 on 17 October only two reports of the convoy's movements were correct, both from *U-413*. In the event both reports were ignored and contact with the convoys was never regained. Various attacks were made by Poel on other convoys but no ships were sunk. He returned to port on 21 November. His sixth patrol began on 26 January 1944, when *U-413* left for the coast of Ireland. In the early morning of 11 February, Poel made contact with Convoys KMS41 and OS67. He made several unsuccessful attacks against destroyers of the escorts. On the 20th Poel sighted the British destroyer HMS *Warwick* and fired two torpedoes. She was hit by one of them and her stern broke off aft of the engine room she stayed afloat for almost four minutes until the bulkhead collapsed and she sank. Three officers and sixty-four ratings were lost. *U-413* returned to Brest on 27 March.

On 25 April 1944, Poel left the U-boat service to become a unit leader at the Naval Warfare Academy in Flensburg. From 29 January 1945, he served on the staff of *Admiral*

HMS Warwick *(D 25) was built in 1918 and saw action during the last months of the First World War, and was at Scapa Flow when the German Imperial Navy surrendered to the British. She was re-commissioned in August 1939, and served as a convoy escort ship. On 20 February 1944,* Warwick *was hit by two torpedoes fired by* U-413 *at about 11:37 hours, 15 miles from Trevose Head, Cornwall. She sank with the loss of three officers and sixty-four ratings.* (Author's collection)

Hans-Georg von Friedeburg, Commanding Admiral of U-boats. He was briefly interned by the Allies at the end of the war. Upon his release in October 1945, he studied metallurgy at Aachen. During the winter of 1948-1949 he was a member of the *Corps Montania Aachen*. In 1951 he graduated with a diploma in engineering and between 1963 and 1970 was a board member of various companies in the Rhine steel industry. He retired in 1982 and settled in Hamburg where he died on 17 January 2009.

Other awards:
06 Jun 1939: Spanish Cross in Bronze
08 Nov 1939: U-Boat War Badge
28 Feb 1940: Iron Cross 2nd Class
03 Apr 1940: Long Service Award 4th Class
01 Nov 1941: Spanish War Cross
26 Nov 1942: Iron Cross 1st Class
17 Dec 1943: German Cross in Gold
27 Apr 1945: U-Boat Combat Clasp in Bronze

Hans-Georg Friedrich (<u>Fritz</u>) POSKE
Kapitän zur See
16 ships sunk, 85,299 tons

Knight's Cross: Awarded on 6 November 1942, as *Korvettenkapitän* and as commander of *U-504* after sinking fifteen ships for a total of 80,112 shipping tons during four war patrols.

Fritz Poske was born on 23 October 1904 in Berlin-Schöneberg, a small suburb which became part of Greater Berlin after the First World War. Poske entered the *Reichsmarine* in April 1923 and was initially assigned to a training unit in Wilhelmshaven. Between October 1923 and March 1926 during his basic training he served aboard the battleship *Braunschweig*, and the light cruisers *Hamburg* and *Berlin*. He was commissioned as a *Leutnant zur See* in October 1927 and after various training course was promoted in July 1929 to *Oberleutnant zur See*. Poske served on minesweepers and was for a time Watch Officer aboard the battleship *Schleswig-Holstein*. From September 1930 he served as Second Watch Officer and later as adjutant aboard the torpedo boat *Albatros*. In October 1934, he took command of the torpedo boat *T155*, and in April 1935 was promoted to *Kapitänleutnant*. From July 1936 he was assigned to various training positions in Kiel and even took a three-week military psychological training course in Berlin. In March 1939 he was promoted to *Korvettenkapitän*, and from April 1939, he served aboard the battleship

(Scherzer)

Schlesien and the light cruisers *Nürnberg* and *Königsberg*. In April 1940 he was transferred to the staff of the Admiral of the Norwegian West Coast Otto von Schrader. In June he took over command of the fleet tender *Grille* and took part in patrols in the Baltic area as a gunnery training ship.

In October 1940, Poske was transferred to the U-boat service, and he took command of *U-504* in July 1941, a Type IXC boat built in Hamburg by Deutsche Werft. After its sea trials were completed he took his boat out from Kiel to its new base in France, arriving in Lorient on 20 January 1942. He left on his first war patrol five days later heading for US waters. From mid-February he was patrolling at the northern end of the Straits of Florida. On 22nd Poske sank the US SS *Republic* about four miles north-east of Jupiter Island Lighthouse, Florida. She was hit by two torpedoes; the explosions destroyed the engine room, killing one officer and two crewmen. She was severely damaged and the following day drifted onto reefs and sank on the afternoon of the 23rd. Earlier Poske had sunk the American SS *W.D. Anderson* about 12 miles north-east of Jupiter Island Lighthouse. On the 26th he sank the Dutch tanker MV *Mamura* east-north-east of the Bahamas. A hunt by destroyers for *U-504* began and on the 28th an aircraft from Key West dropped two depth charges on an object. Surface vessels arrived and carried out their own attacks, but *U-504* had left the area. On 16 March, during his journey back to port, Poske sank the British SS *Stangarth* on her maiden voyage. She sank immediately about 300 miles north of San Juan, Puerto Rico. Her entire crew of forty-six were lost. For years it was thought that Poske had sunk the SS *Manaqui* and not the *Stangarth*, but it has become clear that the SS *Manaqui* was in fact sunk by the Italian submarine *Morosini* on 12 March. Poske returned to Lorient on 12 April.

During his next patrol Poske was ordered to patrol at the western end of the Caribbean, where on 29 May he sank the British SS *Allister* about 54 miles south of Grand Cayman. The ship broke in two and quickly sank with the loss of fifteen of her crew. The eight survivors were later picked up and landed at Port au Prince, Haiti. In early June *U-504* moved eastwards and in six days Poske sank five ships. On 8 June he sank the Honduran SS *Tela* and the British SS *Rosenborg*. On the 11th he sank the Dutch passenger ship SS *Crijnssen*. She was struck by two torpedoes about 85 miles south-west of Grand Cayman. That same evening he sank the US SS *American*, struck by two torpedoes off Honduras. About an hour later Poske sank the Latvian SS *Regent* with the loss of eleven of her crew. She was hit by the *U-504*'s last two torpedoes and quickly sank. Poske returned to Lorient.

On 19 August *U-504* left for the South Atlantic, together with *U-68*, *U-156* and *U-172* as *Eisbär* Group. From the 26th, the group operated west of Spain against Convoy SL119, during which time *U-156* sank one ship. The four boats then swept south to the Cape Verde Islands and after refuelling sailed on to St. Helena. There they were joined by *U-159*, replacing *U-156* which had been ordered elsewhere. The four boats continued south and eventually reached their operational area off Cape Town. Between 4 October and mid-November twenty-four ships were sunk by *Eisbär* boats, six of them by Poske. On the 17th he sank the British SS *Empire Chaucer*: three crew members were lost. Six days later he sank the British SS *City of Johannesburg*. She was struck by one of two torpedoes fired; all but four of her crew of ninety were rescued. On the 26th he attacked the US SS *Anne Hutchinson* about 60 miles east of East London, South Africa. Poske had missed the ship five minutes earlier with a spread of two torpedoes because she did a turn to starboard on her zigzag course after the torpedoes were fired. She was hit by a single torpedo from a second spread, which struck her near the engine room and the explosion buckled the side of the ship, creating a hole 14ft by 16ft, broke the propeller shaft, stopped the engines, knocked out the electrical systems and killed three men. Despite the bulkheads on either side of the hold remaining intact, the crew of eight officers and twenty-nine men abandoned ship in three lifeboats. About fifty minutes after the first torpedo had hit Poske fired a *coup de grâce* which struck the fire room, causing the boilers to explode. The ship stayed afloat until the 29th, and trawlers and tugs from South Africa tried to tow the ship to port but were not powerful enough. So she was blown up with dynamite which split her in two and she was declared a total loss. On 31 October, Poske sank two more ships, the British SS *Empire Guidon* and SS *Reynolds*. Returning south, Poske sighted the Brazilian SS *Porto Alegre* and fired his last two torpedoes. She was struck on the starboard side in the engine room by one torpedo. All but one of the fifty-eight men on board survived. With the *Eisbär* operations a success, the four boats returned to Lorient, arriving on 11 December.

On 6 January 1943, Poske took command of the 1st U-boat Training Division in Neustadt, later moving its headquarters to Hamburg-Finkenwerder. On 1 February he was promoted to *Fregattenkapitän* and in October was promoted to *Kapitän zur See*. Poske remained in this position until February 1945, when he became chief of the special staff for marine infantry, whilst attached to the naval High Command. In May he was captured by Allied troops and spent the next eleven months in captivity. He joined the *Bundesmarine* in May 1951, retiring with the rank of *Kapitän zur See* in March 1963. He lived in Wachtberg-Niederbachen near Bad Godesberg, Germany until his death on 1 October 1984. He is buried in the local cemetery along with his wife Paula, who died on 8 December 1983.

Other awards:
02 Oct 1936: Long Service Award 4th to 3rd Class
02 Oct 1939: Iron Cross 2nd Class
02 Apr 1942: U-Boat War Badge
03 Apr 1942: Iron Cross 1st Class
09 Oct 1942: High Seas Fleet Badge
01 Sep 1944: War Service Cross 2nd Class with Swords
30 Jan 1945: War Service Cross 1st Class with Swords

Friedrich August Wilhelm <u>Günther</u> PULST
Kapitänleutnant
1 ship sunk, 7,176 tons

Knight's Cross: Awarded on 21 December 1944, as *Oberleutnant zur See* and as commander of *U-978* in recognition of his sinking of three Allied ships for a total of 22,000 shipping tons (although the Allies' records show he only sank one ship), and for his sixty-eight day underwater patrol, the longest of the Second World War.

Günther Pulst was born on 26 March 1918 in Braunschweig, the uncle of the American scientist Stefan M. Pulst, Chairman of the Department of Neurology at the University of Utah, Salt Lake City, USA. He joined the *Kriegsmarine* in October 1937, and he was assigned to the 2nd Company of the Naval Ships Training Unit in the Baltic.

From February 1938 he served on the sail training ship *Albert Leo Schlageter* and he continued with his training when he was transferred to the destroyer *Z9 Wolfgang Zenker*, which played a major role in the opening phase of the invasion of Poland and consequently the Second World War. In January 1940, whilst still serving aboard *Z9 Wolfgang Zenker*, he took part in minelaying operations off Cromer, Norfolk, together with her two sister-ships *Z8 Bruno Heinemann* and *Z13 Erich Koellner*. Pulst also took part in a similar minelaying operation on the night of 9/10 February, together with the same two ships. There mines claimed three ships, totalling 11,855 shipping tons. *Z9 Wolfgang Zenker* suffered ice damage in mid-February and was forced to return prematurely when she was escorting the battleships *Gneisenau* and *Scharnhorst* when they attempted to intercept British convoys to Scandinavia. Once repaired, *Z9 Wolfgang Zenker* was allocated to Group 1 for Operation *Weserübung*, the German invasion of Norway. The group's task was to transport the 3rd Mountain Division's 139th Mountain Infantry Regiment under *Generalleutnant* Dietl to seize Narvik. On 10 April, five destroyers of

(Author's collection)

the British 2nd Destroyer Flotilla surprised the German ships in Narvik harbour. Two German destroyers were sunk and the three others received minor damage. As they began to withdraw they encountered the three British destroyers. The German ships opened fire first, but due to the mist and the smokescreen laid by the British the shots were not effective. *Kapitän zur See* Erich Bey, commander of the *Z9 Wolfgang Zenker* was ordered to return Germany with all seaworthy ships. Only Pulst's ship and her sister-ship the destroyer *Z12 Erich Giese* were ready for sea and they slipped out of the Narvik Fjord and turned south. However they spotted the British light cruiser HMS *Penelope* and her two escorting destroyers and Bey decided to turn back. While at anchor, *Z9 Wolfgang Zenker* briefly grounded during the night and damaged her port propeller, which limited her speed to 20 knots.

On 13 April, the British battleship HMS *Warspite* and nine destroyers appeared and caught the Germans by surprise. *Z9 Wolfgang Zenker* charged out of Narvik harbour to engage the British ships. She made a torpedo attack on the British ships but these all missed. Lack of ammunition had forced the Germans to retreat to the Rombaksfjorden, east of Narvik. *Z9 Wolfgang Zenker* had exhausted her ammunition and she was beached at the head of the fjord. Her crew placed demolition charges and abandoned ship. By the time the British reached the ship she had rolled over onto her side. She was then scuttled and the crew joined the army to fight on land against the Allies. Pulst then fought alongside these troops during the battle ashore and for this was awarded the Narvik Combat Shield, a decoration received by few U-boat commanders (another notable recipient was Rolf Thomsen). Pulst fought as a company commander having won his commission to *Leutnant zur See* in May 1940. From July Pulst was appointed commander of small boats along a stretch of the Norwegian west coast. In the autumn he returned to Germany and from November became a training officer at the Naval Academy.

On 18 March 1942, Pulst was promoted to *Oberleutnant zur See*, and the following month he joined the U-boat service. From October he was serving as a Watch Officer aboard *U-752*, taking part in two war patrols whilst under the command of *Korvettenkapitän* Karl-Ernst Schroeter. Pulst took command of his own boat, *U-978*, on 29 May 1943, a Type VIIC boat built in Hamburg and launched in April. With her trials complete, Pulst took her out on her out from Kiel to Horten in August 1944, and from there set-out for Bergen via Flekkefjord and Egersund. He arrived at his new base on 8 October, and set out on his first war patrol the following day. He headed for British coastal waters, arriving on 2 November. On 19th he claimed his first ship, torpedoed just north of Barfleur but this remains unconfirmed. In the same area he attacked the US SS *William D. Burham*. She was badly damaged and eighteen of her crew were lost when the ship exploded. However she refused to sink, and was taken in tow by a US tug and beached off Cherbourg but declared a total loss. Pulst returned to Bergen on 16 December. What is remarkable about this first patrol was that it was made completely submerged. In fact *U-978* was submerged for a total of sixty-eight days, and it was the longest submerged patrol of the Second World War, longer than *U-997*'s famous voyage to Argentina after the war. It was made possible by using the 'Schnorchel' or snorkel, an underwater air tube. Pulst was promoted to *Kapitänleutnant* on 1 January 1945 and made a second patrol and claimed another ship sunk but this was never confirmed. He put in at Trondheim on 20 April.

Pulst surrendered to British troops at Trondheim on 5 May and sailed *U-978* under British escort from Norway to Loch Ryan, Scotland. There, along with 116 other U-boats, it was destroyed by the Royal Navy. Pulst spent almost three years in captivity before being released on 26 March 1948. He entered the *Bundeswehr* in September 1957 as a civilian staff member and worked for a number of years as a financial controller for NATO in Paris. He retired in March 1983, and settled in Bonn-Bad Godesberg, Germany, where he died on 5 January 1991.

Other awards:
11 Feb 1940: Iron Cross 2nd Class
18 Dec 1944: Iron Cross 1st Class
11 Oct 1940: Destroyers War Badge
10 Nov 1940: Narvik Campaign Shield
21 Feb 1943: U-Boat War Badge
19 Nov 1944: U-Boat Combat Clasp in Bronze
09 Oct 1941: Long Service Award 4th Class

Hermann RASCH
Kapitänleutnant
12 ships sunk, 78,553 tons
2 ships damaged, 12,885 tons

Knight's Cross: Awarded on 29 December 1942 as *Kapitänleutnant* and as commander of *U-106* for the sinking of twelve ships for a total of 78,553 shipping tons and for damaging another two ships.

Hermann Rasch was born on 26 August 1914 in Wilhelmshaven and joined the *Reichsmarine* in April 1934 at the age of nineteen. In November 1935 he entered the Naval Academy in Flensburg with the rank of *Fähnrich zur See*. He was commissioned as *Leutnant zur See* in April 1937, and from November he was serving aboard the 'pocket battleship' *Admiral Scheer*. In April 1939, he was promoted to *Oberleutnant zur See* and twelve months later he transferred to the U-boat service. From September 1940 Rasch served as First Watch Officer aboard *U-106*, under the command of *Kapitänleutnant* Jürgen Oesten. He took part in three war patrols during which time ten ships were sunk.

In July 1941 he attended commander training at the Naval Academy, and in October he took command of his old boat, *U-106*, succeeding Oesten. On 21 October he took his boat out of Lorient and headed for the North Atlantic. Two days later during the outbound journey he lost three men when a bridge watch was washed overboard in heavy seas. On the 28th Rasch sank

(Wehrkundearchiv)

the British MV *King Malcolm* about 630 miles west of Ireland. From the 28th, *U-106* operated together with *U-73*, *U-77*, *U-568* and *U-751* they were in contact with Convoy ON28 but were driven off by the escort each time they tried to attack. On the morning of the 30th, Rasch torpedoed and damaged the US fleet oiler USS *Salinas*, about 610 miles east of Newfoundland. The damaged tanker managed to reach Argentina under her own power. In early November Rasch joined *Raubritter* Group which had been deployed on the 3rd against Convoy SC52. However contact with the convoy was lost and the boats moved eastwards and formed a patrol line south-east of Cape Farewell from the 8th. Rasch returned *U-106* to Lorient on the 22nd.

After some repairs, *U-106* was ready for its next patrol and Rasch took her out on 3 January 1942 to operate in the Western North Atlantic. He headed for the Newfoundland area, later moving south to patrol off the US east coast. On the 24th he sank the British SS *Empire Wildebeeste*, from Convoy ON53. On the 26th in the same area east of New York he sank another British ship, the SS *Traveller*. She was struck by two torpedoes and sank within six minutes, and there were no survivors. Four days later he sank the US tanker SS *Rochester* by torpedo and gunfire, and when hit the ship developed a list almost immediately and sank within an hour, with the loss of four crew members. During the early hours of 3 February, Rasch sighted the Swedish MV *Amerikaland* and sunk her with a single torpedo. All of her crew abandoned ship in three lifeboats but weren't picked up for three days, most suffering from frostbite. On the 6th Rasch sank the British MV *Opawa* north-north-west of Bermuda. She was hit by one torpedo amidships and was later shelled until she sank, with the loss of fifty-six men. Rasch returned to Lorient on the 22nd.

On 1 March Rasch was promoted to *Kapitänleutnant* and on 15 April, he left port for his third war patrol, to operate in the Western Atlantic. On 2 May, en route to the Gulf of Mexico *U-106* was attacked by a US destroyer, probably the USS *Broome*, but suffered no damage. Three days later Rasch sank the Canadian passenger ship SS *Lady Drake* about 90 miles north of Bermuda. She was hit by one of two torpedoes and sank within twenty-five minutes with the loss of twelve – she was carrying a total of 268 passengers. After passing through the Straits of Florida into the Gulf, Rasch sank the Mexican tanker SS *Faja de Oro* off Key West, on 21 May. Five days later he sank the US tanker SS *Carrabulle* by torpedo and gunfire, with the loss of twenty-two crew. Rasch damaged the US SS *Atenas* on the 17th, with the boat's deck guns. During the early hours of the following day Rasch sank the British SS *Mentor*. She was struck by a single torpedo north of Cabo Catoche and sank within six minutes. On 1 June, he sank the US SS *Hampton Roads* north-west of Cape San Antonio, Cuba. One torpedo was fired and struck the ship at the No. 3 hatch, causing her to sink in less than a minute. Twenty-three crew abandoned ship and were later rescued, but five died on board. *U-106* returned to Lorient on 29 June.

During his next patrol Rasch headed across the Bay of Biscay. On 27 July, two days into the patrol *U-106* was attacked by a Wellington bomber of 311 (Czech) Squadron, north-west of Brest. The boat was seriously damaged – one officer was killed and Rasch was wounded. He returned to port immediately. It would be almost two months before *U-106* was repaired and ready for another patrol. Rasch took her out on 22 September and headed for the North Atlantic, and onto the Newfoundland area. In October he was ordered into the Gulf of St. Lawrence and on the 11th he sighted Convoy BS31 and sank the British SS *Waterton* in Cabot Strait south-west of Cape Ray. She was struck by two torpedoes and sank by the stern. The entire crew was picked up by the armed yacht HMCS *Vision*. Rasch then left the

Gulf area and became immediately threatened by Allied aircraft. Rasch was preoccupied with the thought of air attack, and with the previous attack on *U-106* and the loss of one of his officers still on his mind, he refrained from attacking a fourteen-ship convoy. Instead he headed instead to an area south of Newfoundland and Nova Scotia but had no success. Rasch was then ordered to join *Westwall* Group west of the Azores. The group moved westwards until 6 December, wherethe convoys had been passing south of their patrol line, out of range. On the 16th, the *Westwall* Group was dissolved and between the 19th and the 23rd various boats, including *U-106* searched for targets off the coast of Spain and Portugal, without success. On the 23rd all operations by Atlantic boats against convoys bound for the Mediterranean were terminated. Rasch returned to Lorient on the 26th.

In March 1943, Rasch transferred to the Office of the Naval High Command, and from June 1944 was a staff officer on the staff of the Commander of U-boat Operations *Konteradmiral* Eberhardt Godt. From October until the end of the war Rasch was commander of the *Kleinkampfverbände*, being responsible for the *Seehund* (Seal) and *Biber* (Badger) midget submarines. He surrendered to British troops in May 1945 and spent just over a year in Allied captivity. He then worked as a journalist in Hamburg, Berlin and Düsseldorf until his premature death in Hamburg on 10 June 1974.

Other awards:
08 Apr 1938: Long Service Award 4th Class
06 Jun 1939: Spanish Cross in Bronze with Swords
00.00.1940: Iron Cross 2nd Class
11 Jul 1941: Iron Cross 1st Class
00 Feb 1942: U-Boat War Badge

Reinhart RECHE
Kapitänleutnant
10 ships sunk, 54,420 tons

Knight's Cross: Awarded on 17 March 1943, as *Kapitänleutnant* and as commander of *U-255* in recognition for the sinking of ten ships for a total of 54,420 shipping tons.

Reinhart Reche was born on 13 December 1915 in Kreuzburg, Upper Silesia, now part of Poland. Reche entered the *Reichsmarine* as an Officer Candidate in April 1934 and spent the next four years training. He was assigned to the sail training ship *Gorch Fock*, the light cruiser *Emden* and the battleship *Schlesien*. He was commissioned as a *Leutnant zur See* on 1 April 1937 and was promoted to *Oberleutnant zur See* in April 1939, and served aboard the sail training ship *Horst Wessel* as a training officer until April 1940.

(Scherzer)

From January 1941, Reche served as Watch Officer aboard *U-751*, taking part in two war patrols whilst under the command of *Kapitänleutnant* Gerhard Bigalk. In October he was promoted to *Kapitänleutnant* and was given his own command, *U-255*, a Type VIIC boat built by Bremer Vulkan. On 15 June 1942, Reche finally took his new boat out on her first war patrol; he left Kiel to operate in Northern Waters. On 1 July he spotted Convoy PQ17[2] east of Jan Mayen and directed other boats to the area. On the 4th the convoy scattered and the U-boats and aircraft from the *Luftwaffe* moved in. On 6th Reche sank the US Liberty ship the SS *John Witherspoon*. She was torpedoed about 20 miles from the shore of Novaya Zemlya. In the same area on the next day he sank the US SS *Alcoa Ranger*, and on the 8th he sank another US ship, the SS *Olopana*. She was struck by one torpedo about 10 miles west of Moller Bay, Novaya Zemlya. The torpedo hit on the port side in the engine room. The explosion blew in all the bulkheads and killed seven men. On the 13th, Reche sank the Dutch SS *Paulus Potter*, which had been damaged previously by a Junkers Ju 88 during a bombing attack. Out of torpedoes, Reche put in at Narvik on 15 July.

On 4 August Reche took *U-255* out of her new base at Bergen. From the 11th to the 17th he took part in an observation operation with a Bv 138 flying boat, equipped with extra fuel tanks. This was in preparation for Operation *Wunderland*, the planned attack by the 'pocket battleship' *Admiral Scheer* on convoys in the Kara Sea. On the 17th *U-255* rescued the crew of a flying boat when it went down. On 25 August, *U-255* and *U-209* shelled the Soviet wireless station at Cape Zhelania and on the 29th they shelled another station at Khodovarikha. Reche put in at Neidenfjord on 9 September. Four days later he headed out again to operate in the Greenland Sea. From the 20th, *U-255* and six other boats operated against Convoy QP14, which sailed from Archangel, Russia on the 13th. Reche torpedoed and sank the US SS *Silver Sword* from the convoy on 20th east of Shannon, Greenland. The ship was later shelled after thirty minutes by HMS *Worcester* and sank – so that the Germans couldn't capture her. On the 23rd *U-255* was attacked and damaged by a Catalina flying boat of 210 Squadron south of Jan Mayern. Reche put in at Bergen on the 25th.

On 23 January 1943, Reche left for operations in northern waters, and sank two ice breakers in the Barents Sea. He sank the Soviet SS *Krasnyj Partizan* on the 26th. She

2 After the German invasion in June 1941, the Soviet Union and Britain found themselves in alliance against Germany. As a result Britain agreed to supply the Soviets with material and goods via convoys through the Arctic Ocean. These convoys were known as PQ convoys. The first convoy left Britain in August 1941 and by the spring of 1942 only one ship of the 103 that had been sent had been lost and twelve convoys had passed through these waters. On 27 June 1942, the ships of Convoy PQ17 left Iceland and headed northwards. The convoy consisted of thirty-five ships and was heavily loaded with nearly 300 aircraft, almost 600 tanks, 4,246 lorries and gun carriers and an additional 156,000 tons of cargo. This was enough to equip an army of 50,000 men and was valued at $700 million. Early in the voyage one ship ran aground in Iceland and another was seriously damaged, so thirty-three ships headed for the Soviet Union. On the evening of 4 July it was suspected that German surface vessels were preparing to attack the convoy so a decision was made for the ships to scatter. A big mistake. The next day the Germans took full advantage of this and attacked. The total number of ships lost was twenty-four, for a total of 142,518 shipping tons, and 153 merchant men lost their lives. The Luftwaffe sank eight ships and the rest were sunk by U-boats, *U-255* sank four ships. Admiral Dan Gallery of the US Navy, serving in Iceland at that time, called PQ17 'a shameful page in naval history'.

was struck by two torpedoes west of Bear Island. The ship sank with the loss of the entire crew. On the 29th he sank another Soviet ship, the SS *Ufa*, which sank within twenty-five minutes after being hit whilst 40 miles south-south-west of Bear Island. The entire crew of thirty-nine was lost. Reche then sighted Convoy RA52 attacked and sank the US SS *Greylock*. She was hit by one of three torpedoes and the entire crew of seventy abandoned ship. For his last war patrol with *U-255*, he left Narvik for operations in the Norwegian Sea on 22 February. On 1 March he made contact with Convoy RA53, and on the 5th he sank the US SS *Executive*. He then torpedoed and damaged another SS *Richard Bland*, south-west of Bear Island. Five days later he finished off the *Richard Bland* after firing a *coup de grâce* torpedo which struck the stern section. She broke in two just forward of the bridge. The forward section was towed to Akureyri, Iceland where the ship was declared a total loss. Reche returned to Narvik on 15th.

From June 1943, Reche was a staff officer on the staff of the Leader of U-boats in Norway (Operational Department). He surrendered to Allied troops in May 1945, and was released on 30 November 1945. In July 1956 he joined the *Bundesmarine*, and from August 1959 he commanded the U-boat training unit. He later served in several staff positions, and was later awarded the Federal Merit Cross and retired in March 1974, with the rank of *Kapitän zur See*. Reche died in Bad Godesberg on 3 March 1993.

Other awards:
08 Apr 1938: Long Service Award 4th Class
07 Jul 1941: Iron Cross 2nd Class
09 Sep 1941: U-Boat War Badge
23 Jul 1942: Iron Cross 1st Class
02 Nov 1944: U-Boat Combat Clasp in Bronze

Wilhelm Eduard Max ROLLMANN
Fregattenkapitän
23 ships sunk, 98,927 tons

Knight's Cross: Awarded on 31 July 1940, to become the 6th U-boat commander to receive the award, as *Kapitänleutnant* and as commander of *U-34* for sinking twenty-one ships for a total of 93,684 shipping tons.

Wilhelm Rollmann was born in Wilhelmshaven on 5 August 1907, and joined the *Reichsmarine*, as a cadet, at the age of nineteen in April 1926. He was initially assigned to the 5th Company of the II. *Schiffsstammdivision* in the Baltic. For the next four years he trained aboard the sail training ship *Niobe* and the light cruiser *Emden* and also took part in various training courses whilst attached to the Naval Academy. On 1 October 1930, Rollmann   (Scherzer) was commissioned as a *Leutnant zur See*, serving as a company officer in the Baltic. He was promoted to *Oberleutnant zur See* in October 1932 whilst serving with the Coastal Artillery School at Wilhelmshaven as an anti-aircraft instructor. Rollmann served as Watch Officer aboard the light cruiser *Karlsruhe* from August 1933, and then from November 1935 he served in London, England as a Naval Attaché. He was promoted to *Kapitänleutnant* in April 1936 and in May the following year he transferred to the U-boat service.

In October 1938, Rollmann took command of *U-34*, a Type VIIA boat built in Kiel by Germania Werft. He left on his first patrol on 19 August 1939 and whilst he was out in the English Channel Germany invaded Poland, which triggered the start of the Second World War. On 7 September he sank the British SS *Pukkastan*. At 12:50 hours two shots were fired across her bow and the crew abandoned ship in the lifeboats before she was torpedoed. She was only the sixth British ship to be sunk during the war. The next day Rollmann sunk another British ship, the SS *Kennebec*, about 70 miles south of the Scilly Isles. Returning to base he came across the Estonian SS *Hanonia*. She was captured without a shot being fired and taken back to Wilhelmshaven. She was later used by the *Kriegsmarine* as an auxiliary minelayer. During his second patrol he sank another four ships and captured a fifth. He headed for the English Channel and east of the Shetlands where he sank the Swedish SS *Gustaf Adolf* and the British SS *Sea Venture*, both on 20 October. On the 27th he sank another British ship, the SS *Bronte*, and two days later about 180 miles west of Lands End he sank the SS *Malabar* from Convoy HX5A returning from America. On his way back to base he captured the Norwegian SS *Snar* off southern Norway. Rollmann headed back to Wilhelmshaven with another captured vessel.

His next patrol was a minelaying operation off the south-west coast of England. Rollmann laid mines off Falmouth on the 20 January 1940 and later that day the British tanker MV *Caroni River* struck one of these mines and sank. On the 28th, he sank the Greek SS *Eleni Stathaton* by torpedo. She was struck about 200 miles west of the Scilly Isles, she failed to sink and Rollmann had to fire a second torpedo and she sank slowly. Nevertheless twelve crew members died. *U-34* returned to port on 6 February. On 3 April Rollmann left Wilhelmshaven under sealed orders to take part in Operation *Hartmut*, the naval element of the German invasion of Denmark and Norway. The sealed orders were opened and all U-boats were ordered to support German land and naval forces during the invasion and to prevent any interference by British warships. Rollmann was ordered to join the 2nd U-boat group, which was to operate off Trondheim. On the 13th he torpedoed the Norwegian minelayer HNoMS *Froya* in the Tronheim Fjord. Her stern was ripped off by the explosion and she was declared a total loss. He returned to base on the 30th.

On 22 June, Rollmann left Wilhelmshaven on his next patrol, heading to the south-western Approaches and the Bay of Biscay. On 5 July he sank the British destroyer HMS *Whirlwind*, about 120 miles west of Land's End. She was struck underneath the bridge by a single torpedo, and remained afloat until she was scuttled by HMS *Westcott* after picking up her survivors. During the next twelve days Rollmann sank seven ships for a total of 21,334 shipping tons. He sank the Estonian SS *Vapper* on 6 July and the following day he sank the Dutch SS *Lucrecia*, both just off the Scilly Isles. He sank another Estonian ship, the SS *Tiiu*, on the 9th, the

Finnish SS *Petsamo* on the 10th, south of Cape Clear, and on the 11th he sank the Norwegian SS *Janna* and the Greek SS *Evdoxia* south-west of Bull Rock, Ireland. Later just gone midnight on 17th, with all torpedoes used he sank the SS *Naftilos*, another Greek ship, by gunfire. He put in at Lorient for replenishment of food and torpedoes on the 18th and left again on the 23rrd. On the 26th he encountered the westbound Convoy OB188 south-south-west of Rockall and torpedoed and sank the British passenger ship MV *Accra* about 320 miles west of Bloody Foreland. In fact when he fired a spread of three torpedoes he also hit the British MV *Vinemoor* at the same time, and she sank slowly by the stern. *Accra* took an hour and fifteen minutes to sink with the loss of eight crew members and eleven passengers when her motorboat capsized in choppy seas. After pursuing the convoy south for twelve hours Rollmann sank two more ships, the British SS *Sambre* and the British tanker MV *Thiara*. On 1 August during the return journey to Wilhelmshaven he torpedoed and sank the British submarine HMS *Spearfish* just west of Stavanger. There was one survivor, Able Seaman William V. Pester, who was on his first patrol. He was taken to Wilhelmshaven aboard *U-34* as a prisoner of war.

On 2 October Rollmann lost his command of *U-34* and was transferred to the 2nd U-boat Training Division as an instructor. Promoted to *Kapitänleutnant* in December 1940, he spent just over two years in this post before being transferred. In February 1943, he found himself back commanding a U-boat. He took command of *U-848* on the 20th, a Type IXD2 boat built in Bremen, and he took his new command out of Kiel on 18 September, and headed for the Indian Ocean. On 2 November, north-west of Ascension he sunk the British SS *Baron Semple*. Her entire crew of sixty-two were was lost. On the morning of the 5th, *U-848* was sighted on the surface south-west of Ascension Island by a US Naval Liberator. The aircraft dropped six depth-bombs, straddling the boat. Another Liberator arrived thirty minutes later and inflicted further damage. A third aircraft was met by heavy flak and returned to base with one engine knocked out. *U-848* kept firing her deck guns at the two remaining aircraft. In the afternoon two Army B25s from the 1st Composite Squadron of the US Air Force dropped 500lb bombs from 4,000ft but caused no further damage to the boat. The two Liberators made another attack; both aircraft had originally attacked the boat that morning but had returned to their base to be refuelled. Both the aircraft made depth-bomb attacks and *U-848* was hit and destroyed. Lifeboats were dropped and about twenty survivors were seen in the water and a ship was requested to pick them up. However, only one delirious survivor was rescued by the light cruiser USS *Marblehead* a month later. He died within a few days. There were no further survivors from *U-848*: sixty-four men, including their commander Rollmann, were dead. Rollmann was posthumously promoted to the rank of *Fregattenkapitän*.

Other awards:
02 Oct 1936: Long Service Award 4th Class
01 Apr 1938: Long Service Award 3rd Class
26 Sep 1939: Iron Cross 2nd Class
12 Nov 1939: U-Boat War Badge
00 Dec 1939: Commemorative Medal for 01 Oct 1938
07 Feb 1940: Iron Cross 1st Class

Ewald Hugo Helmut ROSENBAUM
Korvettenkapitän
9 ships sunk, 57,863 tons

Knight's Cross: Awarded as *Kapitänleutnant* and as commander of *U-73*, on 12 August 1942 for sinking nine ships, including the British aircraft carrier HMS *Eagle*, for a total of 57,863 shipping tons.

Helmut Rosenbaum was born in Döbeln near Leipzig on 11 May 1913 and joined the *Reichsmarine* in August 1932, completing his basic training as an Officer Candidate whilst serving in the *Schiffsstammabteilung* in the Baltic. In October he was transferred to the sail training ship *Edith* for five weeks and then served on board the light cruiser *Köln* until January 1934. Rosenbaum then attended various training courses at the Naval Academy at Flensburg which included navigation and officer training before being

(Scherzer)

transferred to the light cruiser *Königsberg* in April 1935. From September he attended more training courses and was assigned to the light cruiser *Nürnberg* in December. On 1 January 1936, he was commissioned as a *Leutnant zur See*, and in February the following year he was transferred to the U-boat service, being assigned as Watch Officer aboard *U-35*. He was promoted to *Oberleutnant zur See* in September 1937 and from June 1938 until March 1939 he served as Watch Officer aboard *U-31* and later *U-26*. He was then appointed commander of *U-2*, originally a training boat but by March she had become operational. Between 15 March 1940 and 15 April 1940, Rosenbaum took *U-2* out on two patrols but didn't engage any enemy shipping. *U-2* saw no further operational service and in July she became a training boat, attached to the 21st U-boat Flotilla at Pillau.

Rosenbaum was promoted to *Kapitänleutnant* on 24 January 1940, and from 6 August attended construction training at the Bremer Vulkan shipyard when he was informed he had been appointed commander of *U-73*, a Type VIIB boat. He took her out on her first patrol on 8 February 1941, leaving Heligoland to patrol west of the British Isles. On the 19th a Kondor aircraft of Bomber Wing 40 sighted and attacked ships from Convoy OB287 north-west of the Hebrides, sinking two ships. Rosenbaum was ordered to the area and *U-73* was one of five boats to close in on the convoy. But the boats didn't find any ships because of inaccurate reports. On the 22nd, however, westbound Convoy OB288 was sighted, and *U-73* was directed towards the convoy together with five other boats. In the early morning of the 24th, Rosenbaum attacked and sank the British SS *Waynegate*. She was hit on the starboard side by a single torpedo south of Iceland. Rosenbaum then headed for his new base at Lorient, arriving on 2 March.

His next patrol began on 25 March, when *U-73* left for operations in the North Atlantic. From 2 April, *U-73* and other boats formed a patrol line south-west of Iceland in the path of an eastbound convoy reported by *U-76*. The convoy, SC26, ran into the line during the evening of the 2nd and seven boats made their attacks, eleven ships being sunk. Rosenbaum sank four ships from the convoy. He sank the British SS *Alderpool* at 00:42 hours, south-west of Reykjavik. The ship was abandoned after the first torpedo struck, and it was finished off by a second. At 05:08 hours he sank the SS *Westpool*, another British ship, which was struck by a single torpedo and sank in less than one minute south-south-west of Reykjavik. He then sank the Belgian MV *Indier*. She was hit during the attack on *Westpool*, and sank in less than one minute. The fourth ship was the British tanker SS *British Viscount*, sunk at 08:32 hours, being hit amidships by one torpedo south-south-west of Iceland. The operation ended on the 5th, *U-73* continued to patrol in the area until the 17th, and then headed south. On the 30th Rosenbaum sank the British SS *Empire Endurance*. She was struck amidships by one torpedo, broke in two and sank after being struck underneath her bridge by a *coup de grâce* torpedo. The *Empire Endurance* was carrying as part of her cargo two British patrol craft, HMS *ML-1003* and HMS *ML-1037*, both of which were lost.

On 20 May, Rosenbaum headed for the North Atlantic, where *U-73* was part of a patrol line to help with the plan for the German battleship *Bismarck* and the heavy crusier *Prinz Eugen* to break out into the Atlantic. However, the plan was changed when *Bismarck* was damaged by HMS *Prince of Wales* in May 1941 during the Battle of the Denmark Strait. She would make for St. Nazaire and *Prinz Eugen* would head south-westwards. On the evening of the 25th, *Bismarck* was damaged in a torpedo attack, and to assist her a number of U-boats were sent to support her, including *U-73*. They were directed to form a patrol line running north-west from Cape Ortegal. This was delayed by a heavy storm and the boats were not in position until the 26th. *U-556* sighted the British aircraft carrier HMS *Ark Royal* and the battlecruiser HMS *Renown* in pursuit of *Bismarck* but had no torpedoes left. In the end no U-boat was able to help, *Bismarck* was consequently sunk on the morning of the 27th. *U-48*, *U-73* and *U-108* were ordered to search for survivors. They searched until the 31st but none was found. Rosenbaum then resumed with his patrol, but found no convoys. He put in at St. Nazaire on 24 June.

Over the next six weeks Rosenbaum saw little of the Allied convoys and failed to sink another ship. One of his patrols ended in just three days because of engine problems. On 4 August Rosenbaum left port for the Western Mediterranean and together with *U-331*

The 22,600-ton HMS Eagle *was one of the largest ships sunk by a U-boat during the Second World War. She was originally built for Chile in 1913 as the dreadnought battleship* Almirante Cochrane *but work was suspended in 1914. She was then purchased by the British Admiralty in 1918 and completed in February 1924 as an aircraft carrier.* (Author's collection)

was part of a German-Italian submarine force, which from the 10th was to take up a position between Algiers and the Balearic Islands to await Convoy WS215, heading for Malta. The convoy of fourteen merchant ships had a large naval escort and there was a covering force of battleships, aircraft carriers, cruisers and destroyers. At 13:15 hours on 11 August Rosenbaum attacked the British aircraft carrier HMS *Eagle*. He fired four torpedoes which struck her and she sank about 70 miles south of Cape Salinas, Majorca. She was the third largest warship sunk during the Second World War. Her commander and 926 survivors were picked up by two British ships. One hundred and sixty men were lost. On 14 August, Rosenbaum unsuccessfully attacked the escort force on its return run to Gibraltar. He returned to La Spezia on 5 September.

In October 1942, Rosenbaum was transferred and became commander of the 30th U-boat Flotilla and was on the staff of the Admiral of the Black Sea. Rosenbaum was killed when the aircraft he was in crashed near Constanta, Romania on 10 May 1944. He was posthumously promoted to the rank of *Korvettenkapitän*.

Other awards:
15 Aug 1936: Long Service Award 4th Class
06 Jun 1939: Spanish Cross in Bronze
16 Apr 1940: Iron Cross 2nd Class
04 Mar 1941: U-Boat War Badge
25 Apr 1941: Iron Cross 1st Class
17 Sep 1942: Italian Bravery Medal in Silver

Hans-Rudolf Max RÖSING
Kapitän zur See
12 ships sunk, 60,701 tons
1 ship damaged, 5,888 tons

Knight's Cross: Awarded as *Korvettenkapitän* and as commander of the 7th U-Boat Flotilla and as Commander of *U-48*, on 29 August 1940 for sinking twelve ships for a total of 60,701 shipping tons.

Hans-Rudolf Rösing was born in Wilhelmshaven a province of Prussia on 28 September 1905, the son of *Vizeadmiral* Bernhard Rösing (1869–1947) and his wife Elfriede neé Wünsche (1882–1961). He had three brothers, Wilhelm, Kurt-Wolf and Bernhard, all killed during the Second World War, and a sister. Rösing entered the *Reichsmarine* in March 1924, and underwent his basic training whilst in the 2nd Battalion of the *Schiffsstammdivision* in the Baltic. In September he transferred to the First World War battleship *Elsass* and became a Naval Cadet. He was transferred to the sail training ship *Niobe* in April   (Scherzer)

1925, before continuing his training on the light cruiser *Berlin* until March 1926. During this training period he was promoted to *Fähnrich zur See* in April 1926 and was made an *Oberfähnrich zur See* in May 1928. He underwent a number of officer training courses and was later assigned aboard the cruiser *Nymphe* until March 1929. He was commissioned as a *Leutnant zur See* in October 1928 before being transferred to the light cruiser *Königsberg* six months later. Rösing was promoted to *Oberleutnant zur See* in April 1930, and became one of a small number of officers chosen for an exchange programme with the Swedish navy, to gain experience of submarines, Germany having been forbidden to operate submarines under the Treaty of Versailles.

From September to December 1931, Rösing was assigned to the staff of the Admiral commanding the Baltic Naval Station. He then transferred to the 1st *Schnellboot* (MTB) Flotilla, where he commanded the E-boat *S15*. During his command he attended more training courses, which included a Spanish language course, which he passed in October 1932. From November he was assigned to the 1st *Schnellboot* Flotilla and commanded E-boat *S3* from November 1933. He spent the next two years with the U-boat training school and was promoted to *Kapitänleutnant* in April 1935. In September he was appointed commander of *U-11*, an early boat, a Type IIB, built by Germania Werft in Kiel. From October 1937, he commanded *U-10*, another Type IIB, and at the same time was assigned to the *Torpedoprobungskommando*, responsible for the testing of new torpedo types. Then from August 1938, Rösing was commander of the 5th U-boat Flotilla at Kiel.

In July 1939, Rösing was promoted to *Korvettenkapitän* and after a short time as an officer on the staff of the Commander-in-Chief of U-boats, he was posted to back to Kiel where he took command of the 7th U-boat Flotilla. On 21 May 1940 he took command of *U-48*, a Type VIIB boat, taking over from *Kapitänleutnant* Herbert Schultze. His crew was highly experienced and three went on to become Knight's Cross holders. His First Watch Officer was Reinhard Suhren, his Second Watch Officer was Otto Ites and his chief engineer was Erich Zürn. Rösing left Kiel for his first patrol on 26 May, heading for an area west-north-west of Cape Finisterre. He had been appointed tactical commander of a group of five boats, which were ordered to intercept Convoy US3, expected to pass west of Finisterre on 13 June. On the 6th whilst en route to the operational area he sank the British SS *Stancor* by gunfire north-west of the Isle of Lewis. The next morning he sank the SS *Frances Massey* and damaged the SS *Eros*. On the 11th Rösing sank the Greek SS *Violando N. Goulandris* west-north-west of Cape Finisterre. The ship quickly settled and sank by the stern after about fifteen minutes. The master and five crew members were lost. The interception of Convoy US3 did not take place and Rösings' group was broken up. On the 19th he attacked the Norwegian MV *Tudor* and two British ships, the SS *Baron Loudoun* and SS *British Monarch*, all of which were torpedoed and sunk. On the 20th Rösing sank a straggler from Convoy HX49, the Dutch tanker MV *Moerdrecht* west of El Ferrol. She exploded and sank within two minutes with the loss of twenty-five crew members. Rösing returned *U-48* to Kiel on 29 June. His next patrol which began on 7 August took *U-48* just west of the British Isles where on 16th he sank the Swedish SS *Hedrun* west-south-west of Rockall and soon after midnight on the the 18th he sank the Belgian passenger ship SS *Ville de Gand*, with the loss of fourteen. On the afternoon of the 24th he sank the British tanker SS *La Brea*, and in the early hours of the following day he sank another British tanker, when he torpedoed the MV *Athelcrest* 90 miles east-by-north of the Flannan Isles. During the same attack he also sank the British SS *Empire Merlin*. She was hit by a single torpedo and sank within thirty-five minutes, having broken in two. Of the thirty-five crew, there was only one survivor, Ordinary Seaman John Lee. Rösing put in at Lorient on 28 August.

In September 1940, Rösing was appointed liaison officer to the Italian submarine force operating out of Bordeaux in occupied France. From March 1941 he commanded the 3rd U-boat Flotilla, but he returned to the staff of the commander of U-boats in August. In July 1942, Rösing was appointed commander of U-boat West, with his headquarters in both Paris and at Château de Pignevolle near Angers, being responsible for all boats committed to the Battle of the Atlantic. He was promoted to *Fregattenkapitän* in January 1943, and just one month later was promoted to *Kapitän zur See*. He remained in this post in France until August 1944, when the Allied liberation of France forced the *Kriegsmarine* to transfer the remaining boats of the 2nd and 7th U-boat flotilla to Norway, Denmark and northern Germany. He surrendered to the Allies in May 1945, and spent eighteen months in Allied captivity.

Rösing joined the *Bundesmarine* in March 1956, and was given command of German naval units operating in the North Sea. He eventually rose to the rank of *Konteradmiral* in November 1952, retiring as commander of Military District I in August 1965. Rosing died on 16 December 2004 in Kiel at the age of ninety-nine.

Other awards:
02 Oct 1936: Long Service Award 4th to 3rd Class
13 Feb 1940: Iron Cross 2nd Class
03 Jul 1940: Iron Cross 1st Class
00 Sep 1940: U-Boat War Badge
01 Nov 1941: Italian War Cross with Swords
01 Nov 1941: Italian Commanders Cross of the Order of the Crown

<u>Erwin</u> Arnold Martin Wilhelm ROSTIN
Korvettenkapitän
17 ships sunk, 101,321 tons
2 ships damaged, 15,264 tons

Knight's Cross: Awarded on 28 June 1942, as *Kapitänleutnant* and as commander of *U-158*, for sinking sixteen ships for a total of 97,371 shipping tons.

Erwin Rostin was born on 8 October 1907, in Güstrow, capital of the Rostock district in Mecklenburg, Germany. He joined the *Reichsmarine* at the age of twenty-six and was initially assigned to the 6th Company of the II *Schiffsstammdivision* in the Baltic. In January 1934, Rostin was made a *Fähnrich zur See* or Officer Candidate, transferring to Kiel where he was assigned to the Ships' Gunnery School. He attended a number of various courses over the next four months and served on the light cruiser *Leipzig* from September 1934. In July 1935, Rostin attended a training course on U-boats and was in January 1936 commissioned as a *Leutnant zur See*. From June he was commander of coastal escort boats, and in October was promoted to *Oberleutnant zur See*. From December 1937 until April 1939 Rostin was commandant of the Naval Mine Warfare School in Kiel and later served as adjutant to the commander of security in Kiel and then later in the Baltic. In August 1939, he was made commander of the 7th Minesweeper Flotilla and in April 1940 he was promoted to *Kapitänleutnant*. The following month he took command of the minesweeper *M98* and later the *M21*.

On 31 March 1941, Rostin transferred to the U-boat service, and after training was appointed commander of *U-158*, a Type IXC boat built in Bremen. On 2 February 1942, with her sea trials complete, he took his new boat out from Wilhelmshaven and headed for his new base in Helgoland. On the 7th he left port to operate in the Western Atlantic, where on the 22nd he sighted Convoy ONS67 and was ordered to close in, together with *U-155*, *U-94*,

(Scherzer)

U-587 and *U-588*. Rostin torpedoed two British tankers on the morning of the 24th, east-south-east of Cape Race, the SS *Empire Celt* and the MV *Diloma*. The *Empire Celt* was struck by two torpedoes but continued on her way until she stopped and broke in two; the stern remained afloat, and was last seen on 4 March. The other tanker, the *Diloma*, was struck by a single torpedo and was able to proceed at a reduced speed and reached Halifax on 1 March. She was later repaired and returned to service. On 1 March, Rostin chased the Norwegian tanker MV *Finnanger* for fourteen hours before eventually sinking her by gunfire. Rostin then took his boat down the US coast, where on the 11th he sank the US SS *Caribsea*. She was struck on the starboard side by a single torpedo. She rapidly settled by the head due to her cargo of 3,600 tons of manganese ore and was shaken by a boiler explosion and sank in less than three minutes, about 11 miles east of the Cape Lookout Lighthouse. On the 13th he sank the US tanker SS *John D. Gill*, torpedoed about 25 miles east of Cape Fear, North Carolina. One torpedo struck her on the starboard side amidships under the mainmast in No. 7 tank. The tanker did not burst into flames after being hit, the explosion failing to ignite her cargo. Instead the oil ignited when a seaman tossed a life ring with a self-igniting carbide light overboard. The ship and sea was turned into a blazing inferno, forcing the crew to abandon ship. Whilst the crew were lowering one of the lifeboats there was an explosion, and then another. Of her crew of forty-nine, twenty-three were lost. On the 15th, Rostin torpedoed two US tankers, the SS *Olean* which was damaged and later towed to dry dock where she was repaired and reconstructed and renamed the SS *Sweep* and returned to service. The second tanker was the SS *Ario*, struck by a single torpedo and by gunfire, with the loss of eight of her crew. Rostin then put in at his new base at Lorient on 31 March.

On 4 May, Rostin took *U-158* on another patrol in the Western Atlantic. En route to his operational area he sank two ships, east-south-east of Bermuda. He sank the

British tanker MV *Darina* on the 20th, and the Canadian SS *Frank B. Baird* two days later by gunfire. He later entered the Caribbean area and whilst patrolling had more success, sinking another four ships. On 2 June, he sank the US SS *Knoxville City*, torpedoed about 150 miles south-east of Cape Corrientes, Cuba. The explosion killed two men on watch below, which stopped the engines immediately and caused the boilers to explode. On the 4th he sank the Norwegian SS *Nidarnes*, which went down in less than sixty seconds. The next day he sank the US SS *Velma Lykes* about 20 miles off Puerto Juarrez in the Yucatan Channel. The torpedo had been spotted seconds before it struck and killed three men on watch. She developed a slight list to starboard and sank in around one minute after No. 3 and No. 4 hold were flooded. Fifteen crew members were lost in total. On the 7th Rostin sank the Panamanian SS *Hermis*. Struck by two torpedoes, she burst into flames and burnt for many hours before she sank. Rostin moved *U-158* into the Gulf of Mexico and continued his run of success. On the 11th he sank the Panamanian tanker MV *Sheherazade*. She was struck by two torpedoes about 20 miles west of Ship Shoal Buoy. The tanker capsized after being hit by a third torpedo which struck the engine room and then *U-158* surfaced and fired eight rounds from its deck gun and she sank. He sank the US tanker SS *Cities Service Toledo* the following day with the loss of fifteen of her crew. On the 17th he sank two more ships east of Laguna Madre, Mexico, the Panamanian SS *San Blas* and the Norwegian tanker MV *Moira*. Before leaving the Gulf Rostin sank the US tanker SS *Major General Henry Gibbins* on the 23rd. She was torpedoed about 375 miles west of Key West, Florida. Whilst on his return journey he sank his last ship, the Latvian SS *Everalda*. She was shelled from *U-158*'s deck guns, fire being aimed at the bridge to prevent any distress signal from being sent. The chief engineer stopped the ship when she caught fire and Rostin ordered his men to hold their fire for ten minutes while the crew abandoned ship. *U-158* then fired nine rounds from the deck gun but she still didn't sink. Out of ammunition, Rostin ordered a boarding party to go on board the ship and open her bottom valves, causing her to sink by the bow two hours later. All of her crew managed to get to the lifeboats and were picked up, and landed safely at Morehead City on 5 July. Rostin had by this time sank a total of twelve ships in just forty days, in one patrol!

On 30 June, *U-158* was sighted on the surface by a US Naval Mariner aircraft about 200 miles west-north-west of Bermuda. The aircraft attacked with depth-charges, crew-members, sunbathing on the boat's deck, were taken completely by surprise. One of the bombs dropped lodged in the conning tower and exploded as the boat submerged. *U-158* was destroyed, there were no survivors. Fifty-three men including Rostin were killed. Rostin, who had been notified of his Knight's Cross the day before, was posthumously promoted to *Korvettenkapitän*.

Other awards:
04 Oct 1937: Long Service Award 4th Class
10 Oct 1939: Iron Cross 2nd Class
20 Dec 1939: Commemorative Medal of 01 Oct 1938
21 Nov 1940: Iron Cross 1st Class
03 Jan 1941: Minesweepers Badge
01 Jul 1942: U-Boat War Badge

Paul-Heinrich <u>Gerhard</u> SCHAAR
Kapitänleutnant
4 ships sunk, 8,168 tons

Knight's Cross: Awarded on 1 October 1944, as *Oberleutnant zur See* and as commander of *U-957*, for sinking four ships for a total of 8,168 shipping tons.

Gerhard Schaar was born on 5 March 1919, in Berlin and joined the *Kriegsmarine* in October 1937. He served as an officer cadet in the Baltic until February 1938, when he was assigned first to the sail training ship *Albert Leo Schlageter* and then aboard the light cruiser *Emden* until March 1939. He attended various courses before the war started and was promoted to *Fähnrich zur See* in April 1939 and to *Oberfähnrich zur See* in March 1940. He served on the destroyer *Z12 Erich Giese*, which was sunk during the occupation of Norway

(Scherzer)

in April 1940. He was commissioned as a *Leutnant zur See* in May 1940 and after a few months on shore in Narvik, Schaar served as a training officer at the Naval Academy in Flensburg before transferring to the U-boat service in February 1942. He was promoted to *Oberleutnant zur See* on 18 March and attended various training courses which included navigation and U-boat commander training.

On 20 March 1943, whilst in the Baltic during a training exercise, *U-957* collided with the U-boat tender *Wilhelm Bauer*. The boat's conning tower was damaged and her commander, *Oberleutnant zur See* Franz Saar, was killed. In early April Schaar took over as commander and oversaw the repairs and continued with her crews training until *U-957* was finally ready for her first war patrol. Schaar took his new boat out of Kiel on 14 December and headed for northern waters where he joined *Eisenbart* Group. They were directed towards Convoy JW55B by reconnaissance aircraft but they were quickly driven off by the escorts. On the 21st Schaar was notified by radio of his promotion to *Kapitänleutnant* and four days later the German battleship *Scharnhorst* with a destroyer escort was deployed against the convoy. On the 26th *Scharnhorst* was intercepted by a strong British naval force that included the battleship HMS *Duke of York*. The naval engagement, known as the Battle of North Cape, lasted all day and together with her escort ships the *Duke of York* sank the *Scharnhorst*. Only thirty-six men were rescued, out of a crew of 1,968. Schaar made unsuccessful attacks on the 28th against the same convoy. He put in at Narvik on 12 January 1944.

On 24 January, Schaar left for operations with *Isegrim* Group in the Bear Island Passage. Here the boats waited for Convoy JW56A, which had sailed from Akureyri, Iceland on the 21st. In the afternoon of the 25th the *Isegrim* boats closed in on the convoy of Bear Island Passage, and made torpedo attacks throughout the night. On the 26th, Schaar missed a destroyer but sank the British SS *Fort Bellingham*. This ship had on board the convoy commodore, who along with the master and twenty-three crew members were later rescued by HMS *Offa* when *Fort Bellingham* sank. Two gunners were picked up by *U-957* and were interrogated and they provided some valuable information. Just after the sinking Schaar and his crew noticed the US patrol torpedo boat, the USS *PTC-38* which had been transported on the deck of the *Andrew G. Curtis* and floated free after the ship had been sunk by *U-716* earlier. Schaar ordered the boat sunk and after three or fout shots from her deck guns the torpedo boat sank.

On the 30th, Schaar made unsuccessful attacks on the escort ships of Convoy JW56B, including the destroyer HMS *Hardy*, sunk soon afterwards by *U-278*. Schaar put in at Hammerfest on 2 February. Over the next five months Schaar made two more patrols which were both cut short due to bad weather. On 23 July, he left for further operations, this time in the Kara Sea, where he was to operate together with *U-278*, *U-362*, *U-365*, *U-711* and *U-739*, they made up *Greif* Group. On 26 August he sank the Soviet survey ship *Nord* by gunfire. The vessel was able to send a distress message and fired one shot from the 45mm gun aboard, but missed. *U-957* took the four survivors on board. They were landed in Hammerfest on 3 September, transferred to Narvik by train and later by ship to Danzig and then to a POW camp.

On 7 September, Schaar took *U-957* out to rejoin *U-711* and *U-739* in the Kara Sea. On the 21st they encountered the Soviet Convoy VD1, en route from the Vilkitski Strait to Dickson. On the 23rd he sank the Soviet corvette *Brilliant* north of Krakovka Island. She was hit by a torpedo and sank in two minutes. There were no survivors due to the icy temperature of the sea: three officers and sixty-one crewmen were lost. The three U-boats then landed a party on Sterligova Island on the 24th. A wireless station was destroyed and four prisoners taken. Schaar returned to Narvik on 3 October. During his next patrol, Schaar had moved base to Trondheim and left for operations on 17 October but collided with pack ice and had to make for Narvik heavily damaged. *U-957* reached Narvik on the 21st, and was de-commissioned the same day.

On 23 January 1945, Schaar was named as commander of *U-2551*, a Type XXI Elektro boat. However, while still under construction the boat was slightly damaged in an air raid in Hamburg on 17 February. She was repaired but ran aground during her trials and was scuttled at Flensburg-Solitude on 5 May. Schaar was chief of the naval police in Schleswig-Holstein until shortly after Germany's surrender. He died in Maseru in the Kingdom of Lesotho in South Africa on 24 January 1983.

Other awards:
15 May 1940: Iron Cross 2nd Class
15 May 1940: Iron Cross 1st Class
19 Oct 1940: Destroyers War Badge
20 Oct 1940:Narvik Campaign Shield
00 Feb 1944: U-Boat War Badge
14 Feb 1944: German Cross in Gold

Harro SCHACHT
Fregattenkapitän
19 ships sunk, 77,143 tons
1 ship damaged, 6,561 tons

Knight's Cross: Awarded on 9 January 1943, as *Korvettenkapitän* and as commander of *U-507*, in recognition of sinking seventeen ships in just four patrols for a total of 68,067 shipping tons.

Harro Schacht was born in Cuxhaven in Lower Saxony, Germany on 15 December 1907, after completing his schooling he joined the *Reichsmarine* in April 1926 at the age of eighteen. He joined as a naval cadet and was assigned to the 5th company of the II. *Schiffsstammdivision* in the Baltic. From July he began his basic training, serving aboard the sail training ship *Niobe* as well as the light cruiser *Emden* from October. He attended various training courses at the Naval Academy and became an Officer Candidate in February 1928. In September 1930, Schacht was assigned to the light cruiser *Emden* once again. He was commissioned as a *Leutnant zur See* in October and was appointed radio officer. In August 1932 he was promoted to *Oberleutnant zur See*, and in September he transferred to his hometown of Cuxhaven where he served as commander of a naval artillery company. From December 1933, he served as adjutant and

(Scherzer)

company officer of the II. *Schiffsstammdivision* at the naval headquarters of the North Sea. In October 1935 he served as radio officer aboard the light cruiser *Nürnberg*, and was promoted to *Kapitänleutnant* in April 1936. From October 1937 and for the next three and a half years Schacht served as a staff officer with the High Command of the *Kriegsmarine*.

Promoted to *Korvettenkapitän* in October 1940, he transferred to the U-boat service in April of the following year. After his basic training as a submariner he joined the 'Red Devil Boat', *U-552*, under *Kapitänleutnant* Erich Topp as a 'commander-in-training'. Then on 8 October 1941, Schacht got his own command, *U-507*, a Type IXC boat built by Deutsche Werft in Hamburg. The boat was commissioned in October 1941, and after her sea trials was ready for service. On 12 March 1942, Schacht took her out of Heligoland on his first war patrol as commander. On the 18th he sighted the westbound Convoy ONS76, 200 miles west of the North Channel. During the early hours of the 19th he made several attacks on the convoy, but, although he heard explosions there was no evidence that he sank any ships.

Schacht left for the Western Atlantic on 4 April. This next patrol would be more successful. On the 20th, while operating off Cuba he sank the US SS *Federal* by gunfire. On 4 May he took *U-507* through the Straits of Florida and entered the Gulf of Mexico, the first U-boat to do so. On the evening of the 4th he sank the US SS *Norlindo* about 80 miles north-west of the Dry Tortugas. Early the following day Schacht sank another US ship, the SS *Munger T. Ball*. She was struck by a single torpedo on the port side amidships, followed by a second torpedo, thirty seconds later, which struck the ship in the engine room. The burning tanker sank in less than fifteen minutes, there were only four survivors. Three hours later he sank the SS *Joseph M. Culdahy*, torpedoed about 125 miles west of Naples. On the 6th Schacht sighted another steamer, the SS *Alcoa Puritan*. She had spotted a torpedo passing about 15ft astern, about 15 miles off the entrance of the Mississippi River. The master immediately ordered full speed and swung the ship to keep the U-boat dead astern to present as small a target as possible. *U-507* then shelled the ship from a distance of a mile. In approximately forty minutes seventy-five rounds were fired, scoring about fifty hits. The crew of ten officers, and thirty-seven crewmen and seven passengers abandoned ship in one lifeboat and two rafts. Schacht ordered the ship sunk, and the survivors were picked up the same day. Schacht then moved south-eastwards where he sank two more ships. On the 8th he sank the Honduran SS *Ontario* by gunfire and the Norwegian SS *Torny* the same day. On the 12th, he took *U-507* to the area of Port Eads where during the evening he sank the US tanker, SS *Virginia*, she was hit by a torpedo on the port side whilst lying stopped at the pilot buoy 1½ miles off the entrance to South-west Pass of the Mississippi River. Schachts' final victim of this patrol was the Honduran SS *Amapala*, sunk on 16 May by gunfire. She refused to sink and was later taken in tow, but sank before reaching port. Schacht had to take *U-507* out of the area when an aircraft appeared about three hours after the attack and unsuccessfully dropped depth charges on the German boat. With all of his torpedoes used Schacht headed for home. He arrived at Lorient on 4 June.

Schacht eventually left for the Central Atlantic on 4 July. After some repair work to his U-boat, he headed for an area between the Cape Verde Islands and Brazil but had no success. From early August he was operating off the coast of Brazil and on the 16th sank three ships south of Aracaju, the SS *Baependy*, SS *Araraquara* and SS *Annibal Benévolo*, with the loss of 150 of her crew. Schacht then took *U-507* down the coast to a position south of Salvador where he sank another four ships, sinking the Brazilian SS *Itagiba*, on the 17th, with the loss of thirty-six crew; he then sank the SS *Arará* the same day. Two days later he sank the Brazilian sailing ship *Jacyra*. She was stopped with two rounds from the deck gun about 10 miles off Hacaré, Brazil. At 08:00 hours, she sunk after scuttling charges exploded, just after her crew had abandoned ship in a lifeboat. On the 22nd he sank the Swedish MV *Hammaren* by gunfire. It was this action by Schacht, the sinking of six Brazilian ships, which resulted in the hitherto neutral Brazil declaring war on Nazi Germany on 22 August 1942. Brazil claimed that the ships had been sunk inside her territorial waters but Germany claimed that they were outside. At the end of August *U-507* was ordered to proceed towards Freetown and in early September was south of Liberia. On 12th, *U-156* sank the troop transporter RMS *Laconia*. In addition to her passengers and crew, *Laconia* was carrying 1,800 Italian POWs being taken from South Africa to Great Britain. There was a rescue operation and Schacht was ordered to help. En route to the scene he met up with four of *Laconia*'s lifeboats during the afternoon of the 15th. Schacht took aboard the women and gave comfort to the survivors and took the lifeboats in tow. *U-507* reached the scene the same day and took aboard 164 Italians and two British officers, who were taken to France as prisoners-of-war. The rescue operation was terminated when a US Liberator flew over, and in three separate attacks dropped bombs, destroying a lifeboat full of survivors and damaging *U-156*. Despite orders to stop all rescue operations, the U-boat commanders continued to help. On the 17th the Vichy French cruiser *Gloire* together with two other ships rendezvoused with *U-506* and *U-507* to take aboard the survivors they were carrying or towing in boats. *U-507* was attacked by an aircraft during the transfer, luckily nobody was hurt and Schacht ordered that they leave the area. *U-507* then returned to Lorient on 12 October.

There were minor repairs to be made before Schacht went out again on another patrol. Finally on 24 November *U-507* left for the Central Atlantic and headed for the north-east coast of Brazil. On the 27th Schacht sank the British MV *Oakbank* about 200 miles north-north-west of Fortaleza. On 3 January 1943, he sank the British SS *Baron Dechmont*, torpedoed north-west of Cape San Roque. Seven of her crew were lost. Five days later he sank another British ship, SS *Yorkwood*, north-west of Ascension Islands. On the 13th, *U-507* was located on the surface by a Catalina flying boat of VP-83 north-north-east of Camocim, and was attacked. The boat had no time to dive or take evasive action and was struck by two bombs, sinking almost immediately with the loss of the entire crew, including Schacht. He was posthumously promoted to the rank of *Fregattenkapitän*.

Other awards:
02 Oct 1936: Long Service Award 4th Class
01 Apr 1938: Long Service Award 3rd Class
29 Mar 1940: Spanish Cross in Silver
19 Apr 1940: Iron Cross 2nd Class
06 Jun 1942: Iron Cross 1st Class
06 Jun 1942: U-Boat War Badge

<u>Georg</u> Friedrich Karl SCHEWE
Korvettenkapitän
16 ships sunk, 85,779 tons

Knight's Cross: Awarded on 23 May 1941, as *Kapitänleutnant* and as commander of *U-105* after sinking fourteen ships for a total of 79,511 shipping tons.

Born in Ueckermünde, a small seaport town in Pommern, on 24 November 1909, Georg Schewe entered the *Reichsmarine* in October 1928. From September 1929 he served in the 2nd Torpedo Boat Half-Flotilla and in November 1931 he served aboard the sail training ship *Niobe*. From February 1932 he attended the Ships Gunnery School in Kiel before commencing his officer training, being assigned to various course at the Naval Academy. He was commissioned as a *Leutnant zur See* in January 1936 and in October he transferred to the U-boat service. From April 1937, Schewe served aboard *U-15* and later *U-21* as Watch Officer, being promoted to *Oberleutnant zur See* in October.

(Author's collection)

In July 1939, Schewe took command of *U-60*, a Type IIC boat built by Deutsche Werke in Kiel. In October that same year he was promoted to *Kapitänleutnant* and in December he left port for a minelaying operations off the east coast of England. He laid mines off Cross Sound on the 17th. Two days later the British SS *City of Kobe* struck one of his mines and sank. This was the only known victim of these mines. On 4 April 1940, his third patrol, he left Wilhelmshaven under sealed orders to take part in Operation *Harmut*. The orders were opened on the 6th – all participating boats were given their positions off the Norwegian coast, where from the 9th they were to support German transports and naval forces landing troops and to prevent interference by British warships. Schewe was ordered to join the 3rd U-boat Group, which was to operate off Bergen. The boats were later refuelled by German supply ships and afterwards *U-60*, in company with *U-56* and *U-62*, went along the Norwegian coast to Folda Fjord to oppose any British landings. His patrol ended without enemy contact and he returned to port on 11 June.

In August 1940, Schewe was appointed commander of *U-105*, a Type IXB boat built in Bremen. He left Kiel for his first war patrol with his new command on Christmas Eve to operate west of the British Isles. In early 1941, he was on weather-reporting duties, when on the 9th he sighted and sank the British SS *Bassano* north-west of Rockall. On the 26th, west of Ireland he sank the British SS *Lurigethan*. She had been part of Convoy SLS61 and had been bombed and set on fire by a German Fw 200 Kondor about 280 miles west of Galway Bay, Ireland on 23 January. The survivors abandoned ship in the lifeboats. Later a boarding party returned to the ship in an attempt to put out the fire, but it was out of control. During the night of the 25th/26th Schewe became aware of an orange glow and went to investigate. He torpedoed the burning ship to record a successful sinking. The ship had been misidentified as the SS *Heemskerk* but this ship had been previously bombed on 20 January, and was seen to sink the next day by HMS *Arbutus*. The description of the wreck and the date of the sinking prove the ship sunk by Schewe was the *Lurigethan*.

For his next patrol Schewe left port on 22 February, to operate in the Central Atlantic, heading for the Freetown area. He then moved south in the company of *U-106* and *U-124*. Between 3 and 6 March, the three boats were refuelled by the supply ship *Charlotte Schliemann*, and from the 7th operated against the northbound Convoy SL67. Early the following day Schewe sank the British SS *Harmodius* with the loss of thirteen crew members. From the 15th, together with *U-106*, he operated around the Cape Verde Islands and it was here that he sighted Convoy SL68 and sank five ships in just four days. Early on the 18th, Schewe torpedoed and sank the British SS *Medjerda*. She broke in two upon impact and quickly sunk about 90 miles east of the Cape Verde Islands, with the loss of her entire crew. Soon after midnight he sank the Norwegian SS *Mandalika*. Struck in the engine room on the port side by a single torpedo, she quickly sunk. During the early hours of the 21st he sank the British SS *Benwyvis* followed shortly by the SS *Clan Ogilvy*. Later that same evening Schewe sank another British ship, the SS *Jhelum*, which sank about 500 miles west of Cabo Blanco, French West Africa. On the 19th, *U-105* and *U-106* were refuelled by the supply ship *Nordmark* and the two boats then proceeded to the Freetown area. However, in early April they were ordered to Rio de Janeiro to meet the German blockade-runner *Lech* and escort her up through the South Atlantic. During this time Schewe sank another British SS *Ena de Larrinaga* about 205 miles east of St. Paul Rocks. He had sighted the ship about ten hours earlier and decided to wait for night to attack: five of her crew of thirty-nine as well as two gunners were lost. On 3 May, *U-105* was again replenished by the *Nordmark*, and on her way back towards Freetown Schewe attacked and sank the SS *Oakdene*, another British ship from Convoy OG59. In mid-May he sank a further three ships, all British. The SS *Benvrackie* was sunk on the 13th, the SS *Benvenue* on the 15th and on the 16th he sank the 11,803-ton *Rodney Star* about 420 miles west-south-west of Freetown. She was hit in the stern by two torpedoes and later she was struck in the bow and amidships by two more but remained afloat. *U-105* surfaced and fired ninety-one high-explosive rounds and twenty-two incendiary rounds from her deck gun. Eventually, after an explosion the ship sank, without loss of life as the crew had been allowed to abandon ship sometime before. On his way back to Lorient, Schewe sank the British SS *Scottish Monarch* from Convoy OB319, south-west of the Cape Verde Islands. He arrived at Lorient on 13 June, and was informed he had been awarded the Knight's Cross. In one patrol he had sunk twelve ships for a total of almost 72,000 tons.

With the celebrations over and the boat replenished, Schewe left Lorient on 3 August and once again headed for the North Atlantic. He joined a new group, operating south-west of Iceland, and after some unsuccessful attempts to intercept the convoys, the group were reformed on the 28th as *Markgraf* Group south-west of Iceland. On 4 September, the group was ordered to form a new patrol line further west. Over the next few days several convoys were re-routed to avoid the line. However, the eastbound Convoy SC42 could not change course because of bad weather. The convoy was sighted by *U-85* on the 9th near Cape Farewell. Attacks were made on the 9th, 10th and 11th. Altogether a total of sixteen ships were sunk. On the 11th, Schewe, who had no success against Convoy SC42, sank the Panamanian SS *Montana*, north-east of Cape Farewell. He returned to Lorient on 20th.

On 8 November, Schewe left port to operate once again in the North Atlantic, patrolling south of Iceland, and from the 13th he moved south-westwards towards Cape Race. *U-105* joined five other boats and moved towards Newfoundland as *Steuben* Group. Later boats with enough fuel were ordered eastwards to an area west of Gibraltar, but had no success due to Allied air patrols. Schewe had no choice but to return to Lorient on 13 December. On 5 February, he was transferred and became a staff officer assigned to the U-boat command in the Mediterranean. After more than two years in this position, and after being promoted to *Fregattenkapitän* in August 1943, he took over command of the 33rd U-boat Flotilla. From 27 October 1944, he was a staff officer with the Naval High Command, a position he held until the end of the war. He was captured by British forces in May 1945 and was released in April 1946. Schewe returned to Germany and to civilian life, eventually settling in Hamburg where he died on 16 October 1990. (Scherzer, *Die Ritterkreuzträger 1939-1945*, gives the date as 14 October 1990.)

Other awards:
02 Oct 1936: Long Service Award 4th Class
20 Dec 1939: Iron Cross 2nd Class
20 Dec 1939: Commemorative Medal for 01 Oct 1938
24 Jan 1940: U-Boat War Badge
13 Jun 1941: Iron Cross 1st Class

Egon-Reiner Freiherr von SCHLIPPENBACH
Korvettenkapitän
6 ships sunk, 18,390 tons
2 ships damaged, 16,610 tons

Knight's Cross: Awarded as *Kapitänleutnant* and as commander of *U-453* on 19 November 1943, for sinking four ships for a total of 17,220 shipping tons and for damaging two others.

Egon-Reiner Freiherr von Schlippenbach was born on 10 April 1914, the son of Ulrich Karl Ernst Gustav, an engineer, in Köln-Lindenthal a district of Cologne, Germany. Schlippenbach joined the *Reichsmarine* in April 1934, just before his twentieth birthday. From November 1935 he was assigned to the Naval Academy at Flensburg where he trained to be an officer, attending various courses. He was commissioned as a *Leutnant zur See* in April 1937, and served aboard the battleship *Schleswig-Holstein* until October 1938. Promoted to *Oberleutnant zur See* in April 1939, Schlippenbach served as First Watch Officer aboard *U-18* from October. He continued with his training and from September was assigned to *U-3* and in November transferring to *U-101* as Watch Officer.

On 31 March 1941, Schlippenbach took command of *U-121*, a Type IIB boat. The boat saw no operational service and served only as a training vessel throughout the war. On 9 July, he took command of *U-453*, a Type IIC boat built by Deutsche Werke in Kiel. After her sea trials were completed in November he took her out on her first war patrol and headed for the Mediterranean. *U-453* passed north of the British Isles en route to Gibraltar, passing through the Straits during the night of 8/9 December. On the 13th he torpedoed and sank the Spanish tanker MV *Bedalona*. Schlippenbach surfaced and ordered the *Bedalona* to stop, but the tanker tried to escape and used her radio until a shot

from the U-boat's deck gun was fired across her bow. She stopped and her crew abandoned ship. One of the lifeboats was swamped during the hasty launch, drowning three of the occupants. Schlippenbach ordered a torpedo to be fired at the ship and on impact she broke in two and sank. He put in at La Spezia on 17 December and was informed he had been promoted to *Kapitänleutnant*.

He left for his next patrol on 17 January 1942, but had no success and put in at Pola on 1 February. There was a delay before he sailed again, a slight leak was thought to be the reason, but he left for the Eastern Mediterranean on his next patrol on 22 March. Together with *U-205* and *U-431*, he was ordered to attack Allied shipping sailing in and out of Tobruk. At 12:57 hours on 7 April Schlippenbach fired a spread of four torpedoes at a steamer, he heard three detonations after

(Scherzer)

forty-seven seconds. He had hit HMHS *Somersetshire*,[3] a hospital ship of almost 10,000 tons. Fortunately the ship wasn't carrying any patients, although seven crewmen were killed. She had been struck on the starboard side and she settled by the head with a list. The 114 crew and 64 medical staff all abandoned ship in 13 lifeboats. The crew later returned to the ship and with assistance from tugs managed to make it to Alexandria where she was repaired and back in service once again by 1944. Schlippenbach returned to Pola on 21 April.

In the next few months Schlippenbach made five more war patrols, all without success. On 13 October, there was an accident during a weapons practice and one crewman was killed and another three were wounded. During his ninth patrol he sank the Belgian SS *Jean Jadot* on 20 January 1943, about 30 miles west of Cape Ténès with the loss of fifteen of her crew. On 1 April, he took *U-453* out on another patrol in the Western Mediterranean, and during the evening of the 20th, attacked Convoy UGS7. He reported sinking a large freighter and damaging two other ships near Algiers, but there is no confirmation for these claims. On the 23rd *U-453* was sighted by a Hudson aircraft of 500 Squadron. As the aircraft approached, it was seriously damaged by anti-aircraft fire from the U-boat and the pilot was fatally wounded. No depth charges had been dropped and *U-453* escaped without a scratch. The navigator had managed to take the controls and fly the aircraft back to his base, but it was too badly damaged and the crew were seen to bail out and the aircraft crash into the sea. Schlippenbach returned to base on 5 May.

During another patrol once again in the Eastern Mediterranean, Schlippenbach torpedoed and damaged the British fleet oiler the SS *Oligarch* on 30 June, about 40 miles north-west of Derna, Libya. On 6 July he attacked a troop convoy carrying men and supplies for the invasion of Sicily. He sank the British SS *Shahjehan*, with the loss of only one person. During his next patrol he was operating just off the coast of Sicily where he attacked a battleship escorted by six destroyers, but failed to sink anything. On 2 November he left for a mining operation off Bari. The destroyer HMS *Quail* struck one of his mines on the 15th and was seriously damaged. She was later abandoned, and in April 1944 was towed to Taranto and then onto Malta but she sank on the way, being declared a total loss. On the 20th the Yugoslavian sailing ship *Jela* struck a mine and sank and then two days later the minesweeper HMS *Hebe* struck another of Schlippenbach's mines and sank with the loss of thirty-eight crew. His time with *U-453* ended on 1 December after an unsuccessful mining operation. On 13 January 1944, Schlippenberg took a staff position in the Naval High Command. In July he transferred to the Naval College in Schleswig where he served as deputy commander of a battalion. From 26 March 1945, until the end of the war he served on the staff of the 1st Naval Infantry Division as adjutant, under

---

3 HMHS *Somersetshire* participated in the withdrawal from Narvik in April 1940 and on 6 December. She was bombarded from shore as her launches brought wounded from Tobruk. In February 1941, she joined her sister-ship HMHS *Dorsetshire* in evacuating the wounded from the besieged Tobruk before operating from the Red Sea to South Africa, Australia and New Zealand repatriating wounded soldiers. From 1944 to 1946, the *Somersetshire* sailed all over the world as a hospital ship and finishing up in the Pacific. She was decommissioned in February 1948, and rebuilt later as a passenger liner, with accommodation of 550 passengers. She was broken up in March 1954.

the command of *Konteradmiral* Wilhelm Bleckwenn. Schlippenberg was promoted to *Korvettenkapitän* on 20 April.

He was briefly interned by the Allies at the end of the war and was released in August. In January 1956, Schlippenberg joined the *Bundesmarine*, and in February 1957 attended various training courses at the Royal Naval College at Greenwich and later at Woolwich. He was promoted to *Fregattenkapitän* in May 1957 and served in many different staff positions for the next fifteen years. Promoted to *Kapitän zur See* in August 1953, he retired in September 1972. He settled in Kiel where he died on 11 May 1979.

Other awards:
08 Apr 1938: Long Service Awards 4th Class
25 Feb 1941: Iron Cross 2nd Class
25 Feb 1942: U-Boat War Badge
06 Aug 1942: Iron Cross 1st Class

Karl Heinrich Richard Hermann <u>Herbert</u> SCHNEIDER
Kapitänleutnant
7 ships sunk, 45,826 tons
2 ships damaged, 12,479 tons

Knight's Cross: Awarded on 16 January 1943, as *Kapitänleutnant* and as commander of *U-522*, for the sinking of six ships for a total of shipping tons and for damaging another two ships.

(Scherzer)

Herbert Schneider was born on 25 June 1915, in Nuremberg and joined the *Reichsmarine* as a Cadet in April 1934. He was initially assigned to the II. *Schiffsstammabteilung* in the Baltic, and was attached to the 4th Company where he underwent his basic training. He was then assigned to the sail training ship *Gorch Fock*, and from June he served aboard the light cruiser *Emden*. From June 1935 he attended various training courses, Schneider was commissioned as a *Leutnant zur See* in July 1937 and from October he served as an observer with the coastal artillery during the Spanish Civil War.

From August 1940, Schneider served as a pilot with 2nd Squadron of Observer Group 406, part of Naval Coastal Command. In October he transferred to the U-boat service and was assigned to the 1st U-boat Training Division in Pillau. After attending further training courses he was appointed

First Watch Officer aboard *U-123*, under the command of future Knight's Cross holder *Kapitänleutnant* Reinhard Hardegen. From December Schneider underwent commander training and in April 1942 was promoted to *Kapitänleutnant*. On 11 June he was appointed commander of *U-522*, a Type IXC boat built by Deutsche Werft in Hamburg. He left for his first war patrol on 8 October and headed for Canadian waters, and was ordered to an area off Newfoundland and together with *U-520* and *U-521* waited for eastbound convoys. However, with the weather deteriorating the boats were ordered south towards Halifax. On the 30th *U-522* sighted Convoy SC107 east-north-east of Cape Race and the three boats closed in. *U-520* was sunk and *U-521* was driven off by aircraft. Schneider made an unsuccessful attack in the early evening on one of the escorts, the destroyer HMS *Columbia*. The following day *U-522* was driven off. On the morning of 2 November, whilst still shadowing Convoy SC107, Schneider fired four single torpedoes at the convoy about 450 miles east of Belle Isle, where he hit an ammunition ship and a large oil tanker and reported that both ships were sinking. In fact he had hit four ships. He had struck the British SS *Hartingdon* which only sank after Schneider fired a second torpedo. He also sank three Greek ships, the SS *Maritima*, SS *Mount Pelion* and the SS *Partheon*, south-east of Cape Farewell. Schneider then joined *Kreuzotler* Group, formed on 9 November east-south-east of Cape Farewell by boats with limited fuel. On the 15th, the westbound Convoy ONS144 passed through the *Kreuzotler* patrol line. Over the next five days, despite the fog, five ships and a corvette were sunk. On the morning of the 18th, Schneider sunk the US SS *Yaka*. She was struck on the starboard side between No. 2 hold and the bridge.

Kapitänleutnant *Herbert Schneider is welcomed home by Admiral Schmundt and* Reichsstatthalter *(Reich Governor) of Bavaria General Franz Ritter von Epp.* (Author's collection)

The explosion destroyed a lifeboat, caused the foremast and jumbo boom to fall onto the bridge and blew debris through the hull on the port side. At 08:05 hours, some two hours after the first torpedo had struck a spread of four torpedoes was fired at a group of steamers. There were two explosions and Schneider claimed the sinking of two freighters. However, these claims were never confirmed and it's thought that his torpedoes struck the abandoned wreck of the SS *Yaka*. The operation ended on the 21st. A few boats that still had enough fuel, including *U-522*, formed *Drachen* Group on the 24th. They were ordered to search for independents – ships sailing on their own, not attached to a convoy. Several ships were sighted and two were sunk by *U-262* and *U-663*. *Drachen* Group was dissolved on the 26th. Schneider began his return journey to Lorient. He arrived on 2 December.

On New Year's Eve 1942, Schneider left for operations in the Central Atlantic. On 7 January 1943, *U-522* and other boats were ordered to join *Delphin* Group in an attack on tanker Convoy TM1, which had been seen heading for Gibraltar. On the morning of the 9th Schneider closed in on the convoy and torpedoed two tankers, the Norwegian MV *Minister Wedel* and the Panamanian MV *Norvik*. They were abandoned by their crews and HMS *Havelock* made an unsuccessful attempt to sink them both. In further attacks during the afternoon of the 10th *U-522* sank both ships west of the Canaries. Just after midnight the same day Schneider torpedoed and damaged the British tanker SS *British Dominion*. She was hit by three torpedoes and abandoned. She was sunk on the 11th by *U-620*. Schneider remained as part of *Delphin* Group, which had reformed on the 16th, south of the Azores after six of its original members had been refuelled. The group moved westwards in search of the convoys and then turned eastwards again on the 18th. Between the 21st and 29th, it waited south-west of the Azores but nothing appeared so the group moved further eastwards. From the 31st the patrol line was north-west of the Canaries, but moved to a new position west of Gibraltar for 6 February. The next day the five southern boats of *Delphin* went to attack Convoy Gib No. 2. *U-522* together with the other boats from the group moved northwards and took up positions west of Portugal from the 11th. On the 12th, the *Delphin* boat were ordered to close in on Convoy KMS9, but the operation failed when the convoy's air escort forced the boats to remain submerged. The situation got worse the nearer the convoy got to Gibraltar and attacks became impossible and *U-442* and *U-620* were both sunk. On the 22nd, *U-522*, now patrolling alone, reported the south-west bound Convoy UC1 west-north-west of Madeira, and *Rochen* Group and two boats from *Robbe* Group moved in. On the morning of the 23rd, Schneider torpedoed and sank the British tanker MV *Athelprincess*. She was struck by two torpedoes and sank with the loss of just one crew member. On the 24th, *U-522* was located and attacked. Schneider ordered the boat to crash-dive to try and escape, but the sloop HMS *Totland* made a depth-charge attack and *U-522* was sunk. There were no survivors.

Other awards:
01 Oct 1937: Observers' Badge
08 Apr 1938: Long Service Award 4th Class
11 Jun 1940: Iron Cross 2nd Class
04 Dec 1942: Iron Cross 1st Class

Georg Heinrich 'Hein' SCHONDER
Korvettenkapitän
15 ships sunk, 29,368 tons
2 ships damaged, 1,845 tons

Knight's Cross: Awarded on 19 August 1942, as *Kapitänleutnant* and as commander of *U-77* for sinking fifteen ships for a total of 29,368 shipping tons and for damaging two others.

Heinrich Schonder was born on 23 July 1910 in Erfurt, Germany and entered the *Kriegsmarine* as an Officer Candidate in April 1935. He spent the next few months in basic training before being assigned to the torpedo boat *Falke* as Third Watch Officer. He was commissioned as a *Leutnant zur See* in April 1937 and in January 1938 Schonder transferred to the U-boat service. He attended the usual training courses at the Naval Academy in (Scherzer)

Flensburg and later at the Naval College in Neustadt, before being assigned as Watch Officer aboard *U-51* in August. He continued with his training aboard *U-51* and later aboard *U-53* and was promoted in April 1939 to *Oberleutnant zur See*. On 7 January 1940, he was transferred to *U-9* as First Watch Officer and as commander in waiting, under the command of *Oberleutnant zur See* Wolfgang Lüth, a future holder of the Knight's Cross with Oakleaves, Swords and Diamonds. He took part in four war patrols during which time *U-9* sank three ships, Schonder was learning from the best.

On 10 June 1940, Schonder took command of his own U-boat, *U-58*, a Type IIC boat built in Kiel. He left Bergen to begin his first war patrol on 6 July, heading for the North Channel. On the 15th, he claimed a hit on the MV *Scottish Minstrel* in the Butt of Lewis area but this was never confirmed. On the 18th he sank the Norwegian SS *Gyda*. She was struck by a single torpedo north-west of Ireland. The torpedo hit close to the bridge on the starboard side, opening up the side, destroying the radio room and blowing away half of the bridge. She sank in about a minute with the loss of eleven crew members. Schonder put in at Lorient for replenishment on 22 July. Seven days later *U-58* returned to the area west of Scotland. En route he sank the Greek SS *Pindos*, part of Convoy HX60, on 4 August. The survivors, twenty-nine of them, abandoned ship in the lifeboats and made landfall with the help of local fishermen. Schonder returned to port on the 12th. On 2 October he left Lorient and went north, passing west of Ireland. He hoped to have more success. On the 9th he sank a straggler the British SS *Confield* west of Barra. He put in at Bergen on the 12th.

On 18 January 1941, Schonder was transferred and became commander of *U-77*, a Type VIIC boat built by Bremer Vulkan. He left Kiel on his first patrol and headed for the North Atlantic on 29 May, to operate in area south-east of Newfoundland. On 13 June he sank the British SS *Tresillian*. She was struck by a single torpedo amidships, south-east of Cape Race. The ship had been spotted three hours before and was struck by a dud torpedo which alerted her crew. They prepared the lifeboats and sent out an emergency distress call, so Schonder gave the order to open fire on the ship with the deck gun. He then fired another torpedo which caused the ship to break in two and sink. Miraculously the entire crew were saved. From mid-June *U-77* was part of *West* Group in search of convoys. Late on the 22nd, Schonder sank the British SS *Arakaka*, about 450 miles east of St. Johns, Newfoundland. She sank in less than a minute with the loss of her entire crew. On the 25th he sank the Greek SS *Anna Bulgaris*, south-south-east of Cape Farewell. Over the next few days he had no further success and headed for St. Nazaire, arriving on 7 July.

On 2 August Schonder left for operations in the North Atlantic, and two days later, together with *U-43*, *U-71*, *U-96* and *U-751*, was directed to a convoy sighted by *U-565* but they had no success. Towards the end of August the boats moved further east. On 1 September, *U-77* and six other boats formed *Kurfürst* Group west of the North Channel when Schonder was informed he had been promoted to *Kapitänleutnant*. Then together with *Bosemüller* Group the boats searched for convoys but again without success. On the 3rd the operation was called off and Schonder returned to base. His next patrol was a similar story: he linked up with other boats to form a patrol line in the North Atlantic but failed to make contact with any convoys. Disappointed he put in at Lorient on 13 November. On 10 December, *U-77* left once again for the North Atlantic, but by the following day he had been ordered to head to the Mediterranean. On the 15th, he sank the British SS *Empire Barracuda* of Convoy HG76, west of Asilah, Morocco. He put in to Messina on 19th. Two days later he left for the Eastern Mediterranean to operate off the coasts of Egypt and Cyrenaica. On 12 January 1942, he torpedoed and damaged the British destroyer HMS *Kimberley*. He fired a *coup de grâce* torpedo but this missed. The destroyer was later towed to Alexandria by HMS *Heythrop* and was repaired. Schonder then headed towards Salamis, arriving on the 14th. On 11 April, after another unsuccessful patrol, Schonder took *U-77* to La Spezia. On 6 June he left to operate against supply shipping along the coast of Cyrenaica. On the 12th, he sank the British destroyer escort HMS *Grove*. She was struck by two torpedoes off Sollum. Two officers and one-hundred and eight ratings were lost. There were sixty survivors.

On 16 July, Schonder left on another patrol, his eighth, and headed for further operations in the Eastern Mediterranean, between Cyprus and Lebanon. During this patrol he sank seven ships and damaged one other. On the 22nd he sank the Greek sailing ship *Vassiliki* and on the 24th a Syrian sailing ship, the *Toufic El Rahmen*, both by gunfire. On the 30th he sank the *Fany*, an Egyptian sailing ship, by torpedo and the following day he sank another Egyptian sailing vessel, the *St. Simon*, this time by gunfire. On 6 August he sank another ship, the *Ezzet*, and damaged the *Adnan*. Four days later he sank the Palestinian sailing ship *Kharouf* about 20 miles west-north-west of Sidon. His final victim of this patrol was another Palestinian ship, the *Daniel*, sunk with sixteen rounds from the deck gun about 55 miles west of Beirut. Schonder had sunk seven ships and damaged an eighth in twenty-six days. He put in at Salamis to be informed that he had been awarded the Knight's Cross.

On 22 December, Schonder became commander of *U-200*, a Type IXD2 boat built by AG Weser of Bremen. He left Kiel on 12 June 1943, on what would be his last war patrol. He left port in the company of *U-194* and *U-420* and the three boats headed for the Indian Ocean, to reinforce *Monsun* Group, which were operating in the Arabian Sea. *U-200* was carrying a detachment of coastal troops of the crack Brandenburg Division.[4] On the 24th *U-200* was sighted and attacked with depth charges by a Liberator of 120 Squadron and was sunk about 800 miles south-south-west of Reykjavik. There were no survivors and sixty-two men were lost. Schonder was posthumously promoted to the rank of *Fregattenkapitän*.

Other awards:
05 Apr 1939: Long Service Award 4th Class
01 Oct 1939: Iron Cross 2nd Class
01 Dec 1939: U-Boat War Badge
23 Jul 1940: Iron Cross 1st Class
25 Mar 1942: Italian Bravery Medal in Bronze

<u>Dietrich</u> Adalbert SCHÖNEBOOM
Oberleutnant zur See
4 ships sunk, 265 tons

Knight's Cross: Awarded on 20 October 1943 aa *Oberleutnant zur See* and as commander of *U-431* in recognition of his leadership and for sinking four ships for a total of 265 shipping tons.[5]

Dietrich Schöneboom was born in Amdorf a district in the south-west of East Frisia on 4 December 1917. He joined the *Kriegsmarine* as a young Cadet in April 1937, and was initially attached to the 2nd Company of the II. *Schiffsstammabteilung* in the Baltic. In June he was assigned to the battleship *Schlesien* where he continued with his training and also attended various courses at the Naval Academy in Flensburg. From April 1939 he served aboard the escort ships *F10* and *F6* in the North Sea, and was commissioned as a *Leutnant zur See* in August. From July 1940 he served aboard the minesweeper *R152* as part   (Scherzer)

---

4 The Brandenburg Division was an elite German special forces during the Second World War. Originally formed by and operated as an extension of the military's intelligence organ, the *Abwehr*. Members of this unit took part in seizing operationally important targets by way of sabotage and infiltration. The division was generally subordinated to the army groups in individual commands and operated throughout Eastern Europe, in southern Africa, Afghanistan, the Middle East and in the Caucasus. In the later course of the war, parts of the special unit were used in the fight against partisans in Yugoslavia before the division during the last months of the war was reclassified and merged into one of the Panzer Grenadier divisions.

5 Schöneboom claimed sinking three freighters for 26,000 tons, and probably the sinking of another of 10,000 tons and damaging another two for 12,000 tons. Although none of these claims can be confirmed he nonetheless was awarded the Knight's Cross by the *Kriegsmarine* High Command. His claims were all proved to be false after British documents were found after the war.

of the 11th Minesweeper Flotilla and took part in security duties around the Dutch and Belgian coastal waters. From April 1941, his ship was transferred to Northern Norway where she carried out similar duties. On 1 September Schöneboom was promoted to *Oberleutnant zur See* and by the end of the month he had been reassigned to the U-boat service.

On 29 September, Schöneboom began his training with the 1st U-boat Training Division in Pillau. In April 1942, he was assigned to *U-205* as First Watch Officer, under the command of *Kapitänleutnant* Franz-Georg Reschke. From July until August 1942, he attended the U-boat commander school, before taking up his own command. *U-58* was a training boat, a Type IIC used to train new crews and officers alike. In December Schöneboom took command of an operational boat, *U-431*, a Type VIIC built by the Schichau Company in Danzig. He left on his first war patrol as commander on 7 January 1943, heading for the Eastern Mediterranean. On the 23rd he sank the Egyptian sailing ship *Alexandria* by gunfire. After firing ten rounds of 88mm and forty-eight rounds of 20mm, Schöneboom ordered the guns to stop. The *Alexandria*, which was by then a burning wreck, quickly sank. On the 25th he sank a Syrian sailing ship, the *Mouyassar*, and later the same day he sank another, the *Omar el Kattab*. She was rammed by the U-boat and sank about 13 miles south of Cape Apostolos Andreas, Cyprus. The next day he sank the *Hassan*, which Schöneboom ordered rammed but this failed and so she was sunk by gunfire. *U-431* returned to port on 8 February.

On 11 March, Schöneboom left for his second patrol to operate against convoys off the Algerian coast. He was unsuccessful, but claimed he had sunk three ships. One was the SS *City of Perth*, or so he claimed, but later research showed that she had in fact been sunk by *U-77*; the other claims made by Schöneboom have never been confirmed by Allied sources. From May to September, *U-431* sailed on two more patrols but both were unsuccessful. On 22 August Schöneboom had attacked but missed two cruisers, HMS *Aurora* and *Penelope*, about 65 miles north-north-east of Palermo. On 26 September, Schöneboom took *U-431* out of Toulon to operate off the Italian coast, together with other boats deployed against Allied shipping in the Salerno bridgehead. In mid-October he took *U-431* into the Western Mediterranean where on 19th he claimed to have sunk two ships, but again these have never been confirmed. On the night of the 23rd *U-431* was attacked and sunk by a Leigh Light Wellington bomber of 179 Squadron, south-east of Cartagena. There were no survivors – fifty-two men were lost.

Other awards:
00 Jul 1940: Iron Cross 2nd Class
00 Sep 1940: Minesweepers Badge
01 Aug 1941: Iron Cross 1st Class
12 Feb 1943: U-Boat War Badge
10 Aug 1943: Italian Bravery Medal in Bronze

Heinrich Andreas SCHROETELER
Kapitänleutnant
1 ship sunk, 335 tons
1 ship damaged, 7,345 tons

Knight's Cross: Awarded on 2 May 1945, as *Kapitänleutnant* and as commander of *U-1023* for damaging one ship, although he claimed he had damaged another four. He was a convinced National Socialist and favourite of Dönitz, which may be the reason why he was decorated for just damaging the one vessel.

Heinrich Schroeteler was born on 10 December 1915 in Essen-Katernberg, one of eleven children and followed in his family's tradition of naval service when he joined the *Kriegsmarine* in April 1936. During his basic training he saw service aboard the battleship *Schlesien* from June and attended courses from April 1937. Schroeteler was commissioned as a *Leutnant zur See* in October 1938, and was appointed Watch Officer of a minesweeper on 3 September 1939 – eventually he took over as commander, being promoted to *Oberleutnant zur See* in October 1940. His ship performed security tasks in the North Sea, on the Dutch coast and in northern France, initially as part of 14th Minesweeper Flotilla, and from 1 September 1941,

(Scherzer)

as part of the 22nd Flotilla, performing security operations, minesweeping patrols and escort duty in the North and Baltic Seas.

At the end of September 1941, Schroeteler transferred to the U-boat service and he spent the next twelve months training. On 21 October 1942, he was appointed commander of *U-667*, a Type VIIC boat built by Howaldtswerke in Hamburg. He left Kiel for the North Atlantic on 20 May 1943, but on the 24th Dönitz suspended U-boat operations against North Atlantic convoys until the high command could assess the situation. All boats with sufficient fuel were ordered to the area west of Gibraltar. To give the Allies the impression that a strong U-boat presence was still being maintained across the convoy routes, a number of boats with limited fuel were assigned to radio-deception, to move about transmitting messages. Schroeteler was ordered to join these boats. The scheme was abandoned in early July. Schroeteler headed for his new base at St. Nazaire, arriving on 26 July.

For his next patrol Schroeteler took *U-667* out on 14 September and headed towards the Mediterranean. On the 24th the boat was attacked and damaged just west of Gibraltar by two Leigh Light Wellingtons of 179 Squadron. *U-667* managed to escape damage but was attacked again, this time by two Hudson aircraft and another Wellington bomber. Schroeteler escaped again with only minor damage, and was able to pass through the Straits of Gibraltar and returned to his base on 11 October. On 18 November he took *U-667* out on operations in the Atlantic. In early December *U-667* was one of a number of boats which had assembled west of the North Channel as *Coronel* Group and began searching for convoys but without success. From mid-December *Coronel* Group was enlarged and split into two sub-groups but again with no success, they couldn't find the convoys. From the 20th, the *Coronel* Sub-group 3 boats joined with new arrivals to form a new patrol line, *U-667* joined this group to try and intercept Convoys MKS33 and SL142 but again they failed to make contact. On the 22nd and 23rd an escorted carrier was sighted by German aircraft and attacks were made. The destroyer USS

Leary was one of the ships sunk, but not by *U-667*. In the evening of the 24th some boats of *Borkum* Group encountered Convoys OS62 and KMS36 and during the attacks *U-415* sunk HMS *Hurricane*, the only success. The group continued to operate until late December then broke up and some boats, including *U-667*, returned to St. Nazaire on 6 January 1944. On 8 March, Schroeteler began his next patrol. He briefly joined *Preussen* Group in the Atlantic before the group was broken up on 22nd, and the boats then could operate independently near the British Isles. On 16 April, Schroeteler made an unsuccessful attack on a destroyer north of the Azores. During this time *U-667* had been equipped with a *Schnorkel* and on his return to St. Nazaire on 19 May, Schroeteler reported that he had run submerged for nine days and spoke most enthusiastically about the device.

In July Schroeteler was transferred as a Staff Officer in the Operational Department of the U-boat Tactical Command Section, replacing *Kapitänleutnant* Adalbert Schnee. From January 1945, Schroeteler was appointed commander of *U-1023*, a Type VIIC-41 boat built by Blohm und Voss. From mid-March he operated in the Irish Sea and made an unsuccessful attack on a convoy just south of Ireland. On 23 April he attacked and damaged the British SS *Riverton* in the Bristol Channel. She was later towed to Swansea where she was repaired and returned to service. When the U-boat war ended on 4 May, *U-1023*, in accordance with instructions, headed for Weymouth. En route, Schroeteler torpedoed and sank the Norwegian fleet minesweeper HNoMS *Nyms-382* on the evening of the 7th, east-south-east of Torbay. Schroeteler put in at Weymouth and surrendered on 10 May. *U-1023* was one of 116 boats disposed of by the Royal Navy during Operation Deadlight. In January 1946, *U-1023* was towed from Lisahally but foundered under tow on the 9th north-west of Malin Head and sunk.

Schroeteler spent the next three years as a prisoner of the British and was released in May 1948, returning to Germany. During the post war years Schroeteler pursued a career in art history and archaeology. In 1965 he began to study art history, archaeology and medieval history at the Ruhr University Bochum. He graduated in 1969 and worked as a research associate at the Institute of Archaeology. His success as a renovator of ancient works of art was honoured with the University Medal from the Ruhr University in 1981. Later he was awarded an honorary doctorate. He remained a National Socialist his entire life and had from the late 1930s been a member of the Nazi Party. On 6 January 1981, Schroeteler attended the funeral of *Großadmiral* Karl Dönitz in Aumühle. There he was one of the six pallbearers who carried Dönitz to his grave: all were wearing their wartime Knight's Cross. Schroeteler allowed himself to be photographed in uniform, wearing his Knight's Cross, and would send signed postcards for anyone who asked. He died in Bochum on 19 January 2000.

Other awards:
24 Oct 1940: Iron Cross 2nd Class
14 Nov 1940: Minesweepers Badge
14 Apr 1941: Iron Cross 1st Class
06 Jul 1942: U-Boat War Badge
07 Oct 1944: U-Boat Combat Clasp in Bronze
10 Nov 1944: German Cross in Gold

Gottfried Ludwig <u>Horst</u> von SCHROETER
Kapitänleutnant
7 ships sunk, 32,240 tons
1 ship damaged, 7,068 tons

Knight's Cross: Awarded on 1 June 1944, as *Oberleutnant zur See* and as Commander of *U-123* for sinking seven ships for a total of 32,240 shipping tons and for damaging one other ship.

Horst von Schroeter was born on 10 June 1919 in Bieberstein, Meissen, north-west of Dresden. He joined the *Kriegsmarine* in October 1937, and was initially assigned to the 3rd Company of II. *Schiffsstammabteilung* in the Baltic where he began his basic training. Von Schroeter served aboard the sail training ship *Albert Leo Schlageter* and the light cruiser *Emden* between February 1938 a September 1939, as part of his training. He then spent five months aboard the battleship *Scharnhorst*, taking part in two patrols during the first months of the war. He took part in her first operation on 21 November 1939, patrolling with her sister-ship *Gneisenau*, the light cruiser *Köln*, and nine destroyers in the area between Iceland and the Faroe Islands. They were there to draw out British units and ease the pressure on the 'pocket battleship' *Admiral Graf Spee*, which was being pursued in the South Atlantic. Von Schroeter also took part in the early stages of the German invasion of Denmark and Norway. Both *Scharnhorst* and *Gneisenau* were the covering force for the assaults on Narvik and Trondheim, being joined later by the heavy cruiser *Admiral Hipper*. The ships came under constant attack by the British but managed to escape any

(Author's collection)

damage. On 9 April, *Scharnhorst* and *Gneisenau* both came under attack from the British battlecruiser HMS *Renown*, and the battleship *Gneisenau* was hit twice and *Scharnhorst*'s radar was put out of action. Both ships escaped and by the 12th *Scharnhorst* was in Kiel being repaired. Von Schroeter was thankful he was back safe: he had experienced so much and the war was only seven months old. Commissioned as a *Leutnant zur See* in May, he attended torpedo school from June, and the following month he was assigned to the 1st U-boat Training Division, where he served for a time as adjutant.

From April 1941 he was posted to *U-123* where he served as Second Watch Officer and later as First Watch Officer, whilst under the command of *Kapitänleutnant* Reinhard Hardegen. Von Schroeter took part in four patrols and was promoted to *Oberleutnant zur See* in April 1942. On 1 August he succeeded Hardegen as commander of *U-123*, and before he left on his first patrol as commander he had to oversee her repairs and refitting. Finally on 5 December, with all repairs completed von Schroeter took *U-123* out of Kiel for operations in the Atlantic. He joined *Spitz* Group, formed from the 23rd, in the central North Atlantic, west of Ireland. The group began to move southwards and during the afternoon of the 26th they sighted a convoy. *Spitz* and *Ungerstüm* Groups were ordered to close in. Four ships were sunk on the 27th, and more on the night of the 28th/29th. By the end of the operation fourteen ships had been sunk. Von Schroeter had sunk the British SS *Baron Cochrane* and damaged the SS *Empire Shackelton*. By January 1943, he had been ordered to join *Jaguar* Group north-east of Newfoundland. He reached the operational area in late January but bad weather prevented any ships being sunk. Von Schroeter headed for home, arriving at Lorient on 6 February.

On 13 March, *U-123* left for operations in the Central Atlantic where it joined *Seeräuber* Group south of the Canaries. A patrol line was formed and on the 28th, three ships were sunk, none by *U-123*. At the beginning of April the group was dispersed and von Schroeter took *U-123* south to the Freetown–Liberia area. On the 8th he sank the Spanish SS *Castillo Montealegre*. She capsized after being struck by two torpedoes. Von Schroeter questioned the survivors and soon realized he had sunk a neutral Spanish ship, having failed to recognize her when he attacked. Of her crew of forty-one, twelve were killed. They had abandoned ship in a lifeboat but were never seen again. On the 18th, he sank the British submarine HMS *P-615* with the loss of all her crew. The same day he sank the British SS *Empire Bruce*. She was struck by one torpedo about 100 miles south-west of Freetown. She capsized and sank after being hit by two more torpedoes. All of her crew managed to scramble into the lifeboats and survived. Von Schroeter then operated in the area south of Monrovia where on 29th he sank the Swedish MV *Nanking*. She was unescorted and was struck by two torpedoes, the crew immediately abandoned ship in the lifeboats. *U-123* fired a *coup de grâce* torpedo and within a few minutes the ship sank. On 5 May von Schroeter sank the British SS *Holmbury* by gunfire, about 170 miles west of Cape Palmas. He sank another ship on the 9th, a straggler from Convoy TS38, the British SS *Kanbe*. She was hit by two torpedoes and sank approximately 60 miles south-south-west of Monrovia. Von Schroeter returned to base on 8 June. He took *U-123* out on three more patrols between August 1943 and April 1944, but had no success. On 7 November during the journey back to base *U-123* was attacked by a Mosquito of 248 Squadron, near the Bay of Biscay. The boat was only slightly damaged but one crew member was killed. On 17 June 1944, *U-123* was decommissioned at Lorient, later being refitted and re-commissioned after the war by the French Navy.

In June von Schroeter was appointed commander of *U-2506*, a Type XXI Elektro boat, which he took out of Bergen, Norway during the last days of the war, but she never saw action. He had been promoted to *Kapitänleutnant* on 21 December 1944, and he surrendered his boat to the British at Bergen on 9 May 1945. She was later taken to an assembly point and was disposed of together with 116 U-boats in January 1946. Von Schroeter was taken prisoner by British forces and was released in June 1947 and returned to Germany. In July 1956 he joined the *Bundesmarine*. From November 1958 until April 1963 he commanded a destroyer and then a torpedo boat. In April 1970 he was promoted to *Flotillenadmiral* and from October 1971 he held the rank of *Konteradmiral*. From October 1976 until his retirement, von Schroeter was commander of NATO naval forces in the Baltic Sea Approaches with the rank of *Vizeadmiral* (the highest rank of any former U-boat commander of the Second World War). He retired in September 1979 and settled in Bonn where he died at the age of eighty-seven on 25 July 2006.

Other awards:
25 Aug 1941: Iron Cross 2nd Class
10 Feb 1942: Iron Cross 1st Class
12 Dec 1943: German Cross in Gold
25 Aug 1941: U-Boat War Badge
01 Oct 1944: U-Boat Combat Clasp in Bronze
15 Mar 1945: U-Boat Combat Clasp in Silver

Otto SCHUHART
Korvettenkapitän
13 ships sunk, 89,777 tons

Knight's Cross: Awarded on 16 May 1940, as *Kapitänleutnant* and as commander of *U-29* for sinking eight ships for a total of 56,916 shipping tons, in just three patrols. He was also credited with the sinking of the aircraft carrier HMS *Courageous*, the first British warship to be sunk during the Second World War, and was the fifth U-boat commander to be awarded with this award.

Otto Schuhart was born in Hamburg on 1 April 1909 and began his naval career with the *Reichsmarine* in April 1927. He underwent basic training in the II. *Schiffsstammdivision* at Stralsund in the Baltic, before he transferred to the sail training ship *Niobe*. From January 1930, he saw service aboard the light cruisers *Emden* and *Karlsruhe*. At the time *Emden* was under the command of Lothar von Arnauld de la Perière, a U-boat commander of the First World War. Schuhart was aboard her third

(Scherzer)

training cruise and sailed to Madeira, as well as Saint Thomas, New Orleans, Kingston in Jamaica, San Juan in Puerto Rico, Charleston and back to Germany. From May 1930 he served on the *Karlsruhe* and went through the Suez Canal via the Mediterranean Sea and continued down to the African coast, around the Cape of Good Hope to the Angra Pequena and the Walvis Bay. He arrived back in Kiel on 12 December.

Schuhart underwent further training and was commissioned as a *Leutnant zur See* in October 1933. After service as a company commander in the 3rd Artillery Battalion, where in June 1935 he was promoted to *Oberleutnant zur See*, Schuhart joined the U-boat Flotilla *Weddingen* as an aide-de-camp in October 1936. He attended a torpedo course at Flensburg-Mürwick from 5 October 1937 before being appointed company officer with the U-boat Flotilla Emsmann and Hundius until January 1938. In July he was appointed Watch Officer aboard *U-25*, based in Wilhelmshaven. He was promoted to *Kapitänleutnant* in August and took command of *U-25* on 10 December. It was a brief command and from April 1939 he was commander of *U-29*, a Type VIIA boat built in Bremen by AG Weser. His first patrol was on 19 August 1939, leaving Wilhelmshaven for the Atlantic, to operate west of the British Isles and in the English Channel. While on patrol he was notified that Great Britain had declared war on Germany and the Second World War had started. On 8 September he torpedoed and sank the British tanker MV *Regent Tiger* about 250 miles west-south-west of Cape Clear. He continued to patrol in the area and the 13th and sank the steam tug *Neptunia* by gunfire. After her crew had abandoned ship and headed for the lifeboats, Schuhart gave them cigarettes, matches and brandy before *U-29* left. The following day he sank another British tanker, the MV *British Influence*. She was carrying 12,000 tons of diesel. Schuhart ordered the crew to abandon ship when he was told what she was carrying and when her crew were safely in the lifeboats he sank the ship with a torpedo and she burst into flames. He then led a Norwegian ship the SS *Ida Bakko* to their lifeboats and wished them well. Then in possibly a unique incident the British and German crews gave each other three cheers just prior to the boats' departure. An unusual incident in wartime, but perhaps like so many the two crews hoped the war would be over soon.

On the evening of 17 September Schuhart sank the British aircraft carrier HMS *Courageous*, one of the largest ships sunk in the war, weighing 22,500 tons. She was also the first British warship to be lost during the war. *Courageous* was part of the Home Fleet and on board she had 811 and 822 Squadrons, each equipped with a dozen Fairey Swordfish aircraft. On 31 August 1939, she went on alert and left Plymouth on the evening of 3 September for an anti-submarine patrol in the Western Approaches, escorted by four destroyers. On the evening of the 17th she was on patrol off the coast of Ireland. Two of her escorts had been sent to help a merchant ship under attack. During this time Schuhart had been stalking her, ready to attack. The carrier then turned into the wind to launch her aircraft: she was now right across the bow of *U-29*. Schuhart took his chance and fired a spread of three torpedoes. Two of them struck the aircraft carrier on her port side before any aircraft took off, knocking out all electrical power. She capsized and sank in under twenty minutes, with the loss of 519 members of crew, including her Captain W.T. Makeig-Jones. The German commander of U-boats *Kommodore* Dönitz regarded the sinking of the *Courageous* as 'a wonderful success', and the Commander-in-Chief of the *Kriegsmarine*, *Großadmiral* Raeder awarded Schuhart the Iron Cross 1st Class and the rest of his crew were awarded the Iron Cross 2nd Class. When *U-29* reached Wilhelmshaven on 26 September, Adolf Hitler was there to congratulate and decorate Schuhart and his crew.

The aircraft carrier HMS Courageous *was one of the largest warships sunk by a U-boat during the Second World War. She was struck by two torpedoes fired from* U-29 *on 17 September 1939, about 350 miles west of Land's End. She sank in seventeen minutes about 190 miles south-west of Ireland. All of her Swordfish aircraft were lost, together with 518 of her crew.* (Author's collection)

On 14 November, *U-29* left Wilhelmshaven for a minelaying operation near Milford Haven but this was abandoned due to bad weather. Schuhart took *U-29* to Heligoland on 6 February 1940, and from there on the 11th left for another minelaying operation in the British Channel. He laid eight mines and on 3 March the British SS *Cato* struck one of these mines and sank. During the early hours of the following day Schuhart torpedoed and sank the British SS *Thurston*. She sank within sixty seconds with the loss of all but four of her crew. Later the same day he sank the SS *Pacific Reliance* west of Newquay, when he fired a torpedo at the SS *San Florentino* that missed and struck the *Pacific Reliance*. On 16 March the Yugoslavian SS *Slava* struck one of Schuhart's mines and sank. He then returned to Wilhelmshaven on 12 March. For the next few weeks *U-29* was on transport duties, carrying small arms and anti-aircraft ammunition. On 27 May, Schuhart left to patrol the western entrance of the English Channel, with *U-101*. They were later ordered to join the *Rösing* Group, made up of five boats under the tactical command of *Korvettenkapitän* Hans Rösing. On 12 June the boats were in an area west of Cape Ortegal waiting for Convoy US3, which included the *Queen Mary* and other large liners carrying 26,000 troops from Australia and New Zealand. However, the convoy failed to appear, and *Rösing* Group was disbanded on the 17th. On the 26th, he sank the Greek SS *Dimitris* by gunfire after her crew abandoned ship. He sank another Greek vessel on 1 July, the SS *Adamastos*, again by gunfire. The crew abandoned ship immediately upon the first two rounds hitting the ship. The crew of *U-129* boarded the ship for fresh provisions and then sank her. On the 2nd, Schuhart sank two more ships, the Panamanian SS *Santa Margarita* and the British tanker MV *Athellaird*, which sank about 350 miles north-west of Cape Finisterre. He returned to base on 11 July.

On 11 September *U-29* left Bergen to operate west of the British Isles and on 25th sank the British MV *Eurymedon*, part of Convoy OB217. She was struck by a single torpedo about 366 miles west of Achill Head. Twenty-nine of her crew were lost. By 1 October *U-129* was back at Lorient for repairs. Schuhart took his boat out again on two more patrols, both were short and one was to act as a weather boat west of Britain. He failed to sink anything. On 2 January 1941, he was transferred, and *U-29* became a training boat. Schuhart was assigned to the 1st U-boat Training Division, and later took command of the 21st U-boat Training Flotilla at Pillau. Promoted to *Korvettenkapitän* in April 1943, he remained at Pillau until September 1944. Schuhart then took command of the 1st Department at the Naval College at Flensburg-Mürwik, where he surrendered to British troops in May 1945. After the capitulation he served as commander of a naval battalion until August and later served in the German mine-clearance service until the end of 1945. He worked in a factory in Satrup in Schleswig-Flensburg from January to July 1946 and underwent training at the Gothaer fire insurance company in Hamburg until July 1947. From August 1947 until September 1948 he worked for a transport company in Hamburg and was head of the Vocational Education Department of the H.C. Stülcken Sohn shipbuilding company from April 1951 to November 1955. In 1956 he rejoined the Navy and served as commander of the Naval College at Flensburg and later as base commander. He ended his career with the rank of *Kapitän zur See* and as base commander in Kiel. He retired in September 1967, and settled in Stuttgart, Baden-Württemberg where he died on 10 March 1990.

Other awards:
02 Oct 1936: Long Service Award 4th Class
26 Sep 1939: Iron Cross 2nd Class
26 Sep 1939: Iron Cross 1st Class
16 Dec 1939: U-Boat War Badge
00.00.1944: U-Boat Combat Clasp in Bronze
30 Jan 1944: War Service Cross 2nd Class with Swords
01 Sep 1944: War Service Cross 1st Class with Swords

Heinz-Otto SCHULTZE
Kapitänleutnant
20 ships sunk, 67,991 tons
2 ships damaged, 15,666 tons

Knight's Cross: Awarded on 9 July 1942, as *Kapitänleutnant* and as commander of *U-432* for sinking eighteen ships for a total of 61,813 shipping tons and for damaging another two ships.

Born in Kiel on 13 September 1915, Heinz-Otto Schultze was the son of Otto Schultze, commander of *U-63* during the First World War and holder of the *Pour le mérite* and later *Generaladmiral* in the *Kriegsmarine*. Schultz entered the *Reichsmarine* in April 1934, and received his basic training whilst attached to the II. *Schiffsstammabteilung* in the Baltic. He was transferred to the sail training ship *Gorch Fock* in June, and served on the light cruiser *Karlsruhe* from September as a Cadet.

Schultze transferred to the U-boat service in November 1937, having been commissioned as a *Leutnant zur See* seven months previously. From March 1938 he served as Second Watch Officer and later First Watch Officer aboard *U-31*. Promoted to *Oberleutnant zur See* in April 1939, he attended U-boat commander training from January 1940. He was appointed commander of *U-4* in June. It was a training boat and so Schultze didn't take her out on any war patrols. On 31 March 1941, Schultze was ordered to the Schichau-Werke shipyard in Danzig for construction familiarization with his new command, *U-432*, a Type VIIC boat. He left Kiel on his first patrol on 25 August, joining other boats in an assembly area south-west of Iceland. From the 28th, they formed *Markgraf* Group and waited for the convoys. Finally on 9 September, after being moved twice, a convoy was sighted by *U-85*. On the 10th Schultze sunk three ships, all from Convoy SC42, first the British SS *Muneric* during the very early hours, with the

(Scherzer)

loss of her entire crew. Five hours later he sank the Dutch SS *Winterzwijk* and the Norwegian SS *Stargard*, both during the same attack. The following day he sank the Swedish SS *Garm*, also from Convoy SC42. A total of sixteen ships were lost from the convoy. Schultze put in at Brest on the 19th.

On 11 October *U-432* headed for the central North Atlantic. Schultze had been ordered to join a new group forming south-east of Cape Farewell. The convoy was sighted by *U-553* on the night of the 14th/15th, and the boats were ordered to close in. Although they kept being driven off by the escorts, the boats persisted in their attacks on the convoy. On the 17th, Schultze sank three ships, first the Panamanian SS *Bold Venture*.[6] She was struck by a single torpedo and the explosion set her cargo of cotton on fire, collapsing the mainmast and breaking off the poop deck which caused the ship to sink by the stern within ten minutes. He also sank the Greek SS *Evros* and the Norwegian tanker MV *Barfonn*. The operation against the convoy ended on the 18th. Nine ships, a destroyer and a corvette had been sunk. Schultze then joined other boats to form *Reissewolf* Group from the 22nd, 450 miles south-east of Greenland. With no convoys passing their line they were directed to Convoy ON28, sighted by *U-74* some 500 miles west of Ireland. Soon after, Schultze left the group and headed for base. However, on the 28th he was directed to Convoy HG75 and made an attack. He sank the British SS *Ulea* and he also claimed another ship sunk but this has never been confirmed. He finally reached

---

6 Latest research shows that it was *U-432* that sank the SS *Bold Venture* and not *U-553* as previously thought.

his base, St. Nazaire on 2 November, hearing the news that he had been promoted to *Kapitänleutnant* the day before.

During his next patrol *U-432* was damaged by a Swordfish of 812 Squadron as it attempted to pass through the Straits of Gibraltar. Schultze returned to base soon afterwards. On 21 January 1942, *U-432* left port for the Western Atlantic, and was one of a number of boats in the third wave of Operation *Paukenschlag*. Outward-bound, *U-432* acted as escort for the German blockade-runner *Doggerbank*. After being refuelled Schultze headed for the Nova Scotia area and south into US waters. In the early morning of 15 February he sank the Brazilian SS *Buarque*, 30 miles south-west of Cape Henry she sank after being struck by three torpedoes. On the 18th he sank another Brazilian ship, the SS *Olinda*. She was stopped by gunfire east of Parramore Island and the crew took to the lifeboats. The captain and radio operator were taken aboard the U-boat and questioned. After they returned to their lifeboat the ship was sunk by gunfire and a torpedo. Early on the 19th, Schultze sank the British SS *Miraflores* about 50 miles east of Atlantic City, New Jersey. Two days later he sank the US SS *Azalea City*. She was struck in heavy seas by a single torpedo amidships and sank quickly: there were no survivors. Schultze then took *U-432* further south where he sank another ship east of Cape Hatteras, the US SS *Marore*, on the 27th. Schultze then decided to return to base, arriving at La Pallice on 16 March.

His next patrol began on 30 April and took *U-432* to an area south of Nova Scotia where on 17 May he sank the US trawler *Foam* by gunfire about 85 miles south of Halifax. The boat then joined seven other boats to form *Pfadfinder* Group and headed south, and by the 21st they were 400 miles east of New York. Early on the 23rd he sank the British SS *Zurichmoor*. She was struck by two torpedoes and sank within ninety seconds with the loss of forty-five men, the entire crew. *Pfadfinder* Group dispersed soon afterwards and Schultze took *U-432* into the Gulf of Maine and later into the Cape Sable area. On the 31st Schultze torpedoed and sank the Canadian SS *Liverpool Packet* south-west of the Cape, and on 3 June he sank two fishing vessels, *Ben & Josephine* and the *Aeolus*, both by gunfire south-west of Yarmouth, Nova Scotia. On the afternoon of the 9th he torpedoed and damaged the Norwegian MV *Kronprinsen* and the British MV *Malayan Prince*. Schultze then made for base, arriving at La Pallice on 2 July. Schultze took *U-432* out of port once again on 15 August, and headed for the North Atlantic as part of *Lohs* Group east of Newfoundland. The operation ended on the 26th, and the group moved west of the Azores. The group then moved to form a patrol line 400 miles north-east of Cape Race, to await the eastbound convoys. A convoy was intercepted but only a single ship was sunk, by *U-596*, before the group abandoned the operation on 22 September. Schultze then sighted a ship from Convoy SC100, the US SS *Pennmar*. She was sunk with a single torpedo which struck her on the port side about 30ft from the bow near the forepeak oil tank. The crew of sixty-two abandoned ship in one lifeboat and two rafts. Two men were lost, and the remaining survivors were picked up safely the same day. *U-432* returned to La Pallice on 4 October. For his next patrol, Schultze took *U-432* to an area west of Gibraltar, and by mid-December was patrolling along the coast of Morocco where on the evening of the 17th he torpedoed and sank the French trawler *Poitou*. Only two of her crew of twenty-two survived. After an unsuccessful patrol off Huelva, on the southern coast of Spain, Schultze headed for home. He arrived at La Pallice on 5 January 1943.

In February Schultze was appointed commander of *U-849*, a Type IXD2 boat built in Bremen by AG Weser. He took his new boat out on her first patrol on 2 October, leaving

Kiel and heading for the Indian Ocean. The boat was sighted on 17 November by the light cruiser USS *Memphis* and a search was made by US Liberators. On the 25th, the boat was sighted by a Liberator, about 600 miles east-north-east by Ascension. Schultze and his crew were taken by surprise; the boat was straddled by six depth charges from 25ft. *U-849* began to sink and the crew quickly abandoned her before she exploded. A lifeboat was dropped by the aircraft but was never found. *Kapitänleutnant* Schultze and his crew of sixty-two were lost.

Other awards:
01 Sep 1939: Long Service Award 4th Class
16 Sep 1939: Commemorative Medal for 01 Oct 1938
02 Oct 1939: Iron Cross 2nd Class
13 Sep 1941: U-Boat War Badge
23 Sep 1941: Iron Cross 1st Class

Georg-Wilhelm SCHULZ
Korvettenkapitän
19 ships sunk, 89,886 tons
1 ship damaged, 3,900 tons

Knight's Cross: Awarded on 4 April 1941, as *Kapitänleutnant* and as commander of *U-124* for sinking thirteen ships for a total of 68,415 shipping tons and for damaging one other.

Georg-Wilhelm Schulz was born on 10 March 1906 in Cologne. He initially entered the merchant navy, spending ten years in it, including time on sailing ships. In October 1933 he joined the *Reichsmarine* and was assigned to the 6th Company in the II. *Schiffsstammdivision* in the Baltic where he began his basic training. From March 1934 he was attending courses on gunnery and torpedoes before joining the U-boat service in September 1935. He spent the next three years training on submarines, and during this time Schulz was among members of the German forces who were sent to help the Spanish Nationalists during the Spanish Civil War. He had already been commissioned as a *Leutnant zur See* in January 1936, and was promoted to *Oberleutnant zur See* in October 1937.

In January 1939, Schulz was appointed commander of *U-10*, a Type IIA boat used as a training boat until the outbreak of the (Scherzer)

Second World War. He was promoted to *Kapitänleutnant* in April 1939 and carried out two short war patrols before being transferred. In December he took command of *U-54*, a Type IXB boat built by AG Weser in Bremen. On 6 April 1940, he took his new command out of Wilhelmshaven, escorting the auxiliary cruiser *Schiff 36* through the North Sea to the Atlantic. On the 9th he was ordered to Vest Fjord, to operate against British forces taking part in the battle of Narvik. Whilst patrolling in the Herjangsfjord, north of Narvik, *U-64* was spotted on the 13th by a Swordfish floatplane from HMS *Warspite*. The aircraft attacked the boat with two 350lb bombs and sank *U-64* in shallow water. Eight men were killed and the thirty-eight survivors, including Schulz, managed to escape and were rescued from the water by German mountain troops. They were fed and rested and then took a train through Sweden and then by passenger ship back to Kiel, arriving on 26 April. As for *U-64*, she was raised in August 1957 and scrapped.

On 11 June 1940, Schulz was appointed commander of *U-124*, a Type IXB boat built in Bremen. He left Wilhelmshaven on 19 August to operate west of the British Isles. In the late evening of the 25th he attacked Convoy HX65A north of the Isle of Lewis where he sank the British SS *Harpalyce*. She was struck with a single torpedo and sank in less than sixty seconds, possibly due to her cargo of 8,000 tons of steel and iron. The crew had little time to abandon ship and it's unsurprising that only five of the forty-seven crew survived. He also torpedoed two more British ships during the same attack. He sank the SS *Fircrest* and damaged the SS *Stakesby*. On 2 September, he was sent to an area further west to supply weather reports, required for the planning of a possible German invasion of England. Schulz put in at Lorient on 16th. From 5 October until 22 January 1941, Schulz took *U-124* out on two war patrols. On 16 October he sank the Canadian SS *Trevisa* about 218 miles west of Rockall. During the early hours of the 20th he sighted Convoy OB229, and sank the Norwegian SS *Cubano*, 360 miles west of Rockall and then sank the British SS *Sulaco* in the same area. At 21:58 hours on the 31st he sank another British ship, the SS *Rutland*, a straggler from Convoy HX82. On the morning of 1 November he sank the SS *Empire Bison*, another British ship, about 200 miles north-west of Rockall. On 6 January 1941, during the next patrol he sank the British SS *Empire Thunder*, north-north-east of Rockall, his only success on this patrol.

He left port on his seventh patrol on 23 February and headed south in the company of *U-105* and *U-106*. From the 7 March Schulz operated with *U-105* against the northbound Convoy SL67 and during the early morning of the 8th he sank four ships after firing six single torpedoes. They were all British, the SS *Nardana*, SS *Hindpool*, SS *Tielbank* and SS *Lahore* – for a total of 24,159 shipping tons, sunk in less than an hour. The convoy had been sighted on the 7th by the battleships *Scharnhorst* and *Gneisenau*, 300 miles north-east of the Cape Verde Islands. *U-105* and *U-124* had been directed to attack the convoy. However, the boats were driven off by the battleship HMS *Malaya*, which was with the convoy. Schulz now turned south until the 18th and then after he refuelled and stocked up with food and fresh water he headed east to the Freetown area. On the 30th he sank the British SS *Umona* about 90 miles south-west of Freetown, claiming the lives of 101 members of her crew. During the second week of April, Schulz sank five ships in the area south-west of Freetown. On the 4th he sank the British SS *Marlene*, on the 7th he sank the Canadian SS *Portadoc*, the British SS *Tweed* on the 8th, the Greek SS *Aegeon* on the 11th and finally the British SS *St. Helena* on 12 April. She was sunk about 100 miles south-west of Freetown. After he sank SS *Tweed*, *U-124* surfaced and Schulz noticed that the survivors' lifeboat had been damaged and they were swimming towards the submarine. He ordered his men to help them aboard including the ship's Third Officer Baker who had a broken leg and a dislocated shoulder. He was in a bad way. While members of *U-124*'s crew fixed the lifeboat Schulz ordered the boat's doctor to help the British officer. The doctor administered morphine for the pain and so he could relocate his shoulder. After three injections the officer finally passed out, the German doctor fixed his shoulder and leg and when the lifeboat was repaired the survivors including Baker were put aboard. Schulz made sure they had food and fresh water and even gave them a bottle of cognac. By placing his boat in danger he had saved the lives of ten men. Third Officer Baker never forgot this kind act and sixteen years later he managed to track down Schulz. He wrote to the former U-boat commander and invited him to his home in Poole, Dorset. Schulz agreed to visit and the two men met in 1958. They clasped hands when they met at the dock in Poole and introduced their wives to each other. They became good friends.

On 15 July 1941, Schulz left port again to begin his eighth patrol, and headed for the Gibraltar area. From the 23rd he joined *U-93*, *U-95* and *U-109* in a southward sweep covering an area north to west, joining with *U-123* west of Morocco. The sweep was unsuccessful in that no convoys were sighted. From 3 August, the five boats were ordered north to make another sweep towards Gibraltar. They joined other boats between Gibraltar and the Azores from the 6th to await Convoy HG69. The convoy was sighted by *U-79* on the 10th but the escorts prevented any attacks. The operation was soon abandoned, and with no ships sunk the boats headed for Lorient. Schulz was then transferred, and left *U-124*, handing her over to Johann Mohr. Schulz was then appointed commander of the 6th U-boat Flotilla, initially based in Danzig and later in St. Nazaire. Promoted to *Korvettenkapitän* in April 1943, he was attached to the staff of the Commander Training Flotilla in Gotenhafen from October. He later spent time as a staff officer and leader of the *Erprobungsgruppe* (Testing Group) *U-Boote*, and was from 22 April 1945 commander of the 25th U-boat Flotilla in Travemünde, Lübeck. He surrendered to British forces on 6 May and remained in captivity until July 1945. Little is known of his post-war activities, apart from the fact he didn't join the *Bundesmarine*. He died in Hamburg on 5 July 1986.

Other awards:
15 Oct 1937: Long Service Award 4th Class
06 Jun 1939: Spanish Cross in Bronze
01 Oct 1939: Commemorative Medal of 01 Oct 1938
23 Dec 1939: U-Boat War Badge
25 Sep 1940: Iron Cross 2nd Class
25 Sep 1940: Iron Cross 1st Class
30 Jan 1945: War Service Cross 2nd Class with Swords
30 Jan 1945: War Service Cross 1st Class with Swords

Günther Ernst Friedrich SEIBICKE
Korvettenkapitän
7 ships sunk, 36,499 tons
2 ships damaged, 15,575 tons

Knight's Cross: Awarded on 27 March 1943, as *Kapitänleutnant* and as commander of *U-436* for sinking seven ships for a total of 36,499 shipping tons and for damaging two others.

Günther Seibicke was born in Eggersdorf, Germany on 30 August 1911, and entered the *Reichsmarine* as an Officer Candidate in August 1932. He was assigned to the II. *Schiffsstammdivision* in the Baltic initially and attended various training courses before spending time aboard the sail training ship *Edith* and the light cruiser *Köln* from November 1932. He was promoted to *Fähnrich zur See* in January 1934 (Scherzer) and to *Oberfähnrich zur See* in September 1935. During this time he attended many other training courses and served aboard the battleship *Schleswig-Holstein* and the light cruiser *Königsberg* before being commissioned as a *Leutnant zur See* on 1 January 1936. In September Seibicke was attached to the 1st Minesweeper Flotilla and served as First Watch Officer aboard the minesweeper *M111* from November 1936 until February 1938. Promoted to *Oberleutnant zur See* in October 1937, he served in various posting, which included adjutant aboard the minesweeper *M146* and as commander of minesweepers *M89* and *M4*. He was promoted to *Kapitänleutnant* on 1 April 1940.

Exactly a year later, Seibicke transferred to the U-boat service and was appointed commander of *U-436* in February 1942. She was a Type VIIC boat built by Schichau Company in Danzig. With her trials complete she was ready for her first war patrol. Between February and April, Seibicke took his new boat out on three patrols and although he claimed one ship sunk and one damaged, they cannot be confirmed. But on 1 March north-east of Cape Teriberskij he did sink the Soviet trawler *RT19 Komintern*, although Soviet reports claim she was sunk on 16 March. During his third patrol he sank the Soviet SS *Kiev* on 13 April in the Barents Sea. She was struck by a single torpedo and sank within seven minutes with the loss of her entire crew. On 12 May he took *U-436* out on another patrol to intercept the eastbound Convoy PQ16 which had left Reykjavik on the 21st. By the 24th the convoy was being protected by a strong surface force and was found by German aircraft the following day and came under attack from the air. Seibicke made an unsuccessful attack on the 26th, missing a steamer and a corvette. The convoy lost 43,205 tons, all by air attack, except one ship sunk by *U-703*. The patrol ended on the 27th.

On 6 October, *U-436* had moved to its new base in Kiel and had left for operations in the Atlantic on the same day. On the 22nd Seibicke joined *Puma* Group in the central North Atlantic. The group moved westwards and then northwards at high speed to intercept a convoy. On the 26th, Seibicke sighted Convoy HX212, and the following day he attacked and torpedoed three tankers, sinking the British whale factory ship SS *Sourabaya*, which was carrying 7,800 tons of oil. She sank south-east of Cape Farewell. On her deck was the landing craft HMS *LCT-2281*, which was also lost. Seibicke also went onto damage the US tanker SS *Frontenac* and the US SS *Gurney E. Newlin* during the same attack. On the evening of the 29th he sunk the British SS *Barrwhin* from Convoy HX212, struck by a single torpedo and sank quickly just south of Iceland. The ship had previously rescued sixty survivors from the Norwegian whale factory ship *Kosmos II* which had been sunk by *U-624* the same day. On 1 November together with three other boats, Seibicke was ordered to form a patrol line, *Natter*, west of Ireland. During the next few days seven new boats arrived to join the line, and on the 4th *U-92* sighted Convoy ON143 but lost contact soon afterwards. Only two ships were sunk, none by Seibicke, who put in at Lorient on the 12th.

On 17 December, Seibicke left for Atlantic operations as part of *Delphin* Group and formed a patrol line west of Gibraltar. Here they operated against US–Mediterranean convoys carrying supplies for the Allied armies in North Africa. However, nothing was seen and on 3 January 1943, the group was ordered south to intercept a convoy heading for Gibraltar. On the evening of the 8th, Seibicke torpedoed two tankers of Convoy TM1, south of the Azores. He had fired three torpedoes at the convoy and two had struck the British tanker SS *Oltenia II* sinking her. The third had hit the MV *Albert L. Ellsworth* which had fallen back behind the convoy and was abandoned by all hands. Seibicke had left the scene thinking she would sink. Her survivors were later picked up by HMS *Havelock*. However, the *Albert L. Ellsworth* remained afloat and Seibicke returned to the area on the 9th and recognized the wreck in front of him and shelled her until she sank. Seven tankers had been sunk during the operation, which ended near Madeira on the 11th. *Delphin* Group reformed south of the Azores on the 16th. From the 21st to the 29th *Delphin* waited south-west of the Azores for the convoy but without success and from the 31st the line was north-west of the Canaries moving then towards Gibraltar on 6 February. On the 11th *Delphin* Group moved north, a southbound convoy was reported on the 12th, 200 miles west of Cape Finisterre. The group was ordered to close in but the convoy's air cover kept the boats submerged. Attacks on the convoy became impossible and two U-boats were sunk. The operation was called off. Seibicke put in at St. Nazaire on the 19th.

He left again for the Atlantic on 25 April, and *U-436* was one of eleven outward-bound boats which became part of patrol line *Drossel*, north-west of Cape Finisterre. On 3 May German aircraft sighted a convoy and the group moved eastwards to attack. However, the operations were cancelled because the ships were landing craft (LCTs) with flat bottoms, and these were impossible to sink using torpedoes. *Drossel* Group then moved southwards to search for more convoys. Only one ship was sunk during the next few days and so the group moved again, westwards to intercept Convoy HX237. A strong surface escort and carrier-borne aircraft kept the boats off. Before the operation ended on the 13th, three ships had been sunk, but three U-boats had been lost. *U-436* set course for home. On the 26th, *U-436* was attacked with depth charges from the frigate HMS *Test* and the corvette HMS *Hyderabad* west of Cape Ortegal in north-west Spain. Forty-seven men were lost, including Seibicke. He was posthumously promoted to *Korvettenkapitän* on 1 June 1943.

Other awards:
02 Oct 1936: Long Service Award 4th Class
17 Sep 1939: Iron Cross 2nd Class
20 Dec 1939: Commemorative Medal for 01 Oct 1938
16 May 1940: Iron Cross 1st Class
24 Apr 1942: U-Boat War Badge

Heinz Hans SIEDER
Oberleutnant zur See
4 ships sunk, 22,850 tons
1 ship damaged, 7,240 tons

Knight's Cross: Awarded on 8 July 1944, as *Oberleutnant zur See* and as commander of *U-984* for sinking four ships for a total of 22,850 shipping tons and for damaging one other.

Heinz Sieder was born in Munich on 28 June 1920, and joined the *Kriegsmarine* in October 1938 at the age of eighteen. He entered as a cadet and was attached to the 2nd Company of the VII. *Schiffsstammdivision* before continuing his training aboard the sail training ship *Gorch Fock* and the battleship *Schlesien* from February 1939. He attended the Naval College at Flensburg-Mürwik from October and was assigned to the battleship *Scharnhorst* in April 1940. He took part in two war patrols aboard the battleship, operating in Norway from June 1940 with her sister-ship the battleship *Gneisenau*, the cruiser *Admiral Hipper* and four destroyers. They were used to relieve the pressure on German troops fighting in Norway by interrupting the Allied efforts to resupply the Norwegians. Later, from December, *Scharnhorst* was made ready for Operation *Berlin*, a planned raid into the Atlantic Ocean to wreck havoc on Allied shipping. Sieder took part in the first phase of this plan, before the battleships *Scharnhorst* and *Gneisenau* once again had to battle severe storms before they returned to port for repairs. Sieder continued with his officer training and on 1 April 1941 was commissioned as a *Leutnant zur See* and shortly after he transferred to the U-boat service. He was assigned to the 2nd U-boat Training Division and in September was

Above: *Heinz Sieder shortly after joining the Navy as a Cadet in October 1918.*
(Author's collection)

Left: (Scherzer)

appointed First Officer whilst attached to the 26th U-boat Flotilla in Pillau. On 24 January 1942, Sieder transferred to *U-440* as First Watch Officer, taking part in three war patrols under the command of *Kapitänleutnant* Hans Geissler. In April 1943 Sieder was promoted to *Oberleutnant zur See* and attended commander training at the Naval College.

On 17 June 1943, Siedler was appointed commander of *U-984*, a Type VIIC boat built by Blohm und Voss in Hamburg. After her sea trials were complete, Sieder took her out on his first war patrol as commander. He left Egersund, Norway, on 4 January 1944 and headed for the North Atlantic where he joined *Stürmer* Group to await a convoy. German aircraft sighted Convoy ON221 on the 27th, but the convoy was not found by the U-boats. The operation was cancelled, following a report by an aircraft of a suspected invasion of Western France. With this apparent information all available U-boats in the North Atlantic were ordered to proceed at speed to the Biscay coast. However, it soon became clear that the so-called 'invasion fleet' was a group of Spanish trawlers and the U-boats were ordered back to their operational areas. In early February *U-984* was with *Igel 1* Group, north-west of Scotland, but no convoys were sighted until the 14th, no hits were recorded. During the morning of the 15th, Sieder made an attack on a destroyer, but was unsuccessful. He put in at Brest on the 24th.

On 22 May, *U-984* left for the English Channel, with the new *Schnorkel* attached, and joined *U-269*, *U-441*, *U-764* and *U-953* to form *Dragoner* Group. The group was to operate in the western part of the Channel against Allied cruiser and destroyer formations. The objective was to test the effectiveness of the *Schnorkel* and to assess tactics required in areas that were patrolled by enemy aircraft. However, the general results were discouraging. Sieder put in at Brest on the 27th. After a brief patrol from 6 June lasting just four days, Sieder left once again for the Channel on 12th and on the 18th he put in at St. Peter Port, Guernsey, to recharge batteries. A few hours after he arrived, Allied fighter-bombers arrived and attacked the port area but *U-984* escaped with no damage. The U-boat left Guernsey on the 21st and four days later Sieder torpedoed the destroyer-escort HMS *Goodson* south-south-west of Portland. She was towed to Portland by HMS *Bligh* and declared a total loss. On the 29th, he attacked Convoy EMC17 south-south-west of the Isle of Wight and torpedoed four ships. The US SS *Henry G. Blasdel* was struck by a torpedo on the port side. The explosion damaged the interior of the ship and the entire stern section sagged, leaving the after gun platform partially submerged. The ship caught fire, and was anchored to keep her from drifting into a minefield. She was towed to Southampton but broke in two during the journey and was declared a total loss. Sieder also damaged the US SS *Edward M. House* and sank two other US ships, the SS *John A. Treutlen* and SS *James A. Farrell*. He returned to Brest on 5 July.

His next patrol began on 26 July, when Sieder left for operations in the English Channel. He had no success, and had started his return journey when on 20 August, *U-984* was detected by the destroyer HMCS *Ottawa*. Two other destroyers were with the *Ottawa*. The U-boat was attacked with depth charges by one of these ships, but there is no concrete evidence to what caused her destruction, apart from the report the *Ottawa* gave of attacking a U-boat in that area. Needless to say there were no survivors: all forty-five men were lost.

Other awards:
16 Oct 1942: High Seas Fleet War Badge
16 Nov 1942: U–Boat War Badge
29 Jan 1943: Iron Cross 2nd Class
28 Feb 1944: Iron Cross 1st Class

Georg Friedrich Ernst STAATS
Kapitänleutnant
14 ships sunk, 74,087 tons

Knight's Cross: Awarded on 14 July 1943, as *Kapitänleutnant* and as commander of *U-508* for sinking thirteen ships in just four patrols, for a total of 68,744 shipping tons.

Georg Staats was born on 13 March 1916 in Bremen and he joined the *Reichsmarine* as an Officer Candidate in April 1935, at the age of nineteen. He was initially attached to the 2nd Company of the II. *Schiffsstammabteilung* in the Baltic Sea, and continued with his training from June 1935 with service on the sail training ship *Gorch Fock* and the light cruiser *Emden*. He attended various training courses from March 1937, and was commissioned as a *Leutnant zur See* on 1 April 1938. He served on the light cruiser *Karlsruhe* from November 1937 and from May 1938 served aboard the battleship *Gneisenau* until April 1939, when he transferred to the U-boat service.

From August 1939 Staats served aboard *U-5*, as Watch Officer, and was promoted to *Oberleutnant zur See* in October. From January 1940, he served as First Watch Officer aboard *U-A*, a very early boat, under the command of *Korvettenkapitän* Hans Cohausz. From February 1941, he served as deputy commander of the U-boat tender *Isar*, before being appointed commander of *U-80* on 8 April. It was a Type VIIC which saw no operational service, being used only as a training boat. On 6 October he was appointed commander of a Type IXC boat, *U-508*, and he was ordered to report to Hamburg where his new boat had been commissioned. He supervised the training of his crew and

the boat's sea trials. In early 1942 he took his new command from Hamburg to Kiel to await further orders. On 25 June Staats took his new boat out of Kiel and headed for the Antilles. On 6 July he fired two torpedoes at a ship but missed. Six days later he attacked Special Convoy 12, which was en route from Key West to Havana. He torpedoed and sank the Cuban SS *Manzanillo* and SS *Santigo de Cuba*. On the 18th, he attacked Convoy TAW13 south of Portillo, Cuba. He fired two torpedoes which missed and was driven off by the escort. Staats then went to operate off the Florida coastline but had no success. He then put in at his new base Lorient on 15 September.

Before he left on his next patrol *U-508* was replenished with food and extra ammunition and a few minor repairs were completed. Finally Staats took her out on 17 October, and once again headed for the Antilles. He crossed the Atlantic and during the night of 5/6 November sighted Convoy TAG19 south-west of Grenada.

(Scherzer)

He torpedoed two ships, the US Liberty Ship SS *Nathaniel Hawthorne* and the British SS *Lindenhall*. Both sank with loss of life. On the 17th, he sank the British SS *City of Corinth* off Galera Point, Trinidad, with the loss of eleven of her crew. On the 27th, about 95 miles south-east of Galeota Point, he sank the British SS *Clan Macfadyen*, and the following day he sank another British ship, the SS *Empire Cromwell*, about 160 miles south-east of Galeota Point. He then moved north where he sank two British ships east-north-east of Boca Loran, the MV *Trevalgan* on 1 December and the SS *City of Bath* the following day. On the 3rd he sank the British SS *Solon II*, north-east of Georgetown, British Guiana. She was hit by a single torpedo and sank within twenty seconds, with the loss of seventy-five of her crew. Six days later he sank another British ship, the SS *Nigerian*, about 130 miles south-east of Trinidad. With all torpedoes gone he began the journey home, arriving at Lorient on 6 January 1943.

During his next patrol, this time in the North Atlantic, *U-508* was attacked by a Liberator of 224 Squadron on 26 February, north-east of the Azores. Temporary repairs were made and Staats had to return to port, arriving at Lorient on 15 March. His next patrol was even shorter, leaving port on 29 May but having to turn back two days later due to a mechanical defect. Finally with repairs made he left port for the Central Atlantic on 7 June, to operate in the Gulf of Guinea, a distance of 3,044 miles. On 9 July, Staats sank two ships about 60 miles south-west of Lagos in the Gulf of Benin. The first was the British passenger ship, SS *De la Salle*. There were 249 people aboard and only ten lost their lives. Sunk at the same time was the British SS *Manchester Citizen*, with the loss of twenty-nine. On the 18th, he sank the British passenger ship MV *Incomati*, torpedoed about 200 miles south of Lagos. About twenty minutes after the torpedo struck the ship, Staats ordered the ship to be shelled until she sank. There were 222 survivors who were picked up by HMS *Boadicea* and HMS *Bridgewater*. *U-508* was then ordered to join *U-257*, *U-382*, *U-600* and *U-618* to form a reconnaissance line close to the Ivory Coast from 23 July to 2 August. No ships were sighted and the line was broken up a few days later. On the 27th *U-508* was sighted by an Avenger aircraft from USS *Card*, south-west of the Azores. She was attacked with depth-charges and acoustic torpedoes but escaped by diving deep. She finally reached Lorient on 14 September.

On 1 November, Staats had been ordered to take *U-508* from Lorient to St. Nazaire to pick up new radar equipment and torpedoes. With everything loaded he left St. Nazaire on the 9th for operations with *U-515*, under *Kapitänleutnant* Werner Henke. Early on the 12th *U-508* was attacked by a US Naval Liberator aircraft of VB103, north of Cape Ortegal. *U-515* had just departed and so escaped any attack. *U-508* wasn't so lucky: she was sunk by the depth-charges and everyone on board was killed. The Liberator failed to return to base after the attack: all of her crew was lost too.

Other awards:
05 Apr 1939: Long Service Award 4th Class
28 Aug 1940: Iron Cross 2nd Class
28 Aug 1940: U-Boat War Badge
09 Jan 1943: Iron Cross 1st Class

Hans-Gerrit Adalbert Karl Theodor von STOCKHAUSEN
Korvettenkapitän
12 ships sunk, 66,174 tons
3 ships damaged, 22,490 tons

Knight's Cross: Awarded on 14 January 1941, as *Korvettenkapitän* and as commander of *U-65* for sinking twelve ships for a total of 66,174 shipping tons and for damaging two other ships, to become the 23rd U-boat recipient of the award.

Hans-Gerrit von Stockhausen was born on 11 August 1907, in Kassel and joined the *Reichsmarine* in April 1936, at the age of nineteen. He was assigned to the II. *Schiffsstammdivision* in the Baltic as a cadet, and began his basic training aboard the sail training ship *Niobe* and later on the light cruiser *Emden* from July 1926. After attending various training courses he saw service onboard the battleship *Schlesien* from January 1930. Von Stockhausen served for twelve months with the torpedo boat *Jaguar* as Third Watch Officer from September 1930 and in October was commissioned as a *Leutnant zur See*. He was then assigned to the I. *Schiffsstammdivision* in Wilhelmshaven as a platoon leader and was promoted to *Oberleutnant zur See* in January 1932. For the next three years he served as Watch Officer aboard the tender *Elbe* and later the *Weser* and was also from December 1934 commander of *Peilboat V* (Survey Ship V).

At the end of 1935 he served as commander of *U-13*, a training boat stationed in Kiel. From early 1938 he was appointed staff officer attached to the office of the commander of U-boats, after being promoted to *Kapitänleutnant* in April 1936. From August 1938 he saw brief service aboard the 'pocket battleship' *Admiral Scheer* before joining the U-boat service in December 1939. He took command of *U-65* on 15 February 1940, a Type IXB boat built in Bremen. Von Stockhausen left Wilhelmshaven on 9 April whilst undergoing sea

trials and was ordered to take *U-65* to Norwegian waters, primarily to the Nams Fjord – Vaags Fjord area to oppose any British landings. On the 15th he unsuccessfully attacked the troop transport ship *Batory*, from Convoy NP1, and on the 18th he attacked the cruiser HMS *Emerald* but the torpedo failed. On the 19th all boats were ordered away from the fjords and *U-65* and others moved to an area north of the Shetlands, and then headed for Wilhelmshaven, arriving on 14 May.

On 8 June, von Stockhausen took *U-65* to patrol west of the English Channel and the Bay of Biscay. On the 21st he sank the Dutch SS *Berenice*, with the loss of thirty-nine of her crew. The next day he sank the French tanker SS *Monique*, struck by two torpedoes about 70 miles south-west of Penmarsh in the Bay of Biscay. The ship was immediately covered in burning oil and broke in two before she sank. On the 30th, he torpedoed and damaged the

(Scherzer)

British SS *Clan Ogilvy*, and on 1 July he also damaged the Dutch SS *Amstelland* about 380 miles south-west of Lands End. On his next patrol, von Stockhausen left Wilhelmshaven on 8 August, on a special mission, on board *U-65* were two Irish agents of the *Abwehr* (German Military Intelligence). The plan was to land these agents near Smerwick Harbour, Kerry, Ireland in what was called Operation Dove, a plan of sabotage and to train people to design or camouflage explosives as everyday objects. The two agents, Sean Russell (the IRA chief of staff) and Frank Ryan, were to be taken to Kerry on the 15th, but the mission was aborted after Russell died on the 14th. Apparently he became ill during the journey and complained of stomach pains. *U-65* did not have a doctor onboard and Russell died and was buried at sea. *U-65* returned to Lorient with Ryan still on board. There was an inquiry into Russell's death and the conclusion was that he had suffered a burst gastric ulcer and without medical attention had died.

On 28 August von Stockhausen took *U-65* out on another patrol to the area near the British Isles, where on 5 September he sighted Convoy SC2 north-west of Rockall. He was unable to make an attack as the escort kept *U-65* away. Over the next few days *U-28* and *U-47* joined in attacks on the convoy, and as a result five ships were sunk, but none by von Stockhausen. On the 15th, however, he did sink the Norwegian MV *Hird*, struck by a single torpedo on the starboard side between the bridge and the forward mast, about 180 miles from Barra Head, Scotland. All thirty of her crew abandoned ship in one overcrowded lifeboat, and were all picked up safely by an Icelandic tanker. Von Stockhausen put in at Lorient on the 25 September. On 15 October he left for the Freetown area and on the way *U-65* was replenished by the German supply ship *Nordmark*, near the Cape Verde Islands. Two days later he sank the British SS *Tregenna*, 78 miles north-west of Rockall. On 1 November he was promoted to *Kapitänleutnant*, and on the 15th he sank two ships south of Freetown. The first was the British SS *Kohinur*, from Convoy OB235 about 250 miles north of the Equator. The second officer was taken prisoner by von Stockhausen, and thirty-one of the crew was lost when the second ship he had torpedoed, the Norwegian tanker MV *Harbor*, exploded. During the next three days he sank another two ships in the general area west-south-west of Freetown. He sank the British SS *Fabian* on the 16th, and the British motor tanker, MV *Congonian* was sunk on the 18th. *U-65* remained in the area for a further four weeks, but had no further success until 21 December, when von Stockhausen sank the Panamanian tanker SS *Charles Pratt* about 220 miles off Freetown. He had seen the ship's flags, and she was clearly displaying the identification of Panama, a neutral country, but he decided to attack without warning as the tanker was heading for an enemy port. The ship caught fire immediately and there were two large explosions, but miraculously most of the crew escaped, only two being killed. On the 24th he sank the British tanker SS *British Premier*, a straggler from Convoy SLS60; she was struck by two torpedoes and sank 200 miles south-west of Freetown. On the 27th, during his return journey, von Stockhausen sank the Norwegian SS *Risanger*, hit amidships by a stern torpedo off Freetown. On the 31st he torpedoed and damaged the British tanker MV *British Zeal*, east of the Cape Verde Islands. His final success from this patrol was the sinking of the British SS *Nalgora*. She was from Convoy OB261 and was struck by a single torpedo about 350 miles north of the Cape Verde Islands and sunk within twenty minutes. *U-65* finally docked at Lorient on the 10 December.

In April 1941, von Stockhausen was transferred and appointed commander of the 26th U-boat Training Flotilla in Pillau. He now became responsible for the training of the U-boat commanders of his flotilla in torpedo firing. He remained in this position until 15 January 1943, when he was killed in a car accident in Berlin.

Other award:
02 Oct 1936: Long Service Award 4th Class
24 Jun 1938: Long Service Award 3rd Class
20 Dec 1939: Commemorative Medal of 01 Oct 1938
00.00.1940: Iron Cross 2nd Class
12 Jul 1940: Iron Cross 1st Class
00 Sep 1940: U-Boat War Badge

Siegfried STRELOW
Korvettenkapitän
13 ships sunk, 57,023 tons

Knight's Cross: Awarded as *Kapitänleutnant* whilst commander of *U-435* on 27 October 1942 for the sinking of seven ships for a total of 34,582 shipping tons.

Born on 15 April 1911 in Kiel, Siegfried Strelow joined the *Reichsmarine* in April 1931, just two weeks before his twentieth birthday. His basic training began when he was assigned to the II. *Schiffsstammdivision* in the Baltic and from June 1931 he served aboard the sail training ship *Niobe* and later the light cruiser *Karlsruhe*. He attended various training courses over the next four years, when in April 1935 he was commissioned as a

Leutnant zur See. In June he was assigned aboard the battleship *Schleswig-Holstein* and served as Second Torpedo Officer. From December 1935 he served aboard the 'pocket battleship' *Admiral Graf Spee*, serving as the Second Torpedo Officer from January 1936. From October he commanded the torpedo boat *S9* and later the *S11*. On 1 January 1937, Strelow was promoted to *Oberleutnant zur See*, and from October served as Second Watch Officer and Torpedo Officer aboard the destroyer *Z4 Richard Beitzen*. From October 1938 he commanded the torpedo boat *G11* and on 1 October 1939 was promoted to *Kapitänleutnant*.

During the early days of the Second World War, Strelow commanded the torpedo boat *Albatros* and later the *Löwe* between December 1939 and November 1940. On 18 November, he transferred to the light cruiser *Leipzig*, serving as Torpedo Officer. During this time the *Leipzig*

(Scherzer)

was operating as a training ship. Having gained experience of almost every type of vessel in the *Kriegsmarine,* Strelow joined the U-boat service in April 1941. After attending a commanders' training course from May he was appointed commander of *U-435*, a Type VIIC boat, in July. On 20 January 1942, with her sea trials a success, Strelow left on his first war patrol and headed for the North Atlantic. *U-435* was one of twelve boats ordered to assemble west of Rockall as *Schlei* Group, for a south-westerly sweep across the convoy routes. Further orders were received and eight boats were ordered to go to the Iceland-Faroes-Scotland area. However *U-435* together with *U-352*, *U-455*, *U-586* and *U-591* had their previous orders cancelled and went northwards. They searched for possible convoys off the coast of Iceland and investigated the Seydis Fjord, but found no evidence of shipping activity. Strelow was ordered to northern waters and put in at Kirkenes, Norway on 16 February. Two days later he took *U-435* to her new base in Trondheim to await new orders.

On 16 March he left base and on the morning of the 27th German aircraft sighted Convoy PQ13, which had been scattered in a storm. Strelow together with other U-boats, destroyers and aircraft were ordered to attack the convoy. On the 30th, Strelow torpedoed and sank the US SS *Effingham* north-east of Kola Inlet, with the loss of twelve of her crew. The operation ended that day with five ships sunk and one damaged. Strelow took *U-435* back into Kirkenes on 5 April. He left for further operations on 7 April and sighted Convoy QP10 on the 11th. He made an unsuccessful attack on the destroyer HMS *Punjabi* on the night of the 12th/13th, but he sank the Panamanian SS *El Occidente* and the British SS *Harpalion*, both off Bear Island. The *El Occidente* was struck by a single torpedo which hit the engine room, nearly breaking her in two. She sank stern first in two minutes, so fast there was no time to launch the lifeboats. Twenty of her crew of forty-one was lost. Strelow returned to base on 26 April.

By 25 July, Strelow was attached to the 11th U-boat Flotilla in Narvik and left for operations the same day. Between 11th and 15 August, *U-435* landed at the Knospe weather-reporting unit on Spitsbergen, to provide information for a German naval operation against shipping on the Siberian sea route. The operation was completed by 31 August. On 16 September, *U-435* left Skjomenfjord and joined six other boats, which from the 20th were operating against Convoy OP14. In the early morning of the 20th, Strelow attacked the convoy west of the southern tip of Spitsbergen and sank the minesweeper HMS *Leda*. He continued to shadow the convoy, and on the 22nd sank three ships west of Jan Mayern, the US SS *Bellingham*, the British fleet oiler SS *Grey Ranger* and the British SS *Ocean Voice*. His next patrol began on 30 November when he left for the North Atlantic. He arrived in the area south-west of Iceland during the closing stages of *Draufgänger* Group's operation against Convoy HX217. From 13 December, there were new arrivals which combined with the boats from *Draufgänger* to form a new group, *Ungestüm*. Later that same day Convoy ONS152 was sighted and the boats moved in. But with bad weather and poor visibility the operation ended on the 22nd. From the 24th, boats from *Ungestüm* Group formed a new patrol line in the central North Atlantic. Another convoy was sighted north-north-east of the Azores and the group moved to intercept. Again there was poor visibility but four ships were sunk on the 27th. On the 29th, Strelow attacked but missed a destroyer, but he did sink the British catapult-armed ship SS *Empire Shackleton*. She was sunk by a single torpedo and then by gunfire. All of her crew abandoned ship and were all rescued. Later that same afternoon *U-435* sank the Norwegian SS *Norse King*. She was struck by a torpedo and then shelled with over 100 rounds. She was finally sunk by a *coup de grâce* torpedo. Unfortunately none of her crew was ever found. On the evening of the 30th, Strelow sank the British special service ship HMS *Fidelity*, which had fallen behind the convoy due to engine trouble. She was hit by two torpedoes and sank immediately. The survivors were later seen on overcrowded rafts and some were swimming in the water. Strelow couldn't stay in the area to help because it wasn't safe and 368 men lost their lives.

Strelow left for the Atlantic once again on 18 February 1943, to join *Burggraf* Group, west of Ireland. From the 26th, the group swept westwards and from 4 March joined up with *Wildfang* Group to form a patrol line. Convoy SC121 slipped by without being sighted, and *Neptune* Group and boats from *Newland* Group joined the line to form *Raubgraf* Group on the 7th east of Newfoundland, to await Convoy HX228. Over the next few days the convoy wasn't sighted and with bad weather the boats were also hampered by strong Allied air cover. Contact was finally made with the convoy on the 16th, and the following day Strelow torpedoed and damaged the US SS *William Eustis*. Two hours later he claimed hits on another three ships and a tanker but there is no confirmation of this. The damaged *William Eustis* was sunk seven hours later by *U-91*. The four-day operation was the biggest convoy action of the war, with twenty-one ships sunk from the two convoys. Strelow returned *U-435* to Brest on 25 March.

On 20 May, he left for Atlantic operations and was ordered to an area south-west of the Azores, to await expected Convoys UGS9 and GUS7A. A patrol line was formed but nothing was sighted. The group was broken up and moved 600 miles to the north. The UGS convoy was sighted by an outward-bound boat on the 8th, 100 miles south of the *Trutz* patrol area, near the Azores. On the 16th *Trutz* Group reformed into three parallel north-south lines, *Trutz 1, 2,* and *3*, 1,000 miles east of Bermuda. Strelow's *U-435* was part of *Trutz 3*. The boats waited for two convoys, but nothing was sighted for six days, the line continued eastwards until the 27th, when they halted some 200 miles south-west of the Azores. They then waited for another convoy but by the 29th it was realized that it too had by-passed the line. The boats reformed into three new patrol lines, *Geier 1, 2* and *3*, and from 2 July they moved eastwards towards the coast of Spain. *U-435* was in *Geier 2*. Air attacks began on the U-boats at about 500 miles from the coast, and on the 9th *U-435* was attacked by a Wellington bomber of 179 Squadron west-north-west of Lisbon. *U-435* was sunk by a depth charge. There were no survivors: forty-eight men were dead. On 1 July, Strelow had been promoted to *Korvettenkapitän*.

Other awards:
25 Apr 1940: Iron Cross 2nd Class
25 May 1940: Iron Cross 1st Class
02 Oct 1936: Long Service Award 4th Class
01 Aug 1939: Commemorative Medal of 01 Oct 1938
19 Feb 1941: Destroyer War Badge
15 Apr 1942: U-Boat War Badge

Wilhelm <u>Hermann</u> STUCKMANN
Oberleutnant zur See
1 ship sunk, 2,938 tons
2 ships damaged, 11,673 tons

Knight's Cross: Awarded on 11 August 1944 as *Oberleutnant zur See* and as commander of *U-621* after sinking one ship and damaging another for a total of 14,611 shipping tons.

(Scherzer)

Hermann Stuckmann was born on 2 January 1921, in Wuppertal-Barman, North Rhine-Westphalia, Germany. He entered the *Kriegsmarine* shortly after the start of the Second World War on 16 September 1939. Stuckmann began his basic training with the 2nd Company of VII. *Schiffsstammabteilung* where he was assigned as an Officer Candidate. From November he served aboard the battleship *Schleswig-Holstein* and took part in the occupation of Denmark in April 1940. From May he attended various training courses and in July was promoted to *Fähnrich zur See*. In June 1941, Stuckmann attended artillery school and was promoted to *Oberfähnrich zur See* the following month. On 28 July, he transferred to the U-boat service and was attached to the crew of *U-571*, under the command of *Kapitänleutnant* Helmut Mohlmann. He took part in seven patrols, from 21 December 1941, serving as Third Watch Officer, being commissioned as *Leutnant zur See* in March 1942. From 10 March he served as Second Watch Officer aboard *U-571* and from December 1942 he served aboard as First Watch Officer. In May 1943, Stuckmann left the boat and continued his training to become a U-boat commander.

On 5 August 1943, he was named as commander of *U-316*, a Type VIIC boat used as a training vessel. On 1 October Stuckmann was promoted to *Oberleutnant zur See*, and on 5 May 1944 he took command of *U-621*, another Type VIIC boat. He left on his first war patrol on 6 June, leaving Brest as part of *Landwirt* Group. *U-621* was equipped with a *Schnorkel*, and Stuckmann was ordered to go to the area north of Cherbourg, enter the English Channel and inflict what loses he could on the invasion forces on D-Day. It was a difficult and dangerous mission and there was a very heavy concentration of air and surface forces he would have to face. Soon after midnight on the 7th, he attacked some destroyers but his torpedoes missed. On the 15th, he managed to penetrate the screen escorting six LSTs north of Seine Bay and fired three torpedoes, all of which exploded prematurely, but he still managed to damage one target, USS *LST-133*. On the 18th, Stuckmann made an unsuccessful attack on two US battleships, which failed because his torpedoes exploded prematurely again. He was then driven off by the escorts. *U-621* returned to Brest on the 23 June.

Stuckmann left for the English Channel on 15 July, reaching his operational area on the 23rd. During attacks he made on the 29th, south-east of the Isle of Wight, Stuckmann sank the British landing ship HMS *Prince Leopold*. She capsized and sank almost immediately with the loss of her entire crew. He also claimed a hit on a steamer, which was unconfirmed. On the 30th, in the same area he torpedoed and damaged the British SS *Ascanius*. She was later towed into Liverpool and repaired. On 2 August, closer to the French coast, he claimed two other ships sunk, but again they were never confirmed. He put in at Brest on the 11th. Two days later he left Brest for La Pallice – his new base. On the 18th, during the voyage, *U-621* was located and sunk by depth charges by three Canadian destroyers, HMCS *Ottawa*, *Kootenay* and *Chaudière*, west-south-west of La Rochelle. There were no survivors; fifty-six men were lost. Stuckmann was only twenty-three.

Other awards:
11 May 1942: Iron Cross 2nd Class
15 May 1942: U-Boat War Badge
18 Nov 1942: Iron Cross 1st Class

<u>Max-Martin</u> Detlef TEICHERT
Kapitänleutnant
6 ships sunk, 31,528 tons
2 ships damaged, 17,921 tons

Knight's Cross: On 19 December 1943, posthumously awarded, as *Kapitänleutnant* and as commander of *U-456* for sinking six ships for a total of 31,528 shipping tons and for damaging another two.

Max-Martin Teichert was born on 31 January 1915 in Kiel, joining the *Reichsmarine* in April 1934. He entered as an Officer Candidate assigned to the 2nd Company of II. *Schiffsstammabteilung* in the Baltic. From June 1934 he served aboard the sail training ship *Gorch Fock*, and from September until July 1936 served on the light cruiser *Emden*.

(Scherzer)

On 10 October, Teichert served on the torpedo boat *Itlis* as Watch Officer, being commissioned as a *Leutnant zur See* in April 1937. From March 1939, he served on the destroyer *Z14 Friedrich Ihn*, taking part in twenty-two patrols during the first months of the war. He served as Second Watch Officer and Torpedo Officer and was promoted to *Oberleutnant zur See* in April. His ship was initially deployed to blockade the Polish coast, later being transferred to the German Bight to lay defensive minefields in German waters, off the coast of the Netherlands and Denmark. In late 1939 and early 1940, the ship laid multiple offensive minefields off the English coast that claimed eighteen merchant ships and a destroyer. The ship was under repair during the Norwegian Campaign and transferred to France later that year.

On 1 June 1940, Teichert transferred to the U-boat service, and from February 1941, after completing various training courses he was assigned to *U-94* as First Watch Officer. He served on two war patrols under *Kapitänleutnant* Herbert Kuppish (Knight's Cross holder), during which time six ships were sunk. On 19 August, Teichert was named as commander of *U-456*, a Type VIIC boat built in Kiel. The boat was commissioned in September and with her sea trials complete, Teichert took her out from Kiel and headed for northern waters on 31 January 1942. Teichert, who had already been promoted to *Kapitänleutnant* in December 1941, put in at Kirkenes on 15 February, after an uneventful patrol. On 29 March he left port on another patrol and together with four other U-boats was directed to Convoy PQ13, as were destroyers and aircraft. On the 30th, he torpedoed and damaged the US merchant SS *Effingham*. She was struck amidships on the port side and most of her crew immediately abandoned ship. *Effingham* was sunk some two hours later by *U-435*. The U-boats sank three ships of PQ13, but the main action was between German and British surface forces. The Germans lost one destroyer and the Royal Navy had one damaged. Teichert returned to Kirkenes on 2 April.

On 7 April he began his next patrol, meeting with several other boats near Kola Inlet against Convoy QP10. Teichert failed to sink any ships: in fact only *U-435* had any success, sinking two ships. His next patrol began on 29th and the following day he sighted the British cruiser, HMS *Edinburgh*. In the afternoon he made his attack, she was hit by two torpedoes just north of Murmansk and was seriously damaged. On 2 May, she was under tow back to the Kola Inlet when she was attacked by three German destroyers. A spirited battle to defend the stricken warship was fought over the next three days, particularly by the destroyers HMS *Foresight* and HMS *Forester*, which fought off the three German ships. On 1 May, the German destroyer *Z27 Hermann Schoemann* was so badly damaged

HMS Edinburgh *was hit by two torpedoes fired from* U-456 *on 30 April 1942, north of Murmansk while escorting Convoy QP-11. She was later under tow when attacked by three German destroyers and was hit by a torpedo from the destroyer Z-24. She was scuttled by a torpedo from HMS* Foresight *on 2 May.* (Author's collection)

that she was scuttled. *Foresight* and *Forester* were damaged and *Edinburgh* was hit by another torpedo. The surviving crew of the *Z27 Hermann Schoemann* were taken off, 200 of them by the German destroyers *Z24* and *Z25* and a further sixty on rafts and in boats were picked up by *U-88* later on the 2nd. *Edinburgh* was sunk by *Foresight*'s last torpedo on the 3rd – she wasn't going to be left for the enemy.

On 7 May, Teichert moved *U-456* to her new base at Bergen, and he left on his next patrol on 25 June. On 1 July, together with *U-255* and *U-408*, he sighted the eastbound Convoy PQ17. Brief contact was made and there were some unsuccessful attacks. Teichert continued to shadow the convoy. Later the convoy suspected that German surface vessels were preparing to attack, soon on the evening of the 4th the convoy began to scatter. A disastrous error, as the escorts couldn't protect all the ships. The next day U-boats and German aircraft moved in. That afternoon Teichert sank the US SS *Honomu* in the Barents Sea. During the nine-day operation against Convoy PQ17, twenty-four ships were sunk, eight by aircraft. It was the greatest convoy disaster of the Second World War, for as well as the ships lost, 153 merchant seamen were lost also. Churchill called the event, '... one of the most melancholy naval episodes in the whole war'.[7] Teichert put in at Neidenfjord on the 6th.

From 4 August to 4 December Teichert took *U-456* out on two more patrols, both were uneventful and almost without success. He did sink the Soviet motor boat *Chaika* on 22 August. On 14 January 1943, he left for the North Atlantic, his tenth war patrol, and he joined *Landsknecht* Group west of Ireland. After waiting seven days for an expected convoy that did not materialize, the group dispersed on the 28th. En route to join a new group Teichert sighted Convoy HX224 on 1 February in the area of the Central Atlantic. He kept the convoy in sight and radioed the other boats to join him. Within four days he was joined by *U-257*, *U-632* and *U-614*. Early on the 2nd he sank the US SS *Jeremiah Van Rensselaer* and the British tanker MV *Inverilen* the following day. During a later attack he reported damaging the sloop HMS *Londonderry*, but this was never confirmed. The operation against the convoy ended on the 3rd. On the 4th, the eastbound Convoy SC118 passed through the centre of the *Pfeil* Group's patrol line and the boats were ordered to close in, as were five boats of *Handegen* Group. Twenty boats took part in the operation, including *U-456*, and before it ended on the 9th, eleven ships had been sunk and two U-boats lost. On the 23rd en route to Brest Teichert sank the Irish SS *Kyleclare* with the loss of all of her crew. He had fired a spread of three torpedoes. She disappeared in the explosions that followed and after surfacing Teichert noted only debris and wreckage. He reached Brest on the 26th.

On 24 April, Teichert took *U-456* out for operations in the Atlantic and was one of eleven boats which formed a patrol line, *Drossel*, north-west of Cape Finisterre from late April. On 3 May aircraft sighted a convoy and so the group moved in. It proved to be fifteen LCTs and two escorts. Sea conditions made torpedo attacks on these flat-bottomed vessels almost impossible and so the operation was abandoned. *Drossel* Group then moved southwards in search of other convoys. On the 6th Convoy SL128 was located by aircraft but an incorrect position report prevented the boats making contact until early morning the following day. Only one ship was sunk before the operation ended on the 8th. The

---

7 Winston Churchill, *The Second World War*, Volume IV, Cassell, 1951.

group moved westwards to intercept Convoy HX237, which it finally did on the 11th, north of the Azores where Teichert torpedoed and sunk the British SS *Fort Concord*. She was carrying 8,500 tons of grain and 700 tons of military stores, including aircraft in crates. She was struck on the port side about 440 miles north of the Azores. She sank within four minutes with the loss of most of her crew. On 11 May, *U-456* was damaged during an attack by a Liberator of 86 Squadron. The next day *U-456* was seen on the surface by aircraft of 423 Squadron. They contacted surface vessels in the area. The frigate HMS *Lagan* and the corvette HMS *Drumheller* were called up, and although *U-456* could dive, she had been damaged and couldn't dive deep enough to escape the depth charges. *U-456* was lost and there were no survivors: forty-nine men died.

Other awards:
01 Apr 1938: Long Service Award 4th Class
15 Dec 1939: Iron Cross 2nd Class
15 Jan 1940: Commemorative Medal of 01 Oct 1938
19 Oct 1940: Destroyers War Badge
07 Jun 1941: Iron Cross 1st Class
07 Jun 1941: U-Boat War Badge

Franz Wilhelm <u>Karl</u> THURMANN
Korvettenkapitän
13 ships sunk, 62,315 tons
2 ships damaged, 15,273 tons

Knight's Cross: Awarded on 24 August 1942, as *Korvettenkapitän* and as commander of *U-553* in recognition of the sinking of twelve ships for a total of 57,042 shipping tons and for damaging two others.

Karl Thurmann was born in Mülheim an der Ruhr, a city in the western Ruhr region of North Rhine-Westphalia, Germany on 4 September 1909. His naval career began when he entered the *Reichsmarine* as an Officer Candidate on 1 April 1928, at the age of eighteen. He began his basic training aboard the sail training ship *Niobe* from July, and was assigned to the light cruiser *Emden*, before being transferred to the 4th Company of the II. *Schiffsstammabteilung* in the Baltic. From March 1931 he attended various training courses, which included practical experience aboard the light cruisers *Köln* and *Emden* and aboard the 'pocket battleship' *Deutschland* from April 1933. He was commissioned as a *Leutnant zur See* in October 1932 and promoted to *Oberleutnant zur See* in September 1934. From December he attended a coastal artillery course at Swinemünde, before being assigned to the light cruiser

(Scherzer)

Köln as *Rollenoffizer* and as 2nd Gunnery Officer. He was promoted to *Kapitänleutnant* in June 1937 and from October 1938 Thurmann served as a company commander in 2nd Naval Artillery Battalion. In August 1939 he was appointed commander of 122nd Naval Artillery Battalion in Helgoland and later becoming Artillery Commander *Helgoland*.

In April 1940, Thurmann transferred to the U-boat service and after completing various courses joined *U-29*. From 26 October he served aboard as a 'Commander-in-Training', under the watchful eye of *Kapitänleutnant* Otto Schuhart, taking part in one war patrol. On 23 December, he was named as commander of *U-553*, a Type VIIC boat which had been newly commissioned. With her sea trails complete she was ready for her transit voyage from Kiel to her new base in St. Nazaire. She arrived on 2 May 1941 and Thurmann took her out on his first war patrol as commander on 7 June and headed for the North Atlantic. On the morning of the 13th he sank the British SS *Susan Maersk* about 370 miles north-north-east of the Azores. She was struck by one torpedo and sank in ninety seconds with the loss of her entire crew. That same afternoon Thurmann sank the Norwegian tanker SS *Ranella*. He then joined *West* Group south-east of the Newfoundland Bank and began to operate in a widely-spaced formation in the central North Atlantic. No convoys were sighted. On the 24th Convoy OB336 was sighted by *U-203* south of Greenland. However, fog prevented any attacks, and only one ship was sunk, a straggler, by *U-108*. Five days later another convoy was sighted by aircraft but the boats failed to find it, then on the 30th yet another convoy was sighted but fog prevented any attack. A disappointed Thurmann returned to St. Nazaire.

His next patrol, began on 7 April. *U-553* joined a large group of boats operating south-west of Iceland. They had no success in locating any convoys. From 1 September, *U-553* and six other boats formed *Kurfüst* Group west of the North Channel. The group was directed to Convoy OG73 by aircraft and together with *Bosemüller* Group they search for the convoy but couldn't find it. Thurmann returned *U-553* to base on 16 September. His next patrol began on 7 October, and he headed to an area south-east of Cape Farewell, where a new group was formed. As the group was forming, Convoys ONS23, ON24, SC48 and TC14 were re-routed to the south. During the night of the 14th/15th, Thurmann sighted Convoy SC48 in the central North Atlantic. He sank two ships on the 15th, the British MV *Silvercedar* and the Norwegian SS *Ila*. Early on the 17th he sank the British corvette HMS *Gladiolus*. She went down immediately with the loss of her entire crew of sixty-five. Thurmann put in at St. Nazaire on 22 October. For his next patrol he headed for Canadian waters, and on the evening of 15 January 1941, he torpedoed and damaged the British tanker MV *Diala*, east-south-east of St. John's. On the 22nd Thurmann sank the independent-sailing Norwegian tanker MV *Innerøy* south of Sable Island.

From 24 February until 1 April, Thurmann took *U-553* out on his sixth patrol. He left for the Faroes and the Hebrides and was one of about six boats sent to this area to protect German troops near Norway as Hitler feared an Allied landing. Starting on 11 March four boats, including *U-553* were put under the control of Naval Group Command North and, as *York* Group, they waited between the Shetlands and Faroes for the British naval forces. However they never showed and after two weeks the boats returned to base. On 19 April, Thurmann left for Canadian Waters, and arrived in the Newfoundland Bank area on 3 May. On the 6th he located a steamer with a corvette escort, and an attack was made but it failed, but the attack alerted the corvette which dropped a depth charge which damaged *U-553*'s periscope. The boat was then attacked by aircraft and three more depth charges were dropped which caused more damage. Thurmann decided to make for the Gulf of St. Lawrence, the first incursion there by a U-boat. On the 10th *U-553* was spotted on the surface by a USAF aircraft and was once again subject to a depth-charge attack, which caused technical problems for *U-553*. Thurmann managed to get his boat away by diving deep and the attack was called off. The aircraft had seen debris from the boat and believed it had sunk. *U-553* was damaged but still operational. Thurmann took her into the St. Lawrence River and on the morning of the 12th, he sank the British SS *Nicoya* and the Dutch SS *Leto*. On the 21st *U-553* left the Gulf of St. Lawrence via the Cabot Strait and went south, passed Halifax and entered the Bay of Fundy. Thurmann observed the comings and goings at the harbour for several days and soon realized that it wasn't a terminal for convoys. He had nine torpedoes left and enough food and water for twenty-five days, so on 1 June he moved back into the Atlantic. On the morning of the 2nd, he torpedoed and sank the British MV *Mattawin* 190 miles east-south-east of Nantucket Island. He began the homeward journey on the 5th, but on the 10th he turned back after receiving a wireless message of a nearby convoy. The following evening *U-553* was attacked on the surface by a flying boat that dropped depth charges but Thurmann managed to dive and escaped any further damage. He couldn't approach the convoy and with a damaged boat he headed for St. Nazaire, arriving on the 24th.

After major repairs *U-553* was ready for her eighth patrol, leaving for the Antilles on 19 July. On the 29th Thurmann was directed to Convoy ON115 located about 480 miles south-east of Cape Farewell, but *U-553* and other boats were driven off. On 1 August, together with *U-164*, *U-210*, *U-217* and *U-511* they formed a patrol line, *Pirat*, ahead of the convoy. On the 22nd the convoy was located and on the morning of the 3rd, Thurmann attacked the Belgian SS *Belgian Soldier*, which was damaged by the torpedo and was later sunk by *U-607*. It was also thought that Thurmann had sunk the British MV *Lochkatrine* but she was in fact sunk by the U-boat ace *Kapitänleutnant* Erich Topp on 3 August. When contact was lost with the convoy a few days later the operation was called off. Thurmann resumed his journey southwards to the Caribbean where he encountered Convoy TAW13 on the 18th, north of Jamaica. In three morning attacks he sank three ships, the British MV *Empire Bede*, the Swedish MV *Blankaholm* and the US SS *John Hancock*, about 95 miles west of Guantanamo Bay. Shortly after the third attack *U-553* was attacked herself by the corvette HMS *Pimpernel* and Thurmann had to make an emergency dive and was kept away from the convoy. He eventually took *U-553* away from the operational area and headed for port, reaching St. Nazaire on 17 September. Once back at base Thurmann was informed he had been promoted to *Korvettenkapitän* on 1 August.

On 23 November, he headed for the North Atlantic, where *U-553* joined *Draufgänger* Group. It had been formed on the 30th west of Ireland to operate against a convoy but it never appeared. On 7 December, the group was ordered north-west to close in on another convoy and *U-553* attempted an attack on a destroyer but this failed. On the morning of the 9th, Thurmann sank the British MV *Charles L.D.*, about 405 miles east of Cape Farewell. Thirty-six of her crew were lost. One other ship was sunk, but not by Thurmann, and the operation ended on the 11th, after strong Iceland-based air cover appeared. *U-553* reached La Pallice on the 18th. After some leave and minor repair work to *U-553*, Thurmann headed out on his tenth, and what would be his last, patrol. He headed out to the North Atlantic on 16 January 1943 and joined *Landsknecht* Group west of Ireland.

On the 20th, he met up with *U-465* and passed a nautical yearbook to her commander Heinz Wolf. That was the last time anyone saw *U-553* or Thurmann. The location and cause was never determined. It was known, however, that *U-553* had sent a message on 20 January which said, '*Sehrohr unklar*' ('periscope unready for action'): it could be that a fault with the periscope led to the boat sinking. Other sources claim that *U-553* was a victim of an aircraft from RAF Coastal Command but whatever the reason Thurmann and his crew were officially reported '*Verschollen*' (missing) on 28 January 1943.

Other awards:
02 Oct 1936: Long Service Award 4th Class
21 Jul 1941: Iron Cross 2nd Class
23 Oct 1941: Iron Cross 1st Class
23 Oct 1941: U-Boat War Badge

Hans-Diedrich Freiherr von TIESENHAUSEN
Kapitänleutnant
2 ships sunk, 40,235 tons
1 ship damaged, 372 tons

Knight's Cross: Awarded on 27 January 1942, as *Kapitänleutnant* and as commander of *U-331* for the sinking of the British battleship HMS *Barham* (31,000 tons) on 25 November 1941.

Hans-Diedrich Freiherr von Tiesenhausen was born on 22 February 1913 in Riga, Latvia, at the time part of the Russian Empire. He was a member of the

(Author's collection)

Baltic German nobility and was the son of Gerhard von Tiesenhausen, a noted architect. The young von Tiesenhausen joined the *Reichsmarine* in April 1934 and was assigned to the II. *Schiffsstammabteilung* in the Baltic. From June he served aboard the sail training ship *Gorch Fock*, and the light cruiser *Karlsruhe* as well as attending various training courses at the Naval Academy. From October 1936 von Tiesenhausen served aboard the light cruiser *Nürnberg*, and in April 1937 was commissioned as a *Leutnant zur See*. From May he served as adjutant aboard *Nürnberg*, taking part in neutrality patrols in Spanish waters. In March 1938 he served with the 5th Naval Artillery Battalion and later as adjutant with an anti-aircraft regiment in Pillau. Von Tiesenhausen was promoted to *Oberleutnant zur See* in April 1939, before he transferred to the U-boat service in October. In December he was assigned as Second Watch Officer to *U-23*, under the command of *Kapitänleutnant* Otto Kretschmer. He served with Kretschmer until 6 May 1940, taking part in three successful war patrols during which Kretschmer sank five ships for a total of 27,000 tons, as well as one destroyer. He was then posted to *U-93* as First Watch Officer, serving under *Kapitänleutnant* Claus Korth.

On 31 March 1941, von Tiesenhausen was named as commander of *U-331*, a Type VIIC boat built by Nordseewerke in Emden. He took his new boat out from Kiel on 2 July for operations in the North Atlantic, one of a number of boats operating in loose formation south of Greenland. No convoys were sighted until the 17th, but only two ships were damaged in attacks. From 6 August von Tiesenhausen joined other boats near Gibraltar and the Azores, waiting to operate against an expected convoy, but the escorts prevented any attacks. *U-331* put in at Lorient on the 19th. About a week later von Tiesenhausen left for the Mediterranean, and *U-331* passed through the Straits of Gibraltar during the night of the 19th/20th. She was one of six boats of the newly-formed *Goeben* Group, the first Type VII boats to enter the Mediterranean. On 10 October he engaged three British tank landing craft off Sidi Barrani, Egypt, inflicting slight damage to HMS *TLC-18* with his deck guns. The attack was broken off after *U-331* was hit by 40mm shells fired from one of the ships, which wounded two of the crew and damaged the U-boat's conning tower. The following day von Tiesenhausen put in at Salamis, Greece.

On 12 November, *U-331* left port on a special operation, and during the night of the 17th/18th, von Tiesenhausen landed seven men of the *Lehrregiment Brandenburg* east

Leutnant zur See *Hans-Diedrich von Tiesenhausen with his father* Oberst *Gerhard von Tiesenhausen, 1939.* (Author's collection)

of Ras Gibeisa, on a mission to blow up a railway line near the Egyptian coast. After completion of the mission von Tiesenhausen was given a free hand to patrol and attack Allied targets along the coast. On the morning of 25th, *U-331* detected the faint engine noises of numerous ships and von Tiesenhausen moved his boat to intercept them. The ships were the 1st Battle Squadron, three British battleships, HMS *Barham*, *Queen Elizabeth* and *Valiant*, with an escort of eight destroyers. Von Tiesenhausen got ready to act and fired all four bow torpedoes at a range of 410 yards. He hadn't had time to aim at the leading battleship, and just fired and then quickly dived, without knowing for certain of the results of his attack. He heard the torpedoes explode and radioed to say he had sunk the battleship *Queen Elizabeth* with a single torpedo. In fact he had hit HMS *Barham* with three torpedoes. She had been struck between the funnel and 'Y' turret with devastating consequences for the ship and her crew. There had been no time for evasive action when the torpedoes had struck; they caused a single massive water column to throw up in the air. The impact caused *Barham* to list heavily to port, and with a slight pause at an angle of about 40 degrees, she continued to list for about four minutes and then water flooded in through her funnel. She was by now lying on her side when a massive magazine explosion occurred, and *Barham* suddenly disintegrated and the wreck was shrouded by a huge pall of smoke. The entire British Battle Squadron was watching the dramatic scene. Admiral Cunningham who was aboard HMS *Queen Elizabeth*, said, 'It was ghastly to look at, a horrible and awe-inspiring spectacle when one realized what it meant'. The explosion was captured on film by British news cameraman John Turner. The sinking of HMS *Barham* remains one of the most lasting images of the Second World War. Due to the speed of her sinking, 862 officers and ratings were lost, including two who later died from their wounds after being rescued. The destroyer HMS *Hotspur* rescued 337 survivors and the Australian destroyer *Nizam* rescued another 150 men. Von Tiesenhausen returned to Salamis on 3 December. He then went directly to Berlin, where he was treated as a hero, although the sinking of *Barham* had not been confirmed by the British. Her loss wasn't announced by the British Admiralty until 27 January 1942. At the end of his fourth patrol von Tiesenhausen was greeted at La Spezia and immediately presented with his Knight's Cross. He was also informed that he had been promoted to *Kapitänleutnant*.

With the celebrations over, von Tiesenhausen left for a minelaying operation on 4 April, *U-331* had been ordered to lay mines off the coast of Beirut. Later on the 15th von Tiesenhausen made an unsuccessful attack on the SS *Lyder Sagen* and on the 16th reported sinking two sailing vessels by gunfire off the Lebanese coast, but this has never been confirmed. He returned to Salamis on the 19th. His next four patrols passed without incident. On 7 November, he left La Spezia on his tenth patrol and headed for the Algerian coast. On the afternoon of the 9th von Tiesenhausen sighted the American troop transport USS *Leedstown* near Algiers. She had been previously attacked by two German Ju 88 aircraft, and had been hit by an aerial torpedo. One of the aircraft had been shot down but the USS *Leedstown* had been seriously damaged. At 14:04 hours, von Tiesenhausen fired a spread of four torpedoes. The ship was struck on the starboard side by two of these torpedoes and abandoned after ten minutes when she started to list heavily, and sank soon after. Her commander and 103 survivors were later picked up by HMS *Samphire*. At dawn two days later *U-331* was moving westwards on the surface close to Algiers when she was sighted by a Hudson aircraft of 500 Squadron.

HMS Barham *was one of the largest British warships sunk by a U-boat during the Second World War. On 28 December 1939, she was struck by a torpedo fired from* U-30 *and was damaged on the port side. She was out of action for six months while being repaired at Birkenhead and she returned to service on 30 June 1940 – but worse was to follow.* (Author's collection)

When the aircraft appeared to turn towards the boat von Tiesenhausen ordered a crash dive to escape. The Hudson returned two hours later and sighted the U-boat back on the surface. The aircraft dived out of the sun from 10,000ft and dropped four depth charges, straddling the boat. The damage caused made it impossible for the boat to dive. *U-331* was now a sitting duck, unable to dive and escape an attack. Another attack was made by two newly-arrived Hudsons, also from 500 Squadron, and *U-331* was damaged further. Two hours after the initial attack von Tiesenhausen raised a white flag, and the aircraft flew off. During the lull members of his crew that gone overboard were pulled back on the U-boat and von Tiesenhausen helped with the injured. The Hudsons returned and circled the boat, awaiting the arrival of the destroyer HMS *Wilton*. However, a force of three Albacores and three Martlet aircraft arrived from the carrier HMS *Formidable* and were apparently unaware that the boat had surrendered. One Martlet made a strafing attack, killing most of the men on the U-boat and wounding von Tiesenhausen. Then one of the aircraft launched a torpedo, hitting *U-331* and exploding causing her to begin to sink. Thirty-three crew members were lost but von Tiesenhausen and sixteen others survived.

Von Tiesenhausen spent the next few years as a prisoner-of-war, first in England and later in Canada. He returned to Germany in 1947 working as a joiner. During the autumn of 1951 he left Germany and went back to Canada. He settled in Vancouver where he remained for the rest of his life, working as an interior designer, and becoming an excellent nature photographer. Von Tiesenhausen died on 17 August 2000, in Vancouver, Canada.

Other awards:
08 Apr 1938: Long Service Award 4th Class
30 Jan 1940: Iron Cross 2nd Class
26 Feb 1940: U-Boat War Badge
25 Jun 1940: Return of Memel Commemorative Medal
06 Sep 1940: Commemorative Medal of 01 Oct 1938
00 Nov 1941: Italian Bravery Medal in Bronze
07 Dec 1941: Iron Cross 1st Class
25 Mar 1942: Italian Bravery Medal in Silver

Nikolaus Heinrich TIMM
Korvettenkapitän
9 ships sunk, 53,782 tons

Knight's Cross: Awarded on 17 September 1944 as *Korvettenkapitän* and as commander of *U-862* for sinking seven ships for a total of 39,426 shipping tons.

Heinrich Timm was born on 30 April 1910 in Bremen and joined the *Reichsmarine* in October 1933, being initially assigned to the 6th Company of II. *Schiffsstammdivision* in the Baltic. Between August 1934 a September 1936 Timm served aboard the light cruiser *Leipzig* and the 'pocket battleship' *Admiral Scheer*. During this time he was commissioned as a *Leutnant zur See* and in October 1937 was promoted to *Oberleutnant zur See*. He then served as First Watch Officer aboard the minesweepers *M132* and *M110* before taking command of *M7* in July 1939. His first success was at Helgoland, where he located and attacked the British submarine HMS *Starfish* on 9 January 1940. He caused so much damage she was forced to surface and was scuttled. Timm then rescued her crew. He

was promoted to *Kapitänleutnant* on 1 February 1940 and won the Iron Cross 1st Class for action in the Norwegian invasion, and in May 1941 he transferred to the U-boat service.

He underwent commander training at Pillau before being appointed commander of *U-251* in August 1941. She was a Type VIIC boat built by Bremer Vulkau in Vegesack, and commissioned in September. In mid-April 1942, Timm took his new boat out from Kiel for operations in Northern Waters, he then put in at Kirkenes on the 25th. Four days later he left port and joined other boats of *Strauchritter* Group deployed to intercept Convoy QP11. Contact was made on the 30th, and some of the boats carried out successful attacks on the convoy. Timm missed a destroyer. Early on 3 May he was more successful, sinking the British SS *Jutland*. She had already been attacked from the air south of Bear Island the day before and her crew

(Scherzer)

had abandoned her. She sank at 00:14 hours north of Vannöy, Norway. Timm returned to Kirkenes on the 7th.

He left for his new base at Skjomenfjord on 7 June, then four days later he joined *U-376* and *U-408* in taking up positions in the Denmark Strait, shadowing convoys and attacking warships. On 1 July they located Convoy PQ17 east of Jan Mayen and were joined by *U-88*, *U-355*, *U-457* and *U-657*. They formed a new patrol line, *Eisteufel*. They made brief contact with the convoy on the 2nd and 3rd and made some unsuccessful attacks. The convoy dispersed a few days later and the sinking of the ships by U-boats and aircraft began. During the early hours of the 10th, Timm torpedoed and sank the Panamanian SS *El Capitan*, north-east of Kharlovka, Russia. She was one of twenty-four ships of PQ17 sunk. Timm put in at Narvik on the 15th. During his next patrol, his fourth, he left on 14 August to carry out an ice reconnaissance ahead of the *Admiral Scheer*, en route to the Kara Sea to attack convoys and shore installations in Operation Wunderland. Once he reached the Kara Sea he surfaced close to Uyedineniya Island and destroyed a Soviet weather station with shells from his deck gun. Then together with six other boats they operated against the westbound Convoy QP14 between 20 and 22 September in an area west of the southern tip of Spitsbergen. Four ships were sunk during the operation, none by Timm. He returned to Narvik on the 26th.

From 30 September 1942 until 29 May 1943 Timm took *U-251* out on three patrols in the area around Narvik and Trondheim. There are no details of these patrols but we do know that Timm failed to sink any ships. In June 1943, *U-251* was temporarily decommissioned, and returned to Germany for an extended refit. Since her crew and as commander could not be left standing idle, they were ordered to proceed to Bremen where, after some leave, they joined a much large boat, *U-862*. It was a Type IXD2 and was to become a *Monsun* boat, one of those operating in the Indian Ocean and the Far East. Timm took his new boat from Bremen to Kiel and then back to Narvik, his old home base. On 3 June 1944, he left port and headed for the Indian Ocean, passing through the Denmark Strait into the North Atlantic. On the 25th he sank the US SS *Robin Goodfellow* west-south-west of St. Helena, with the loss of sixty-nine men, her entire crew. On 1 July Timm was informed that he had been promoted to *Korvettenkapitän*. On 13 August he torpedoed and sank the British SS *Radbury* west of Madagascar, with the loss of twenty-three crew.

U-862 moved up through the Channel and at the northern end sank another British ship, the SS *Empire Lancer*. Three days later he sank the SS *Nairung*, another British merchant ship, about 100 miles north-east of Mozambique. On the 19th he sank the British SS *Wayfarer* about 150 miles east of Mozambique, struck on the port side by a single torpedo. The following day, whilst on the surface an aircraft was spotted, it was a *Catalina* flying boat of 265 Squadron, and *U-862* stayed on the surface and fired at the aircraft. It came straight towards them, very low, so low that Timm thought it might hit the conning tower. The aircraft flew over the boat, inches from the conning tower and crashed into the sea, killing all of its crew. Timm knew that the aircraft must have radioed the position of his boat before it crashed and so he abandoned any thought of going to the Gulf of Aden and instead headed for base at Penang, arriving on 9 September.

On 18 November Timm began his eleventh patrol and took *U-862* out of Batavia and headed for the coast of Australia. He arrived on the 28th and moved eastwards along the southern coastline. On 9 December he attacked the SS *Ilissos* but couldn't sink her due to the rough sea conditions. *Ilissos'* naval gunners returned fire and *U-862* was forced to dive to escape any damage. The ship escaped in heavy rain and Timm managed to evade the ships looking for him and made his way to Tasmania. In the early hours of Christmas Eve he sank the US SS *Robert J. Walker*. She was sunk by a single torpedo while steaming a zigzag course about 165 miles south-east of Sydney. The torpedo struck the starboard side of the stern, blew off the rudder, bent the shaft and destroyed the steering gear. She was struck by a further two torpedoes which created a hole 10ft by 20ft on the starboard side and another hole 6ft by 8ft on the port side. The crew began to abandon ship and remarkably only two crew members were lost. *U-862* became the only German U-boat to sink a ship in the Pacific Ocean. Timm took the boat north-eastwards from the 27th, until 1 January 1945, when he headed due east across the Tasman Sea. From the 7th until the 21st no ships were sighted and Timm headed back towards Australia. On 6 February he sighted the US SS *Peter Silvester* and fired two torpedoes. She sank with the loss of thirty-three of her crew, although the remaining crew together with 142 troops were picked up by the US SS *Cape Edmont*. Timm returned to base on 15th.

During his last two patrols Timm had *U-862* fitted with a *Bachstelze* (Water Wagtail), a small folding autogyro. It carried a man and when towed behind a U-boat on 500ft of cable, it could rise to 400ft, lifted by the unpowered three-blade rotor, which revolved as the *Bachstelze* was towed into the wind. At maximum height, the pilot could see 25 miles in every direction, as opposed to the view from the conning tower of five miles. The *Bachstelze* could only be used in remote areas when no enemy shipping or aircraft were present, however, as the U-boat was completely unable to submerge while it was being used. In normal use there were also a pair of landing skids near the front so that it could land back on the U-boat. There was also an emergency landing system – if the U-boat was attacked or needed to dive the pilot could eject the rotor and parachute to safety. The pilot also could communicate with the U-boat via a telephone. *U-862*'s pilot was Josef Schaefer, the boat's doctor.

Timm was to return *U-862* to Europe but had not left Singapore before the German surrender was announced. On 7 May, the Germans remaining in the Far East were interned by the Japanese Empire and *U-862* became part of the Imperial Japanese Navy, renamed *I-502*. When the British liberated Singapore in late August 1945 the Germans were marched to Changi Prison and in June 1946 they were taken to England. Timm was released in April 1948. He joined the *Bundesmarine* in December 1955 and served in various positions, including that of the first commander of the frigate *Scharnhorst* in 1959. Timm rose to the rank of *Fregattenkapitän* and retired in September 1966. He died on 12 April 1974 in Axstedt, Lower Saxony, Germany. During his time as commander, Timm had the habit of playing music over the boat's loudspeakers. He was given the nickname of 'Tüte', which referred to the cone-shaped paper bag used for sweets and which also resembled an old-fashioned gramophone horn. This was later used for *U-251*'s emblem, which was a '*tüte*' with a torpedo in it.

Other awards:
04 Oct 1937: Long Service Award 4th Class
26 Oct 1939: Return of Memel Commemorative Medal
20 Dec 1939: Commemorative Medal of 01 Oct 1938
10 Jan 1940: Iron Cross 2nd Class
16 May 1940: Iron Cross 1st Class
12 Feb 1942: German Cross in Gold
00 Sep 1942: U-Boat War Badge
29 Sep 1944: U-Boat Combat Clasp in Bronze

Hans-Hartwig TROJER
Kapitänleutnant
21 ships sunk, 70,348 tons
1 ship damaged, 7,197 tons

Knight's Cross: Awarded on 24 March 1943, as *Oberleutnant zur See* and as commander of *U-221* for sinking twenty ships for a total of 60,916 and for damaging another.

(Scherzer)

Hans-Hartwig Trojer was born on 22 January 1916 in Birthälm, Siebenbürgen, part of the Austro-Hungarian Empire and later part of Romania. His village was in Transylvania and earned him the nickname of 'Count Dracula'. Trojer joined the *Kriegsmarine* in April 1936 and was assigned to the II. *Schiffsstammdivision* in the Baltic, before serving aboard the sailing ship *Duhren* and the battleship *Schleswig-Holstein*. From January 1938, he attended an officers' training course at Kiel and then at Flensburg, before returning aboard the *Schleswig-Holstein* in October. Commissioned as a *Leutnant zur See* the same month, Trojer entered the U-boat service shortly afterwards. In August 1938, he served aboard *U-34* as Second Watch Officer, and from September 1940 he served as First Watch Officer. He took part in six war patrols, serving under *Kapitänleutnant* Wilhelm Rollmann, during which time twenty-one ships were sunk. He was promoted to *Oberleutnant zur See* in October 1940, and served briefly aboard *U-67* as Second Watch Officer from January 1941, under *Kapitänleutnant* Heinrich Bleichrodt. In June he attended a commanders training course, and the following month he was appointed commander of *U-3*, a training boat at Pillau.

On 10 March 1942, Trojer was named as commander of *U-221*, a Type VIIC boat built by Germania Werft in Kiel. He left on his first patrol on 1 September, as part of *Lohr* Group heading towards Newfoundland. The boats were directed to Convoy SC99, but *U-221* was driven off and contact was lost until the next day, when *U-440* found the convoy. Again the boats were driven away by the escorts and the pursuit was abandoned. On the 15th, outward-bound boats in the area west of Ireland were formed into *Pfeil* Group. The same day Trojer sighted Convoy ON129 and the boats prepared for an attack, but the convoy was lost in fog. It was briefly sighted again two days later but again was lost and the operation was terminated. *Pfeil* Group then moved north-eastwards on the 18th and north-westwards the day after. *U-221* sighted the convoy and *Pfeil* Group joined *Lohs* Group in an attack. However, the weather turned and a gale became a hurricane and on the 22nd the operation was once again called off. A new patrol line, *Blitz*, was formed 500 miles south-east of Cape Farewell and it moved south-westwards towards another convoy, again an attack was delayed because of the weather. *Blitz* Group was by now scattered and before they reformed another convoy was located. The boats searched for the convoy as *Tiger* Group but failed to locate it: yet again bad weather had prevented any attack and so the operation was called off. On the 29th, the boats were then ordered to a refuelling area near the Azores. The *Tiger* boats formed a new patrol line, *Wotan*, from 8 October east of Newfoundland and waited for a convoy. During the early hours of the 12th, the group was ordered to intercept Convoy SC104, which had been sighted during the night in the central North Atlantic. On the 13th, Trojer sank three ships, the Norwegian SS *Fagersten* and SS *Senta* and the British SS *Ashworth*, about 500 miles east of Belle Island Strait. Soon after midnight on the 14th he sank the US SS *Susana*, which broke in two and sank in less than ten minutes with the loss of thirty-eight of her crew. On the same day he sank the SS *Southern Empress*, a British whale factory ship, carrying landing craft and 11,700 tons of oil. Allied aircraft then appeared overhead and the operation was called off on the 15th. Trojer returned to base on the 22nd. He had sunk five ships and another ten landing craft were lost with the *Southern Empress*. As a result of his success, Trojer and his crew were mentioned in the daily Armed Forces Bulletin, the *Wehrmachtsbericht*, of 14 October 1942, 'In the convoy battles in the North Atlantic, the U-boat of *Oberleutnant zur See* Trojer was particularly successful, destroying five vessels for a total of 29,681 tons.' It was the highest confirmed score of any U-boat on the North Atlantic run in the autumn of 1942.

His second patrol began on 23 November, again in the North Atlantic, where he joined a new group, *Draufgänger*, west of Ireland. The group waited for a convoy that failed to show. On 7 December, the group was ordered to close on Convoy HX217, but the operation was called off due to strong air cover. On the 8th, *U-221* collided with *U-254*, when on the surface having failed to see each other in the dark and rough sea. *U-254* sank immediately, killing its commander and forty-one of her crew. The crew of *U-221* dived into the sea tied to ropes in an effort to rescue their comrades. Four cold and bedraggled survivors were dragged out and onto the deck. Unable to dive, Trojer was forced to abort his patrol and return to his base. Later the Norwegian corvette *Potentilla* arrived at the scene of the incident and came upon wreckage and human remains, her captain speculated that a B24 aircraft must have sunk a U-boat. Dönitz later said of the incident, 'Generally speaking, it's not practical to have more than thirteen to fifteen U-boats on a single convoy.' He exonerated Trojer, saying that it was a freak accident.

When the major repairs were complete on *U-221*, Trojer took her out to the North Atlantic on 27 February 1943. He joined *Neuland* Group west of Ireland, and on 7 March he sank the Norwegian MV *Jamaica*. She was hit by a single torpedo and broke in two and sank in less than two minutes. The survivors launched the lifeboats, but two had been damaged and could not be used. The motor lifeboat was sucked down as the ship sank and came up capsized. The boat was righted, bailed out and later held thirteen survivors. Trojer questioned the survivors and the U-boat accidently rammed a lifeboat, throwing the occupants into the sea. The lifeboats were sighted on 9 March by aircraft that reported their position and dropped medical supplies and water. However, they weren't rescued until the 18th, when they were picked up by HMS *Borage*. Trojer then took *U-221* northwards, still with *Neuland* Group, and on the 9th began to search for Convoy HX22. They found the convoy the following day and attacked. Trojer sank two ships, the British SS *Tucurinca* and the US SS *Andrea F. Luckenbach*. He also hit the SS *Lawton B. Evans*, another US ship, but she was only damaged and managed to reach port. Immediately after this, *U-221* was located and attacked with depth charges but escaped. On the 13th the operation against HX228 ended and *U-221* and eight other southern *Neuland* boats formed *Dränger* Group, west of Ireland, to operate against Convoy HX229. On the morning of the 16th, a convoy was sighted and *Dränger*, *Stürmer* and *Raubgraf* Groups were ordered to attack. Later the same day a second convoy appeared. The largest convoy action of the war then took place. More than forty U-boats took part and sank twenty-one Allied ships. On the 17th, *U-221* came under attack again by a Liberator but managed to escape. The following day Trojer sank two more ships from HX229, the US SS *Walter Q. Gresham* and the British MV *Canadian Star*. Trojer then headed for home, arriving in St. Nazaire on 28 March.

Trojer was promoted to *Kapitänleutnant* on 1 April and left port on his next patrol just over a month later. He was directed towards the eastbound Convoy HX237. On the 12th he sank the Norwegian tanker MV *Sandanger* in thick fog. She was hit amidships in the pump room by three torpedoes and immediately caught fire. Some of her survivors tried to abandon ship in boats and rafts but they died in the burning sea. After the tanker broke in two the stern sank while the burning forepart remained afloat. Of her crew of thirty-nine, twenty were lost. From the 18th, *U-221* became part of a new group, *Oder*, and waited for another convoy, but it passed well to the north of the *Oder* boats. A new patrol line, *Mosel*, was formed on the 21st, about 400 miles south of Cape Farewell. The operation was cancelled after one boat was damaged and *U-752* was lost. Trojer then took his boat to an assembly area south-west of the Azores. Convoy operations in the North Atlantic had been halted and it was decided to try and intercept convoys between the US and the Mediterranean out in the Atlantic beyond the range of land-based aircraft. A new patrol line, *Trutz*, was formed during the night of the 30th/31st, to await Convoys UGS9 and GUS7A. However by the evening of 5 June, the convoys had failed to show and it was thought that they must have passed to the north of the patrol line. The group was broken up and moved 600 miles to the north, and from the 8th until the 29th, *U-221* chased various convoys as part of *Trutz*, but the convoys were never sighted. *U-221* left the group, together with *U-558*, and patrolled in the Lisbon area before returning to St. Nazaire on 21 July.

Trojer and his crew were granted leave before leaving for their next patrol on 20 September, and headed out to the North Atlantic. On the 27th, *U-221* was attacked by a RAF Halifax, 800 miles south-west of Ireland. Eight depth charges were dropped and *U-221* quickly sank. During the action the Halifax's starboard fuel tank was hit by anti-aircraft fire from the boat and caught fire. The wireless operator and the radar operator were killed. The pilot ditched the aircraft and six survivors climbed into a dinghy. Among the survivors was Group Captain Mead, the station commander of RAF Holmesley South, who had been flying as second pilot to gain experience. The six men were adrift for eleven days before being picked up by the destroyer HMS *Mahratta*. For the action the pilot, Flying Officer Hartley, was awarded the Distinguished Flying Cross. As for Trojer and his crew they were never seen again, believed drowned.

Other awards:
12 Nov 1939: U-Boat War Badge
07 Feb 1940: Iron Cross 2nd Class
03 Apr 1940: Long Service Award 4th Class
05 Aug 1940: Iron Cross 1st Class

Otto Emil WESTPHALEN

Oberleutnant zur See
5 ships sunk, 24,286 tons
1 ship damaged, 8,129 tons

Knight's Cross: Awarded on 23 March 1945, as *Oberleutnant zur See* and as commander of *U-968* for sinking five ships for a total of 24,286 shipping tons and for damaging one other.

Born in Hamburg on 12 March 1920, Otto Westphalen began his naval career in October 1938, when he joined the *Kriegsmarine* at the age of eighteen. He began his basic training aboard the sail training ship *Gorch Fock* from February 1939 and five months later was assigned to the battleship *Schlesien*. From March 1940, he attended the Torpedo School at Flensburg and in May was assigned to the torpedo boat *Kondor* for six months. Promoted to *Oberfähnrich zur See* in August, Westphalen was assigned to *U-566* as Second Watch Officer from March 1941, taking part in three patrols whilst under *Kapitänleutnant* Dietrich Borchert. Commissioned as a *Leutnant zur See* a month later, Westphalen was appointed commander of *U-968*, a Type VIIC boat, in March 1943. He was promoted to *Oberleutnant zur See* in April and from September he took part in trials in the Baltic, testing equipment to counter airborne radar aboard *U-986*.

In January 1944, together with another U-boat commander Wolfgang Dittmers, he was asked to serve on the panel of a court martial of the commander of *U-154*, Oskar Heinz Kusch. He had been accused of defeatism by his First Officer Dr. Ulrich Abel, who had been angered by a negative report Kusch gave him and plotted his downfall. The report stated that Abel was, 'inflexible, rigid and a one-sided officer' of 'average talent'. On 12 January Abel filed a formal complaint accusing Kusch of sedition, followed by a second complaint on the 25th, accusing him of cowardice.

The first report triggered legal proceedings and Kusch was arrested by the Gestapo and confined at the Angers Military Prison in France. Abel's charges of sedition were backed up by two other officers on *U-154*. All three men swore that Kusch had openly ridiculed Hitler. Kusch had thrown out the standard photograph of Hitler in his U-boat with the comment, 'There will no more idol worship on this boat'. He had also said that he thought Germany would soon lose the war. On 26 January he was found guilty, and three days later he was sentenced to death. Both Westphalen and Dittmar had pushed for the death sentence. Dönitz did nothing to save Kusch and on 12 May 1944 he was executed by firing squad in Kiel-Holtenau. In 1996 Kusch's record was wiped clean and he was deemed a victim of Nazi injustice. Dr. Abel himself died three weeks before Kusch when his boat, *U-193*, was sunk on its first patrol.

(Scherzer)

On 7 March, with the trial behind him, Westphalen returned to *U-968* and left Kiel for northern Waters, joining *Hammer* Group in its search for Convoy JW58. When the boats made contact with the convoy Westphalen was one of the first to attack but was unsuccessful. His boat was damaged whilst making another attack. Westphalen then decided to put in at Narvik on 2 April. The repairs to the boat took more time than expected and it wasn't until July that Westphalen left for operations once again. On the 18th, *U-968* was sighted by a Liberator aircraft and two depth-charge attacks were made despite heavy anti-aircraft fire from the U-boat and as a result the aircraft was shot down. *U-968* was damaged in three more attacks on the morning of the 19th and one crewman was killed and another six were wounded. The Allies seemed to have control of the skies. Westphalen put in at Bogenbucht two days later. On 29 August, he left for his next patrol, a minelaying operation as part of *Dachs* Group. Records show that no ships were sunk or damaged as a result of these mines. The operation ended on 10 September. His third and fourth patrols were both short and unsuccessful, Westphalen sighted no convoys.

In early February 1945 he left for operations, joining *Rasmus* Group in Bear Island Passage. The group was attempting to reach the eastbound Convoy JW64 but failed because of the strong escort. On the 14th he torpedoed the Norwegian tanker SS *Norfjell*, damaging her and killing two crew members when the torpedo struck the engine room. She was later towed to Rosta and taken over by the Soviet Navy in June 1945. On 16 February a combined force of British and Soviet naval vessels attempted to drive the waiting U-boats away before their return journey. The next day Westphalen sighted the convoy and attacked and torpedoed two ships, damaging the escorting sloop HMS *Lark* and the US SS *Horace Gray*. Both were seriously damaged: the *Lark* was later handed over to the Soviets and declared a total loss. The *Horace Gray* began to sink whilst being towed and was also later declared a total loss. That same day he also sank the US SS *Thomas Scott*, 13 miles south-west of Kilden Island as the ship tried to get into her assigned station when the convoy was being formed. The torpedo struck by hatch No. 3 and caused an immediate list to starboard. The ship went out of control, broke in two and after just ten minutes the crew abandoned ship. The Soviets later took the ship in tow, but she broke in two and sank. The patrol ended on the 20th and *U-968* headed for its new base at Kilbotn in Norway

On 12 March, Westphalen took *U-968* out for operations where he joined *Hagen* Group in Bear Island Passage, awaiting Convoy JW65. Although two patrol lines were formed the convoy passed the first line in a snowstorm. One ship was torpedoed and damaged but not by Westphalen. The second line was passed at noon. On the 20th, Westphalen sunk the US SS *Thomas Donaldson*, together with the British sloop HMS *Lapwing*. After the convoy entered Kola Inlet on the 21st, the boats attempted to operate against the aircraft carriers, HMS *Campania* and *Trumpeter*, but this proved unsuccessful. Unable to make any more attacks Westphalen returned *U-968* to base on 30 March. On 21 April, the day after Hitler's fifty-sixth and last birthday, Westphalen left once again for the Kola Inlet. En route some of the boats he was with sighted a Soviet coastal convoy on 21st and 22nd. Westphalen did not take part in the action. On the 29th he attacked a group of ships which included HMS *Alnwick Castle* and HMS *Honeysuckle*, but failed to hit any with his torpedoes.

When Dönitz, the new Reich President of Nazi Germany, declared the end of the U-boat war on 4 May 1945, Westphalen was still at sea. When he heard the order on the radio he put in at Harstad on the 6th and then left for Skjomenfjord on the 7th. He left again heading for Narvik where he surrendered to British troops. Westphalen was taken into captivity and *U-968* was together with 116 other boats disposed of by the Royal Navy during Operation Deadlight. Westphalen returned to Germany just over a year later and worked in civilian life. He was asked about the Kusch affair when he served on his court martial, and tried to defend his actions by saying that Kusch's political views had somehow made his U-boat less effective during the war. A questionable statement at best! He did admit that he would have supported a petition for clemency, with probation to a fighting unit, had such a plea been heard. Westphalen later settled in Hamburg where he died on 9 January 2008, at the age of eighty-seven.

Other awards:
08 Oct 1941: Iron Cross 2nd Class
08 Oct 1941: U-Boat War Badge
03 Apr 1944: Iron Cross 1st Class
18 Feb 1945: German Cross in Gold

Werner WINTER
Korvettenkapitän
15 ships sunk, 79,302 tons

Knight's Cross: Awarded on 5 June 1942, as *Kapitänleutnant* and as commander of *U-103* for sinking fifteen ships (eight in just eleven days) for 79,302 shipping tons.

Werner Winter was born in Hamburg on 26 March 1912, and joined the *Reichsmarine* as an Officer Cadet in April 1930. He spent the next four years training and was assigned to the light cruiser *Emden* and the survey ship *Meteor* as well as a torpedo boat. He attended

various different training courses at Flensburg and was commissioned as a *Leutnant zur See* in October 1934. He joined the U-boat service in July 1935 and from January 1936, Winter was assigned to *U-17* as Watch Officer and was promoted to *Oberleutnant zur See* in June. In October 1937 he took command of *U-22*, a Type IIB boat, and made two successful patrols during the Polish campaign in September 1939. He was promoted to *Kapitänleutnant* in June 1939 and from November served as a staff officer attached to the office of the commander of U-boats.

On 15 July 1941, Winter took over command of *U-103* from Viktor Schütze. His new command was a Type IXB boat built in Bremen. Winter left for his first patrol on 10 September. He left to operate in the Freetown area, and from the 18th, together with *U-67*, *U-68* and *U-107*, proceeded south. On the 21st *U-107* sighted Convoy SL87 west of the Canaries. There he sank two British merchant

(Wehrkundearchiv)

ships on the evening of the 22nd, the SS *Niceto de Larrinaga* and the MV *Edward Blyden*. The attacks were made over three days and a total of seven ships were sunk from the convoy. After the operation Winter and the other boats continued south to the area west of Freetown, with *U-67* and *U-68* going to Tarafal Bay. Winter had no success and together with the other boats began the return journey. On 2 October *U-103* and *U-107* joined *Störtebecker* Group west of Spain, where a patrol line had been planned for the 5th, to operate against the expected Convoy HG76 from Gibraltar. However, air reconnaissance failed to find the convoy and on the 7th the boats were directed instead against Convoy SL91. Winter, however, had to leave as he was running short of fuel and so headed for Lorient, arriving on 9 November.

On 3 January 1942, Winter left to operate off the US east coast and *U-103* was one of the first U-boats of Operation *Paukenschlag*. Attacks on US shipping, however, did not begin until the 13th. On 2 February, Winter sank the US tanker SS *W.L. Steed* about 90 miles off the mouth of the Delaware River. She was struck on the starboard side by two torpedoes, and after the crew had abandoned ship and headed for the lifeboats, the U-boat began to shell the ship with eighty-three rounds from its deck gun, which resulted in the ship catching fire. A *coup de grâce* torpedo was fired at 21:20 hours which caused her cargo of oil to explode, sending flames 500ft in the air. The tanker settled by the bow, capsized and sank within ten minutes. The four lifeboats had by now drifted apart in a snowstorm with rough seas and icy temperatures, and most of the survivors died of exposure. Thirty-four crew were lost, only four surviving. On the 4th he sank the Panamanian SS *San Gil*, south-east of Ocean City, Maryland by torpedo and gunfire. He moved south and on the 5th he sank two US ship the SS *India Arrow* and SS *China Arrow* south-east of Delaware Bay. Winter had no further success and reached his new base of St. Nazaire on 1 March.

The next patrol, his fifth, began on 15 April when he left for operations in the Caribbean. On 5 May, Winter sank the British SS *Stanbank* north-east of Bermuda. He continued to the coast of Florida, passed through the Straits of Florida and entered the Caribbean through the Yucatan Channel. On the 17th he sank the US SS *Ruth Lykes*, north-east of Cauguira, Honduras and on the 19th he sank the US SS *Ogontz*. She was hit by a single torpedo about 70 miles south-east of Cozumel Island off Yucatan. Nineteen crewmen died when a falling mast hit one of the lifeboats causing most of the casualties. *U-103* operated from the 20th in an area south of Cuba. Early on the 21st he sank two US ships, the SS *Clare* and SS *Elizabeth*, both were about 30 miles south of Cape Corrientes, Cuba. On the 23rd he sank the American tanker SS *Samuel Q. Brown*, followed by the Dutch MV *Hector* the following day. On the 26th Winter claimed the US SS *Alcoa Carrier*, sunk by torpedo and gunfire, and two days later he sank the US tanker SS *New Jersey* south-east of Grand Cayman. In eleven days Winter had sunk eight ships for a total of 36,203 shipping tons. It was no surprise that he had been recommended for the Knight's Cross. He was also mentioned in the *Wehrmacht* Communiqué of 1 June 1942, which reported: 'During the successes of German U-boats off the American coast, the boat of *Kapitänleutnant* Winter has been particularly successful.'

In July Winter was taken off operational duties and appointed commander of the 1st U-boat Flotilla in Brest. Promoted to *Korvettenkapitän* on 21 February 1943, Winter was captured by US troops on 6 September 1944 whilst serving on the staff of the Sea Commandant of Brest. He was later transferred to Britain where he remained in captivity until he returned to Germany in November 1947. Almost ten years later in April 1957, Winter entered the *Bundesmarine* and was soon appointed commandant of Kiel in the December with the rank of *Fregattenkapitän*. From August 1961 he served as commander of *Zerstörer 1*, which had been the USS *Anthony* during the war, being transferred to the West German Navy in January 1958. From October 1963 he was attached to the Navy Telecommunications Section and was appointed its commander in April 1965. Winter retired from active service in March 1970 with the rank of *Kapitän zur See*. He remained in Kiel where he died at the age of sixty on 9 September 1972.

Other awards:
02 Oct 1936: Long Service Award 4th Class
18 Sep 1939: Iron Cross 2nd Class
18 Sep 1939: U-Boat War Badge
20 Dec 1939: Commemorative Medal of 01 Oct 1938
10 Nov 1941: Iron Cross 1st Class
30 Jan 1944: War Service Cross 2nd Class with Swords

<u>Hans</u> Ludwig WITT
Korvettenkapitän
19 ships sunk, 100,773 tons

Knight's Cross: Awarded on 17 December 1942, as *Kapitänleutnant* and as commander of *U-129* for the sinking of sixteen ships for a total of 74,183 shipping tons.

Hans Witt was born on 25 December 1909, in Bantzen, Saxony and joined the *Reichsmarine* as an Officer Candidate in April 1929. He spent five years in training on the sail training ship *Niobe* and later saw service aboard the light cruisers *Emden* and

Karlsruhe. Witt was commissioned as a *Leutnant zur See* in October 1933 and was assigned to the battleship *Hessen* for twelve months. He then transferred to the 1st Naval Artillery Battalion, serving as a company officer, and was promoted to *Oberleutnant zur See* on 1 June 1935. Shortly after his promotion he was transferred to a training battalion of the 1st Destroyer Division. In January 1937, he took command of the torpedo boat *Leberecht Maaß* and from May 1938 served as *Rollenoffizier* aboard the battleship *Schlesien*, being promoted to *Kapitänleutnant* in July. From March 1940 Witt served aboard the sail training ships *Gorch Fock* and *Albert Leo Schlageter* as a training officer. He later served aboard the cadet training ship *Tannenberg* in a similar capacity.

In October 1941 he transferred to the U-boat service and was attached to the U-boat

School at Pillau until December. He then took command of *U-181*, a training boat, and attended various training courses. In May 1942, Witt was appointed commander of *U-129*, a Type IXC boat built in Bremen by AG Weser. His first patrol began on 20 May when he left for operations in the Caribbean where on 10 June he sank the Norwegian MV *L.A. Christensen*. She sank vertically with a heavy list to port after about twelve minutes, which gave time for the crew to escape in the lifeboats and they were all safely picked up. On the 12th he sank the British SS *Hardwicke Grange*. She was struck by two torpedoes north of Puerto Rico. Witt surfaced about a mile away and ordered the deck guns to open fire. The ship was hit by twenty-six high explosive rounds. First the navigating bridge was hit, which caused fires to break out amidships then fire was concentrated on the hull until the vessel sank. Three crew members, the third engineer and two greasers, were lost below. The rest of the crew including the master landed at Monte Cristi, Dominican Republic thirteen days later in a lifeboat. Witt then took *U-129* to an area north of Cuba where on the evening of the 18th, he torpedoed and sank the US SS *Millinocket* in the Nicholas Channel. By late June *U-129* was in the Gulf of Mexico where on the 17th Witt sank the Mexican SS *Tuxpam*. After being struck by the torpedo the ship settled by the stern, but did not sink, so Witt surfaced and ordered the deck guns to open fire. The ship caught fire and sank after fifty-two rounds had been fired. Eight crewmen were lost. That same afternoon he also sank another Mexican ship, the tanker SS *Las Choapas*. She was struck by a single torpedo and quickly sank. On 1 July, Witt sank the Norwegian SS *Cadmus*, hit on the port side by a single torpedo and sank in the Gulf of Mexico. *U-129* then surfaced so Witt and his First Officer could question the crew, they also picked sixteen banana tiers out of the sea, which had been part of the cargo of the ship. The next day he sank the Norwegian MV *Gundersen* before leaving the Gulf. On the 14th he sank the Soviet tanker MV *Tuapse* north-west of Havana after the ship had been spotted four hours earlier. She was later finished off with a third torpedo and sunk soon after with the loss of eight of her crew. Witt took *U-129* in the western Caribbean and on the 12th, just before midnight he sank the US SS *Tachirá*. She was hit on the starboard side by a single torpedo about 375 miles west of Jamaica. The torpedo struck No. 4 hatch and caused the ship to sink in three minutes, but most of her crew were able to escape in lifeboats. On the 19th he sank the Norwegian SS *Port Antonio*, hit on the starboard side amidships by a single torpedo and sank in two minutes. Witt then made his way towards the Atlantic and on the 2nd he sank the US SS *Onondaga*, five miles north of Cayo Guillermo. Twenty of her crew were killed, while eight officers and twenty-five crewmen and one passenger abandoned ship by jumping overboard and swimming to the lifeboats. In early August *U-129* was refuelled by *U-463* and made her way to Lorient, arriving on the 21st. Witt had been extremely successful, he had sunk eleven ships in forty-three days for a total of 41,570 tons. When he arrived back at Lorient he was awarded the Iron Cross 2nd and 1st Classes.

On 28 September, Witt left for the Western Atlantic to an area east of the Lesser Antilles. On 15 October he sank the Norwegian MV *Trafalgar*, about 110 miles north-east of Guadeloupe. On the 23rd he sank the US SS *Reuben Tipton* about 400 miles north-east of Trinidad. She was hit by a single torpedo on the starboard side in the No. 1 hold. Witt ordered another torpedo to be launched and it hit the ship on the port side in the engine room and the No. 4 hold, which caused her to sink in four minutes. Seven days later he sank the SS *West Kebar*, struck by a single torpedo about 350 miles north-east of Barbados. The torpedo hit amidships in the No. 3 deep tank, blew a hole 25ft by 30ft in the bulkhead between No. 3 hold and the engine room, stopped the engines, destroyed both starboard lifeboats and killed one officer and two crewmen. Witt fired a *coup de grâce* torpedo about an hour and twenty minutes after the first torpedo had hit. The ship broke in two and sank. Eight officers, twenty-seven crewmen and eleven armed guards made it to the remaining two lifeboats, and were picked up in November. From early November Witt was in the eastern Caribbean, and on the morning of the 5th had sighted Convoy TAG18 north of Curaçao. Here he sank two tankers, the US SS *Meton* and the Norwegian SS *Astrell. U-129* was then driven off by the escorts. In mid-December the boat was refuelled south of the Azores and Witt then decided to head for port. He arrived in Lorient on 6 January 1943.

Before he started his next patrol Witt was granted some leave and was promoted to *Korvettenkapitän* on 1 February. On 11 March he left for the Western Atlantic and on 2 April sank the British MV *Melbourne Star*. She was struck by three of the four torpedoes fired about 480 miles south-east of Bermuda. She blew up and sank in less than two minutes. Of her crew of 117, only four survived. Witt then received orders to patrol off the coast of the US between Cape Hatteras and Cape Lookout. During the night of the 21st/22nd he attempted to attack a New York–Guantanamo convoy but was driven off by the destroyer USS *Swanson*. On the 24th he sank the American SS *Santa Catalina* about 370 miles south-east of Cape Hatteras, North Carolina. On 4 May he sank a straggler from the convoy, the Panamanian tanker MV *Panam,* off the coast of North Carolina. She had been left behind by Convoy NK538 due to engine problems. She had been struck by the torpedo on the port side in the engine room, completely wrecking it and killing two crew members. Six minutes later a second torpedo struck the ship and she sank within a matter of minutes. The remaining crew had abandoned ship in three lifeboats and were later picked up by USS *SC-664* a few hours later. Witt put in to Lorient on the 29th.

From July 1943, Witt was attached to the Naval Operations Office in Berlin as a staff officer. In October 1944 he returned to active duty when he was appointed commander of *U-3524*, a Type XXI Elektro boat, manufactured in an attempt to turn the tide in the battle of the Atlantic. In early May, he took his new boat from Kiel to the bays in Northern Germany, one of many boats ordered there to await orders. On 5 May she was scuttled in Gelting Bay, Flensburg, together with eighty-seven other boats to avoid capture by the Allies in what was called Operation Regenbogen, but it was contrary to the surrender terms. On 8 May, Witt surrendered to the British at Flensburg. He was released in less than eighteen months and returned to civilian life. He settled in Poppenbüttel a suburb of Hamburg, where he died on 13 February 1980.

Other awards:
30 Sep 1936: Long Service Award 4th Class
23 Aug 1942: Iron Cross 2nd Class
23 Aug 1942: Iron Cross 1st Class
23 Aug 1942: U-Boat War Badge
07 Oct 1944: U-Boat Combat Clasp in Bronze

Helmut Friedrich WITTE
Korvettenkapitän
23 ships sunk, 119,554 tons
1 ship damaged, 265 tons

Knight's Cross: Awarded on 22 October 1942, as *Kapitänleutnant* and as commander of *U-159* for sinking fifteen ships for a total of 77,681 and for damaging another three in just three patrols.

Helmut Witte was born in Bojendorf in Holstein, Germany on 6 April 1915. He enlisted in the *Reichsmarine* in April 1934 and served aboard the sail training ship *Gorch Fock* and later aboard the light cruiser *Karlsruhe* until June 1935. His training continued at the Naval School at Flensburg and was commissioned as a *Leutnant zur See* in April 1937. From October Witte served as Watch Officer aboard the light cruiser *Köln*, and later served in a

(Scherzer)

similar capacity aboard the torpedo boat *Kondor*, taking part in security patrols at the time of the Spanish Civil War. In April 1939 Witte was promoted to *Oberleutnant zur See* and transferred to the destroyer *Z22 Anton Schmitt* from September, taking part in the occupation of Narvik. When the destroyer was sunk Witte found himself on land fighting alongside the infantry. He fought well and made his way to the German lines.

In July he transferred to the U-boat service, and after several training courses was appointed First Watch Officer aboard *U-107* under *Kapitänleutnant* Günther Hessler. He joined Hessler on his his second patrol, which became the most successful patrol of a U-boat during the Second World War. Hessler sunk fourteen ships for a total of 86,699 tons. For his part in the patrol, Witte was awarded the Iron Cross 1st Class. Now an experienced officer, he undertook a commanders' training course and was promoted to *Kapitänleutnant* in September 1941. In October he was named as commander of *U-159*, a Type IXC boat built in Bremen. He left Kiel on 22 April to take *U-159* to her new base in western France; en route Witte laid some weather buoys. He arrived at Lorient on 3 May.

His next patrol began on 14 May, leaving for operations in the Western Atlantic where he soon encountered Convoy OS28 east-south-east of the Azores. In the early hours of the 21st he attacked and sank the British SS *New Brunswick*, about 140 miles east-south-east of Santa Maria. He had fired four torpedoes at a group of ships and had also sunk the British fleet oiler SS *Montenol*. She was so seriously damaged that HMS *Woodruff* whoich had turned up with HMS *Wellington* to help, later scuttled the ship. HMS *Wellington* picked up the sixty-one survivors. Witte then continued westwards and in early June approached the Caribbean. On 2 June he sank the USS *Illinois*. She was unescorted and unarmed. Two torpedoes struck her amidships and she sank in about forty seconds, 400 miles north-east of Puerto Rico, with the loss of all but six of her crew. Witte then took

U-159 into the Caribbean, through the Mona Passage, and on 5th he attacked two sailing vessels by gunfire south of the Dominican Republic. He damaged the Brazilian sailing ship *Paracury* and sank the Honduran sailing ship *Sally*. On the 7th, during the late evening, he sank the USS *Edith*, hit by a single torpedo about 200 miles south-east of Jamaica. On the 11th, Witte sank the British SS *Fort Good Hope*, on her maiden voyage, which sank in thirty minutes with the loss of two crew members. Her forty-five survivors were later picked up by the US gunboat USS *Erie*. In the same area two days later he sank two more ships. At 04:12 hours he torpedoed the US passenger ship, SS *Sixaola*. She was hit on the starboard side by two torpedoes about 50 miles off Bocas del Toro, Panama. The first torpedo struck in the bow and the second in the centre of No. 2 hold. Most of the eight officers, seventy-nine crewmen, six armed guards and 108 passengers aboard abandoned the ship in five lifeboats and six rafts two minutes after the second strike which stopped the engines, twenty-nine were lost. The survivors were questioned by the Germans and were offered medical aid and were given the exact course and distance to the nearest land. At 19:38 hours Witte sank the US steamer *Solon Turman* about 100 miles north of Cristobal, Canal Zone. Witte moved to just off the coat of Colombia where on 18th he sank the Dutch SS *Flora*, and on the 19th, he sank the Yugoslavian SS *Ante Matkovic* by gunfire. On the 22nd he sank the US tanker, SS *E.J. Sadler*, set on fire and after four hours a boarding party was sent aboard and planted scuttling charges, which sank the ship. Witte decided to return to port and whilst approaching Lorient on 12 July the U-boat was attacked after being spotted by a Leigh Light Wellington of 172 Squadron. The boat dived and four depth charges, were dropped damaging the boat. Witte reached Lorient on the 13th.

His next patrol was to prove just as successful, beginning on 24 August when he left for operations in the South Atlantic. Witte took *U-159* south and was ordered to join *Eisbär* Group and replaced *U-156*, which had been damaged by aircraft in the *Laconia* rescue operation. On 24 September the *Eisbär* boats, *U-68*, *U-172*, *U-504* and *U-159* refuelled about 600 miles south of St. Helena, after which they moved towards Capetown. On 7 October he torpedoed and sank the British MV *Boringia*, 200 miles west-south-west of Capetown with the loss of twenty-five of her crew. On the morning of the 8th, in the same area, Witte sank the British SS *Clan Mactavish*, struck on the port side in No. 2 hold by a single torpedo. The vessel settled rapidly by the head and sank by the bow within a few minutes with the loss of sixty-one of her crew. The next day Witte sank the US SS *Coloradan*, struck on the port side by a single torpedo. It hit the vessel between the No. 5 and No. 6 hatches and destroyed the bulkheads between the holds and blew out the double bottom. The ship sank in less than eight minutes. Witte ordered the boat to surface so he could question the survivors in the lifeboats. The third mate answered question concerning the ship and her cargo, and Witte then gave them course and distance to land and wished them a pleasant voyage and good liberty. The forty-eight survivors were later picked up by HMS *Active*. On the 10th, *U-159* was attacked by a Ventura of the Australian Air Force with four depth charges but was undamaged. Witte began to move further south, and on the 13th he sank the British SS *Empire Nomad* about 230 miles south of Cape Point. On the 29th, he sank two more ships and both were British, the MV *Ross* and SS *Laplace*. On 7 November, in the area of Mossel Bay, Cape Province, Witte sank the US SS *La Salle*, struck by a single torpedo about 350 miles south-east of the Cape of Good Hope with the loss of her entire crew of sixty. The torpedos had ignited her cargo of ammunition and the ship exploded, creating a fireball hundreds of feet high and completely destroying the vessel. Bits of wreckage fell around the ship for several minutes afterwards, wounding three of the crew of *U-159* who were on watch in the conning tower. It was reported that the explosion was head at Cape Point Lighthouse some 300 miles away. Whilst still attached to *Eisbär* Group, *U-159* now began her return journey through the South Atlantic. On the 13th, Witte sank by gunfire the US sailing ship the *Star of Scotland* about 900 miles west of Luderitz Bay, South-west Africa. The first shot went over the ship, the second fell short and the third struck the vessel and started a fire. The crew immediately began to abandon ship in a lifeboat while *U-159* continued shelling the ship. Miraculously only one member of the crew was killed. Witte kept the US flag from the ship as a souvenir. He then took the lifeboat with eighteen survivors in tow, despite the obvious risk to his own boat and its crew by staying on the surface. The US Captain Constantine Fink was taken aboard *U-159* and found Witte to be a kind and considerate man, who supplied blankets, food and medicine and then allowed Fink to return to his men. The two captains formed a friendship after the war and remained in contact until Fink's death in 1976.

During the last week of November *U-159* patrolled an area west and south-west of St. Paul Rocks and in early December was refuelled. On the 13th Witte sank the British SS *City of Bombay*, with the loss of her crew. On the 15th he sank the Egyptian SS *Star of Suez*, hit amidships by one torpedo, which sank after seventeen minutes about 100 miles south of St. Paul Rocks. The next day he sank another British ship, the SS *East Wales* with the loss of seventeen. He returned to Lorient on 5 January 1943, having sunk eleven ships in one patrol. At Lorient he was met as usual by a crowd but also was presented with his Knight's Cross.

His fourth patrol began on 4 March, when *U-159* joined *U-67*, *U-103*, *U-109* and *U-524* in the Central Atlantic to an area south of the Azores, where they formed *Wohlgemut* patrol line. They set out to hunt for Convoy UGS6 which had left New York on the 5th. *U-130* from *Unverzagt* Group sighted the convoy first but was sunk by the American destroyer USS *Champlin* with all crew lost. The boats from *Wohlgemut* and *Unverzagt* Group joined forces to form a new patrol line and the convoy passed through on the 14th. Although at least six boats made contact with the convoy and there was no aircraft cover, only four ships were sunk, and none by *U-159*. The operation ended on the 19th. Witte together with *U-67* continued southwards and joined a new patrol line, *Seeräuber*, south of the Canaries to intercept Convoy RS3. It was sighted on the 27th, and the next day *U-159* sank the British MV *Silverbeech*. The boat dived after firing a spread of four torpedoes and heard several detonations, but *U-172*, which had been chasing the same convoy, was badly shaken when the ship blew up at a distance of 2,000m. A total of fifty-one crew of *Silverbeech* were lost, only eight surviving. Witte left the area and began to patrol independently but had no further success, returning to Lorient on 25 April.

Witte missed the next patrol due to illness, which was fortunate since *U-159* was sunk on 28 July south-east of Haiti with the loss of all hands. After his recovery Witte attended the Naval Academy and thereafter served on the Ship Constructors' Commission before becoming a staff officer at the Naval Operations Office. He was promoted to *Korvettenkapitän* on 20 April 1945, and served as the representative of *Vizeadmiral* Hellmuth Heye, commander of the Small Naval Combat Forces, which included midget submarines. He surrendered to British troops in May, being released from captivity just two months later. He returned to Germany and was employed by several major manufacturing firms, becoming a director of Ruhrkohl *AG*. Witte died on 3 October 2005, at the age of ninety in Duisberg.

Other awards:
01 Apr 1938: Long Service Award 4th Class
06 Jun 1939: Spanish Cross in Bronze
12 Jan 1940: Iron Cross 2nd Class
19 Oct 1940: Destroyers War Badge
10 Jul 1941: Iron Cross 1st Class
10 Jul 1941: U-Boat War Badge
27 Apr 1943: Wound Badge in Black
18 Jul 1943: Wound Badge in Silver
24 Nov 1944: Combat Badge for Small Battle Units 1st Class
23 Dec 1944: U-Boat Combat Clasp in Bronze

Heinrich Wilhelm <u>Herbert</u> WOHLFARTH
Kapitänleutnant
21 ships sunk, 66,032 tons
3 ships damaged, 20,455 tons

Knight's Cross: Awarded as *Kapitänleutnant* and as commander of *U-556* on 15 May 1941, for sinking eighteen ships for a total of 46,593 shipping tons and for damaging another three ships. He was presented with his Knight's Cross by Dönitz to become the 30th U-boat commander to be honoured with the award.

(Scherzer)

Herbert Wohlfarth was born on 5 June 1915 in Kanazawa, Japan, the son of a teacher. He later attended school in Berlin-Schöneberg and in March 1933 passed his final exams. Wohlfarth entered the *Reichsmarine* a month later, and after his basic training was assigned to the 'pocket battleship' *Admiral Graf Spee*. Commissioned as a *Leutnant zur See* in October 1936, he entered the U-boat service in May 1937. In September Wohlfarth was assigned as a staff officer with the 3rd U-boat Flotilla in Kiel. In February 1938 he attended a signal officer's course at Flensburg, before returning to the U-boat Flotilla as an adjutant. In April he was promoted to *Oberleutnant zur See*, and in June was appointed Watch Officer aboard *U-16*, under the command of *Kapitänleutnant* Hannes Weingaertner.
     On 19 October 1939, Wohlfarth took command of *U-14*, a Type IIB boat. During his first three

patrols he sank nine mainly smaller ships in Scottish and Norwegian waters. On 25 January 1940, he sank the Norwegian SS *Biarritz* about 36 miles north-west of Ymuiden. On 15 February, he sank the Danish SS *Sleipner* about 50 miles north of Rattrey Head. The following day he sank three ships, the Danish SS *Rhone* and two Swedish ships, the SS *Osmed* and SS *Liana*. During his third patrol in the southern North Sea, early on the morning of 7 March, Wohlfarth sank the Dutch SS *Vecht*. She sank in less than twenty minutes with the loss of her entire crew, just north of Zeebrugge. On the 9th he sank three more ships in the same area; all were British, the SS *Borthwick*, SS *Abbotsford* and SS *Akeld*.

His fourth patrol began on 4 April, when Wohlfarth left Kiel under sealed orders to take part in Operation *Hartmut*, supporting the German invasion of Norway. From the 9th, his boat was called upon to support German transports and naval forces landing troops and to prevent any interference by British warships. Wohlfarth was later ordered to join the 3rd U-boat Group, which was to operate off Bergen. By the 15th the group had moved off Trondheim to oppose any British landings in the area. However, by the 25th the expected landings had not taken place and the group was ordered to an area east of the Shetlands. Wohlfarth put in at Kiel on 5 May, having not fired one torpedo.

On 15 June, Wohlfarth was appointed commander of *U-137*, also a Type IIB boat, referred to as a *Einbaum1* or dugout canoe. They were small boats but very successful

Kapitänleutnant *Herbert Wohlfarth after receiving his Knight's Cross from Admiral Dönitz in May 1941.* (Author's collection)

and other well-known commanders including Hardegen, Kretschmer and Lüth won their successes in them. With her sea trials complete Wohlfarth took his new boat out of Kiel on 14 September on a transfer voyage to Stavanger, arriving on the 17th, without any problems. On the 21st he left for his first operational patrol to operate west of the British Isles. During the early hours of the 26th he sank two ships, and damaged a third. At about 00:50 hours he fired three torpedoes at Convoy OB218 west of Malin Head. He sank the British SS *Manchester Brigade* and SS *Stratford* and damaged the SS *Ashantian*, which was eventually sunk by *U-415* on 21 April 1943. Wohlfarth put in at Lorient on the 29th. During his next patrol, again off the coast of the British Isles, he torpedoed and damaged the cruiser HMS *Cheshire*. She was later towed to Belfast Lough where she was beached and later taken to Liverpool for repairs, which took six months. On 3 November, Wohlfarth began his next patrol, operating west of the British Isles, where he sank the British SS *Cape St. Andrew* on the 13th. She was a straggler from Convoy OB240 and was torpedoed west-north-west of Aran Island. On the 16th, Wohlfarth torpedoed and sank the British SS *Planter* about 30 miles north-north-west of Bloody Foreland. Twelve crew members and one passenger were lost. In the same area the following day he sank two more ships, the British MV *Saint Germain* and the Swedish SS *Veronica*, with the loss of seventeen crew members. Wohlfarth put in at Lorient on the 22nd.

In December Wohlfarth left *U-137*, and transferred to the 1st U-boat Flotilla without a command. On 6 January 1941, he took command of the U-boat construction department in Hamburg. The following month he was appointed commander of *U-556*, a Type VIIC boat built in Hamburg and Wohlfarth had in fact supervised her construction and sea trials. On 1 May he took his new boat out on patrol and headed for the North Atlantic. He was patrolling west of the British Isles when on the 6th he sank a Faroese trawler, SS *Emanuel*, by gunfire near the Faroe Islands. When on the 7th, *U-94* sighted the westbound Convoy OB318 south of Iceland, Wohlfarth was ordered to intercept it. On the morning of the 10th, he torpedoed and damaged the British SS *Aelybryn*, south-east of Cape Farewell. The ship managed to get to Reykjavik on the 17th, but was sunk on 11 March 1943 by *U-160*. Later the same day, Wohlfarth sank another British ship, the SS *Empire Caribon*, about 465 miles south-west of Reykjanes, with the loss of thirty-four crew members. Wohlfarth joined up with *U-93*, *U-94* and *U-98* on the 11th, to form a patrol line south-east of Greenland. From the 13th these boats joined *U-74*, *U-97*, *U-109* and *U-111*, and moved south-west and formed a patrol line south-south-east of Cape Farewell. On the 19th, *U-94* sighted Convoy HX126 and the other boats closed in. The first to arrive was Wohlfarth, and on the afternoon of the 20th he torpedoed three ships, the MV *Darlington Court*, the tanker MV *British Security* and the SS *Cockaponset*. On the 24th Wohlfarth began his return journey, the day the battleship *Bismarck* and the heavy crusier *Prinz Eugen* attempted to break out into the Atlantic via the Denmark Strait. The plan was for a group of U-boats to form a patrol line running north-west by south-west, south of Cape Farewell. After the two battleships had passed through the line the boats would then deal with any British warships pursuing them. But the plan was changed when *Bismarck* was damaged in the Denmark Strait by HMS *Prince of Wales* on 24 May. She then made for St. Nazaire and *Prinz Eugen* headed south-westwards. On the evening of the 25th, *Bismarck* was damaged in a torpedo attack by Swordfish aircraft. The U-boats were directed to assist her into the comparative shelter of the Bay of Biscay but all of this was delayed by a heavy storm. On the evening of the 26th, *Bismarck* was at the north-west end of the patrol line and any boats with torpedoes were ordered to assist her, but they couldn't locate her due to worsening storms. On the morning of the 27th, *Bismarck* was sunk by the British Navy. Wohlfarth put in at Lorient on 30 May with a crew in shock, as Germany's greatest ship had been lost. When they arrived they were met by a crowd and much to Wohlfarth's surprise *Vizeadmiral* Dönitz, commander of the U-boats, was there to present him with the Knight's Cross.

With the celebrations over, Wohlfarth took *U-556* out on 19 June on another patrol and headed for the North Atlantic. On the 23rd a convoy was sighted by *U-203*, but after one ship was sunk all contact was lost. The next day *U-556* was attacked by the British corvettes, HMS *Nasturtium*, HMS *Celandine* and HMS *Gladiolus* south-west of Iceland. Wohlfarth had no choice but to surrender, when he surfaced in his badly-damaged boat. Apart from five of his crew who had died during the attack, forty men were taken prisoner. Wohlfarth spent more than six years in English and Canadian POW camps, finally being released on 14 July 1947. He returned to Germany, where he died on 13 August 1982 in Villingen.

Other awards:
31 Mar 1937: Long Service Award 4th Class
06 Oct 1939: Iron Cross 2nd Class
20 Dec 1939: Commemorative Medal of 01 Oct 1938
20 Dec 1939: U-Boat War Badge
01 Oct 1940: Iron Cross 1st Class
01 Nov 1941: Italian War Service Cross

Erich Karl Ferdinand WÜRDEMANN

Kapitänleutnant
15 ships sunk, 76,714 tons
3 ships damaged, 23,358 tons

Knight's Cross: Awarded on 14 March 1943, as *Kapitänleutnant* and as commander of *U-506* for the sinking of fifteen ships for a total of 76,714 tons and for damaging another three ships.

Erich Würdemann was born in Hamburg on 15 January 1914 and began his naval career in the *Reichsmarine* in April 1933. His first fourteen months he spent in basic training, first with II. *Schiffsstammdivision* in the Baltic then aboard the sail training ship *Gorch Fock* from June 1933. From April 1936, Würdemann served aboard the light cruiser *Leipzig*, and was later promoted to *Oberfähnrich zur See*. From October he was assigned to the torpedo boat *Iltis*, where he trained as a navigation officer and was commissioned as a

(Scherzer)

Leutnant zur See. He was then assigned to the 3rd Destroyer Division from December where he trained as a platoon leader, later being assigned to the 3rd Torpedo Boat Flotilla serving as Adjutant and Third Watch Officer.

From June 1937, Würdemann was assigned to the destroyer *Z5 Paul Jacobi* as Third and later as Second Watch Officer, and from October 1940 he served as First Watch Officer as well as the Torpedo Officer. In late 1937 the ship participated in manoeuvres as part of the 2nd Destroyer Division. *Z5 Paul Jacobi* and her sister-ship *Z8 Bruno Heinemann* sailed to Norway in 1938 to test a new 15cm (5.9in) gun. In August she took part in a Fleet Review as part of the 2nd Destroyer Division. From 1 September 1939, the destroyer was tasked to inspect neutral shipping for contraband goods in the Kattegat, the sea area bounded by the Jutland Peninsula near Denmark, until early 1940. Würdemann then took part in the early stages of the Norwegian Campaign, when the ship transported troops to the Trondheim area from early April 1940 and was transferred to France later that year where she made several attacks on British shipping. During his time aboard he was promoted to *Oberleutnant zur See* in June 1938 and on 1 November 1940 he was promoted to *Kapitänleutnant*.

In November 1940, Würdemann transferred to the U-boat service and began his training. From April 1941, he served aboard *U-43*, under *Kapitänleutnant* Wolfgang Lüth, taking part in one patrol in the North Atlantic. During the patrol Lüth sunk three ships: he was to add many more – Würdemann was learning from one of the best. In July he was given his own command, a Type IXC boat, *U-506*, built in Hamburg. With her sea trials complete Würdemann took her out of Hamburg to Heligoland on 2 March 1942. A week later he left again in transit to France, putting in at his new base of Lorient on the 25th.

He left port for US waters on 6 April and headed for the coast of Florida. On 3 May, Würdemann sank the Norwegian MV *Sama*, she was struck on the port side amidships by a single torpedo about 60 miles south-south-west of Miami. The explosion blew away the entire midsection on the port side and felled the mast aft. The entire crew abandoned the ship in seven minutes, and they were picked up later by the British tanker SS *Athelregent* later the same day. A few days later Würdemann took *U-506* into the Gulf of Mexico, the second U-boat to do so, just behind *U-507*. The two boats made a joint attack on the US tanker MV *Aurora* on the 10th about 40 miles off South-west Pass, Louisana. She was hit by a torpedo fired from *U-506* and immediately took on a list to starboard, she was then hit by two more torpedoes and *U-506* surfaced and shelled the ship. All the crew then abandoned ship in two lifeboats and three rafts. Würdemann thought the tanker would sink and left, but she remained afloat. Later the *Aurora* was towed to Algiers, Louisiana, where she was at first declared a total loss, but was later repaired. On the 13th and 14th, he sank two US tankers, the SS *Gulfpenn* and SS *David McKelry*, the latter being declared a total loss. On the 16th Würdemann attacked and damaged two more US tankers, the MV *Sun* and MV *William C. McTarnahan*. The badly-damaged *William C. McTarnahan* was towed to the entrance of South-west Pass by the US Coast Guard tug USS *Tuckahoe* and the US tug *Baranca*. She was repaired and returned to duty a year later. On the 17th he sank the US tanker SS *Gulfoil*, torpedoed about 75 miles south-west of the Mississippi River Delta. The explosion blew the catwalk away from the mainmast to the midships house. Fifteen seconds later a second torpedo struck the engine room, killing three men on watch below. The tanker sank in two minutes with the loss of twenty-one of her crew.

Würdemann took *U-506* further west and on the 19th sank the SS *Heredia*, another US ship two miles south-east of the Ship Shoal Buoy. She was hit by three torpedoes and sank in less than three minutes with the loss of thirty-six of her crew. The following day he sank the US tanker SS *Halo* about 50 miles from the South-west Pass of the Mississippi River: there were only three survivors. Würdemann took *U-506* through the Straits of Florida into the Atlantic, where on the 28th he sank the British SS *Yorkmoor*. The boat surfaced and fired shells from the deck gun, as Würdemann had used his last torpedo. It was night and the U-boat gunners could just about see the outline of the ship, but the gunners aboard *Yorkmoor* could not see the U-boat and could only fire at the flashes of the boat's own guns. After firing fifty-five rounds the boat ceased fire when the crew was seen getting into the lifeboats. Würdemann questioned the master and then left. *Yorkmoor*'s crew of forty-five survived, mainly due to his ceasing fire. On the 31st, about 200 miles south-east of Bermuda, Würdemann sank the British SS *Fred W. Green*. She was sunk by *U-506*'s deck gun. He returned to Lorient on 15 June having sunk eight ships and damaging another three and for this achievement Würdemann was awarded the Iron Cross 1st Class.

He left for operations in the Central Atlantic on 28 July, and initially operated south-west of Freetown. On 21 August he torpedoed and sank the British SS *City of Wellington*. Two days later he sank another British ship, the SS *Hamla* about 200 miles south-south-west of Freetown. She was struck by two torpedoes and Würdemann watched as the ship immediately disappeared upon being hit, sinking in less than twenty seconds. The master and his crew of thirty-seven and four gunners were lost. On 5 September, south-east of Cape Palmas, he sank the British MV *Myrmidon* who at the time was being escorted by the destroyer HMS *Brilliant*. Her crew of 245 passengers all managed to abandon ship and was picked up by the escorting warship. On the 13th, he sank the Swedish MV *Lima* just off the coast of Liberia.

On 12 September, *U-156* sank the troop transport *Laconia* north-east of Ascension Island. She was carrying 2,732 crew, passengers, soldiers and prisoners-of-war. When the commander of *U-156* realized the situation he called upon other boats in the area to mount a rescue. *U-506*, *U-507* and the Italian submarine *Capellini* were ordered to the scene to assist. *U-506* arrived on the night of 14th/15th, and Würdemann took aboard 132 Italian POWs from the 263 survivors. By the morning *U-506* had more than 200 aboard. The rescue operation halted as soon as a US Liberator came overhead and dropped three bombs, destroying a lifeboat full of survivors and damaging *U-156*, which had been under Red Cross flags at the time. Despite the orders to discontinue all rescue operations, the U-boat commanders continued to help. On 17th, the rescue boats left the area carrying and towing survivors in lifeboats. *U-506* was again attacked but managed to dive and escape any damage. The US aircraft killed dozens of *Laconia*'s survivors with bombs and strafing attacks, which forced *U-156* to cast their remaining survivors into the sea and crash dive to avoid being destroyed. In fact the pilots of the bombers mistakenly reported that they had sunk the U-boat and were even awarded medals for their bravery. Würdemann surfaced and ordered the survivors from the lifeboats on board so he could transfer them to the Vichy French sloop *Annamite* that had turned up with two other ships. A total of 1,113 survivors were eventually rescued, but 1,619, mostly Italian prisoners, died. The event changed the attitude of Germany's naval personnel towards rescuing Allied seamen. Dönitz would later issue what was known as the '*Laconia* Order' which forbade any such attempts at rescue: this order more than any other helped to usher in unrestricted submarine warfare for the rest of the war. Neither the US pilots nor their commanders were punished for the attacks on the U-boats and the matter was quietly forgotten by the US authorities.

Würdemann then took *U-506* back to the Freetown area and continued with his patrols. On 30 September, he attacked the British SS *Siam II*, south-west of Monrovia after being hit by a second torpedo on 1 October. She was his final victory of an eventful patrol. Würdemann headed for Lorient, arriving on 7 November.

On 14 December, he took *U-506* out on his fourth patrol, heading for the Central Atlantic. From New Year's Day 1943, *U-506* was in a waiting area between the Canaries and the Cape Verde Islands. In mid-January Würdemann joined, *U-160*, *U-182*, *U-509* and *U-516* to form *Seehund* Group, for operations in South African waters. By late February the boats were operating off the southern coast of Cape Province. On 7 March, Würdemann torpedoed and sank the British SS *Sabor* south-east of Mossel Bay. Two days later he sunk another ship, the Norwegian SS *Tabor*, struck by a single torpedo south-east of Cape Agulhas. On the 19th he began the journey home, reaching Lorient on 8 May, after being refuelled by *U-117* south of the Azores.

His fifth patrol would be his last. He left for the South Atlantic on 6 July, part of *Monsun* Group. Würdemann headed for an operational area south of the Cape and into Indian Ocean. On the 12th, *U-506* was attacked and sunk by a Port Lyautey-based Liberator of the USAAF. Forty-eight men, including Würdemann were lost, there were only six survivors. (Some sources give the date as 14 July 1943.)

Other awards:
01 Apr 1937: Long Service Award 4th Class
19 Oct 1940: Destroyer War Badge
26 Mar 1942: U-Boat War Badge
24 Apr 1942: Iron Cross 2nd Class
18 Jun 1942: Iron Cross 1st Class

Robert <u>Richard</u> ZAPP
Fregattenkapitän
16 ships sunk, 106,200 tons
1 ship damaged, 12,502 tons

Knight's Cross: Awarded on 23 April 1942, as *Korvettenkapitän* and as commander of *U-66* for sinking thirteen ships for a total of 82,709 shipping tons.

Richard Zapp was born on 3 April 1904, in Germersheim, Pfalz in the German state of Rhineland-Palatinate. His naval career began when he joined the *Reichsmarine* in May 1923, he was initially attached to the II. *Schiffsstammdivision*. Between May 1924 a October 1926, Zapp served aboard the sail training ship *Niobe* as a Cadet. He then served on the light cruiser *Emden* before attending various training courses at the Naval School in Flensburg. On 1 October 1930, Zapp was commissioned as a *Leutnant zur See*, whilst serving aboard the battleship *Hessen*. From April 1931 he served as Second

Watch Officer aboard the minesweeper *M145* and was promoted to *Oberleutnant zur See* in May 1933. He then served as a company officer with a naval anti-aircraft unit before being assigned as commander of various small minesweepers. In April 1936 he was promoted to *Kapitänleutnant* and from September 1938 was appointed commander of the minesweeper *M122* and then the *M1*.

In April 1940, Zapp transferred to the U-boat service and after the usual training was assigned to *U-46*, under the command of *Oberleutnant zur See* Engelbert Endraß. He took part in his fourth patrol from 13–19 October during this time Endraß sank five ships. In November he was transferred to the Construction Training Group at Bremen where he learnt everything needed to command a boat himself. Then in January 1941 he took command of *U-66*, a Type IXC boat, and after he completed her sea trials was promoted to *Korvettenkapitän* in April, he was ready to take

(Scherzer)

her out on a war patrol. On 13 May he took *U-66* out from Wilhelmshaven for operations south of Greenland. On the 22nd Zapp was operating together with other boats against Convoy HX126, without success. On the 24th, *U-66* was one of seven boats ordered to form a new patrol line south of Cape Farewell, ahead of the fleeing *Bismarck*, in the hope of sinking some of her pursuers after she had passed. The plan was later cancelled when *Bismarck* changed plans and headed for St. Nazaire. *U-66* together with *U-43*, *U-46*, *U-111* and *U-557* were ordered to form a new patrol line south-east of Cape Farewell, but no convoys were sighted and *U-66* put in at Lorient on 11 June.

On 23rd, Zapp left for the Central Atlantic and the Freetown area. During the outward-bound journey he sank three ships west of the Canary Islands. On the 29th he sank two Greek ships, the SS *George J. Goulandris* and SS *Kalypso Vergott*. The next day he sank the British SS *Saint Anselm* from Convoy SL78, with the loss of thirty-four of her crew. After a short unsuccessful patrol off Freetown he began the journey home. On the morning of 19 July, he sank the British SS *Holmside*, struck by three torpedoes sinking in fifteen minutes north-east of the Cape Verde Islands. Zapp reached Lorient on 5 August and was immediately awarded both the Iron Cross 1st and 2nd Classes for sinking four ships in this one patrol.

Zapp left for his third patrol on 28 August and again headed for the Freetown area. He later moved south-west across the Central Atlantic where on 26 September he sank the Panamanian tanker SS *I.C. White*. She was struck by one of the two torpedoes fired despite flying the flag of a neutral country. The ship had been sighted by Zapp on the 24th and he radioed headquarters for advice after seeing the Panamanian markings and was told that he was only to sink the vessel outside of the Pan-American security zone. He attacked the ship after she left the zone because she was transporting oil to a British port. The torpedo which struck caused an explosion which threw flaming oil high over the deck. Two more torpedoes were fired, both of which hit and the ship broke in two, she later sank about 500 miles off Recife with the loss of three members of her crew. The thirty-four survivors were picked up and were landed four days later late in Rio de Janeiro. Zapp returned to his base on 9 November.

His fourth patrol began on Christmas Day when he left for operations in the Western Atlantic. *U-66* was one of the first three U-boats to enter US waters for Operation *Paukenschlag*, along with *U-123* and *U-125*. Whilst patrolling off Cape Hattera, Zapp sank the US SS *Allan Jackson* on 18 January about 60 miles east-north-east of Diamond Shoals, North Carolina. The next day he sank the Canadian SS *Lady Hawkins*. She was struck by two torpedoes about 150 miles east of Cape Hatteras. The master, eighty-six crew members, one gunner and 163 passengers were lost. Seventy-one survivors were picked up five days later by the US SS *Coamo*. On the 22nd, Zapp sank the Panamanian tanker SS *Olympic*, with the loss of thirty-five, her entire crew. Two days later, about 15 miles south-east of the Diamond Shoals buoy, he sank the British tanker MV *Empire Gem* and the US SS *Venore*. With all torpedoes gone Zapp returned to Lorient on 10 February.

On 21 March Zapp left for the Caribbean on his next patrol, a very successful one. On 14 April, whilst patrolling in the eastern Caribbean area, south-west of Bridgetown, Barbados he sank the Greek SS *Korthion*. She was struck by one torpedo amidships and sank immediately with the loss of fourteen. On the 16th, he sank the Dutch tanker SS *Amsterdam*, which was struck by two torpedoes. The first hit amidships and the second in the engine room. Most of the crew abandoned ship in the two starboard lifeboats before the tanker sank 60 miles west of British Grenada. Two days later Zapp sank the 11,000-ton Panamanian tanker MV *Heinrich von Riedemann*. She was struck by a single torpedo on her port side, and the explosion wrecked the steering gear and the port diesel engine. The ship was pouring oil from the tank while steering in circles until the other engine stopped, the crew abandoned ship in three lifeboats. Zapp then fired two more torpedoes and eventually the ship sank after four hours. All of her crew were later picked up and landed safely at Trinidad the following day. On the 26th, about 80 miles north-north-east of Bonaire, Zapp sighted another ship, the US SS *Alcoa Partner*. She was sunk by torpedo and gunfire in less than three minutes with the loss of ten of her crew. Zapp continued with his run of luck when three days later he sank the 10,000-ton Panamanian tanker the MV *Harry G. Seidel*. She was hit on the port side by two torpedoes about 12 miles north-east of Los Testigos Islands. The forty-eight crew began to abandon ship and unfortunately two had to be left behind as they were too badly injured. After about twenty minutes *U-66* surfaced to attack the ship with her deck guns but the ship had sunk by the stern before a shot was fired. One of the three lifeboats which had an outboard motor towed the other two boats. They headed for the coast of Venezuela some 60 miles away. They made land fall in the Bay of Caribes after twenty-one hours, and were eventually led by a police officer over mountains and through jungle to a launch that took them to the village of Rio Caribes. The British authorities in Trinidad had sent a tug and a yacht to pick them up and they landed at Port of Spain on 1 May. Zapp continued on north of Tobago where on the 2nd he sank the Norwegian tanker MV *Sandar*. She was hit by two torpedoes amidships, but still continued at slow speed although on fire. Zapp fired another torpedo and the ship sank after about ten minutes, the survivors abandoning ship in a lifeboat and a motorboat. The only deaths were the first mate and the boatswain. The thirty-four survivors were picked up the next day after being spotted by an aircraft.

On the morning of the 3rd, Zapp attacked and damaged the 12,500-ton British tanker MV *Geo W. McKnight* of Convoy ON87. She had been chased for some time and struck by Zapp's last torpedo about 40 miles west of Tobago. *U-66* then surfaced and fired three rounds from her deck gun and scored two hits, but the ten gunners aboard the ship fired back, forcing Zapp to call off his attack and dive. With no more torpedoes Zapp headed for Lorient, arriving on the 27th. The boat was met by a cheering crowd and as soon as Zapp stepped off the boat he was presented with his Knight's Cross.

On 22 June Zapp was transferred and had to leave *U-66* and was appointed commander of the 3rd U-boat Flotilla in La Rachelle, France. In January 1945 he was promoted to *Fregattenkapitän* and during the last months of the war he also became leader of Naval Regiment *Zapp* which defended the U-boat base at La Rochelle as well as protecting the remaining U-boats. On 9 May he surrendered to French Forces and spent more than two years in captivity, in various different prison camps, being released in July 1947. He returned to Germany and settled in Kiel where he died on 17 July 1964.

Other awards:
02 Oct 1936: Long Service Award 4th to 3rd Class
14 May 1941: U-Boat War Badge
06 Aug 1941: Iron Cross 2nd Class
06 Aug 1941: Iron Cross 1st Class
30 Jan 1944: War Service Cross 2nd Class with Swords
00.00.1945: U-Boat Combat Clasp in Bronze

German Awards and Decorations

Knight's Cross with Oakleaves, Swords and Diamonds: Instituted by Hitler on 28 September 1941. The Diamonds could only be awarded to previous winners of the Swords. There were just twenty-seven recipients of this prized award and only two recipients were U-boat commanders. With the Diamonds came a lavish document, printed on high-grade parchment in gold. The diamonds were hand-crafted by a jeweller using real diamonds set in the Oakleaves and on the handles of the Swords. All recipients were presented with the award personally by Hitler.

Knight's Cross with Oakleaves and Swords: Instituted by Hitler on 28 September 1941, and could only be awarded to previous winners of the Oakleaves. The Swords was presented to the recipient in a box and was attached below the Oakleaves crossed at a forty-degree angle, with the right sword overlapping the left. The band clip on the back was slightly larger than the one attached to the Oakleaves. There were 159 confirmed recipients of the Swords – only three were U-boat commanders.

Knight's Cross with Oakleaves: Instituted by Hitler on 3 June 1940 and was worn above the Knight's Cross and held in place by means of a silver loop that would also secure the neck ribbon. The decoration consisted of a cluster of three oak leaves with the centre leaf superimposed on the two lower leaves. The original clasp had the digits 800 or 900 added, like the Knight's Cross to show it was made from 800-grade silver and measured 2cm in diameter. Hitler frequently made the presentations of the Oakleaves to the recipients personally, either at the Reich Chancellery in Berlin or at the Berghof on the Obersalzburg near Berchtesgaden. There were 890 recipients of the Oakleaves and twenty-three were U-boat commanders.

Knight's Cross of the Iron Cross: The Knight's Cross was instituted by Hitler on 1 September 1939, and is probably one of the most recognizable decorations of the Second World War. It was similar in design to the Iron Cross except it was larger. It measured 48mm x 48mm with a silver ring on top which measured 6mm. At the top of the cross there was an elongated ribbon top which went through the silver ring and this is where the ribbon went that was used to hold it in position around the recipient's neck. With the Knight's Cross came an impressive-looking citation presented in a red leather binder and stamped with an embossed German Eagle in gold on the front cover and signed by Hitler. There were over 7,000 recipients of the Knight's Cross of which 95 were U-boat commanders.

German Cross: The award was created in two classes: Gold and Silver, independent of one another, and was instituted on 28 September 1941. The Gold type was awarded in recognition of repeated acts of bravery or exceptional command not justifying the award of the Knight's Cross. The Silver type was to reward significant performance in military conduct of the war. A total of 24,204 Gold and 1,114 Silver types were awarded.

Iron Cross 1st Class: Instituted on 1 September 1939, for three to five acts of bravery above and beyond the call of duty. Approximately 450,000 were awarded.

Iron Cross 2nd Class: Instituted on 1 September 1939, for one act of bravery above and beyond the call of duty. Approximately 3,000,000 were awarded.

War Service Cross: Instituted by Hitler in October 1939, it was graded the same as the Iron Cross. The award had two variants: 1st and 2nd Class and without or without Swords. The War Service Cross with Swords was given to soldiers for exceptional service 'not in direct connection with combat', and was given to civilians. The ribbon of the War Service Cross was red–white–black–white–red.

Spanish Cross: Instituted on 14 April 1939, for German service personnel who had fought in the Spanish Civil War. It was awarded in four grades with and without Swords – Bronze, Silver, Gold and Gold with Diamonds.

Commemorative Medal of 1 October 1938: Instituted on 18 October 1938, for those who participated in the annexation of the Sudetenland or Bohemia and Moravia, and approximately 1,162,000 were awarded.

Return of Memel Commemorative Medal: Instituted on 1 May 1939, awarded to those who participated in the annexation of Memel on 23 March 1938. Approximately 31,300 were awarded.

Long Service Award (Wehrmacht): Instituted on 16 March 1936, it was awarded in four grades: Silver Medal: for 4 years service; Gold Medal: for 12 years service; Silver Cross: for 18 years service and Gold Cross: for 25 years service.

Wound Badges: Instituted on 1 September 1939, and were awarded in three grades: Black, Silver and Gold. Wound Badge in Black: awarded for being wounded once or twice or during an air raid or by frostbite in the line of duty. Wound Badge in Silver: awarded for being wounded three or four times in fighting or in an air raid or serious injury in the line of duty. Wound Badge in Gold: awarded for being wounded five times or more during combat or for being wounded extremely seriously (loss of a limb, loss of eyesight) in the line of duty.

U-Boat War Badge: Instituted on 13 October 1939, it was awarded to submarine crew members after two operational trips or one if it was particularly successful or if the man in question had been wounded.

U-Boat War Badge with Diamonds: It was instituted by *Großadmiral* Karl Dönitz sometime in 1941 after he had received the award himself from *Großadmiral* Erich Raeder, the first C-in-C of the German Navy. It was awarded to U-Boat commanders who had received the Knight's Cross with Oakleaves. It was the same as the basic pattern but with nine small diamonds inlaid in the Swastika. This award was more of a personal award made by Dönitz – only thirty were awarded.

U-Boat Combat Clasp: Instituted on 15 May 1944 by *Großadmiral* Dönitz. It was awarded to U-Boat personnel for continuous service in the submarine forces, in order to reward them for their courage during the desperate struggle to turn the tide in the Battle of the Atlantic for five years. The badge existed in two classes: Bronze and, from 24 November 1944, Silver.

Minesweeper War Badge: Instituted on 31 August 1940, and was awarded to men who had completed three operational sorties or had been wounded in action, or having completed an extra-dangerous mission or had completed a mission that had lasted twenty-five days or more of escort duty.

Destroyer War Badge: Instituted on 4 June 1940, for having been wounded in action, for having one's ship sunk in action, performing acts above and beyond the call of duty, participation in three engagements with the enemy, participation in twelve non-enemy sorties or for participation in the Battle of Narvik.

High Seas Fleet War Badge: Instituted on 30 April 1941 by *Großadmiral* Erich Raeder. It was to recognize actions, mainly against England. It was normally awarded after twelve weeks service on a battleship or cruiser. The number of weeks was reduced if the person was wounded or killed or for performing acts above and beyond the call of duty.

Glossary

Abwehr:	German Military Intelligence service: from 1938 it was under the command of Admiral Wilhelm Canaris
Admiral:	British Navy Admiral
Bundesmarine:	Post-war German Navy
Fähnrich zur See:	Equivalent to Midshipman (junior)
Flottillenadmiral:	The lowest flag officer rank in the postwar German Navy, equivalent to a Commodore in the British Navy.
Fregattenkapitän:	Equivalent to Commander
Generaladmiral:	No equivalent
Generaloberst:	Colonel-General
Großadmiral:	Equivalent to Admiral of the Fleet in the British Navy. Nazi Germany had two *Groß*admirals – Erich Raeder 1935–43 and Karl Dönitz 1943–5
Kapitänleutnant:	Equivalent to Lieutenant
Kapitän zur See:	Equivalent to Captain
Kleinkampfverband:	Small Action Units of the German Navy, which included midget submarines and frogmen
Kommodore:	Equivalent to Commodore
Konteradmiral:	British Navy Rear-Admiral
Korvettenkapitän:	Equivalent to Lieutenant Commander
Kriegsmarine:	The Navy of Nazi Germany from 1935 to 1945. It superseded the Imperial Navy and the inter-war *Reichsmarine* of the Weimar Republic
Leutnant zur See:	Equivalent to Sub-Lieutenant
Marinepanzerjagd:	Naval Anti-tank (Regiment)
Oberfähnrich zur See:	Equivalent to Midshipman
Oberleutnant zur See:	Equivalent to Sub-Lieutenant
Reichsmarine:	The Navy during the Weimar Republic years 1919–35
Rollenoffizier:	The Role Officer – had to divide the entire crew of a ship into the individual roles, he was the right-hand man of the First Officer
Schiffsstammdivision:	Naval Headquarters – training division (North Sea or Baltic area)
Schiffsstammabteilung:	Training Battalion (subordinate to Naval Headquarters)
Staffelkapitän:	Squadron Leader
Vizeadmiral:	British Navy Vice-Admiral
Volksschule:	German term which refers to compulsaory education, equivalent to a combined primary school and lower secondary education
Volkssturm:	National militia established during the last months of the war. Established by

Hitler and staffed by conscripting males between the ages of 16 and 60 years. Headed by Joseph Goebbels and Martin Bormann

Wehrmachtbericht: Wehrmacht communiqué or Armed Forces report. This was the daily report from the German High Command and a key component of Nazi propaganda during the Second World War.

Bibliography

Alman, Karl, *Ritter der Sieben Meere. Ritterkreuzträger der U-Boots-Waffe*, Rastatt: Erich Pabel Verlag, 1975.

Angolia, John R., *On the Field of Honor* Volume 1, San Jose, California, USA: Roger James Bender Publications, 1979.

_____, *On the Field of Honor* Volume 2, San Jose, California, USA: Roger James Bender Publications, 1980.

Blair, Clay, *Hitler'sU-Boat War: The Hunters 1939-1942*, London: Weidenfeld & Nicolson, 1997.

_____, *Hitler's U-Boat War: The Hunted 1942-1945*, London: Weidenfeld & Nicolson, 1999.

Brustal-Naval, Fritz, and Suhren, Teddy, *Nasses Eichenlaub: als Kommandant und F.d.U. im U-Boot-Krieg* [Wet Oak Leaves: as Commander and F.d.U. in the U-boat War], Frankfurt/Main, Berlin Germany: Ullstein, 1999.

Buchheim, Lothar-Gunther, *U-Boat War*, London: Collins, 1978.

Busch, Rainer, and Hans-Joachim Röll, *German U-Boat Commanders of World War II: A Biographical Dictionary*, Annapolis: Naval Institute Press, 1999.

_____, *Der U-Boot-Krieg 1939-1945: Die Ritterkreuzträger der U-Boot-Waffe von September 1939 bis Mai 1945*, Hamburg, Verlag E.S. Mittler & Sohn, 2003.

Cremer, Peter, *U-333: The Story of a U-Boat Ace*, London: Bodley Head, 1984.

Dixon, Jeremy, *The Knight's Cross with Oakleaves 1940-1945. Vol 1 & 2*, Atgen, PA, USA: Schiffer Military History, 2012.

Dörr, Manfred, *Die Ritterkreuzträger der U-Boot-Waffe. Band 1: A-J*, Osnabrück: Biblio Verlag, 1988.

_____, *Die Ritterkreuzträger der U-Boot-Waffe. Band 2: K-Z* Osnabrück: Biblio Verlag, 1989.

Edwards, Bernard, *Dönitz and the Wolf Packs*, Barnsley: Pen & Sword, 2014.

_____, *The Wolf Packs Gather*, Barnsley: Pen & Sword, 2011.

Frank, Wolfgang, *Enemy Submarine: the Story of Günther Prien, Captain of U-47*, London: William Kimber, 1954.

Fraschka, Günter, *Mit Schwertern und Brillanten: aus dem Leben der siebennundzwanzig Träger der höchsten deutschen Tapferkeitsauszeichnung*, Baden: E. Pabel, 1958.

Gannon, Michael, *Operation Drumbeat. The Dramatic True Story of Germany's First U-boat Attacks along the American Coast in World War II*, New York: Harper & Row, 1990.

Gasaway, E.B., *Grey Wolf, Grey Sea. Aboard the German submarine U-124 in World War II*, London: Arthur Barker, 1972.

Hadley, Michael L., *U-boats against Canada. German Submarines in Canadian Waters*, Kingston & Montreal: McGill-Queen's University Press, 1985.

Hoyt, Edwin P., *The Sea Wolves*, New York: Avon Books, 1987.

_____, *The U-boat Wars*, New York: Arbor House, 1984.

Jones, Geoffrey, *U-Boat Aces*, London: William Kimber, 1988.

Kemp, Paul, *U-boats Destroyed. German Submarine Losses in the World Wars*, London: Arms & Armour Press, 1999.

Kurowski, Franz, *Die Trager des Ritterkreuzes des Eisenen Kreuzes der U-Boot Waffe*, Friedberg: Podzun Pallas Verlag, 1987.

Lüdde-Neurath, Walter, *Unconditional Surrender: A Memoir of the Last Days of the Third Reich and the Dönitz Administration* Barnsley: Frontline Books, 2010.

McIntyre, Donald, *U-Boat Killer*, Annapolis: Naval Institute Press, 1976.

Morgan, Daniel, and Taylor, Bruce, *U-Boat Attack Logs. A Complete Record of Warships Sinkings from Original Sources 1939-1945*, Barnsley: Seaforth Publishing, 2011.

Mulligan, Timothy P., *Lone Wolf. The life and death of U-boat ace Werner Henke* Westport, Conn: Praeger, 1993.

Niestle, Axel, *German U-Boat Losses during World War II: Details of Destruction*, London: Frontline Books, 2014.

Padfield, Peter, *Dönitz. The Last Führer*, London: Victor Gollanz Ltd., 1984.

Patzwall, Klaus,and Scherzer,Veit, *Das Deutsche Kreuz 1940-1945 Band II*, Norderstedt:Verlag Klaus D. Patzwall, 2001.

Paterson, Lawrence, *U-564 auf Feindfahrt—70 Tage an Bord* [*U-564* on War Patrol—70 Days on Board], Stuttgart, Germany: Motorbuch-Verlag, 2005.

Persico, Joseph E., *Nuremberg: Infamy on Trial*, London: Allison & Busby, 1995.

Range, Clemens, *Die Ritterkreuzträger der Kriegsmarine*, Stuttgart: Motorbuch, 1974.

Robertson, Terence, *The Golden Horseshoe*, London: Evans, 1955.

Rust, Eric C., *Naval Officers Under Hitler: The Story of Crew 34*, New York: Praeger, 1991.

Saves, Theodore P. (ed.), *Silent Hunters.German U-Boat Commanders of World War II*, Barnsley, Pen & Sword, 2004.

Schaeffer, Heinz, *U-boat 977*, London: William Kimber, 1952.

Scherzer, Veit, *Die Ritterkreuzträger. Die Inhaber des Ritterkreuzes des Eisernen Kreuzes 1939 von Heer, Luftwaffe, Kriegsmarine, Waffen-SS, Volkssturm*, Ranis: Scherzers Militaer-Verlag, 2007.

Showell, Jak P. Mallmann, *The German Navy in World War II*, London: Arms & Armour Press, 1979.

———————————, *U-boat Command and the Battle of the Atlantic*, London: Conway Maritime Press Ltd, 1989.

———————————, *U-Boat Commanders and Crews 1935-1945*, Marlborough, Wiltshire: The Crowood Press, 1998.

———————————, *U-boats under the Swastika*, London: Ian Allen, 1973.

Sprecher, Drexel A., *Inside the Nuremberg Trial: A Prosecutor's Comprehensive Account* 2 vols. University Press of America, 1999.

Tarrant, V.E., *The Last Year of the Kriegsmarine: May '44-May '45*, London: Arms & Armour Press, 1994.

—————, *The U-boat Offensive: 1914-1945*, Annapolis: Naval Institute Press, 1989.

Topp, Erich, *The Odyssey of a U-Boat Commander: Recollections of Erich Topp*,Westport, Conn.: Praeger, 1992.

Turner, Barry, *Karl Doenitz and the Last Days of the Third Reich*, London: Icon Books, 2015.

Van der Vat, Dan, *The Atlantic Campaign*, New York: Harper & Row, 1988.

Vause, Jordan, *U-Boat Ace: The Story of Wolfgang Lüth*, Shrewsbury: Airlife Publishing Ltd., 1990

Vause, Jordan, *Wolf. U-Boat Commanders in World War II*, Annapolis: Naval Institute Press, 1997.

Werner, Herbert A., *Iron Coffins: a personal account of the German U-boat battles of World War II*, New York: Holt, 1969.

Williamson, Gordon, *Aces of the Reich*, London: Arms & Armour Press, 1989.

Wynn, Kenneth, *U-Boat Operations of the Second World War. Volume 1: Career Histories, U1–U510*, London: Chatham Publishing, 1997.

_____, *U-Boat Operations of the Second World War. Volume 2: Career Histories, U511–UIT25*, London: Chatham Publishing, 1998.